Counseling Ethics
for the 21st Century

To our family, the light of our lives, and source of inspiration

Counseling Ethics for the 21st Century

A Case-Based Guide to Virtuous Practice

Elliot D. Cohen
Indian River State College / Florida State University College of Medicine

Gale Spieler Cohen
Indian River State College

$SAGE

Los Angeles | London | New Delhi
Singapore | Washington DC | Melbourne

ⓈSAGE

FOR INFORMATION:

SAGE Publications, Inc.
2455 Teller Road
Thousand Oaks, California 91320
E-mail: order@sagepub.com

SAGE Publications Ltd.
1 Oliver's Yard
55 City Road
London, EC1Y 1SP
United Kingdom

SAGE Publications India Pvt. Ltd.
B 1/I 1 Mohan Cooperative Industrial Area
Mathura Road, New Delhi 110 044
India

SAGE Publications Asia-Pacific Pte. Ltd.
3 Church Street
#10-04 Samsung Hub
Singapore 049483

Acquisitions Editor: Abbie Rickard
Editorial Assistant: Jennifer Cline
Production Editor: Laureen Gleason
Copy Editor: Deanna Noga
Typesetter: Hurix Digital
Proofreader: Susan Schon
Indexer: Mary Mortensen
Cover Designer: Scott Van Atta
Marketing Manager: Jenna Retana

Copyright © 2019 by SAGE Publications, Inc.

All rights reserved. No part of this book may be reproduced or utilized in any form or by any means, electronic or mechanical, including photocopying, recording, or by any information storage and retrieval system, without permission in writing from the publisher.

Printed in the United States of America

Library of Congress Cataloging-in-Publication Data

Names: Cohen, Elliot D., author. | Cohen, Gale Spieler, author.

Title: Counseling ethics for the 21st century: a case-based guide to virtuous practice / Elliot D. Cohen, Indian River State College, Gale Spieler Cohen, Indian River State College.

Description: Thousand Oaks, Calif.: SAGE, [2019] | Includes bibliographical references and index.

Identifiers: LCCN 2017044642 | ISBN 9781506345475 (pbk.: alk. paper)

Subjects: LCSH: Counselors—Professional ethics. | Counseling psychologists—Professional ethics. | Counseling—Moral and ethical aspects. | Counseling psychology—Moral and ethical aspects.

Classification: LCC BF636.67 .C64 2019 | DDC 174/.91583—dc23 LC record available at https://lccn.loc.gov/2017044642

This book is printed on acid-free paper.

18 19 20 21 22 10 9 8 7 6 5 4 3 2 1

CONTENTS

Preface   xi
Acknowledgments   xiii
Introduction   xv
    What Is Counseling Ethics?   xv
    Codes of Ethics and Law   xvi
    References   xx

PART I • BECOMING A VIRTUOUS THERAPIST

Chapter 1 • Building Character: Virtues of Excellent Practitioners   3
    What Being Virtuous Means   3
    The Counselor Virtues   5
    Questions for Review and Reflection   20
    Cases for Analysis   21
    References   22

Chapter 2 • Being Trustworthy   25
    CASE STUDIES: TWO RESISTANT CLIENTS
    A Client Who Tests Her Therapist's Trustworthiness   25
    Maintaining Trust in a Client Who Tests Her Therapist's Commitment   27
    A Suspicious, Apprehensive Client   29
    Establishing Trust With a Suspicious, Apprehensive Client   31
    Questions for Review and Reflection   33
    Cases for Analysis   34
    References   35

PART II • RESOLVING ETHICAL ISSUES

Chapter 3 • Applying Ethical Standards   39
    CASE STUDY: A CLASH OF VALUES INSIDE A FUNDAMENTALIST CHRISTIAN FAMILY
    A Clash of Values Inside a Fundamentalist Christian Family   40
    The Standards: An Overview   40
    Responsibilities to Clients   50

Applying the Ethical Standards to the Case of Shelly ... 52
Questions for Review and Reflection ... 53
Cases for Analysis ... 54
References ... 55

Chapter 4 • Using an Ethical Decision-Making Process ... 57

CASE STUDY: A HATEFUL CLIENT

A Case of a Hateful Client ... 58
What a Moral Problem Is ... 59
The Six Steps of Ethical Decision Making ... 61
Questions for Review and Reflection ... 74
Cases for Analysis ... 76
References ... 77

PART III • NAVIGATING KEY CONCEPTS: CONFIDENTIALITY AND INFORMED CONSENT

Chapter 5 • Exercising Discretion ... 81

CASE STUDY: A DANGEROUS CLIENT

A Case of a Dangerous Client ... 82
Ethical Limits of Confidentiality: Professional Codes of Ethics ... 82
The Legal Limits of Confidentiality ... 83
Decision Making in the Case of Arty ... 84
Confidentiality and Privileged Communication ... 89
Questions for Review and Reflection ... 92
Cases for Analysis ... 93
References ... 94

Chapter 6 • Being Candid and Honest ... 97

CASE STUDY: WITHHOLDING INFORMATION FROM A DEPRESSED CLIENT

A Case of Suspected Child Abuse ... 97
Legal Limits of Informed Consent ... 99
When Is Informed Consent Informed? ... 100
Circumstantial Information as Part of Informed Consent ... 104
Capacity as a Condition of Informed Consent ... 105
Informed Consent and the Termination of Therapy ... 107
Informed Consent in Couples and Family Counseling ... 108
Informed Consent and Therapist-Client Trust ... 109

Questions for Review and Reflection	110
Cases for Analysis	111
References	111

PART IV • EMPOWERING AND ADVOCATING FOR VULNERABLE POPULATIONS

Chapter 7 • Empowering Adult Victims of Domestic Abuse — 115

CASE STUDIES: PHYSICAL AND EMOTIONAL ABUSE

A Physically Abused Client	115
Empowering a Physically Abused Client	117
An Emotionally Abused Client	119
Empowering an Emotionally Abused Client	121
Questions for Review and Reflection	123
Cases for Analysis	124
References	124

Chapter 8 • Exercising Courage in Protecting Children — 125

CASE STUDY: CHILD SEXUAL ABUSE

A Case of Advocacy for Victims and Their Families	126
Questions for Review and Reflection	133
Cases for Analysis	134
References	134

PART V • COUNSELING ACROSS MULTIPLE ROLES AND CULTURES

Chapter 9 • Being Loyal and Fair to Clients — 137

CASE STUDY: SEX WITH A FORMER CLIENT

Conflicts of Interest	138
A Case of Sexual Attraction to a Client	140
Sexual Relations With Current Clients	141
Sexual Relations With Former Clients	142
Sexual Attraction to Clients	144
Online Relationships	146
Bartering for Fees	148
Pro Bono Counseling Services	149
Sliding Scales	150
Receiving Gifts From Clients	151

Questions for Review and Reflection 152
Cases for Analysis 154
References 155

Chapter 10 • Being Respectful Across Diverse Cultures 157

CASE STUDY: SUPERVISING A SUPERVISEE DOING CROSS-CULTURAL COUNSELING

A Case of Cross-Cultural Counseling 157
The Role of the Supervisor 159
Barriers to Resonating With the Client's Phenomenological World 160
Client Informed Consent in the Supervisory Context 162
The Supervisory Relationship 163
Online Supervision 165
Questions for Review and Reflection 166
Cases for Analysis 167
References 168

PART VI • COUNSELING IN CYBERSPACE

Chapter 11 • Being Diligent in the Digital Age 173

CASE STUDY: A CASE OF RECORD HACKING

The Primary Purpose of Counseling Records 173
What Counseling Records Include 174
The Hacking of a Vulnerable Network 175
The HIPAA Security Rule 175
Maintaining and Destroying Records 179
Questions for Review and Reflection 180
Cases for Analysis 181
References 182

Chapter 12 • Providing Competent Online Counseling Services 185

CASE STUDY: A SUICIDAL CLIENT

A Case of a Suicidal, Online Client 185
State Law and Ethical Responsibility 187
Interstate Agreements 189
Three Possible Models for Resolving Instate Conflict and Ambiguity 189
Informed Consent in Distance Counseling 191
Practicing Responsibly in Cyberspace 194

Questions for Review and Reflection — 194
Cases for Analysis — 195
References — 196

PART VII • DEFINING LIMITS OF CONFIDENTIALITY

Chapter 13 • Being Benevolent — 201

CASE STUDY: A TERMINALLY ILL CLIENT CONTEMPLATING SUICIDE

A Terminally Ill Client Contemplating Suicide — 202
The Conventional Moral View of Suicide — 202
Rational Suicide — 203
Legal Concerns — 206
Applying the Ethical Standards — 209
Qualifications for Conducting End-of-Life Counseling — 210
Permitted Suicide With Irremediably Ill Patients Who Are Not Terminally Ill — 211
Standards for Permitting Suicide in Mental Health Practice — 213
Questions for Review and Reflection — 215
Cases for Analysis — 216
References — 217

Chapter 14 • Being Nonmalevolent — 221

CASE STUDY: A SEXUALLY ACTIVE CLIENT WITH HIV

HIV and AIDS — 221
Discrimination Against Persons With HIV — 222
The Case of an HIV Positive Client and His Unsuspecting Fiancée — 223
The Ethical Challenge — 225
State Professional Regulations — 225
Respect for Client Self-Determination — 227
Facilitating Client Self-Disclosure — 228
Therapist Disclosure — 230
Building Trust and Preventing Harm — 235
Questions for Review and Reflection — 236
Cases for Analysis — 237
References — 239

Index — 241
About the Authors — 249

Sara Miller McCune founded SAGE Publishing in 1965 to support the dissemination of usable knowledge and educate a global community. SAGE publishes more than 1000 journals and over 800 new books each year, spanning a wide range of subject areas. Our growing selection of library products includes archives, data, case studies and video. SAGE remains majority owned by our founder and after her lifetime will become owned by a charitable trust that secures the company's continued independence.

Los Angeles | London | New Delhi | Singapore | Washington DC | Melbourne

PREFACE

This book is written for a wide range of mental health practitioners and students. It seeks to bring the mental health professions into the burgeoning digital age amid an ever changing kaleidoscope of ethical and legal challenges. For example, the Internet as a medium for conducting counseling sessions, communicating with clients, and storing records has raised new ethical and legal problems that call for careful reflection. In this new age, fundamental ethical and legal concepts such as confidentiality and informed consent have at once become more complex and vulnerable. Cyberattacks have undermined privacy. With the rise of social media, personal information, including that of therapists and their clients, may now be publicly accessed, thereby obscuring the boundaries of privacy. Multiple role relationships have expanded to include online relationships, which can potentially place a strain on both therapist and client objectivity.

The expanding ability to sustain human life past a meaningful quality has led to the revisiting of established norms such as proscriptions against physician assisted suicide and euthanasia, the former of which is now legal in some states. In the mental health fields, this rethinking has prompted changes in how therapists approach terminally ill clients who wish to hasten their own deaths. Here, professional codes of ethics have begun to address the subject, while legal standards are still unclear, hence leaving therapists in a quandary about what to do. Indeed, if therapists simply follow their own religious and/or moral lights, they risk imposing their own values on their clients, thereby violating client autonomy. If they play it safe by avoiding any potential legal risk, then they place self-interest above client autonomy and, potentially, the best interest of their clients.

In cases in which HIV positive clients are sexually active with partners who are unaware of the client's HIV positive status, professional codes of ethics as well as state laws have often left to the discretion of the therapist the question of whether to disclose confidential information to inform the client's sex partner of the potential health risk. Therapists may therefore, once again, be left in a quandary about what to do. Indeed, in such unsettled territory, the understanding and balancing of respect for client autonomy and harm to others require closer inspection to provide rational guidance about what to do.

These among many other ethical challenges broached in this book make abundantly clear that what is now needed, perhaps more than ever before, is a new moral compass: a new, clearly articulated and illustrated guide for mental health practitioners to identify and appropriately discharge their ethical and legal responsibilities to their clients. This is not readily accomplished by mechanical thinking, as though the moral and legal challenges of contemporary practice could be resolved by applying an algorithm. To the contrary, what is needed is a more robust, compassionate, authentic approach, where therapy remains a human encounter, not a robotic one. Such a counseling posture cannot be captured in a how-to approach, where resolution of ethical and legal problems becomes just another set of techniques applied. Instead, it is best captured in the Rogerian idea of persons relating to one another AS PERSONS.

This idea has profound implications for the type of ethics needed in the contemporary environment in which counseling and psychotherapy are conducted. Utilitarian ethics, which detach actions from the persons performing them and speak exclusively in terms of actions and their consequences, are inadequate in meeting the stated person-centered goal. In contrast, the ancient idea of virtue ethics can fill the void. According to the latter approach gleaned from such philosophers as Aristotle and Plato, effective therapy cannot be separated from the person conducting it. Being a good (effective) therapist and being a person who possesses human attributes such as trustworthiness, benevolence, empathy, genuineness, discretion, loyalty, and diligence are not distinct; for who one is in the counseling room cannot be separated from who one is outside it.

Such an ethics can be demanding, indeed. It requires moral sensitivity, including multicultural insight and understanding, attained through consistent practice. It involves development and reinforcement of cognitive, emotional, and behavioral skills in sensing and relating to the phenomenal worlds of the diverse clients served. It is an ethics that sets aspirational goals toward excellence in mental health practice. While this includes due care in adhering to basic legal requirements (for example, avoiding sexual relationships with current and former clients), it is much more.

Thus, the primary goal of this book emerges: to provide a guide for counselors and psychotherapists in cultivating the human virtues that equip them for meeting the challenges of the contemporary counseling scene. If we are successful in helping those who are the current and future members of the mental health practice community carefully reflect on and hone their human skills within the context of a growing body of state and federal law and codified professional ethics, then our primary goal in writing this book will have been achieved.

Elliot D. Cohen, PhD
Gale Spieler Cohen, EdD, LMHC, NCC

ACKNOWLEDGMENTS

This book owes its origins to many individuals with whom we both have shared information and experiences, or who have otherwise been instrumental in making this book possible. Those explicitly mentioned here are therefore not exhaustive of those to whom we owe a debt of gratitude. We are especially grateful to: Michael Davis, Senior Research Fellow, Illinois Institute of Technology Center for the Study of Ethics in the Professions, for his insights on conflicts of interest and related concepts; the late Michael Bayles, Professor of Philosophy, Florida State University, for his insights into the nature of the fiduciary relationship in the professions, especially as it pertains to virtuous practice; the late John Ladd, Professor Emeritus of Philosophy, Brown University, for his profound influence overall on my (Elliot D. Cohen) work in professional ethics, and especially on the concept of moral responsibility embedded in this book; the late Robert C. L. Moffat, Professor of Law, Levin Law Center, University of Florida, for introducing us to Lon Fuller's profoundly important distinction between the morality of aspiration and that of duty, a distinction that rebounds throughout this book; the late Albert Ellis, the father of cognitive-behavior therapy, for his personal friendship, exemplification of what being a devoted mental health practitioner portends, and fundamental concepts that undergird our approach such as Unconditional Self- and Other-Acceptance; Dr. William P. Knaus, original trainer at the Albert Ellis Institute in New York City, for his many insights and discussions on procrastination and related problems that can affect the ethical decision-making process; Jeffrey Spike, professor at the McGovern Center for Humanities and Ethics, The University of Texas Health Science Center at Houston; and Dr. Bruce Dutra, Dean, Division of Liberal Arts, College of Morris County, for his insightful comments on the ethics of online counseling. I (Gale Spieler Cohen) would also like to acknowledge Carl Rogers for his ever present influence on this book. While neither of us knew him personally, my thinking on counseling and counseling ethics was strongly influenced by his work, having written analyses, during my graduate school years, of most of the audio- and videotapes that he made. I (Elliot D. Cohen) am, in turn, greatly indebted to Gale Spieler Cohen for our enlightening discussions about Rogers' Person-Centered Approach, especially as it relates to virtue ethics.

Special thanks goes to Kassie Graves, our former editor at SAGE, for taking on this project with us; Nathan Davidson, our interim editor, for his patient support; and Abbie Rickard, our present editor, for her professionalism and assistance in overseeing this project in its final stages.

Thanks also go to the reviewers whose feedback helped shape the development of this text: Monique Levermore, University of Central Florida; Don MacDonald, Seattle Pacific University; Christine McNichols, The University of Texas at Tyler; Anna M. Viviani, Indiana State University; and Jessica S. Waesche, University of Central Florida.

INTRODUCTION

WHAT IS COUNSELING ETHICS?

The term *ethics* has different senses. Sometimes it is used to mean the same thing as *morality* as when one questions another's ethics. However, the term *ethics* can also be used to refer to a *discipline* that studies morality. It is in this latter sense that we are using the term *counseling ethics*. In this sense, counseling ethics is the discipline that studies the morality of counseling.

Counseling ethics belongs to the broader area of inquiry known as *professional ethics*, which also includes the ethics of other professions such as medicine, law, business, engineering, journalism, and accounting, among others. In the context of professional ethics, the term *morality* can refer to professional codes of ethics that define morally appropriate conduct within a professional area (e.g., the American Counseling Association *Code of Ethics*, the American Psychological Association *Ethical Principles of Psychologists and Code of Conduct*, and The National Association of Social Workers *Code of Ethics*). It can also refer to general theories, standards, or principles that determine right from wrong conduct (e.g., not harming others, respecting autonomy, and promoting welfare). Finally, it can refer to ideals such as what it means to be a *virtuous* practitioner (e.g., diligence, loyalty, honesty, and candor). Some treatments of counseling ethics concentrate primarily on the examination of codes of ethics and/or principles; others may emphasize virtuous practice. The present book takes a virtue-based approach that demonstrates the importance of all three types of standards.

Some professional ethics approaches hold that professional ethics and personal ethics are separate and distinct. For example, a journalist may be said to be acting ethically in invading the privacy of individuals (e.g., electronically eavesdropping on them) to obtain a story, whereas such an act performed by an ordinary person in a non-journalistic context would ordinarily be considered the pinnacle of immorality (Daniel, 1982). Similarly, a defense attorney may be commended in cross-examining a rape complainant whom he knows to be telling the truth to cast doubt on her truthful testimony; whereas such an act would be considered abhorrent and underhanded if an ordinary person did something similar in a nonlegal context (Fried, 1976). However, regardless of the merits (or demerits) of distinguishing between personal and professional ethics in certain professions such as journalism and law, this distinction is difficult to maintain in the case of counseling ethics (Cohen & Cohen, 1999).

As this book demonstrates, being an ethical counselor requires being an ethical person, both inside and outside professional practice. For example, clients do not generally trust phonies, so being an authentic (genuine) person is not just part of what it means to be an ethical practitioner; it is also part of what it means to be an effective one; for without trust a client would not venture to disclose her deep, dark secrets; and without such disclosure, a counselor could not help his client work through her unfinished business. This convergence between being a good person and being a good therapist makes the distinction between ethical counseling practice and being an ethical person quite artificial, and potentially harmful to client welfare. This, in turn, makes ethical counseling practice quite challenging because it requires more than simply a commitment to learning and applying a set of techniques. Clearly, being a good person is not a set of techniques, learned and applied. To the contrary, it involves a lifetime commitment in the course of one's everyday life as well as inside the counseling room. But such an aspirational dimension of counseling ethics is also what makes it such an exciting pursuit!

CODES OF ETHICS AND LAW

> Todd Seabert, LMHC, has been seeing his client, Peter Portobello for 2 months. His presenting problem is existential anxiety. "I feel like my life is meaningless" he states. "Tell me about that," Seabert asks, but Peter is unwilling to disclose. Finally, after 2 months, Peter reposes his trust in Seabert and drops a bombshell.
>
> "I have HIV. My wife doesn't know it. I had an affair, and that's where I think I got it."
>
> "Are you having intercourse with your wife?" Seabert quickly asks.
>
> "Yes, we are, several times a week," he says in a matter of fact tone, with a hint of uneasiness.
>
> Seabert braces himself as he asks that crucial question. "Are you using protection?"
>
> Silence fills the room as the pause in responding seems like an eternity. Then there is the resounding unmistakable sound of "No."

So what if Peter refuses to stop engaging in unprotected intercourse with his wife? Indeed, Seabert has gotten this far with his client because he now trusts him. Should Seabert betray this trust by contacting Peter's wife to inform her about the situation? On the other hand, should he respect his client's confidence, even if it places Peter's wife in harm's way? How is he to decide?

Codes of ethics can only take one so far. For example, B.2.c of the *ACA Code of Ethics* states:

> When clients disclose that they have a disease commonly known to be both communicable and life threatening, counselors may be justified in disclosing information to identifiable third parties, if the parties are known to be at serious and foreseeable risk of contracting the disease. (American Counseling Association [ACA], 2014)

So he "may be justified," but that does not mean he *must* disclose. The Code stops short of a duty to disclose. So is there a *legal* if not a moral duty to disclose?

As discussed in Chapter 14, state statutes may give the same permission, while leaving the moral judgment in the therapist's court. For example, Florida Statute [FS] 491.0147 (2016) permits disclosure of confidential client information when the counselor believes that "there is a clear and immediate probability of physical harm to the patient or client, to other individuals, or to society . . ." And FS 456.061 (2016), under certain conditions, grants practitioners (including mental health counselors, psychologists, marriage and family therapists, and clinical social workers [Florida Health, n.d.]) immunity from both civil and criminal liability if they decide to disclose information about a client's positive HIV test; but it also provides the same immunity if they decide not to disclose.

The upshot is quite clear. One cannot easily look up and find the answers to the gnawing (indeed exasperating) moral problems encountered in one's practice of counseling and psychotherapy. While such codes and legal standards can provide the general parameters within which decisions are to be made, they often do not settle these problems. So, for example, the aforementioned ethical and legal standards (ACA B.2.c and FS 456.061) make clear that the practitioner must inform the client of his or her intent to disclose to the at-risk sex partner prior to making the disclosure. But the question regarding whether or not to disclose in the first place is left to the discretion of the practitioner.

And this is exactly as it ought to be; for, as this book demonstrates, ethics is about the exercise of judgment. True, some ethical questions are fully addressed by a legal or moral code, such as the universal proscription against having sex with current clients (as addressed in Chapter 9). But notice that such regulations set very basic ground rules of practice, that is, ones that tell you how to avoid malpractice suits. These are not the sort of standards that tell you how to be an excellent therapist. Here we can do well to distinguish between what has sometimes been called the "Morality of Duty" versus the "Morality of Aspiration" (Fuller, 1964, p. 5). The former tells you what is required (such as not sleeping with your clients). Those who violate these basic duties are punished—have their licensed revoked, fined, and/or jailed. In contrast, the "Morality of Aspiration" sets ideals to which to aspire to attain excellence in one's practice. Those who violate the latter are not typically punished through institutionalized means such as fines and imprisonment, but may be criticized for their shortcomings. So no one puts a therapist in prison for failing to be empathetic unless this somehow involves some more basic breach of duty (e.g., exposing the client to a life-threatening harm). On the other hand, we may criticize such a therapist for falling short of what we think a therapist should be like. So if you want to do your basic duties, then moral and legal codes can be reasonably serviceable. But that is not likely to solve those gnawing ethical challenges that come with striving to be an excellent therapist. Here, there is typically need to exercise moral judgment honed by experience and practice.

Codes of ethics and law are also sometimes inconsistent. For example, 1.09(c) of The Code of Ethics of the National Association of Social Workers (NASW, 2017) states:

> Social workers should not engage in sexual activities or sexual contact with former clients because of the potential for harm to the client. If social workers engage in conduct contrary to this prohibition or claim that an exception to this prohibition is warranted because of extraordinary circumstances, it is social workers—not their clients—who assume the full burden of demonstrating that the former client has not been exploited, coerced, or manipulated, intentionally or unintentionally.

In contrast, A.5.c of the ACA Code of Ethics (ACA, 2014) states that

> sexual and/or romantic counselor–client interactions or relationships with former clients, their romantic partners, or their family members are prohibited for a period of 5 years following the last professional contact.... Counselors, before engaging in sexual and/or romantic interactions or relationships with former clients, their romantic partners, or their family members, demonstrate forethought and document (in written form) whether the interaction or relationship can be viewed as exploitive in any way and/or whether there is still potential to harm the former client...

While both codes discourage sex with former clients, notice that the NASW Code does not provide any time limit for exceptions to the rule of non-engagement. In contrast, the ACA Code specifies 5 years. Moreover, the ACA Code requires documentation in writing whereas the NASW Code does not. As such, one could be acting in line with the NASW Code by waiting 6 months to have sex with a former client without documenting in writing the extraordinary nature of the relationship; whereas the latter would be in clear violation of the ACA Code.

Codes of ethics can also conflict with law. For example, FS 491.0112(1) (2016) states that

> any psychotherapist who commits sexual misconduct with a client, or former client when the professional relationship was terminated primarily for the purpose of engaging in sexual contact, commits a felony of the third degree...

And according to FS 491.0112(4)c (2016),

> "Sexual misconduct" means the oral, anal, or vaginal penetration of another by, or contact with, the sexual organ of another or the anal or vaginal penetration of another by any object.

This means that the counselor who waits 6 months to have sex with a former client could be guilty of a third degree felony if he terminated the counseling relationship for the purpose of engaging in sex, even if he believes he can document the nonexploitative nature of the sexual relationship. So this counselor could be acting in conformity with the NASW Code but still be guilty of a third degree felony.

Generally, when codes of ethics and the law conflict, it is in one's best interest to comply with the law; but does that necessarily mean one is acting ethically?

From the institution of slavery to the old racial laws and the oppression of women, the history of law in the United States has supported great iniquity. It cannot, therefore, be assumed that what is legal must also be moral. Indeed, even when laws have a moral basis, their application in some exceptional cases can have profoundly unethical consequences. For example, it is not unreasonable to require a pregnant minor to get parental permission before having an abortion, inasmuch as an abortion is a medical procedure and parental approval should ordinarily be secured before performing a medical procedure on a child. Unfortunately, where the minor's father is also the one who impregnated her, forcing the child to endure the pregnancy because the father refuses to give the legally mandated permission would be a miscarriage of justice. Moreover, while in such cases, there may be legal recourse (i.e., requiring the father to have a paternity test), such processes can often be mired in a maze of legal gymnastics (e.g., the father secures an attorney to help him "assert his legal rights"). Consequently, a legal outcome may be far afield of a moral one.

In this context of morally perplexing legality, it may take great courage to act morally. On the one hand, acting in accordance with settled law can provide self-protection but lead to a morally regrettable outcome; while, on the other hand, acting morally can place one in a legally precarious situation.

Consider this further case involving child custody:

> Clare Vasquez, a clinical social worker has made remarkable progress with Jeannie, a 4-year-old. At first, Jeannie was nondisclosing; however, through play therapy, it became abundantly clear to Clare that Jeannie was a victim of sexual abuse and that the perpetrator was her father, Bill, a very wealthy and influential businessman in the community. With Clare's support, Jeannie's mom, Sarah, separated from Bill and filed for sole custody of Jeannie. However, in response, Bill filed for sole custody on grounds that Sarah was an unfit mother. While Sarah, herself a survivor of sexual abuse, had had a history of drug addiction and depression, she had made much progress, had been clean for the past 2 years, and was committed to keeping her little girl safe and secure from further molestation at the hands of Bill. Unfortunately, Bill had the best legal representation money could buy, whereas Sarah's attorney was inept. To make matters worse, if that was possible, the judge assigned to the case played golf with Bill. It did not come as a surprise, therefore, when the judge awarded sole custody of Jeannie to Bill.
>
> Sarah was despondent and looked to Clare for help. It was evident that turning Jeannie over to her father, as the law required, would mark the end of the progress Jeannie had made and would subject this vulnerable little girl to a hellish life of repeated sexual molestation by a clever and seriously disturbed perpetrator. On the other hand, Clare was well aware of the existence of an underground network that could help Sarah make an escape with Jeannie, turning her into a fugitive from the law but keeping her daughter, at least temporarily, outside the reach of her molester father. Clare knew that this possibility had its own negative consequences, including forcing the child into a life of hiding, and subjecting the mom to the possibility of ending up in prison for the commission of a felony. She also questioned whether Sarah, herself, a survivor of sexual abuse, would have the will and determination to see this through, or would, in the end, cave under pressure. And, of course, there were the legal risks Clare herself would be taking in assisting Sarah to go underground. What was Clare to do?

In such a case as this, the law is clearly not the solution; it is, instead, part of the problem. Here, doing what is morally right is a complex matter that pits respect for law against one's concern for the welfare of one's clients—a vulnerable child and her mom. The morality of duty, which demands obedience to the law, does not begin to capture the complex nature of such a decision. In this case, the question is not what one must do, but what one *should do as a virtuous practitioner*. It is about *courage* in the face of personal risks; it is about deeply *empathizing* with the plights of this mom and her daughter; it is about *benevolence* and *compassion* for others. These are aspects of the morality of aspiration, a virtue-based morality, not of a bare-bones morality of requirement.

In the end, this decision is one that is likely to portend regrets for Clare no matter what she does. Still, the standard response that one must simply do what is legally required misses the point. For it is well within the parameters of an ethical choice for Clare to decide otherwise. Of course, we must pick and choose the battles we wish to fight and the hills we are willing to die on; but the point is that we must choose; and this choice is not simply one a therapist can look up in a volume of laws or code of ethics.

Further, legal responsibility is distinct from *moral* responsibility. The former is about blaming and making someone pay for their unlawful action. In some cases, the person who is blamed and made to pay may not have done anything morally wrong, as in vicarious legal liability where an employee commits an untoward act unbeknownst to the employer, who is made to pay. Sometimes the person held legally responsible is the one who has the financial means to pay. Sometimes this "person" is a corporation, not even a flesh and blood person.

In contrast, moral responsibility arises when a person has the knowledge and ability to affect, for better or worse, the welfare or interests of others who depend on the person (Ladd, 1982). Thus, therapists have moral responsibilities to their clients, who depend on and trust them, because they have special knowledge and power to affect their welfare, for good or ill. So moral responsibility is about helping others, not about casting blame for purposes of making someone pay. It is about compassionate caring for the plights of others; it is about kindness and, in the very least, the sincere desire that others not be harmed by one's actions.

Accordingly, this book is about what is involved in being a *virtuous* practitioner, not just a practitioner who avoids malpractice suits, fines, and imprisonment. To be clear, we cannot overstate the importance of considering applicable laws and professional rules of ethics in making ethical decisions. Indeed, this book integrates careful discussion of relevant federal, state, and case law into the ethical decision-making process. Therapists who do not know such laws or who do but practice with disregard for the laws are not likely to advance the welfare or interests of their clients or themselves. But excellence in the human services professions is a much higher calling, one that goes to the heart of who one is as a human being, both inside and outside the counseling room. In Chapter 1, we describe the virtues of such an excellent practitioner. In subsequent chapters, we examine these virtues within the context of addressing a myriad of case vignettes that illustrate persistent challenges to ethical counseling practice.

References

American Counseling Association. (2014). *ACA code of ethics*. Alexandria, VA: Author. Retrieved from counseling.org/resources/aca-code-of-ethics.pdf

Cohen, E. D., & Cohen, G. S. (1999). *The virtuous therapist: Ethical practice of counseling and psychotherapy*. Belmont, CA: Wadsworth.

Daniel, S. H. (1982). Ethical theory and journalistic ethics. *International Journal of Applied Philosophy, 1*(1), 19–25.

Florida Health. (n.d.). *Licensing and regulation*. Tallahassee, FL: Author. Retrieved from http://www.floridahealth.gov/licensing-and-regulation/

Fried, C. (1976). The lawyer as friend: The moral foundations of the lawyer-client relation. *Yale Law Journal, 85*, 1060–1089. Retrieved from https://dash.harvard.edu/handle/1/23903316

Fuller, L. (1964). *The morality of law*. New Haven, CT: Yale University Press.

Ladd, J. (1982). Philosophical remarks on professional responsibility in organizations. *International Journal of Applied Philosophy, 1*(2), 58–70.

National Association of Social Workers. (2017). *Code of ethics of the National Association of Social Workers*. Washington, DC: Author. Retrieved from https://www.socialworkers.org/About/Ethics/Code-of-Ethics/Code-of-Ethics-English.aspx

BECOMING A VIRTUOUS THERAPIST

PART I

1

BUILDING CHARACTER

Virtues of Excellent Practitioners

As discussed in the introduction, it is one thing to practice within the limits of law and another to be an excellent therapist. The former is a necessary condition for the latter, but not a sufficient condition. Here, aspiring to excellence in counseling and psychotherapy requires commitment to cultivating the moral character that is emblematic of virtuous practice. Accordingly, this first chapter starts with the basics of virtue ethics, which stresses the cultivation of moral character. In particular, it defines what it means to be virtuous, and then develops accounts of 14 interconnected counselor virtues that guide virtuous practice.

WHAT BEING VIRTUOUS MEANS

Virtue ethics received its most elaborate articulation in ancient Greek philosophy, especially in the writings of Aristotle. A key note of this approach is that virtuous practice is akin to skill building. According to Aristotle (2015), becoming virtuous is like becoming good at an art or craft. For example, if one wants to become a good musician, one needs to practice. There are no shortcuts. It takes time, patience, and perseverance. Difficult musical passages are executed (e.g., playing a classical guitar piece) by repeatedly executing the difficult passages. The more one practices, the more one can become adept at executing them. It is similar with respect to becoming virtuous. This is because virtues are *habits*. For example, consider the character trait of truthfulness. What does it mean to be truthful?

One becomes truthful by telling the truth. The more one tells the truth, the more one gets used to it. On the other hand, the more one tells falsehoods with the attempt to deceive or mislead others, the more one gets used to being duplicitous. Indeed, one truth does not make one truthful; for it takes a truthful character to be truthful. This means being in the habit of telling the truth.

Such a habit of truthfulness involves the *intrinsic desire* to tell the truth, not merely truth-telling. So an untruthful person can be forced at gun point to repeatedly speak the truth; but that does not make this person truthful. The truthful person desires to tell the truth for informational purposes. Moreover, a truthful person will also have requisite emotions regarding the truth. For example, a truthful person may feel guilty or uncomfortable about not having been forthright enough in presenting the facts. In contrast, an untruthful person may lie without batting an eyelash. So possessing the *virtue* of truthfulness means that one is in a habit of acting, thinking, and feeling in truthful ways. This is why virtuous practice is so challenging. It is a matter of character, not just right conduct.

Virtues also involve moderation, that is, the avoidance of extremes. Thus, Aristotle (2015) informs us that

> virtue must have the quality of aiming at the intermediate. I mean moral virtue; for it is this that is concerned with passions and actions, and in these there is excess, defect, and the intermediate. For instance, both fear and confidence and appetite and anger and pity and in general pleasure and pain may be felt both too much and too little, and in both cases not well; but to feel them at the right times, with reference to the right objects, towards the right people, with the right motive, and in the right way, is what is both intermediate and best, and this is characteristic of virtue. (Bk. 2, Ch. 6)

So (moral) virtue involves controlling ones passions (anger, fear, desire, pity, etc.) in a manner that avoids the extremes of excess and efficiency. This, in turn, requires having the ability to adjust one's response to the context or situation. So the intermediate with regard to controlling one's fears will invariably depend on such factors as the object of fear, the nature of the impending danger, and what you are trying to accomplish. For example, one may act appropriately in subduing a wild boar that was poised to attack you by shooting it. However, it would be overreacting if you attempted to subdue a yapping Chihuahua in the same way. Indeed, what is extreme and what is intermediate will vary with the nature of the situation. The virtuous person will be able to assess the situation and act accordingly. As Aristotle (2015), admonished, such judgment is not something one can learn entirely from reading a book; rather, it requires time and experience so that we should better trust "the opinions of experienced and older people . . . for because experience has given them an eye they see aright" (2015, Bk. 6, Ch. 11).

In the context of counseling, assessing danger appropriately requires judgment tempered by experience. So, as we build up our client databases, we can draw analogical inferences from our experiences. "I recall that a former client expressed a desire to kill his wife after he found out she was cheating on him. I was able to help him get through it. And the profile of my current client is very similar." Of course, we also learn from trial and error, and failure to take adequate precautions can, in retrospect, help us avoid the same mistake in the future. On the other hand, it would be going to extremes to have one's clients involuntarily detained every time they expressed a desire to kill someone; for this would surely alienate clients and thwart their progress. Experience can indeed light the pathway to virtuous practice, but it provides no algorithm. As you will see, being a virtuous practitioner involves a sort of artful practical knowhow that depends largely on one's ability to hone in on the welfare and interests of clients and other relevant third parties, and to see these factors through the magnifying lenses of experience and professional training. Such ability requires cultivation of a set of mutually supportive habits or *counselor virtues* involving dispositions of thought, feeling, and action.

THE COUNSELOR VIRTUES

The following descriptions provide snapshots of what such a set of mutually supportive virtues looks like.

Benevolence/Nonmalevolence

As helping professionals, who are privy to the most intimate and personal aspects of their clients' lives, virtuous counselors are benevolent, which means that they are deeply committed to advancing the welfare of their clients. Benevolent counselors seek to eliminate pain and suffering of clients as well as advance their positive welfare (Cohen & Cohen, 1999). For example, helping a client overcome a major depression eliminates serious client suffering; whereas helping a client gain greater confidence in social contexts helps promote positive change.

Benevolent counselors' deep commitment to their clients is reflected not only in the provision of competent services that advance client welfare, but also in the expression of caring sentiments and thoughts. Indeed, to be benevolent means to feel joy at client progress and sadness or regret at setbacks. Benevolent counselors also have *intrinsic* regard for the well-being of their clients (Cohen, 1985); that is, they see client progress as good *in itself*, not merely as an instrumental value (such as a means of making money, advancing professional reputation, or receiving praise).

Such practitioners do not stand on ceremony when it comes to client welfare. They are flexibly adaptive, and do not ordinarily "fire" their clients when they refuse to follow their counsel. They view resistance as an inevitable part of the counseling process, and make reasonable efforts to work with resistant clients to overcome barriers to progress. Of course, being benevolent also means avoiding going to extremes to accommodate clients, such as when counseling becomes unhelpful or counterproductive. Benevolent counselors terminate counseling or make a suitable referral when it becomes evident that continuing the counseling relationship is not serving the best interest of the client (American Counseling Association [ACA], 2014, A.11.c).

A condition of benevolence is nonmalevolence (Cohen & Cohen, 1999). This means that the benevolent counselor avoids inflicting harm on the client and seeks to prevent harm. In accord with the premier medical ethic, "First, do no harm" (Latin: *Primum non nocere*), the nonmaleficent counselor perceives infliction of harm on a client as deplorable. Indeed, better to leave the client without improvement than to leave her worse off! Nonmaleficent counselors are therefore strongly inclined toward referring clients when it's evident that counseling them poses a serious risk of inflicting harm. For instance, such a basis for referral may arise when the counselor lacks adequate knowledge and experience in treating a particular type of mental disorder (ACA, 2014, A.11.a).

Nonmalevolent counselors also seek to prevent future harm to clients as well as third parties (Cohen & Cohen, 1999). For example, nonmalevolent counselors will take reasonable precautions in safeguarding a suicidal client from attempting suicide. Such a counselor will also act responsibly to prevent harm to endangered third parties—for example, as when a client makes a credible threat to kill or seriously injure another person.

Empathy

Benevolent counselors are also empathetic persons. This is because one cannot begin to help others if one does not have a clue about what will, in fact, conduce to their well-being. Being empathetic permits a counselor to key into the welfare and interests of clients so that they can, in turn, assist them in making constructive life changes.

The virtue of empathy involves the settled ability to resonate with the plights of others, to sense the subjective meanings of their personal and interpersonal challenges, and to be there for them in helping facilitate constructive change (Cohen, 2015). This state of resonance involves a balance of cognitive, affective, sensitive, and behavioral factors. As Carl Rogers (1961) expressed it, in empathizing, it is "as if" one is in the subjective world of another, but "without losing the 'as if' quality," that is, without losing one's objectivity as an observer (p. 284). The latter "as if" is especially important for counselors because loss of objectivity would prevent the counselor from helping the client engage in self-exploration. Suppose your client has just lost her husband of 20 years in a car accident. A drunk driver ran a stop sign, ending his life instantly. Whether or not you have, yourself, suffered such a tragic loss, you can still empathize; for you can know what it would be like to lose someone so close to you—you can imagine the harsh reality of not ever being able to see, confide in, or experience the love and support of someone who has played such a major role in your life for so many years; and the way it happened, so unexpectedly and tragically (Cohen, 2007). To empathize here is to grasp the *subjective* meaning and import of these facts, which includes *feeling* (viscerally) the client's devastation—the hollowness is in your gut, too, and the lump is in your throat. You are there *with* the client, sensing what she is going through: the incredulity ("How can this be!"); the forlornness ("I have nothing left!"); the futility ("How could this have happened!"); the anxiety ("What's going to happen to me now!?"); the sense of powerlessness ("Nothing will ever bring him back!"). From this point of subjective reference, you are able to reflect back these emotionally charged meanings in a way that conveys insight and understanding, which, in turn, encourages further client disclosure:

"So you are feeling that there's nothing you could ever do to fill the void?"

"Yes, I could never look at another man. That would be disloyal."

Relevant self-disclosure can sometimes add to this resonance:

"I recall when my dad died suddenly of a heart attack, how lost I felt . . ."

"Yes, that's exactly it. I feel so lost!"

Here, as in all virtues, there is an intermediate point attained where there is the right balance of cognitive, emotive, behavioral, and sensitive factors. In empathizing with your client, you do not plunge so deeply into her subjective world that you too are lost. Neither too close, nor too distant—close enough to grasp and sense the client's subjective meanings, but not so close that you become so emotionally involved that the client's desperation becomes your own and you lose the ability to help.

Clearly, the ability to attain this Aristotelian "golden mean" (state of intermediate, harmonic balance between your subjective world and that of your client) is no mere counseling technique. It requires a settled character (habit) of being an empathetic person (Aristotle, 2015; Cohen, 2003). One does not become empathetic when one enters the counseling room. One enters as an empathetic person, and leaves as one. As such, empathizing occasionally no more makes one empathetic than does telling the truth on occasion make one truthful. This does not mean that empathetic people must always feel empathy for the plights of others any more than truthful people must always tell the truth. However, when lack of empathetic regard becomes more the rule than the exception, then it is clear that the person in question is not habitually disposed toward being empathetic.

Empathy, like other counselor virtues can be practiced and improved. This book (especially Chapter 4) will help you cultivate and strengthen your powers of empathy.

Authenticity

Being empathetic leads to client self-disclosure only if the client trusts the therapist with her personal information. However, client trust is not likely to be established if the therapist is not authentic. Authenticity involves genuineness; that is, not being a phony or putting on a façade. Carl Rogers (1977, p. 9) refers to this state of genuineness as "congruence," meaning that what is going on inside (the person's thoughts, desires, and emotions) matches what is going on outside (behavior, intonation, speech, facial expressions, and other body language). When therapists' inner and outer states are in alignment, clients are more likely to confide in them and disclose deeply personal matters. On the other hand, when these states are incongruent (inconsistent), clients are able to pick up on the disparity. For example, some subtle (and not so subtle) outward appearances may betray the attempt to conceal one's anger with a smile; for the smile may appear strained, and one's pupils may contract, presenting a "beady little eye" appearance. Such outward signs can alert the client that the therapist is not trustworthy, thereby chilling off the potential disclosure.

Authenticity is a broader concept than being congruent in a therapy session, however. As a virtue, it portends a habit and tendency to present as a congruent person, both inside and outside the counseling room (Cohen & Cohen, 1999). The authentic person is also an honest person since dishonesty (such as lying) requires misrepresenting one's true motives, emotions, or beliefs. Further, as an honest person, the authentic person accepts responsibility for her actions (Sartre, 1989).

Authenticity is, in fact, a keynote of existential therapy. In such therapy, emphasis is on accepting responsibility for one's actions (or inactions), and not making excuses or hiding behind pretense. Thus, French existentialist philosopher Jean-Paul Sartre (1989) famously drives home the point that

> we have neither behind us, nor before us in a luminous realm of values, any means of justification or excuse. We are left alone, without excuse. That is what I mean when I say that man is condemned to be free. Condemned, because he did not create himself, yet is nevertheless at liberty, and from the moment that he is thrown into this world he is responsible for everything he does. (para. 11)

So, according to Sartre, we always have a choice, even if it is the negative one of refusing to do something. Thus, the teenager, who joins a gang as a way to deal with peer pressure, or the battered housewife, who remains in an abusive relationship because she tells herself that she cannot survive on her own, are simply hiding behind excuses rather than taking responsibility for their choices. The authentic person makes no excuses. Such a person distinguishes between not having any choices and not having any easy choices. So, in the case of the teenager, it may be difficult to withstand peer pressure, and in the case of the battered housewife, it may be difficult to forge a new life on her own, but the challenging nature of such choices is not the same as not having any genuine choices. Indeed, the authentic person does not deny her freedom to decide, even when the available options are difficult or challenging. The authentic person realizes that standing up to the anxiety of choosing amid an uncertain future is exactly the way one grows, morally and intellectually.

Authentic persons are not blind conformists who try to hide their freedom and responsibility by allowing others to choose for them (Cohen, 2017). They avoid the extremes of blind conformity (doing or saying things just because others are) and blind *non*conformity (doing or saying things just to be oppositional). Instead, such persons are guided by their own moral and intellectual lights and avoid needless, groundless, or arbitrary conformity and nonconformity.

Such individuals have a word and can generally be trusted to do what they say they will do. They do not ordinarily cave to social pressure and tend to be true to their moral convictions. Therapists who are authentic persons, therefore, present as models for their clients to emulate. Inasmuch as many clients come to therapy because they feel powerless, trapped, or otherwise not in control of their own lives, therapists who are authentic can inspire their clients to exercise the courage to make constructive changes in their lives rather than make excuses about why they cannot (Kolden, Klein, Wang, & Austin, 2011). In contrast, therapists who model the inconsistent directive of "Do as I say, not as I do" fail to encourage or inspire clients to make constructive life changes.

Courage

Authenticity requires courage because it is not possible to be transparent unless one is willing to risk being negatively judged by others. Indeed, authentic persons do not expect that others will always accept or agree with them; and it may be expedient to avoid others' negative judgments by hiding or disguising one's true convictions, desires, motives, and feelings. Yet the authentic person is true to herself and exercises courage in the face of such adversity.

Courage involves taking risks for the sake of a "noble end" (Aristotle, 2015, Bk. 3, Ch. 7). This means doing what you think is morally right even when you believe that doing so means risking suffering some substantial harm. As Aristotle explains, it is "the mark of a brave man to face things that are, and seem, terrible for a man, because it is noble to do so and disgraceful not to do so" (Bk. 3, Ch. 8).

In professional contexts, the exercise of courage involves standing on principle notwithstanding that this may involve risking loss of time, money, reputation, friendship, popularity, or other personal or professional resource (Cohen, 1985). In counseling clients, there are inevitably situations arising that may involve making choices about what to do when client welfare conflicts (or appears to conflict) with the therapist's welfare.

The courageous therapist seeks to promote the client's welfare notwithstanding the latter personal conflict. For example, as shown in Chapter 8, putting one's reputation or job on the line to challenge an unethical practice in the workplace can take courage; however, if the prevention of serious harm to one's client hangs in the balance, the courageous therapist tends to favor client protection above her own interests in reputation or job security. Clearly, risking loss of one's job to challenge a relatively minor transgression may not be worth the potential personal sacrifice, but it is in the nature of a courageous therapist to make a reasonable and informed assessment of the situation and to act accordingly. Here there is avoidance of the extremes. One such extreme is to act rashly in the face of danger, that is, in a manner that is impetuous and takes unreasonable risks. The other opposite extreme is to act cowardly, that is, in a manner that is motivated primarily by fear and avoidance of risk without due consideration to client welfare. In each extreme, there is an ethically inappropriate response to perceived danger; the former being not afraid enough; the latter being too afraid. In contrast, the courageous therapist is in a habit of avoiding both extremes, and thus tends to be neither insufficiently nor overly fearful (Aristotle, 2015). The courageous therapist is thus disposed, in the course of her counseling practice (and outside it), to make such "intermediate" ethical judgments about whether and how much to fear something and then act accordingly. As such, the courageous therapist has the strength of will to act on her ethical judgment. This is in contrast to the weak-willed or "incontinent" person who may know what is right but nevertheless fails to act according to his better judgment (Aristotle, 2015, Bk. 7, Ch. 1).

Honesty

The courageous therapist is also honest because dishonest people tend to be intentionally manipulative and deceitful to get what they want, whereas courageous people tend to do what they think is right even if that means not getting what they want or prefer.

Conversely, honest people tend to be courageous. This is because such people are accustomed to being truthful and doing what they say they will do (keeping their word). However, this requires exercising courage in situations where speaking the truth or keeping one's word portends personal risk or sacrifice. So, for example, an honest therapist, who had serious monetary problems, would not continue to treat a client who was not making satisfactory progress merely to receive fees for services rendered. Rather, the therapist would act in the best interest of the client, such as by providing an appropriate referral, even though such an action might mean substantial loss of income for the therapist.

Honesty is not the same as truthfulness, but is instead a broader concept. This is because a person can tend to be truthful but nevertheless deceitful and therefore dishonest (Bayles, 1989). For example, some people manipulate others to do things on their behalf through the use of pity or seduction, yet tell the truth about their true intentions when asked later, after they get what they want. Such individuals are not honest but they may still be truthful about their dishonesty! So being truthful does not necessarily make one honest, for honesty involves being *both* truthful and non-deceitful.

Truthful people tend to tell the truth with the intent to provide an accurate and reasonably complete account of the facts. In contrast, people who habitually lie tend to make statements they believe to be false with the intent to deceive others about the facts (Mahon, 2016). Such individuals are therefore deceitful in a particular way. They intentionally make statements about the facts they believe to be false. They may be and often are motivated by self-interest (e.g., to escape being blamed for a misdeed) but this is not necessarily true, since some deceitful people (pathological ones) lie about things even when it is clearly not in their best interest to lie about them.

Lies need to be distinguished from half-truths. A half-truth provides part of the truth while intentionally leaving out other information that is needed to form an informed perspective (Cohen, 2009). For example, when former President William Jefferson Clinton famously stated, "I never had a sexual relationship with that woman, Monica Lewinsky," he did not lie; but what he failed to also say was that he meant "sexual relationship" in the biblical sense. So Clinton told a half-truth by attempting to create a false impression, not by disseminating falsehoods, but by leaving out pertinent facts.

As such, honest people are not only truthful, but they are also not prone to engage in half-truths. In the context of therapy, this means that honest therapists do not engage in deceptive practices such as telling clients that they have credentials without telling them what field they are in, for example, holding oneself out as "Dr." when one's doctorate is in educational leadership or some other non–mental health field, or otherwise misrepresenting one's credentials or training (ACA, 2014, C.4.d). Likewise, honest therapists do not file false, misleading, or incomplete reports to third parties such as courts or insurance companies; for example, sending in a diagnosis to an insurance company that you know to be false just for the sake of being reimbursed (ACA, 2014, C.6.b). They do not guarantee successful treatment or otherwise manipulate prospective clients to enlist them as clients, lie or misrepresent their qualifications to treat certain mental disorders, or manipulate or deceive potential research subjects about the nature and possible adverse effects of the research to enlist them in a research project (ACA, 2014, C.2.c, C.3.a, G.2.a).

Indeed, the honest therapist is also an honest person who has cultivated such an honest habit in his personal as well as professional life. This means that he tends to choose the intermediate in the way of informing others, including those with whom he works, friends, family, and associates, as well as clients (Aristotle, 2015, Bk. 2, Ch. 6). On the one extreme is the telling of lies, half-truths, manipulation, and deception; on the other is over-informing others. Too much information can sometimes be as problematic as not enough. Indeed, some information is relevant, whereas other information can be a needless distraction. The honest therapist does not inundate or waste others' time—clients, coworkers, or other associates—with irrelevant or excessive facts that serve to distract from important matters. For example, the honest therapist does not engage in excessive or irrelevant self-disclosure that serves only to distract the client from addressing her own problems. Such sharing of information is not being honest in the provision of therapy. In contrast, the honest therapist knows what, when, how, and to whom information is appropriately disclosed.

Candor

Such a habit of making appropriate disclosure also makes the honest therapist *candid*. Candor, in the provision of therapy, involves disclosing those facts about therapy that a client would reasonably want to know (*Canterbury v. Spence*, 1972). Such disclosure, to be adequate must be such that comprehension of the information by the client would be sufficient for the client to give informed consent to therapy. So clients' informed consent is, in a sense, the purpose of being candid. This is because, without informed consent, a client is not capable of making an informed decision about therapy. Case law itself has been very clear about the importance of candor in the provision of therapy. In the landmark case, *Canterbury v. Spence* (1972), the point is succinctly expressed:

> In our view, the patient's right of self-decision shapes the boundaries of the duty to reveal. That right can be effectively exercised only if the patient possesses enough information to enable an intelligent choice. The scope of the physician's communications to the patient, then, must be measured by the patient's need, and that need is the information material to the decision. Thus the test for determining whether a particular peril must be divulged is its materiality to the patient's decision: all risks potentially affecting the decision must be unmasked. (Section V, para. 41)

As discussed further in Chapter 6, in this medical case involving the failure of a physician to inform his patient of a 1% risk of thoracic surgery causing paralysis, the court made clear that there is a legal *duty* to disclose, which arises out of the patient's right to informed consent to treatment. The court concluded that a reasonable person in the patient's position (who subsequent to the surgery became paralyzed) would have attached significance to the 1% risk.

While the duty announced in *Canterbury* is one that the candid therapist upholds, it is important to emphasize that such a therapist is not merely driven by concern for avoidance of legal liability and malpractice suits. Indeed, these are concerns; however, the candid therapist is motivated, both inside and outside therapy, to be candid to others because it is the right thing to do. Thus, it is not possible to conclude that a therapist is candid, in the virtuous sense emphasized in this book, purely because she provides informed consent to her clients. To be virtuous, such a tendency must be appropriately *motivated*, not entirely by self-interest, but primarily for the welfare of the client; and it needs to extend outside the counseling room (Cohen & Cohen, 1999). For example, in dealing with coworkers, the candid therapist needs to provide information necessary for their giving informed consent, too. Thus, the candid therapist would not hire a receptionist without providing him with the facts he would need to know to make an informed decision about whether or not to take the job—work hours, pay, opportunity for advancement, and so on. And such a habit of candor would also extend to the therapist's personal life. As such, she would tend to be candid with friends, family, and others outside the work context.

Respectfulness

Candor is also linked to the more general virtue of respectfulness. In the words of the 18th century German philosopher, Immanuel Kant (1964), this means treating others (as well as oneself) "as ends in themselves and not as mere means" (p. 96). In other words, it means treating persons *as persons* and not as mere objects or things. What all persons have in common is that they are *autonomous,* that is, able to rationally decide matters concerning themselves, *for themselves.* Clearly, to make rational decisions about personal matters one needs to have adequate information. So, respectful persons must also be candid, thereby empowering others to make informed decisions about matters concerning them. This is in stark contrast to treating others as mere objects or things, which involves manipulating and using them to one's personal advantage.

According to Carl Rogers, such respect in relating to others is a primary ingredient of any helping relationship. Rogers (1961) describes this state of respect as an unconditional state of acceptance or "positive regard," which treats the other as "a person of unconditional self-worth—of value no matter what his condition, his behavior, or feelings" (p. 34). Such a state of respectfulness or unconditional positive regard, he states, "involves an acceptance of and a caring for the client as a separate person with permission for him to have his own feelings and experiences, and to find his own meanings in them" (Rogers, 1961, p. 284). According to Rogers, "to the degree that the therapist can provide this safety-creating climate of unconditional positive regard, significant learning is likely to take place" (pp. 284–85).

To treat others respectfully involves avoiding using degrading or pejorative labels to characterize others. Thus, the client isn't "stupid," "insane," or "bad." Such characterizations fail to respect the person as possessing the capacity for autonomous, positive change. Clearly, in labeling a person as bad, one has already *pre*judged what can be expected of the individual, namely bad things; and such a closed attitude is likely to influence how one acts and reacts to the person (Cohen, 2007). This does not mean merely not calling a person such things to her face. It means not even *thinking* them. So the respectful person is in a habit of not merely avoiding such outward, verbal condemnations; he is also disposed to accept the intrinsic self-worth of the person on the inside (subjectively), too. This means that the respectful person is also authentic and does not simply put on a façade of being respectful when he is not (Sartre, 1989). As mentioned earlier, clients are likely to pick up on such lack of transparency, thereby affecting the likelihood of constructive change taking place.

As Kant (1961) made clear, respectfulness is a universal disposition. It is not merely respect for some people; it is respect for them all. This includes people who behave in ways you find objectionable. For it is one thing to condemn a person's deed and quite another thing to condemn the doer (Ellis, 1975). The respectful person may disapprove of or disagree with what another does or says, but such a person still tends to respect individuals with whom they disagree as centers of intrinsic worth and dignity. Of course, therapists are only human, and there are some populations with whom they may find holding such unconditional respect difficult or challenging. For example, a therapist may find it difficult to work with clients who have molested children. In such a case, the virtuous therapist realizes the problem and refers the client to a therapist who does not have a similar problem (American Psychological Association [APA], 2016, 2.06; National Association of Social Workers [NASW], 2017, 1.06).

Universal respect also includes respect for oneself (Kant, 1964). This means that respectful therapists do not treat themselves or permit others to treat themselves like objects manipulated. Therefore, such a therapist avoids berating herself and tends to value her own rational autonomy. For example, she is disposed against sacrificing her ethical principles, such as engaging in agency practices that are harmful to herself or her clients; she does not permit her clients to mistreat or take unfair advantage of her, such as by refusing to pay for services rendered; and she does not passively allow clients to make false claims against her. In such cases, the self-respecting therapist courageously stands on principle, does not allow clients to exploit her services, and takes necessary legal action. Indeed, there are ethical limits within which respectful therapists are willing to tolerate disrespectful, degrading, or injurious practices.

Moreover, such therapists avoid self-destructively degrading themselves for their own mistakes or professional misjudgments. Instead, they are disposed to recognize such mistakes and rectify and/or learn from them. For example, a self-respecting therapist who misdiagnoses a client who, as a result, seriously injures or kills himself learns a painful lesson. The costs of this lesson typically exceed legal repercussions (such as a law suit); for it can also take its toll on the therapist's sense of personal and professional self-worth. While it is human to entertain self-doubts in such unfortunate situations and deeply lament what has happened, the respectful therapist (eventually) works through the issue (perhaps with the help of therapy), accepts responsibility for his actions or inactions, and learns from the experience. Here it is important to emphasize that respectfulness, in such circumstances, is not compatible with self-pity and weakness of will. Instead, building self-respect requires honesty (with oneself) and resolve to make constructive changes. Nor is such respect compatible with the refusal to accept responsibility for one's mistakes—since this is effectively to deny one's ability to rationally assess and autonomously make constructive changes. Indeed, in the course of a career in counseling and the human services, one inevitably encounters situations that have the potential to strain one's sense of unconditional self-acceptance or regard. This is part of the landscape of therapy, but it is also the occasion for growing stronger as a person. As Friedrich Nietzsche (1954) suggested, "profound suffering makes noble and separates the sufferer from the uninitiated" (p. 596).

Empowerment

Respectful therapists are also empowering to their clients. This means that they facilitate clients' autonomy or self-determination in making constructive change (Cohen, 2007). Empowering therapists do not manipulate, threaten, trick, intimidate, or cajole clients into making changes; for this would not be consistent with respecting the client as a person; nor would it promote future constructive change. For example, threatening to terminate therapy of a client who has a social phobia unless the client attends a particular social event treats the client like an object manipulated rather than as a person; it also makes the client dependent on the therapist rather than building self-reliance. Further, such manipulative treatment creates an atmosphere of distrust wherein the client is less inclined to confide in the therapist. "If I don't say or do what the therapist wants me to say or do, then he will refuse to see me anymore." Such an environment is clearly not conducive to facilitating constructive change.

Empowering therapists therefore do not tell clients what to do. They are not advice givers but, instead, facilitators (Rogers, 1977). This does not mean that they cannot employ didactic therapeutic modalities for their clients, such as cognitive behavior therapy. Insofar as the latter sorts of therapy teach clients how to avoid self-defeating or irrational beliefs and behavior, they seek to provide a set of cognitive and behavioral tools that can be autonomously harnessed by the client to address her behavioral and emotional issues (Beck, 1979; Ellis, 2001). Indeed, a central goal of such therapies is to help the client avoid forms of self-defeating thinking (such as catastrophic thinking, self-damnation, demanding perfection, and low frustration tolerance) that tend to stifle autonomy by undermining self-confidence and creating a sense of powerlessness and ineptitude. However, empowering therapists who use such modalities do not force clients to engage in "homework assignments" or other cognitive behavioral techniques by threatening or intimidating them into cooperating, for this is inconsistent with treating clients as rational, self-determining persons, and therefore, with the purpose of the therapy in the first place (Cohen, 2017).

The virtue of empowerment is an Aristotelian mean between two extremes or vices (Aristotle, 2015). On the one hand, empowering therapists avoid disempowering their clients through manipulation or telling them what to do. On the other, they avoid promoting a false or unrealistic sense of power. For example, an empowering therapist would not support a client's unrealistic idea that she can (and must) always gain the approval of others. Instead, such a therapist would help to facilitate a more realistic attitude: "I really don't always need the approval of others to be happy." As such, the empowering therapist helps facilitate a *realistic* sense of power or capability.

Empowering therapists are also empowering persons. This means that they seek to facilitate rational autonomy both inside and outside the counseling room. Accordingly, empowerment is not a therapeutic technique. It is a well-formed personal habit that empowering clients bring to the therapeutic arena (Cohen, 2007). As such, empowering therapists do not need to *try not to* manipulate, force, or otherwise impose their will on their clients; for such therapists are already disposed not to do these things. To the contrary, empowering therapists quite naturally create an environment in which clients can feel safe to explore their potentials.

Discretion

Empowering persons are also *discreet* about what they say and do. Otherwise others would not come to trust them, would not confide in them, and, therefore, would not be empowered by them. Exercising discretion involves taking care not to offend or violate others' privacy through the disclosure of their private or personal information (Cohen & Cohen, 1999). Such information can be learned directly from the person whom the information is about, or it can be learned from third-party sources. For example, in the latter case, you might learn from a friend of an acquaintance of yours that she conceived a child out of wedlock. A discreet person would not ordinarily disclose this acquired information to others even if she could have reasonably figured it out on her own (the child was born 5 months after the mother was married). Similarly, you might acquire personal information about another on the Internet. Thus you might learn from public records that the bank has foreclosed on someone you know. Notwithstanding that this information is publicly available, it would still be indiscreet to disclose it to others, inasmuch as public information can still be information that people might not want others to know (Bayles, 1989).

In cases where someone discloses personal or private information directly to you, the person has *entrusted* you with the information. The person has confided in you with the (implied or explicit) understanding that you will not disclose this information to others. In such a case, the discreet individual ordinarily respects this trust by not disclosing the confided information to anyone else. Indeed, one who failed to keep this trust could be said to have *betrayed* it. Barring any exceptional circumstances, such a betrayal would be perceived as a mark of an *untrustworthy* person. This is one extreme. The other extreme is that of one who would not disclose a secret even if the lives of others depended on it. This is the attitude of "Let the heavens fall; I will never betray a trust." However, as discussed in Chapter 5, there are exceptional circumstances under which discreet and trustworthy people may disclose the confidences of others such as to save the life of the person who disclosed the information or the lives of third parties. As such, the virtue of discretion is a mean between the extremes of untrustworthiness and blind, overzealousness regarding the keeping of the personal or private information of others. The discreet person can generally be relied on to keep the trusts of others. However, he is aware that there can be situations in which the exercise of discretion may involve disclosing of information confided in him. In such cases, the discreet person exercises rational judgment about what information to disclose, where, when, and to whom.

The discreet therapist is a discreet person. This means that he is disposed to keep confidences in his private as well as professional life. Thus, it is second nature for him to respect secrets reposed in him by his clients, for doing so is an internalized character trait (or habit) of his, not merely an external requirement included in professional codes of ethics or legal standards (Cohen & Cohen, 1999). As such, the discreet therapist avoids the extremes of untrustworthiness on the one hand, and blind, unconditional adherence on the other. He also does not mislead clients about the limits of confidentiality. He does not tell a client, "Trust me, I will hold whatever you tell me in the strictest confidence and will never disclose anything you tell me to anyone else"; nor does he deceive his clients into trusting him with their confidences only to betray that trust. Instead, the discreet therapist is candid about the limits of confidentiality (ACA, 2014, H.2.c). "What you tell me in the sessions is confidential. However, there are some exceptions. For example, if you tell me that you or someone else you know is abusing a child or an elderly or disabled person, I am required by law to report it to the state. If you tell me that you are going to injure or kill yourself or another, I may also report this to the authorities. But I assure you that I take confidentiality very seriously and will do my utmost to protect it."

Loyalty

Accordingly, the discreet therapist also demonstrates loyalty to his clients. As mentioned, there can be exceptional circumstances in which the welfare of a client may need to be weighed against other competing interests such as the serious welfare of third parties; however, within these rational limits, loyal therapists exercise independence of judgment and steadfast devotion to the welfare and interests of their clients.

As addressed in detail in Chapter 9, such loyalty requires independence of judgment. This, in turn, requires avoiding *conflicts of interests* in counseling practice. A conflict of interests arises for a therapist when the therapist has a personal interest that makes it harder to exercise independent, professional judgment on behalf of a client. The client trusts the therapist to apply his professional training and experience toward the promotion of the client's welfare. That is, because the therapist has knowledge and skills the client lacks, the client depends on the therapist to apply these tools in a manner conducive to client welfare (Bayles, 1989). However, where there is a conflict of interests, the ability of the therapist to honor this trust is called into question. Indeed, there are a myriad of situations with the potential to create such conflicts of interest. For example, a therapist who gets personally involved with a client, such as forming a sexual relationship or friendship with the client, sets herself up for a conflict of interest. This is true because the personal relationship involves expectations incompatible with those involved in the professional relationship (Kitchener, 1988). For example, going into business with a client creates potential for conflict between the self-interested goal of making a profit with the other-regarding professional interest in promoting the client's psychological well-being.

In fact, the loyal therapist is inclined to sacrifice self-interest in favor of client welfare when she *unavoidably* finds herself in situations where the two conflict. For example, a loyal therapist does not keep clients in therapy when the client is not benefitting from therapy (ACA, 2014, A.11.c), even though terminating and/or referring the client to another therapist may place a strain on the therapist's financial situation. Again, the client trusts the therapist to apply her knowledge and skill to promoting the client's welfare, and she does not betray this trust to advance personal interests.

Consequently, loyal therapists exercise temperance or self-control in situations where personal desires are concerned (Aristotle, 2015). This means that loyal therapists must also be loyal persons, possessing the strongly engrained habit of avoiding and standing up to moral and physical temptation. Such a moral habit is the mean between betrayal (being a traitor), in the one extreme, and idolatry (blind devotion), in the other. The loyal person does not sell out those who depend on her; yet she does not stand on ceremony when devotion goes too far—for example, when it involves permitting someone to do something that is morally unacceptable. Thus the loyal therapist does not turn a blind eye while her client puts the lives of innocent third parties at risk. This does not mean that the loyal therapist engages in wholesale sacrifice of client welfare in favor of that of others. Rather, the loyal therapist knows when, how, and where to draw the line. For example, as addressed in Chapter 14, in the case of an HIV positive client who is sexually active with an unwitting sex partner(s), the questions of whether to disclose confidential information, to whom, under what situations, and how much information to disclose must be carefully considered and assessed. The loyal therapist is capable of exercising such discretion in such situations where the welfare of others may conflict with client welfare.

Diligence

The loyal therapist is also diligent. This is because diligence amounts to the settled habit of meeting client responsibilities in a reliable and efficient manner (Cohen & Cohen, 1999). Diligent therapists are disposed against sacrificing the welfare of their clients for personal interests. This does not mean that they do not take care of their own welfare and interests. For example, therapists can benefit from some down time where they can relax away from the stresses of the counseling room. However, taking a vacation is not the same thing as client abandonment. Diligent therapists keep appointments, do not ordinarily cut short sessions, have an answering service (or at least an answer machine), check messages regularly, return calls in a timely way, and leave a competent therapist on call while away (ACA, 2014, A.12; NASW, 2017, 1.15). Diligent therapists maintain and store counseling records, as appropriate, in a safe and secure manner (ACA, 2014, B.6.b; APA, 2016, 6.02; NASW, 2017, 1.07l) and provide appropriate and timely documentation in records (ACA, 2014, A.1.b; NASW, 2017, 3.04.b); stay current on ethical standards and pertinent laws (ACA, 2014, C.1; 1.1.a), new therapies, technologies, multicultural education, and other forms of continuing education (ACA, 2014, C.2.f; APA, 2016, 2.03; NASW, 2017, 3.08, 4.01); and otherwise conduct themselves in all other manners that provide for the efficient operation of their practices conducive to client welfare.

Diligent therapists avoid the extremes of irresponsibility on the one hand, and rigidity on the other. Thus, while diligent therapists are disciplined and scheduled, they are also flexible and have the ability to adjust their schedules when necessary to meet unexpected situations. For example, a diligent therapist may cancel or shorten a client's session to accommodate another client's crisis situation, when this is the only reasonable way to address the crisis. In such exceptional situations, the diligent therapist judiciously and rationally seeks to balance the welfare of all clients concerned so that there is no unnecessary sacrifice of anyone's welfare. For example, having canceled a client's session to address another client's crisis, the diligent therapist reschedules the missed appointment in a timely manner (Cohen & Cohen, 1999).

Diligent therapists are also disposed against overbooking or taking on more clients than they can accommodate. Indeed, they are aware that the quality of their services can be compromised when there is inadequate time to address a client overload. Thus, they decide against taking on new clients, notwithstanding the loss of income, when this means reducing the efficiency and quality of their counseling services.

Competence

Diligence is also a condition of competence because a therapist cannot provide competent counseling services if she is not responsible. Competent therapists are qualified for practice. This includes appropriate course work as well as practical experience (ACA, 2014, C.2.a, C.2.b, C.2.c, H.1.a, A.4.b, A.11.b; APA, 2016, 2.01, 2.03, 2.04; NASW, 2017, 1.04.a, 1.04.b). Competence is therefore relative, and a therapist can be competent for practice in one area but not in another. For example, a therapist who is qualified to work with clients with anxiety disorders may not be qualified to work with other populations such as clients with eating disorders. Competent therapists also know their practice boundaries, that is, what areas in which they are not competent to practice, they know when to make suitable referrals to other competent therapists, and they avoid practicing in areas in which they are unqualified to practice or seek appropriate training in the questionable area of practice. Of course, practical experience is attained only when one endeavors to practice in an unpracticed area; and one does not have such experience until one actually practices in the area. However, the competent therapist takes reasonable precautions in attaining such experience (ACA, 2014, C.2.b; APA, 2016, 2.01e; NASW, 2017, 1.04.b). Thus, if he thinks he can help the client with the guidance of a therapist experienced in the area in question, he seeks out a competent supervisor to provide oversight. Moreover, the competent therapist does not engage in such an undertaking unless he is candid with the client about his practical experience in the area in question. This means explaining to the client his willingness to work with the client under competent supervision and offering the client a suitable referral if the client prefers to work with a therapist who is competent to practice in the area in question. The same applies to use of new or untried modalities of therapy. The competent therapist informs the client of his inexperience in using the modality and attains the client's informed consent to apply the modality to the client's case under the supervision of a competent supervisor (APA, 2016, 10.01.b; Cohen & Cohen, 1999).

Competent therapists also seek ethics consultation from colleagues and/or the ethics departments of their respective professional organizations (e.g., the American Counseling Association Ethics and Professional Standards Department) in cases that present challenging ethical questions (ACA, 2014, C.2.e). For example, therapists may have questions ranging from bartering for fees or entering (or getting out of) multiple role relationships to how to deal with a potentially suicidal client who is suffering from a terminal illness.

The competent therapist seeks ethics consultation, where there is sufficient time, when she has questions about how to respond to such ethical challenges. However, in the end, the competent therapist rationally considers the insights gleaned from the consultation and exercises her own prudent judgment in making a decision (ACA, 2014, Purpose; APA, 2016, Introduction and Applicability; NASW, 2017, Purpose of the NASW Code of Ethics).

Competence also includes knowledge of cultural differences between different groups of people (ACA, 2014, C.2.a). Indeed, adequate diagnoses may well depend on the therapist's knowledge of the client's cultural background (ACA, 2014, E.5.b). Thus a client who claims to hear voices may not have a psychosis if it is part of a religious orientation to hear voices. As such, an understanding of the cultural background of a client may be essential in drawing clinical inferences. Therefore, competent therapists are aware of the profoundly important role that culture may play in making such inferences and take appropriate steps in educating themselves about the cultural backgrounds of the client populations they serve, such as enrolling in courses on multicultural counseling and anthropology and doing independent research (NASW, 2017, 105.c).

Competence also implies prudence or *practical wisdom*. The competent therapist not only has the requisite knowledge to make appropriate clinical decisions, but she also knows how to "deliberate well" about applying this knowledge in the counseling room. This means that, based on her clinical experience, she is capable of determining what actions are likely to best help particular clients (Aristotle, 2015, Bk. 6, Ch. 7); for example, what modalities might be most effectively employed with different clients. This is largely a product of clinical experience, which can be improved through the process of trial and error; for the competent therapist is not immune to making mistakes; however, she tends to be aware of these mistakes and strives to learn from them.

Fairness

Competent therapists also tend to treat clients and others fairly. This is because, as discussed, competent therapists seek to be ethical and equity is an important aspect of the ethical treatment of clients. Fairness (or equity) involves treating *relevantly* similar cases alike (Feinberg, 1973). In the counseling professions, such differences as race, gender, ethnicity, sexual preference, physical attractiveness, and age are not generally considered relevant differences for treating some clients better (or worse) than others. In general, differential treatment of clients can be ethically justified on the basis of therapeutic outcomes. For example, therapists may permissibly not accept, as clients, those whose problems fall outside their areas of competence. Thus, a therapist who is not competent to treat eating disorders might refuse to take on, as a client, someone who is bulimic, referring the individual instead to a therapist who is competent to treat this client population. On the other hand, a therapist would be unfair in refusing to treat a client who is obese simply because he prefers thinner clients. While the former case of differential treatment can be justified on the basis of therapeutic outcomes or goals, the latter cannot.

In unusual circumstances, a fair therapist may treat one client different than another, where ordinarily the differential treatment would be unfair. For example, to address the immediacy of a suicidal client, the therapist may cut short a session of another client who is not in any immediate danger. However, even in such cases, the fair therapist makes reasonable efforts to compensate for the differential treatment, for example, by giving the client, whose session was cut short, additional time in a subsequent session (Cohen & Cohen, 1999).

As discussed in Chapter 9, a therapist who charges differential rates need not be unfair to clients who pay more than other clients for the same counseling services (ACA, 2014, A.10.c). This is the case if the differential rates can be justified on grounds of therapeutic outcomes. For example, a client who is poor and cannot afford the usual and customary rate may be charged a rate based on his ability to pay. This can be a fair arrangement if it enables the client to receive competent therapy, whereas he otherwise would not have been able to receive such therapy under the existing circumstances.

Fair therapists avoid the extremes of rigidity on the one hand, and arbitrariness on the other. Accordingly, the fair-minded therapist is receptive to the individual who requires exceptional help (of time, money, or personal sacrifice); but also she does not take such decisions lightly and carefully considers the merits of the case, the impact the decision may have on her ability to efficiently serve her other clients, and its potential impact on her personal well-being (e.g., her health and financial stability).

Trustworthiness

Fairness, no less than the other counselor virtues, is a human virtue, not merely a therapeutic attitude. And, like all the other virtues, it promotes the virtue of trustworthiness. The therapist-client relationship is a *fiduciary* relationship, that is, one based on trust. The client relies on the expertise (knowledge, training, and experience) of the therapist to help her with her personal problems. The client must therefore trust the therapist to make progress (Bayles, 1989; Cohen & Cohen, 1999).

However, put yourself in the client's seat for a moment. Imagine that you are considering whether to share the most intimate, private details of your life with me, the therapist, whom you really do not know. Indeed, you are not likely to have much trust in me if you believe any of these things about me:

- I am incompetent and incapable of helping you;
- I have evil intentions or just do not really want to help you;
- I will not really do what I tell you I will do;
- I am haphazard or disorganized;
- I will not keep the things you tell me confidential;
- I am dishonest or will misrepresent the facts to you;
- I will not be loyal to you (will use what you tell me against you);
- I really don't understand you;
- I am a big phony;
- I tend to catastrophize, yet you are here to overcome your own issues;
- I am not telling you the whole truth about my services and what I can do for you;

- You really do not respect me as a person;
- I try to force you to do things, or otherwise manipulate you; or
- I am not in some way being fair to you (for example, repeatedly shortchanging you on session time).

If you entertain one or more of these thoughts (as many clients often do), it is not likely that you will trust me enough to make significant changes; or at least it is not likely that you will do as well in therapy as you otherwise would have done had you not entertained such thoughts. On the other hand, imagine that I am benevolent, empathetic, authentic, courageous, honest, respectful, candid, discreet, diligent, empowering, loyal, competent, and fair. Since these are settled personal as well as professional habits, you are likely to (eventually) gain a sense of the person I truly am. In that case, I would venture to claim that you would probably trust me. And this is because I would be trustworthy, that is, worthy of your trust. I will have earned your trust because you will have come to see that I can be relied on to keep my trusts. As such, you will be more likely to tell me things you otherwise would not have told me, offer less resistance, be more attentive, and display greater openness to the therapeutic process. This is precisely why the counselor virtues discussed in this chapter are so vital to successful therapy. They are the basic building blocks of client trust, which, in turn, is essential for client progress.

Questions for Review and Reflection

1. What is virtue ethics, and why is it so demanding?
2. What is the motive that a virtuous person has for telling the truth? How do you think this might relate to being a virtuous therapist?
3. How does a virtuous person decide right from wrong? Is there a formula for doing so?
4. What did Aristotle mean when he maintained that virtues are means between extremes of excess and deficiency?
5. What is benevolence and nonmalevolence, how are they related, and why are they important virtues in counseling?
6. What is empathy, and why is it important in counseling?
7. What is authenticity, and why is it an important counselor virtue?
8. What is courage, and how does it relate to counseling?
9. Is honesty the same as truthfulness? Explain.
10. What's the difference between a lie and a half-truth?
11. What is candor? What sort of information would a candid therapist disclose to a client?
12. What is respectfulness and how does it relate to what psychologist Carl Rogers calls "unconditional positive regard"?
13. What did the philosopher, Immanuel Kant, mean when he said that we should treat others as well as oneself as "ends in themselves" and not as "mere means"?

14. What does it mean to say that respectfulness is "universal"? Why is this aspect of respectfulness significant in counseling?

15. What does it mean to respect oneself?

16. What does it mean to be an empowering therapist?

17. What does it mean to be a discreet therapist? Would a discreet therapist ever disclose something a client disclosed to him or her in confidence? Explain.

18. Why does being loyal to a client require independence of judgment? Why does loyalty also require temperance or self-control?

19. What does it mean to be diligent? List at least five things that we would expect a diligent therapist to do.

20. How does a therapist acquire competence in counseling? Why would multicultural knowledge part of being competent?

21. Would a competent therapist ever seek consultation from other therapists in addressing client issues? Explain.

22. What is fairness, and how do you distinguish between fair and unfair treatment of clients?

23. What is a fiduciary relationship, and why is counseling such a relationship?

24. Why is attaining client trust paramount in counseling?

25. Does one virtue ever support another? That is, do you ever need to have one virtue to have another? Explain.

Cases for Analysis

1. Francine Fuentes is a 48-year-old city councilwoman who has been diagnosed with major depressive disorder with recurrent suicidal ideation. She is in counseling with Dr. Henrietta Ettinger, a clinical psychologist. As election season is drawing near, Fuentes discusses her fears about handling the rigors of her office while struggling with her depression. Ettinger has some doubts about whether Fuentes will be able to perform competently on the job and addresses these concerns with Fuentes. Fuentes is undeterred in finally deciding to run for reelection. Ettinger is concerned about the welfare of her client and how the pressures of her job may affect her. She is also worried about the future of the city in which both she and Fuentes reside. As a virtuous therapist, how should Ettinger proceed? What are her ethical and legal responsibilities? What therapist virtues are relevant to the decisions that Ettinger makes?

2. Catalina Smythe is a clinical social worker with a large private practice. When she first began practicing, Smythe carefully got both oral as well as written informed consent from all her clients. As time goes on, and her practice grows, Smythe decides that it is more expedient to have her receptionist give all new clients the informed consent form before therapy commences. In that way, Smythe can save time and see at least one more client each day. This is important to her because she is saving up for a more spacious home. So far there have been no known negative consequences from only getting written consent. Discuss whether what Smythe is doing comports

with virtuous practice. Which virtues might militate against what she is doing? Which virtues, if any, might be demonstrated by her decision to only get written consent?

3. Xavier Merrill is a 19-year-old male, who lives with a roommate and who graduated from high school last year. He has begun counseling with Elvira Moreau, a licensed mental health counselor, because he is confused about the direction of his life. Although Merrill is no longer a minor child, he is still on his parents' insurance policy. During the course of his counseling, he reveals that he is undergoing treatment for Hepatitis C and is experiencing significant side effects from the medication. He stresses that he does not want his parents to know about his illness. Moreau is concerned about the health and safety of her client; however, she is wary of compromising his autonomy. How should a virtuous therapist handle this situation? Discuss which virtues are most important to consider.

References

American Counseling Association. (2014). *ACA code of ethics*. Alexandria, VA: Author. Retrieved from counseling.org/resources/aca-code-of-ethics.pdf

American Psychological Association. (2016). *Ethical principles of psychologists and code of conduct*. Washington, DC: Author. Retrieved from http://www.apa.org/ethics/code/? item=11#805

Aristotle. (2015). *Nicomachean ethics* (W. D. Ross, trans.). South Australia: eBooks@Adelaide. Retrieved from https://ebooks.adelaide.edu.au/a/aristotle/nicomachean/

Bayles, M. D. (1989). *Professional ethics* (2nd ed.). Belmont, CA: Wadsworth.

Beck, A. (1979). *Cognitive behavior therapy and the emotional disorders*. New York, NY: Meridian.

Canterbury v. Spence. 464 F.2d 772 (D.C. Cir. 1972).

Cohen, E. D. (1985). Pure legal advocates and moral agents: Two concepts of a lawyer in an adversary system. *Criminal Justice Ethics*, 4(1), 38–59.

Cohen, E. D. (2003). *What would Aristotle do? Self-control through the power of reason*. Amherst, NY: Prometheus Books.

Cohen, E. D. (2007). *The new rational therapy: Thinking your way to serenity, success, and profound happiness*. Lanham, MD: Rowman & Littlefield.

Cohen, E. D. (2009). *Critical thinking unleashed*. Lanham, MD: Rowman & Littlefield.

Cohen, E. D. (2015, May 17). How to be empathetic. *Psychology Today*. Retrieved from https://www.psychologytoday.com/blog/what-would-aristotle-do/201505/how-be-empathetic

Cohen, E. D. (2017). *Logic-based therapy and everyday emotions*. Lanham, MD: Rowman & Littlefield.

Cohen, E. D., & G. S. Cohen. (1999). *The virtuous therapist: Ethical practice of counseling and psychotherapy*. Belmont, CA: Wadsworth.

Ellis, A. (1975). *A new guide to rational living* (3rd ed.). Chatsworth, CA: Wilshire Books.

Ellis, A. (2001). *Overcoming destructive beliefs, feelings, and behaviors: New directions for rational emotive behavior therapy.* Amherst, NY: Prometheus Books.

Feinberg, J. (1973). *Social philosophy.* Englewood Cliffs, NJ: Prentice-Hall.

Kant, I. (1964). *Groundwork of the metaphysics of morals* (H. J. Paton, trans.). New York, NY: Harper & Row.

Kitchener, K. S. (1988). Dual role relationships: What makes them so problematic? *Journal of Counseling and Development, 67,* 217–221.

Kolden, G. G., Klein, M. H., Wang, C. C., & Austin, S. B. (2011). Congruence/genuineness. *Psychotherapy Theory Research Practice Training, 48*(1), 65–71.

Mahon, J. E. (2016, Winter). The definition of lying and deception (E. N. Zalta, Ed.). *The Stanford Encyclopedia of Philosophy.* Retrieved from https://plato.stanford.edu/archives/win2016/entries/lying-definition/

National Association of Social Workers. (2017). *Code of ethics of the National Association of Social Workers.* Washington, DC: Author. Retrieved from https://www.socialworkers.org/About/Ethics/Code-of-Ethics/Code-of-Ethics-English.aspx

Nietzsche, F. (1954). Beyond good and evil (H. Zimmern, trans. in *The philosophy of Nietzsche*). New York, NY: Random House.

Rogers, C. R. (1961). *On becoming a person.* Boston, MA: Houghton Mifflin.

Rogers, C. R. (1977). *Carl Rogers on personal power: Inner strength and its revolutionary impact.* New York: Delacorte Press.

Sartre, J. P. (1989). Existentialism is a humanism. In W. Kaufman (Ed.), *Existentialism from Dostoyevsky to Sartre.* New York, NY: Meridian. Retrieved from https://www.marxists.org/reference/archive/sartre/works/exist/sartre.htm

2

BEING TRUSTWORTHY

Case Studies: Two Resistant Clients

As discussed in Chapter 1, the development of trust in a therapeutic relationship is, indeed, predicated on the therapist's character as benevolent, caring, empathetic, honest, candid, authentic, competent, diligent, loyal, and fair-minded. This capacity to be trusted, or that of being trustworthy, supervenes on these virtues and provides the climate that facilitates client well-being, self-determination, connectedness, and equity. This chapter shows how, in furtherance of this trust, virtuous therapists model and embrace the stated virtues. In particular, two cases are presented involving clients who are resistant, insecure, and untrusting with respect to the counseling process. The first case involves a client who tests the therapist to see if she is really trustworthy. The second is suspicious and apprehensive.

A CLIENT WHO TESTS HER THERAPIST'S TRUSTWORTHINESS

The development of trust may be met with challenges and tests. Clients may be unfamiliar with receiving unconditional positive regard and may be doubtful that this is genuine and steadfast. Consider, for example, the case of Dawn Delmar.

> Dawn, a 34-year-old woman, had recently and dramatically lost a teenaged child through a motor vehicle accident. Dawn was struggling to care for her younger child Tom and was living at poverty level. She had been abandoned as a young teen by her mother and did not have any close family members except for her son. Her live-in boyfriend was unemployed and suffered from an untreated chronic illness. Dawn herself had not received medical care for many years and did not appear to be in good health.
>
> Hilda Green, Dawn's outreach therapist, initiated contact and scheduled a series of home visits following a referral from social services. During the times when Dawn was home for the visits, sessions appeared to go well. Hilda actively listened to

Dawn. She used open-ended questions to learn what was most important to Dawn and reflection to enter Dawn's phenomenal world to learn how she must be feeling.

Dawn struggled with feelings of loss, self-doubt, fear, grief, abandonment, and betrayal. Some of Dawn's problems were related either directly or indirectly to poverty. Accordingly, many of her life decisions were strongly influenced by the lack of financial resources. Although Hilda had herself never been in the same economic strata as Dawn, she was familiar with the struggles of those who faced severe economic challenges. Dawn often spoke of the pressures she felt as a result of worrying about paying bills and getting medical services.

Despite the fact that Dawn did speak at great length about a wide array of feelings, there were often feelings that were not fully articulated verbally, but instead communicated nonverbally. She sometimes cried and tugged at her hair when talking about Tom. Hilda was able to actively listen, ask open questions, and discern the fear Dawn felt over the possibility of losing another child. Rapport between therapist and client seemed to grow, but there were many times when Dawn was not at home for scheduled visits. Her reasons for not keeping the appointments were often not convincing. Sometimes, Hilda suspected that Dawn had been running errands and wanted to finish them all before returning home and having to go out yet another time. This might require additional expenses for fuel. Hilda tried and was successful at rescheduling these appointments. On a few occasions when Dawn missed appointments and did not answer phone calls, Hilda dropped in unannounced to see how Dawn was doing. She sometimes feared for her own safety when making these visits in the evening after seeing all her other clients. On several occasions when she arrived after sunset, she felt uneasy because vehicles appeared to surround her car. Nonetheless, no actual physical harm ever occurred.

As time passed, Dawn missed fewer sessions and explored additional issues. She discussed poor choices that she had made in her life and worked with Hilda to develop more effective decision-making skills. She also began to reveal additional details related to her health problems. Hilda, concerned about the possible seriousness of these problems, provided Dawn with a referral for free health care. She discussed her serious concerns with Dawn; however, Dawn remained hesitant about pursuing any treatment. Later in treatment, however, Dawn stated that she might consider medical care, but was intimidated and confused by the process of making an initial contact. She related that many of her experiences in procuring medical care had been fruitless. At this point, Dawn agreed that she would consider seeking medical care if Hilda assisted her.

Dawn subsequently signed a release form allowing Hilda to make initial arrangements to seek care at a local clinic; however, Dawn never followed through with pursuing medical care. Hilda periodically brought the subject up, but demurred to Dawn when she expressed reluctance to discuss the subject. On the whole, Hilda's rapport with her client appeared to be strong.

Because this rapport appeared to be intact, Hilda was surprised when, after about 3 months of counseling services, she arrived at Dawn's house for a scheduled session to find the residence empty. Concerned about the welfare of both Dawn as well as Tom, Hilda set out to locate them both. Despite intensive checking, no one whom she contacted seemed to know where Dawn had gone.

Still, Hilda persevered. Navigating all the pathways that were potentially available, she tried for over 2 weeks to find her client. Finally, she had a lead, a potential address on the opposite side of town. On a Saturday morning, Hilda drove to the location and hesitantly knocked on the door. Dawn answered the door, stared at Hilda, and declared, "What took you so long? I was wondering when you would find me."

Hilda expressed how concerned she had been about Dawn, and the two set up a session for the next week. Dawn subsequently remained a client of Hilda for an additional 9 months. At the time of termination, Dawn had begun to demonstrate more effective parenting skills as evidenced by her son Tom's improved behavior. She also experienced less self-doubt as evidenced by a demonstrable increase in her positive self-statements and a significant decrease in her negative self-statements. In addition, Dawn had begun to socialize with a few neighbors, a departure from her previous stance of not trusting strangers.

MAINTAINING TRUST IN A CLIENT WHO TESTS HER THERAPIST'S COMMITMENT

One of the striking things in this case is the question posed to Hilda as she arrives at Dawn's home after a 2-week search: "What took you so long?" Implicit in this question is the obvious client assumption that, indeed, Hilda *would* show up; it was merely a matter of when. This underscores that Dawn believes that Hilda, most likely, will not abandon her, but she isn't absolutely certain of this. Her moving without leaving a forwarding address appears to set up a test of sorts for Hilda.

Hilda, exhibiting benevolence, acts in the best interest of her client by attempting to locate Dawn regardless of the time or inconvenience that this endeavor entails. Empathetically, she is able to put herself in the client's shoes to feel what it must be like to have a history of betrayal and loss and to feel alone and afraid. Likewise, Hilda reschedules visits when Dawn is a no-show for her at-home sessions. Despite the fact that Hilda seeks to promote client responsibility, she is able to flexibly adapt to these roadblocks because she perceives that Dawn had begun to trust and confide in her. This is laudable as long as Hilda does not sacrifice other clients or put herself at risk of significant harm.

In addition to being benevolent, Hilda is a fair person and provides equitable services for Dawn despite the fact that she does not get reimbursed for the overtime hours devoted to locating her client or for the weekend counseling visit she makes. Since Dawn is often not at home for her scheduled visits, Hilda returns so that she can provide services. Sometimes these visits also go beyond the number of hours that Hilda is required to work each week.

In providing equitable services, Hilda also makes certain that all her counseling is rendered competently and diligently. As a culturally competent therapist, Hilda has a background in counseling clients from diverse multicultural and socioeconomic backgrounds. She understands that Dawn has very limited financial stability and, as such, may schedule all her errands at one time so as not to spend extra money on gas. Sometimes that means missing appointments. Hilda empathizes with her situation and is steadfast and unrelenting in providing equitable and competent counseling services.

In providing such services, Hilda tries to address her client's health problems when they are shared by Dawn. Hilda's concerns about Dawn's health grow stronger as Dawn speaks in increasing detail about these issues. As an empathetic and diligent therapist, Hilda provides timely and reliable medical referral information, recommends medical evaluation, and at one point, with the consent of her client, advocates for such care. She does not, however, badger or exhort Dawn to make an appointment. Dawn is, in fact, a competent adult, and this stance is consistent with treating clients respectfully and refrains from imposing her values on her client (American Counseling Association [ACA], 2014, A.4.b). In this context, Hilda is intent on empowering Dawn; however, she balances her deep concern for her client's welfare with the utmost respect for her autonomy. Since Dawn is mentally competent and is seemingly not in imminent danger, Hilda respects her as a rational, self-determining person.

Although Hilda does not cajole her client on matters related to health care, one may question whether some of Hilda's other behaviors are overzealous and self-defeating. For instance, Hilda often arrives for scheduled visits at Dawn's house only to find that Dawn is not home. Hilda then reschedules these visits, which often involve working on her own time without remuneration. Is Hilda simply being manipulated by Dawn? One could argue that the missing of sessions by Dawn should, of necessity, have consequences that might teach Dawn to become more responsible and to develop respect for other people's time and efforts.

On the other hand, Hilda's benevolent, empathetic understanding of Dawn and her lifestyle allows her to understand the circumstances, feelings, and worldview of her client and still want to help her despite the inconvenience. After all, Dawn is in a state of crisis and turmoil. She is living at poverty level and has never had a stable emotional support network or role model. Although, in an ideal world, Dawn should alert Hilda beforehand that she would not be at home for the missed visits, she may be, on at least some occasions, acting frugally in running all her errands in one fell swoop. As discussed earlier, this minimizes the amount of fuel that Dawn needs to use.

In addition, Hilda senses that over the course of her visits, Dawn has begun to develop increased trust in her. This is evidenced by Dawn's progress in becoming increasingly more disclosing and aware of some of the poor choices that she has made. Hilda and Dawn also work together as Dawn begins to develop more effective decision-making skills. To teach Dawn responsibility at the expense of such therapeutic progress by not discontinuing therapy with her would be to blindly adhere to the practice of "teaching her to tow the line" instead of further fostering Dawn's sense of trust in Hilda. In fact, any discontinuation or abridgment of services may be experienced as betrayal and actual abandonment. This is reminiscent of the types of experiences that Dawn had experienced from childhood onward.

By contrast, Hilda's consistent caring may, in the long run, model the very sense of responsibility, empathy, and unconditional positive regard that might not only free Dawn to act in her own self-interest, but to connect with others in a more empathetic way as well. Because Hilda also embodies the virtue of diligence, she is able to demonstrate flexibility to adjust her schedule in situations wherein such actions appeared to be vital to the client's well-being.

This flexibility appears to be fruitful for the therapeutic relationship. Since Hilda's agency does not require that therapists maintain clients after three missed appointments, she would have been practicing well within the rules of the program to terminate the counseling relationship after the missed sessions. Instead, Hilda determines that canceling or abridging such services might breach the inviolable trust that is foundational for the helping relationship and potentially create issues of abandonment as well in the process. This commitment to her client highlights Hilda's benevolence. Her deep commitment and intrinsic regard for Dawn is evidenced by the satisfaction she experiences as she witnesses her client developing improved decision-making skills and an increased sense of trust. In addition, because Hilda is a salaried therapist, her commitment to Dawn is not influenced or predicated by financial gain, nor is she attempting to garner praise from her supervisor.

This commitment to her client is further expressed as Hilda strives to empower Dawn in a multiplicity of ways. Although Hilda respects her client's autonomy, her benevolence leads her to sometimes drop by to see if Dawn is okay after missed home visits. As discussed, Hilda sometimes fears for her own safety when making these visits. Due to the fact that on several occasions, after sunset, Hilda feels uneasy about her own safety, she has a right to be mindful of her own security. While it is true that counselors must be acutely cognizant of promoting client welfare, as discussed in the next chapter, they must not do so blindly if such actions put them in demonstrably dangerous situations. Hilda, therefore, should consider mitigating any potential danger to herself by limiting her visits to pre-dusk hours. This might allow her to serve her client as well as protect herself without making unnecessary or ill-conceived sacrifices.

As Hilda strives to navigate these often complex therapeutic waters, she is able to make substantial progress with Dawn. At the time of termination, she is beginning to demonstrate improved parenting skills as evidenced by her son Tom's improved behavior. She experiences less self-doubt as evidenced by a demonstrable increase in her positive self-statements and a significant decrease in her negative self-statements. She has also begun to socialize with a few neighbors, a departure from her previous stance of not trusting strangers.

Hilda's relationship with Dawn was likely instrumental in the constructive changes Dawn made in the course of 1 year of therapy. This is largely because the relationship is based on trust. "Clients of effective therapists feel understood, trust the therapist, and believe the therapist can help him or her" (Wampold, n.d.). Indeed, the trust that is established through virtuous practice demonstrates how virtue-based counseling practice can build and foster edifices of trust, therapist-client rapport, and client self-determination (Cohen & Cohen, 1999).

A SUSPICIOUS, APPREHENSIVE CLIENT

Such edifices of trust and client self-determination may be more illusory in situations where most familial and social contacts have been seriously severed and clients display marked suspiciousness and mistrust of others. This is the situation with Harold, a 50-year-old divorced father of two who was self-referred to the practice of Selmon Morales, who is licensed as both a clinical social worker as well as a mental health counselor.

> Harold spoke of pervasive feelings of loneliness and isolation. Divorced for 10 years, he was estranged from his two teenaged sons. He related that his divorce had been rancorous and stated that his ex-wife had "poisoned his children's minds"

against him. Harold spoke of having no friends and expressed that the only person that he could trust was his sister who lived 1,000 miles away from him. He shared that his sister had urged him to move closer to her, but that he had deferred for two main reasons. The first was that he was successfully self-employed as a small shop owner. The second was that he still had hopes of rekindling his relationship with his sons.

Harold told Selmon that he had been hesitant to begin therapy, but that he was becoming increasingly more isolated and that that situation scared him. He shared that he had married his wife on the rebound and that he was now unsure of whether he had ever really loved her. She was 10 years his junior and had been looking to find stability in her life.

Harold also related that he had been engaged prior to his marriage, but that his fiancée had "cheated" on him with a woman with whom she worked. Although Harold stated that he had still wanted to "save" the relationship, his fiancée chose to terminate it. Harold relayed that he "never got over this betrayal."

In addition, he shared that after marrying his wife he became very suspicious of her activities. Although his actions in the relationship were not overtly intrusive, he often imagined that she, too, like his fiancée, would leave him. After several years of repeatedly asking her if she was cheating on him, his spouse filed for divorce. Harold stated that he was too "decimated" to "fight for custody" of his sons and was awarded only "standard visitation." This was visitation every other weekend and 6 weeks in the summer. As his sons grew older, Harold said that he sensed their hesitation to visit him, so he "just stopped asking."

This estrangement appeared to weigh heavily on Harold. As Selmon and Harold explored goals, it became clear that Harold wanted to try to rebuild his relationship with his sons as well as develop some friendships. He shared that he was "full of emotions" but that he had been taught that it was "unmasculine" to "be weak" and to "cry like a baby." He stated that he was, nonetheless, going to try to "do his best" in therapy.

As the two began to discuss Harold's fear of rejection, Selmon sensed his client's ongoing hesitation to disclose too much emotional content pertaining to his present-day feelings. As is often the case, it may be easier for clients early on in therapy to discuss historical feelings than to discuss those that are current (Rogers, 1961). Despite having been given both written as well as oral informed consent, related to the limits of confidentiality as well as other aspects of the therapist-client relationship, Harold seemed to be very concerned that Selmon might share the content of his sessions with others. Though this informed consent was given at the onset of treatment and periodically throughout its duration, Harold seemed to be struggling with the fear of being betrayed and of being discovered in a counseling setting by other clients, particularly customers from his business. He expressed anxiety about these customers possibly seeing him in Selmon's waiting room.

Responsive to Harold's concerns about disclosure of confidential information, Selmon candidly reiterated that codes of ethics and state laws protect client confidentially with certain specific exceptions (ACA, 2014, B.2.a.) and was careful to provide details. For example, he described that client information could be disclosed to prevent serious, foreseeable, and imminent harm to the client or others. At the same time, Selmon was clear that these were exceptions and that confidentiality is otherwise rigorously protected as both a legal and professional duty. To assuage Harold's fear that others would see him in Selmon's office, the therapist also arranged for Harold to be the last appointment of the night.

Nevertheless, Harold continued to question Selmon's professional fidelity to him, often asking if Selmon thought that his issues were silly compared to the concerns of others. Selmon, however, persevered in helping his client meet his goals, including assigning him behavioral homework geared toward helping Harold make friends.

When Harold reported having made a new friend who had been a recurrent customer of his, he appeared to feel some sense of accomplishment, but still lamented not being yet able to reestablish his relationship with his children who were, at the time, ages 16 and 18. He was particularly fearful about attempts to contact his sons, fearing rejection. He told Selmon that he "would fall to pieces" if his sons rejected him again. Selmon used cognitive restructuring and rehearsal exercise wherein various scenarios were practiced to dispel the irrational belief that Harold would fall to pieces if his efforts with his sons were unrequited. Harold ultimately made the choice to contact his sons.

As the relationship between father and sons began to evolve, Selmon suggested referring the three to a therapist to explore a few issues that had begun to emerge. Harold was at first hesitant to see another counselor. Selmon did not coerce or pressure his client in any way. Instead, he explained to Harold that he had made the suggestion because he believed that counseling both Harold as well as his sons, might involve conflicting roles that could be problematic.

After several sessions of exploring the status of his relationship with his sons and the possible benefits of family therapy with another therapist, Harold decided that this course of action would be in his best interest. Accordingly, Harold and Selmon mutually agreed to begin to scale down the number of times they met and to review the goals and progress Harold had made during treatment. Selmon reassured Harold that, should he decide that he wants to resume treatment, Selmon will accommodate him. Harold and his sons subsequently began family therapy, and Harold gleefully reported back to Selmon during his 3-month follow-up visit that he and his children were making significant progress in restoring their bonds.

ESTABLISHING TRUST WITH A SUSPICIOUS, APPREHENSIVE CLIENT

Clearly, Selmon understands that Harold has a history of broken trust and unsuccessful interpersonal relationships and appropriately demonstrates empathy and compassion in working with him. Although Selmon, unlike Harold, has a successful marriage and good relationships with his children, he is able to key into the universality of feelings that human beings experience, albeit in different situations (Cohen, 2015). So, although Selmon has not had the exact experiences as Harold, he still recognizes what it is like to feel betrayal, loneliness, and isolation. As such, Selmon can accurately empathize with his client. He is able to enter Harold's phenomenal world and, in a Rogerian manner, experience this world as if he were the client, but "without ever losing the 'as if' quality" (Rogers, 1957). As such, Selmon tries to understand the persistent fear that Harold has of disclosing sensitive emotional information and of the confidentiality of this information being compromised. As a benevolent counselor, Selmon is devoted to promoting the welfare of his clients and helping facilitate positive change.

The virtue of benevolence, of necessity, encompasses the virtue of nonmalevolence. Accordingly, Selmon carefully works to avoid hurting, or in any way, needlessly compromising the integrity or dignity of his client. In particular, he takes appropriate precautions to candidly provide his client with informed consent (both written and oral) at the outset of therapy and reinforce such consent throughout the course of therapy, including informing Harold of the special circumstances under which codes of ethics and state statutes would permit disclosure (see Chapter 5). In so doing, Selmon treats Harold with the respect and dignity owed to another human being. Such respectful treatment can help not only to empower clients, but also, importantly, assists in creating a stronger edifice of trust between client and helper.

In addition to this, Selmon takes measures to ease Harold's concern about being recognized at a therapist's office, namely, scheduling him at a later hour when there are less people out and about. This helps ease the client's concerns, further empower him, and promote trust.

Promoting trust also entails acting as a competent and diligent therapist. Selmon's competence allows him to use therapeutic techniques and tools effectively. His diligence allows him to be flexible with Selmon in changing appointment times and not blindly adhering to pro forma rules. This fosters an atmosphere of egalitarianism and contributes to Harold's sense of autonomy and self-determination.

This ability to promote self-determination is also evident because Selmon suggests referral to a family therapist. Counselor and client discuss the options and implications over several sessions with Harold ultimately deciding what he feels is best for him. In addition, this referral also demonstrates another therapist virtue, that of loyalty. Selmon clearly puts his client's welfare first when he suggests the referral. He does not, in any way, consider that making this referral will cause him to lose revenue or clients. Rather, Selmon believes that either Harold or his sons may feel uncomfortable with the fact that he has been Harold's therapist and perceive that he might have a conflict of interest. As discussed in Chapter 9, even the *appearance* of such a conflict could be good reason to avoid entering into the counseling relationship.

As a virtuous practitioner, Selmon avoids this perception and facilitates a smooth and seamless referral process for his client. Thus, as Selmon and Harold began the termination process, Selmon reassures Harold that he is free to contact him if he believes that he needs to resume services. Here the client is not made to feel that he is being abandoned, but rather that there is still a support system in place should he perceive the need. This also means that, as a fair-minded therapist, Selmon does due diligence not to overbook clients, thereby allowing for the possibility of accommodating returning clients without lengthy waiting periods. In this manner, Harold is reassured, experiences less apprehension about terminating therapy, and gains a sense of security about "having a net" after termination.

This feeling of security can further contribute to the foundation of trust that develops in a well-functioning therapeutic relationship. Such a relationship is, of course, predicated on a multitude of factors including counselor attributes and attitudes, adherence to counseling best practices, therapist authenticity, and the ability of the therapist to competently assess each situation. While competent therapists can and do approach similar situations differently (such as by employing different counseling modalities), the embodiment of counselor virtues can, indeed, provide an edifice for building trust.

As demonstrated in the above two cases, establishing trust in a therapeutic relationship can be a challenging endeavor. Trust in a therapeutic relationship must constantly be reaffirmed and can continue to grow even though the therapist may believe that it is there in sufficient quantity to further client progress. Therapists often work tirelessly to reinforce that they can, in fact, be trusted. This is most likely accomplished, however, when the therapist is, in fact, a trustworthy person; and such a person, as discussed in Chapter 1, demonstrates all the other virtues broached in this book, such as benevolence, empathy, honesty, candor, authenticity, competence, diligence, loyalty, and fairness.

Questions for Review and Reflection

1. Hilda makes occasional visits to Dawn's home after sunset, even though she sometimes fears for her own safety. What are some pros and cons of doing this in the context of counselor nonmaleficence?

2. When Dawn moves without informing Hilda, Hilda makes great effort to locate her. As it turns out, Dawn appears to be testing the trustworthiness of the therapist. What safety and therapeutic risks could Hilda be making in trying to find Dawn? What might have been some other reasons for Dawn leaving without a trace?

3. Hilda provides equitable services for Dawn even when she is not being paid for her services. What are some therapeutic pros and cons of her doing this in the context of Dawn's personal circumstances?

4. Hilda allows Dawn to miss several counseling sessions without notifying her. What, if any, potential pitfalls could arise from this practice?

5. Dawn has a boyfriend who appears to have a chronic, untreated illness. What, if any, ethical responsibilities does Hilda have to him? Explain.

6. Hilda attempts to conduct herself in ways intended to promote client autonomy and self-determination. Is there a risk that some of the strategies that she uses could backfire and actually promote client dependence? Explain.

7. Why does Harold appear to feel more comfortable discussing historical feelings rather than the feelings that he is currently experiencing?

8. Selmon suggests making a referral to Harold for family therapy to avoid any uncomfortable feelings on the part of the family members and also to avoid the appearance of a conflict of interests. What virtue(s) is Selmon practicing in so doing? Explain. How does this relate to the therapist's trustworthiness?

9. In the case of Harold, how does the counselor's virtue of diligence affect the quality and success of the termination process?

10. How might Selmon's candor, specifically with respect to the potential disclosure of certain confidential client disclosures affect the trust and rapport that he develops with Harold? Is it ethically necessary for Selmon to reiterate over time, state laws and codes of ethics dealing with such disclosures of confidential material?

11. In discussing his sons with Selmon, Harold talks about "falling to pieces" if he is rejected by them. How does Selmon work with Harold's apparent irrational supposition without imposing his values on his client?

Cases for Analysis

Using the concepts discussed in this chapter, discuss and reflect on virtuous practice in the following cases.

1. Martin is a middle-aged male with a history of committing minor crimes and lying to friends and associates when truth telling is often the easier route. The offspring of alcoholic parents, Martin states that he was never able to trust his parents and is having difficulty trusting his psychologist of 3 months' duration, Dr. Silvan Barton. Martin has served time for his criminal behaviors and has stated that he is not afraid that revealing these crimes now could put him in any legal jeopardy; however, he has said that he fears that Barton will use his past against him and judge him unfairly. He has vacillated between beginning to speak of his past and saying that he will never reveal it to Barton. Barton suspects that resolution of issues related to this past are critical to the success of treatment. How can Barton responsibly proceed with treatment?

2. Cynthia is a Hispanic female who has been in therapy with Dr. Brianna Karlton for 3 weeks. She had requested a Latina therapist but was not able to be accommodated because the satellite office of the agency where she receives services does not have one on staff and Cynthia is unable to travel 15 miles to the main office. Cynthia has repeatedly expressed doubts that Karlton, a white woman, will be able to fully understand her experiences and concerns. Karlton is versed in the dynamics and challenges that sometimes occur with multicultural counseling but is sensing that she is at a standstill with Cynthia. How can she ethically and responsibly address Cynthia's concerns?

3. Alvin is a 7-year-old male child who is in therapy because he has been the victim of long-term school bullying. His counselor of 4 weeks, Bernard Jarold, has been able to engage Alvin in limited play therapy but finds that he appears reluctant to speak about his school experiences. Alvin seems to fear expressing what happened to him, stating that he was referred to counseling for some "misunderstandings with other kids." How can Jarold begin to establish trust with this client?

References

American Counseling Association. (2014). *ACA code of ethics*. Alexandria, VA: Author.

Cohen, E. D. (2015, May). How to be empathetic. *Psychology Today*. Retrieved from https://www.psychologytoday.com/blog/what-would-aristotle-do/201505/how-be-empathetic

Cohen, E. D., & Cohen, G. S. (1999). *The virtuous therapist: Ethical practice of counseling and psychotherapy*. Belmont, CA: Wadsworth.

Rogers, C. R. (1957). The necessary and sufficient conditions of therapeutic personality change. *Consulting Psychology, 21*(2), 95–103. Retrieved from https://app.shoreline.edu/dchris/psych236/Documents/Rogers.pdf

Rogers, C. R. (1961). *On becoming a person*. Boston, MA: Houghton Mifflin.

Wampold, B. E. (n.d.). *Qualities and actions of effective therapists*. Washington, DC: American Psychological Association. Retrieved from https://www.apa.org/education/ce/effective-therapists.pdf

RESOLVING ETHICAL ISSUES

PART II

3

APPLYING ETHICAL STANDARDS

Case Study: A Clash of Values Inside a Fundamentalist Christian Family

As seen in Chapter 2, facilitating client trust is a major factor in promoting positive client change. Further, the cultivation and practice of a mutually supportive set of habits or virtues, as examined in Chapter 1, is a major factor in facilitating client trust. Now, in this third chapter, key virtues (namely, benevolence, nonmalevolence, respect, fairness, and empathy) are linked to *standards of ethical practice* that virtuous therapists tend to use in making rational, ethical judgments in professional contexts. As discussed in Chapter 1, virtues are character traits consisting of habits to think, act, and feel in certain morally appropriate ways. Because virtuous practitioners seek to act in morally appropriate ways, that is, to do the morally right thing, they can benefit from having a set of standards that guides them in making such ethical decisions. Standards of ethics provide such guidance.

To be clear, the making of rational, ethical judgments in such contexts is not a mechanical process, and the virtuous therapist does not bring algorithms or mathematical formulae to the counseling room in confronting ethical problems. As Aristotle (2015) long ago made clear, we should not expect the precision of mathematics in ethics, for the subject matter of ethics does not lend itself to such precision, inasmuch as "matters concerned with conduct and questions of what is good for us have no fixity" and, therefore, "must be given in outline and not precisely" (Bk. 1, Ch. 3; Bk. 2, Ch. 2). Further, there are hard cases in counseling ethics that can challenge the knowledge and skills of even the most seasoned practitioner. This chapter begins with such a case and shows how ethical standards can be used to address it.

A CLASH OF VALUES INSIDE A FUNDAMENTALIST CHRISTIAN FAMILY

> Shelly Simon, a 14-year-old, was in therapy for 3 weeks with Dr. Dimsdale, who had diagnosed her with clinical depression. Previously a stellar student, she was receiving failing grades, cutting classes, and had to be "forced" to wake up in the morning, get dressed, and board the school bus. In the evenings, Shelly locked herself in her room, lying in bed and often refused to come out to eat dinner. Fortunately, Dr. Dimsdale began to develop a rapport with Shelly, and she started to open up about her issues. Shelly informed Dimsdale that she was unhappy about not being able to be like the other kids. In particular, she expressed strong desires to go to parties, date, wear makeup, and have fashionable clothes; however, her parents, who were Evangelical Christians, refused to allow her to do any of these things. As a result, she was ostracized by the other children, who thought she was a "weirdo." With Shelly's consent, Dimsdale discussed the matter with her parents; however, they were firm that the things Shelly wanted to do were off bounds for her. What was Dimsdale to do?

Cases like Shelly's are ethically complex because there are competing interests at stake. On the one hand is Shelly's interest in being like the other kids at school. On the other is the interest of Shelly's parents in remaining faithful to their religion. Dimsdale's primary allegiance is to the welfare of his client, but what is truly in Shelly's best interest when her parents, who are her primary caretakers and legal guardians, refuse to give her what she wants? As you can see, this question is not only an ethical one. It is also one that is relevant to how Dimsdale proceeds in attempting to help Shelly beat her depression. Here, ethics and clinical skill seem to coalesce. An ethical solution to the problem at hand is also a clinical one.

On the positive side, the history of ethics has provided a rich source of ethical standards or principles that can be used to enlighten ethical judgment in cases like Shelly's. These standards, in one form or another, have been used to provide serviceable guidelines in diverse areas of professional ethics (Beauchamp & Childress, 1979) and have also found their way into some counseling codes of ethics as establishing "a conceptual basis" for the code of ethics and "the foundation for ethical behavior and decision making" (American Counseling Association [ACA], 2014, Preamble). Accordingly, such standards are presented in this chapter.

THE STANDARDS: AN OVERVIEW

There are five general standards presented here. Three of them can be divided into further more specific standards, equaling 10 standards in all:

1. Beneficence:

    Client Welfare: Do what is in the client's best interest.

    Social Welfare: Act to maximize the good of society.

2. Nonmaleficence:

    Client Nonmaleficence: Do not needlessly or carelessly cause or permit harm to clients.

    Counselor Nonmaleficence: Avoid serious harm to self.

    Third Party Nonmaleficence: Do not cause or permit needless or preventable harm to others.

3. Autonomy:

    Client Autonomy: Treat clients as self-determining agents.

    Counselor Autonomy: Treat oneself as a self-determining agent.

    Third Party Autonomy: Treat non-clients as self-determining agents.

4. Justice: Provide equitable or fair counseling services.

5. Compassionate Caring: Be with and there for clients.

Each of the above general standards represents a major current in the evolution of ethical standards for professional ethics (Beauchamp & Childress, 1979; Cohen & Cohen, 1999; Gilligan, 1982; Kitchener, 1984). Collectively, they can provide a rational, informed perspective for addressing the many ethical challenges that confront mental health practitioners. Each is, itself, supported by a major counselor virtue. Standard 1 seeks to bring about the best consequences for clients (Client Welfare) and society in general (Social Welfare). It is accordingly what a *benevolent* therapist would use in helping clients do and feel better and in making constructive contributions to society. Standard 2 is concerned with avoiding needless harm to both clients and other third parties (*nonmaleficence*) and is therefore a principle that a benevolent or nonmalevolent therapist would naturally apply. Standard 3 seeks to respect the rights and dignity of individuals, both clients (Client Autonomy) and therapists (Counselor Autonomy). It is therefore a standard naturally applied by a *respectful* therapist. Standard 4 extends respect for the rights and dignity of individuals to the equitable distribution of counseling services and is therefore a standard engaged by just or *fair* therapists. Standard 5 seeks to provide emotional support for clients. *Empathetic* therapists obviously apply this standard.

These standards can conflict with each other. For example, Client Welfare can conflict with Client Autonomy when respecting the latter means not doing something that is in the client's best interest. Virtuous therapists are therefore prepared to strike balances between these standards to do what is right in a given context. So in one context the therapist may believe that Client Welfare overrides Client Autonomy because the interest in question is urgent. For example, a therapist may believe that involuntary detainment of a suicidal client is in the best interest of the client, although it would restrict the client's freedom to end his life.

In his classic work, *The Right and the Good*, philosopher W. D. Ross (2002) distinguished between what he called "prima facie" or "conditional duties" and "actual duties" (p. 9). According to Ross, a prima facie duty is a sort of action (for example, promise keeping) that tends to be the right thing to do, as long as there is nothing else that overrides it (e.g., keeping the promise would seriously harm someone). The five standards presented here have this conditional quality. They are conditionally the right things to do as long as they are not overridden by something else. For example, doing what is in the client's best interest tends to be the right thing for a therapist to do, but if the act in question undermines the client's autonomy then it is not necessarily the right thing for the therapist to do. For example, the therapist might reasonably believe that the client would benefit from continuing with a particular sort of therapy; nevertheless, the client prefers to discontinue the current therapy and try a different modality instead. While continuing with the current therapy may be in the best interest of the client, the therapist may concede to changing the modality. In such a case, the prima facie duty to do what best advances Client Welfare is overridden by respect for Client Autonomy. All the standards introduced below are prima facie or conditional duties in this way.

Beneficence

This standard tells one to promote the positive welfare of others, that is, their happiness, pleasure, or contentment and/or to remove or reduce their negative welfare, that is, their unhappiness, pain, or suffering (Beauchamp & Childress, 1979; Frankena, 1973). In the first instance, a therapist may teach a client assertiveness skills, which, in turn, help him advance professionally or forge new interpersonal relationships. In the second instance, a client who is suffering from depression may be helped by a therapist to overcome the depression through the therapy.

Beneficent acts may, and often do, produce negative welfare as an unintended consequence of producing positive welfare. For example, in couples counseling the relationship may become more contentious before it improves, or a client may experience painful emotions as a consequence of applying a certain counseling technique or modality. For example, Gestalt Therapy, Psychoanalysis, or a confrontational approach; or an aversion therapy may be used because the therapist believes that the approach would maximize the clients *overall or net positive welfare*. The overall or net positive welfare of an act refers to *the balance of positive welfare over negative welfare produced by the act* (Sinnott-Armstrong, 2015). Thus, in treating panic disorders a therapist might prefer cognitive-behavior therapy (CBT) over a certain type of drug therapy if the latter had adverse physical side effects, required higher and higher dosages over time, and did not produce lasting, permanent changes; while the CBT avoided the side effects, produced lasting changes, and was at least equally as effective in reducing the symptoms of the disorder. In such a case, the overall or net positive welfare of CBT could be said to be higher than the overall or net positive welfare of the drug therapy in treating panic disorders. However, if the overall positive welfare of the CBT, when combined with the drug therapy, were greater than any other available option (including the solitary use of any of the available treatments), then it could also be said to be in the client's *best interest* to have the combined therapy. In other words, doing what is in the client's *best interest* refers to *maximizing the client's overall or net positive welfare*, or doing what produces a greater balance of positive welfare over negative welfare than any alternative course of action available.

Beneficence is the standard that benevolent people subscribe to when they do things, out of kindness, to help others (Cohen & Cohen, 1999). Helping professionals who are successful in their fields tend to be such individuals. The benevolent teacher, who dedicates many hours in grading papers to provide careful feedback to her students, does so because she genuinely wants her students to acquire knowledge that will be helpful to them. The benevolent physician goes into medicine because he wants to help ill people get well, not because the medical profession is prestigious or lucrative. Beneficence in counseling aims at helping individual clients to deal with their psychological challenges; but it also extends to promoting positive welfare on a social level. Each of these types of beneficence is discussed below.

Client Welfare

This standard of beneficence tells therapists (in their capacity as mental health providers) to do what maximizes the client's overall or net positive welfare; that is, what is in the *client's best interest* (Lo, 2013). This standard is largely served through the provision of competent counseling services. As discussed in Chapter 1, competence includes both classroom knowledge as well as experience in the field and the ability to make accurate diagnoses. It includes knowledge of one's own limitations and abilities; multicultural understanding of the client populations with whom one works; willingness to admit one's mistakes and to learn from them; consult with others when one has ethical as well as technical questions; diligence in the provision of services; and prudence in applying one's fund of knowledge and experience, including the skillful application of counseling modalities to the diverse counseling populations one serves; and the ability to make reasonable prognoses based on acquired data and experience in the field. However, as discussed in Chapter 2, therapists are not disposed to acquire relevant client data unless their clients are disposed toward trusting them. As such, only trustworthy therapists who have attained such a level of professional competence are ordinarily best equipped to apply the Client Welfare standard (ACA, 2014, C2).

What maximizes a client's overall positive welfare may not necessarily be what the client herself desires. Reasonable application of the Client Welfare standard requires awareness of the potential for such disagreement and the ability to work with less cooperative clients short of providing services that are not helping the client address her issues (Shallcross, 2010).

Social Welfare

The human services delivery system consists of a social network consisting of various institutions from private practices, to state and federally funded agencies and hospitals. In its attempt to provide mental health services, this system must deal with further organizations such as insurance companies, managed care institutions, the pharmaceutical industry, and government itself including state and federal legislative and judicial branches. This standard tells therapists, all of whom practice within this massive interconnected network, to act in ways that maximize overall happiness, or the good of society (ACA, 2014, Preamble; Bentham, 2014). As a therapist, this includes making contributions to the profession itself, which may include doing research, publishing, teaching, supervising or training other therapists; serving on local, state, or national committees and task forces; and being active members of professional associations. This standard includes working cooperatively with staff and colleagues and creating a work environment conducive to productivity and the well-being of all concerned. This standard applies to working within the system to improve or remedy systemic problems—for example, issues with managed care that may be affecting the quality of counseling services and the paucity of local, state, and federal budgets affecting access to affordable mental health care. In some cases, it may justify whistle blowing to expose a corrupt practice that is usurping the quality of mental health care. It involves acting in ways that advance rather than undermine the ability of people to receive counseling services at affordable rates. For example, this standard militates against submitting false diagnoses to insurance companies to get paid for client services. This is because such ploys increase insurance companies' operation costs, which raises the cost of insurance premiums, thereby affecting the ability of prospective clients to afford mental health insurance.

Nonmaleficence

This standard consists of three kinds, Client Nonmaleficence, Counselor Nonmaleficence, and Third Party Nonmaleficence. It instructs against *causing* needless or preventable harm or failing to *prevent* it (Beauchamp & Childress, 1979). In the first instance, a therapist might cause needless harm through incompetence or negligence; in the second instance, a therapist might have information about a dangerous client and an identifiable victim, or a suicidal client, but nevertheless fail to protect the potential victim. The Standard of Nonmaleficence is violated through intentionally harmful, malicious, or reckless acts; but it can also be violated through incompetence, negligence, or disregard for or ignorance of professional ethics. Many transgressions of this standard tend to be easily definable and identifiable and thus proper subjects of criminal sanctions—imprisonment, fine, loss of licenses to practice—as well as malpractice suits (Fuller, 1964).

Client Nonmaleficence

This standard proscribes therapists' having sexual or romantic relationships with current clients or their families inasmuch as such dual or multiple role relationships mix inconsistent expectations—such as the client's expectation that the therapist will remain objective in helping to address the client's problems; and the therapist's expectation that the client will provide intimacy or sex (Kitchener, 1988). Other transgressions against Client Nonmaleficence include client abandonment, failure to keep counseling records safe and secure, sharing of confidential client information with others having no need to know; failure to provide informed consent to therapy, taking on cases for which one is not qualified, and failing to disguise a client's identifying information when publishing a case study (ACA, 2014; American Psychological Association [APA], 2016; National Association of Social Workers [NASW], 2017). Such avoidable harms, among others, are often regulated by legal standards of "due care" as well as professional codes of ethics (Cohen & Cohen, 1999).

Counselor Nonmaleficence

This standard justifies therapists in refusing to participate in professional practice that imperils them (ACA, 2014, A.11.c.; APA, 2016, 4.05; Zur, 2007). Therapist's lives matter, too, and they are justified in taking reasonable measures to protect themselves, as well as their families and their staff, against dangerous clients who threaten their lives, limbs, or property, for example, by terminating counseling or calling the police.

Therapists are also not expected to take serious legal risks for clients, for example, risking imprisonment or losing their licenses. Indeed, even courageous counselors carefully consider the hills they are prepared to die on. Nevertheless, therapists who practice long enough will inevitably confront moral challenges that do not necessarily comport with the law and raise questions about whether obedience to law takes precedence over doing what is morally right on behalf of a client.

Therapists are also not expected to risk losing substantial amounts of money or their personal, material possessions on behalf of clients. As professionals, there is ordinarily a line drawn between personal property and professional service. While professional sacrifices of time and money are praiseworthy to make counseling services available to clients (for example, providing pro bono services to indigent clients), a therapist is not expected to open his home up to clients who are destitute or to pay the medical costs of clients who can't afford medical care. However, this does not mean that a therapist should not attempt to help locate public services that could provide the appropriate assistance for clients in need (Meyers, 2014). Indeed, it is a mark of a virtuous therapist to do just that.

Third Party Nonmaleficence

This standard proscribes therapists engaging in conduct that harms or fails to prevent harm to individuals other than clients in the provision of mental health services. Transgressions of this standard include sexual harassment of an employee; engaging in research that does not take adequate precautions against causing psychological or physical harm to subjects; failing to prevent harm to a third party who is endangered by a client; coaching a client on how to "get even with" another person, say an estranged spouse; encouraging or helping a client commit a crime such a theft, assault, or fraud; or enabling or helping a client abuse or otherwise harm another person such as a family member (ACA, 2014; APA, 2016; NASW, 2017).

Autonomy

Client Autonomy: Treating Clients as Self-Determining Agents

This standard is one that a respectful therapist would have internalized. It says to treat clients as persons, not objects. German 18th Century philosopher Immanuel Kant expressed this eloquently. He said, "Treat humanity, whether in your own person or that of another, always as an end in itself, and never as a mere means" (Kant, 1964). By "end in itself" Kant meant a person, that is, a rational being capable of making up his own mind. For Kant, persons are centers of intrinsic value. That is, they have worth and dignity that persists independently of whatever use we may have for them. This is in contrast to "mere means," which are objects whose value depends entirely on the use we may have for them. For example, a pen is a utensil used for writing. When it ceases to serve this function, it ceases to possess value, and we are justified in discarding it and purchasing a new pen. In contrast, persons, as "ends in themselves," are not to be used, then discarded and replaced when we no longer have a use for them.

Kant held that the basis of a person's worth and dignity is his rational nature, which distinguishes persons from objects or mere things. Because persons, as distinct from objects, have a rational nature, they also have a *right* of self-determination, which means that they have a claim not be treated like mere things. In the context of counseling, this means that clients have a basic right to be treated as rational, determining agents. This means that they are not to be tricked, deceived, threatened, coerced, or otherwise manipulated. They have the right to informed consent, which means that they are to be fully informed about matters relevant to their therapy and given the opportunity to decide themselves. Here, "fully informed" means informed, on an ongoing basis, about anything a reasonable person would want to know about his treatment. This includes the purpose or goals of therapy; potential risks and benefits, alternative approaches; diagnoses and their interpretation; the nature and limits of confidentiality; fees and billing arrangements; therapist's qualifications, scheduling; and the status of client records (ACA Code, 2014, A2a–A2b). Clients are not to be used by therapists for self-aggrandizing purposes such as keeping them in therapy when it is no longer useful just to continue to receive payment, or using clients' sessions to work through one's own problems.

As in the case of all other standards, Client Autonomy is a prima facie standard. That is, there may be some occasions when another standard overrides it. For example, in an exceptional situation such as a case of a suicidal client in a crisis, a therapist may withhold information from the client about his diagnosis if the therapist believes that disclosing the information will lead the client to attempt suicide. So, in such a situation, the standard of Nonmaleficence may override the Autonomy standard. However, the therapist should not allow the exception to become the rule. Respectful therapists avoid such exceptions and do what they can to mitigate any abridgment of Client Autonomy. For example, the therapist would disclose the information withheld from the client when she is stable and no longer in a state of crisis.

Counselor Autonomy: Treating Oneself as a Self-Determining Agent

As stated, Kant held that one should treat oneself as well as others as an "end in itself" and not as a "mere means." The standard of Counselor Autonomy is true to Kant's directive. It holds that therapists should not become a vehicle to be exploited by others, including their clients. Therapists are entitled to be paid for services rendered in the amount agreed upon; they are not required to serve clients who are uncooperative or abusive, for example, do not keep appointments, threaten, or sexually harass them; or seek help for frivolous, unethical, or unlawful purposes, for example, to forge a personal or sexual relationship or to seek assistance in the commission of a crime or perpetration of a fraud. While client transference can often be an important aspect of therapy, there is, nevertheless, a difference between clients who act out in the course of working through a problem, and clients whose inappropriate treatment of their therapists has nothing to do with working through an issue. Respectful and competent therapists are aware of the distinction and use discretion in deciding how to proceed.

It is important for therapists to treat themselves as self-determining agents not only for their own sake, but also for the sake of their clients. Therapists who do not appear to respect themselves make poor role models, permit self-defeating client behavior, and do not, therefore, have much success in helping clients meet therapeutic outcomes.

Third Party Autonomy: Treating Non-Clients as Self-Determining Agents

The Kantian standard of respect for persons clearly includes non-clients. This includes the families of clients, colleagues, coworkers, public service providers, medical personnel, insurance providers, court officers, and others with whom mental health practitioners are expected to work cooperatively. Here such respect includes not lying or deceiving others. For example, it is a violation of this standard to submit false diagnoses to an insurance company to gain approval of insurance benefits for a client. Likewise, presenting redacted versions of client records that have been subpoenaed, even for purposes of protecting one's client, is not only unlawful, but it also violates the standard of Third Party Autonomy by treating officers of the court as objects manipulated. Accordingly, "[c]ounselors are accurate, honest, and objective in reporting their professional activities and judgments to appropriate third parties, including courts, health insurance companies, those who are the recipients of evaluation reports, and others" (ACA, 2014, C.6.b). Likewise, lying or otherwise deceiving the families of clients or their legal guardians ordinarily violates this standard. For instance, in the cases of counseling minor clients, or adults with diminished decision-making capacity, therapists not only protect the ethical rights of these clients to make decisions to the extent to which they are capable, but also recognize "parental or familial legal rights and responsibilities to protect these clients and make decisions on their behalf" (ACA Code, 2014, A.2.d).

This does not mean that therapists who adhere to the standard of Third Party Autonomy discount their client's welfare for the sake of respecting the autonomy of others; for, like the other ethical standards discussed here, Third Party Autonomy can be overridden, especially when the client's welfare and/or interests hang in the balance. Thus, when a legal guardian or parent of a client is acting against the welfare of a client, say through abuse or neglect, the therapist takes steps to report such action to the appropriate authority pursuant to state law (Peterson & Urquiza, 1993). Indeed, the client's best interest is a *primary* responsibility of the therapist (ACA, 2014, A.1.a).

Justice: Providing Equitable or Fair Counseling Services

The provision of equitable or fair counseling services involves treating relevantly like cases alike. This is a formal principle of justice that, more exactly, means two things: that we should (1) treat alike those who are the same in relevant respects, and (2) treat differently those who are unalike in relevant respects (Feinberg, 1973). For example, if one person violates a traffic law and is fined $100 and another person, say a celebrity, violates the same traffic law and is not given any fine, then, without there being any relevant difference between them (which being a celebrity is not), such unequal treatment would be unjust. This is because relevantly like cases were treated differently, whereas they should have been treated the same. On the other hand, if a nonhandicapped person who does not have a legal handicap permit parks in a handicapped space, thereby preventing a handicapped person who has the required permit from parking in the space, yet is not fined or made to vacate the space, then this is also unjust. This is because relevantly *different* cases (the truly handicapped person and the nonhandicapped person) were *not* treated differently.

The above Standard of Justice is *formal* because it does not specify what treatment to dole out to relevantly like or relevantly unlike cases; nor does it say what the standard of relevance is. Lest these substantive matters be clearly defined, there is danger of applying this principle in unjust ways. Indeed, it is possible to consistently treat alike all cases that are the same in a certain respect but, in so doing, treat them in ways that are morally reprehensible (Feinberg, 1973). For example, the old racial laws sought to consistently treat blacks equally by systematically segregating them. However, in 1955, in the landmark Supreme Court case, *Brown v. Board of Education of Topeka,* "Separate but equal," as earlier announced in *Plessy v. Ferguson,* was found to be unconstitutional. While all blacks were treated alike, the treatment itself was unjust. Requiring all blacks to have separate facilities (schools, public bathrooms, etc.) was unjust because it discriminated against blacks by sending out the unequivocal message that blacks were inferior to whites and, therefore, not entitled to associate with them. The justice of the treatment itself is a function of whether it respects the rights of the group in question, that is, treats them as persons rather than as mere objects or things. The old racial laws treated blacks like objects instead of respecting their dignity as rational, self-determining agents because they forced blacks to be isolated and looked down on as inferior beings; and it sought to socialize, condition, or brainwash them into believing it.

In saying that the Standard of Justice treats *relevantly* like cases alike and relevantly dissimilar cases differently, what is meant is that the treatment in question must be applied only to cases possessing certain properties that *for the intended purposes* make application appropriate. "We should not discriminate between persons who are alike in all relevant respects; but which respects are relevant depends upon the occasion for justice, on our purposes and objectives, and on the internal rules of the 'game' we are playing" (Feinberg, 1973, p. 102). So, for purposes of education, dining in restaurants, traveling on public transportation, or having access to public facilities, race is irrelevant because it has nothing to do with whether a person is capable of receiving an education, dining, boarding a bus, or using a public bathroom or water fountain. In contrast, the age of a person may be relevant. Thus, a 2-month-old child is exempt from attending first grade because she is not capable of doing the work of a first grader. So, excluding all two month olds from first grade is not unjust according to the Justice Standard as it would be to exclude black, Hispanic, Muslim, or Jewish children from the first grade. This is true because race and religion do not bear on the capacity to do the work (Soble, 1982).

In mental health counseling, the standard of relevance is need for treatment and how beneficial the therapy might be. As such, giving therapy to individuals who are not in need of it, or are unlikely to benefit from the therapy, while excluding others who are truly in need, or are likely to benefit, would be unjust. Unfortunately, to the extent that the cost of adequate mental health treatment in the United States, and the failure of some insurance plans to cover it, excludes suitable candidates from obtaining adequate mental health care, the current system of mental health care in the United States is unjust. As long as indigent or poor individuals in need of therapy receive inferior mental health care—or none at all, in comparison to wealthier individuals who receive superior treatment—the present system fails to satisfy the Standard of Justice and should be reformed. Because approximately one third of the homeless population in the United States has an untreated, serious mental illness, it is clear that government has not done enough to promote just mental health care in the United States (Treatment Advocacy Center, 2014). At the same time, mental health treatment programs and facilities have been on decline while over a half million people with serious mental illness are unable to find suitable mental health care (Szabo, 2014).

Given this environment of iniquity in which mental health services are delivered, virtuous therapists have a moral obligation to do what they can to serve those in need. This does not mean that they give up their livelihood to help underserved populations.

Just therapists are not expected to be martyrs. However, it does mean that they are willing to work within the budgets of their clients to provide needed mental health services. This includes providing services at reduced rates based on a sliding scale of ability to pay. It includes providing pro bono mental health services, for example, at homeless shelters or in state or federally funded or faith-based programs designed to help indigent clients (ACA 2014, C.6.e; NASW, 2017, Principles, Value: Services).

Like the other standards, the Standard of Justice is a prima facie principle and can be overridden in exceptional situations. For example, to treat a client in crisis, it may be necessary to cancel a session originally scheduled with another client. In this situation, the Standard of Nonmaleficence may override the Standard of Justice. However, the just therapist does what he can to ameliorate any iniquity, or appearance of iniquity, as far as possible. For example, this may include providing a double session in lieu of the missed session.

Compassionate Caring: Being With and There for Clients

The Standard of Compassionate Caring involves attentive, nonjudgmental, and genuine caring about clients (Gilligan, 1982; Rogers, 1961). This standard directs therapists to cultivate a caring relationship with their clients. This relationship consists of being *with* the client and being there *for* her. Being with the client means knowing, on an emotional level as well as a cognitive one, what the client is going through. It involves resonating with the client's subjective world by empathetically relating to it. Being there *for* the client involves being available for her, not abandoning her, and being willing to listen attentively to her, without distraction. This emotional presence—being with and for the client—has both intrinsic and instrumental value. Considered apart from its value in helping promote further constructive client change, it is therapeutic in and of itself. That is, the caring relationship is something that should be promoted even if it did not help the client overcome her issues. For example, a client may be depressed as a result of a divorce after 20 years of marriage. The caring therapist sees the client not only from the external perspective of someone who needs to make behavioral changes to accommodate her new life circumstances. Such a behavioral perspective is, indeed, part of caring but it is not the same thing. For, in the caring relationship, there is an irreducible emotional element, one that has therapeutic value in itself apart from any further therapeutic value it may serve. The client wants to know that the therapist "gets it." She does not simply want to fix the situation. She wants the therapist to resonate with what she is going through, for its own sake. It is important to her that the therapist attains this deep emotional perception. The caring therapist understands this desire and wants also to attain such heart-felt insight. Here, such reciprocity and resonance between client and therapist is experienced as a deep personal satisfaction, as meaningful in and of itself, quite apart from its conduciveness to any further positive, therapeutic outcomes. For this value to be actualized, the therapist needs to be able to communicate that he truly cares. Compassionate Caring can and should be conveyed nonverbally through engaged body language and eye contact and through verbal expression (Whitbourne, 2012). "I understand your anguish; the dismal gloom hanging over you as though nothing matters anymore; the haunting feeling of being somehow responsible; the second guessing of your self-worth; the gnawing, persistent, unchangeable, blunt, cold reality that the person with whom you have spent the last 20 years has now left you for another woman." Here there are the elements of a caring relationship coalescing in the therapist's being with and there for the client and in the client meeting the therapist in her subjective space, inviting him in, and being comforted by the communion. From the viewpoint of the Standard of Compassionate Caring, in this resonance, there is substantial therapeutic value.

RESPONSIBILITIES TO CLIENTS

Primary Responsibilities of Therapists

The inherent therapeutic value of being with and there for the client is itself a precursor to further therapeutic change. The virtuous therapist engages in compassionate caring, which, in turn, provides the empathetic insight needed to effectively pursue the best interest of the client. For, in this state of resonance, in entering the subjective world of the client, the therapist is able to help the client identify and clarify the challenges she confronts to constructive change. So Compassionate Caring both inherently and instrumentally adds to Client Welfare: In being with and there for the client, she feels better, and consequently does better.

However, the Client Welfare Standard is constrained by the Client Autonomy Standard inasmuch as the therapist does not impose, force, trick, deceive, or otherwise manipulate the client for her own good but instead respects her right of self-determination. "The primary responsibility of counselors" is accordingly "to respect the dignity and promote the welfare of clients" (ACA, 2014, A.1.a). In the very least, the therapist must do no (avoidable) harm so that Client Nonmaleficence sets a minimum level of client care below which the therapist can be taken to task for being incompetent, negligent, reckless, malicious, or otherwise falling below the level of client care required of a mental health practitioner. Further, in seeking to avoid harming clients, mental health practitioners need to practice mindful of the fact that they serve more than one, and often many clients, who are entitled to the same quality of care. As such, they must strive to be equitable in their distribution of their services among clients.

As the ACA (2014) astutely surmises, the primary responsibility of therapists is twofold: (1) "to respect the dignity" of the client, which means *to treat the client as a self-determining, autonomous agent*; and (2) "to promote the welfare" of the client, that is, to act in the best interest of the client. The former is generally supportive of the latter because empowering clients by respecting their autonomy tends to be in the best interest of the client. Many clients come to therapy feeling disempowered and out of control; hence therapy may aim at facilitating self-reliance, creativity, spontaneity, individuality, and other "fluid values" (Rogers & Skinner, 1975). Manipulating or deceiving clients, even to promote their best interest, as in the case of especially resistant clients (Seltzer, 2013), violates their dignity by treating them like mere things and breaches the therapist-client trust. In contrast, compassionately caring for the client by empathetically, authentically, and respectfully relating to the client tends to enhance client dignity.

The Basic Client Responsibilities

Client Nonmaleficence is a precondition of Client Welfare because a therapist cannot promote a client's best interest by needlessly harming them. Likewise, Justice, that is, treating clients equitably, is also a precondition of respecting clients' dignity inasmuch as to make arbitrary exceptions, for example, giving clients one likes preferential treatment, is demeaning and degrading, and violates the therapist-client trust. As such, Standards of Nonmaleficence and Justice jointly set basic requirements in the provision of counseling services. They may therefore appropriately be called basic responsibilities to clients.

Self-Regarding Responsibilities

While the aforementioned five *client-centered* standards set the primary and basic responsibilities of mental health practitioners, the human services delivery system includes more than simply clients. Obviously, the practitioners themselves are humans, too, and are, therefore, also deserving of respect. As such, the Standard of Counselor Autonomy sets an important constraint on the client-oriented standards. Thus, the therapist himself cannot be expected to seek the best interest of the client while the client is threatening his life, harassing him, or otherwise creating conditions unsuitable for therapeutic progress to occur. In such cases, the therapist has a right to treat himself with the dignity and respect he deserves by not allowing himself to be mistreated.

Other-Regarding Responsibilities

Mental health practitioners may likewise need to weigh and balance their responsibilities to clients against other responsibilities they have to third parties, as when the actions of clients portend serious harm to others. In addition, they must be mindful of the responsibilities they have to others with whom they work, for example, to provide competent consultation to colleagues; and of the responsibilities they bear to the mental health

DIAGRAM 3.1 ■ Basic Client Responsibilities set conditions for compassionate caring, which, in turn, promotes Primary Client Responsibilities. Self-Regarding Responsibilities and Other-Regarding Responsibilities can set rational limits on promotion of Primary Client Responsibilities.

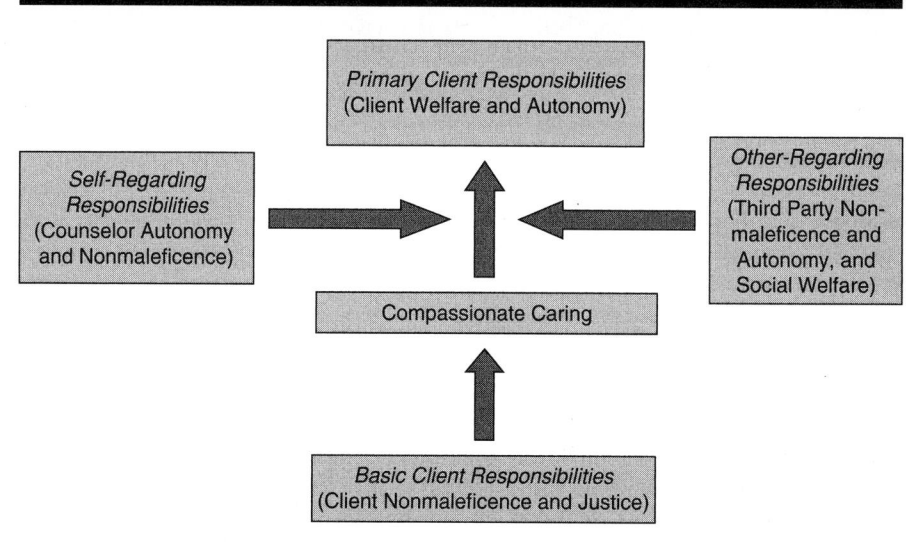

profession itself, for example, to help advance in-field knowledge, or address problems in the human service delivery system. Finally, mental health practitioners have responsibilities to treat non-clients, as well as clients, as self-determining agents, for example, not to engage in false or deceptive advertising, or to otherwise engage in deceptive public practices. These, then, are the *social* responsibilities that therapists have: Third Party Nonmaleficence, Third Party Autonomy, and Social Welfare.

Virtuous therapists are in a habit of applying all the standards contained in Diagram 3.1. When client primary responsibilities conflict with other-regarding or self-regarding responsibilities, the virtuous therapist seriously considers the implications for the client, self, and others, and acts, in a timely way, to limit, to the extent possible, any adverse consequences for the concerned parties. As the client's confidant and helper, the virtuous therapist's primary responsibility is to the client, and therefore protects the client's welfare and dignity as her first priority (ACA, 2014, A.1.a). Still, the therapist realizes that there are occasional, overriding circumstances in which even the client's best interest may yield to the protection of others. Likewise, the therapist's willingness to help the client is not a blank check for the client to violate the rights of the therapist herself any more than it is a free pass to do the same to non-clients (APA, 2016, 4.05; NASW, 2017, 1.01).

APPLYING THE ETHICAL STANDARDS TO THE CASE OF SHELLY

Seeing the case of Shelly, presented at the beginning of this chapter, through the lenses of the above hierarchy of ethical standards can guide the way to helping Shelly do and feel better. For one, by caring, Dr. Dimsdale can be with and there for Shelly, entering into her subjective world, reflecting insight and understanding of what she is experiencing rather than attempting to prove to her that she is being irrational. Such legitimizing of her feelings would have value in itself, even if it never brought about further constructive change; for in this recognition, Shelly is being respected, as a person, not as a thing that must be reprogrammed to function according to a set of instructions. As such, Dimsdale also engages the Standard of Client Autonomy by respecting her dignity as a person. He seeks to empower her by recognizing the legitimacy of her feelings and the importance that she be treated as an "end in itself" and not as a mere thing. In this moral space, she is permitted to be herself, to be authentic, free to express her objections to the way her parents are treating her.

As Shelly's therapist, Dimsdale is concerned about Shelly's depression. He wants to help her overcome it. This is just what the Standard of Client Welfare tells him do, to act in the best interest of his client, to maximize net client welfare so that his clinical goal and this primary ethical responsibility are one and the same.

But there is another consideration that appears to tug in an opposing direction. Shelly's parents have prohibited their daughter from doing certain things that her classmates are doing, based on their religious views. Whether Dimsdale agrees or disagrees with these religious views is plainly irrelevant. Indeed, as a just therapist, he does not attempt to convince any of his other clients, or their families, to surrender their religious beliefs. Instead, he typically works within their value systems in the provision of counseling services. As such, to challenge Shelly's parents' religious convictions about how to raise their daughter would not be to treat relevant like cases alike, and would therefore be inconsistent with the Standard of Justice. Still, it is these religion-based demands that are perceived by Shelly as intolerable and are leading her to be depressed.

As discussed, the virtuous therapist attempts to find the mean between the extremes of excess and deficiency. It appears that there are such extremes in the present case. On the one hand, the parents are unwilling to appreciate, emotionally, Shelly's perspective; on the other, Shelly is unwilling to appreciate, emotionally, her parents' perspective. Neither has attempted to walk in the subjective shoes of the other. As such, there is still room for mutual understanding, which, in turn, can lead to compromise that maintains the dignity of each party. So maybe Shelly and her parents can jointly come to an agreement about what other things she might be able to do. Here there is still respect for Third Party Autonomy (that of Shelly's parents) rather than a wholesale attempt to undermine their parental authority. For example, even if Shelly cannot go to dances or date, maybe she can attend certain concerts or school plays, go with friends to Starbucks, or join an athletic team. Maybe she can't wear short skirts and jeans with holes, but maybe she can wear other types of fashionable clothes, for example, designer jeans without holes; and maybe she can wear lip gloss. Dimsdale could accordingly arrange a joint session with the parents and Shelly, setting the stage for brainstorming about such possibilities. In so doing, the ethical standards—Compassionate Caring, Justice, Client Autonomy, Client Welfare, and Third Party Autonomy and Nonmaleficence—will receive a hearing. Perhaps Shelly may not be completely satisfied with the concessions her mom and dad make. Perhaps her mom and dad may not be wholly convinced that they are doing the right thing for their daughter. The concrete situations in which ethical judgments are made do not ordinarily lend themselves to perfect solutions. Again, as Aristotle reminds us, it is the nature of ethics to be imperfect and inexact. But, as the case of Shelly suggests, if its virtues and standards can help save an adolescent girl from the perils of clinical depression, it can still be incredibly useful.

Questions for Review and Reflection

1. What is the purpose of ethical standards?
2. How do they relate to counselor virtues?
3. What is standard of beneficence? Describe the two different types of beneficence.
4. What is "net or overall positive welfare," and how does it relate to client best interest?
5. What is the standard of nonmaleficence? Describe the three different types of nonmaleficence.
6. What is the standard of autonomy? Describe the three different types of autonomy.
7. What is the standard of justice?
8. What is the standard of compassionate caring?
9. What does it mean to say that the standards of ethics are prima facie or conditional standards? Provide an example that illustrates this property of ethical standards.

10. What are the primary responsibilities of the therapist?

11. What does respecting the dignity of a client mean?

12. What is the relationship between client welfare or best interest and the standard of compassionate caring?

13. What are the basic client responsibilities, and how do they relate to the primary client responsibilities?

14. What are the self-regarding responsibilities, and how do they relate to the primary client responsibilities?

15. What are the other-regarding responsibilities, and how do they relate to the primary client responsibilities?

16. Describe the ethical problem raised in the case of Shelly for her therapist, Dr. Dimsdale.

17. How could each of the following standards be applied in addressing Dimsdale's ethical problem?
    - Compassionate Caring
    - Client Autonomy
    - Client Welfare or Best Interest
    - Justice
    - Third Party Autonomy
    - Third Party Nonmaleficence

18. Do you agree with how Dimsdale handled the conflict between Shelly and her parents? If you were in Dimsdale's shoes, how would you have handled this situation? Explain.

Cases for Analysis

1. Nick, a 28-year-old single male, has been unemployed for 2 years and is actively looking for a job. He is in therapy with Kyra Wilson, a mental health counselor at a local facility that offers pro bono counseling. Nick reports becoming increasingly desperate about not having a job because his funds and public assistance are almost completely depleted. He discloses to Kyra that he has begun to be untruthful on his job applications by creating jobs that he never had and listing his friends as references for these jobs. He expresses some anxiety about being caught in these fabrications and asks Kyra to teach him some relaxation exercises so that he can cope with his apprehension. He states that he will continue to be untruthful on future applications because he is "desperate." Using the above discussed ethical standards, how can Kyra assist Nick with his anxiety and still remain a virtuous therapist?

2. Melanie is a 75-year-old widow who resides with her son, Dan, and his wife, Glenna. She has begun therapy with Asa English, a clinical social worker, because she is having difficulty getting along with Glenna. Melanie states that Glenna often criticizes her for forgetting to turn off the oven or leaving her things in the living room. She states that she is overwhelmed and desolate about these behaviors. Asa suggests family counseling, and the three begin treatment together while occasionally meeting for individual sessions. During one such session, Glenna reveals that she believes that Melanie has dementia. She discloses that Melanie rarely turns off the oven and often puts her belongings in odd places. She says that

she has found Melanie's toothbrush on the living room sofa and her dentures in the freezer. Glenna asks for Asa's help in convincing Melanie to get evaluated for dementia. Using the above discussed ethical standards as guidelines, how should Asa proceed? What are his responsibilities to Melanie, Glenna, Dan, and any potentially endangered third parties?

3. Randall is a 55-year-old gay male who is in a long-term relationship with Lorne, age 50. The couple has moved to a new city and has been having difficulty adjusting because this city is not as accepting of same-sex couples as their previous one. The two have been experiencing subtle and not so subtle forms of discrimination including verbal slurs on the streets as they walk by and graffiti on their front door. They are in counseling with Dara Dolber, a licensed mental health counselor, so they can better cope with these issues. As therapy progresses and Randall and Lorne discuss their experiences, they mention the name of their landlord and state that she has called the two names and ridiculed their relationship saying that they are lucky that she rents to them. Dolber recoils when she hears the landlord's name because she is an acquaintance of hers. Dolber is not certain if she now has a conflict of interest or a dual role relationship because of this and is unsure about how to proceed. Discuss the following. Does Dolber have a responsibility to reveal to her clients that she knows the landlord? Does she have ethical responsibilities to refer her clients to another therapist for treatment? Does Dolber have any ethical responsibilities to help change any of the types of discrimination that are being directed toward Randall and Lorne? Refer to the ethical standards developed in this chapter to formulate your responses.

References

American Counseling Association. (2014). *ACA code of ethics*. Alexandria, VA: Author.

American Psychological Association. (2016). *Ethical principles of psychologists and code of conduct*. Washington, DC: Author. Retrieved from http://www.apa.org/ethics/code/?item=11#805

Aristotle. (2015). *Nicomachean ethics* (W. D. Ross, trans.). South Australia: eBooks@Adelaide. Retrieved from https://ebooks.adelaide.edu.au/a/aristotle/nicomachean/

Beauchamp, T., & Childress, J. (1979). *Principles of biomedical ethics*. New York, NY: Oxford University Press.

Bentham, J. (2014). *Introduction to the principles of morals and legislation*. South Australia: eBooks@Adelaide. Retrieved from https://ebooks.adelaide.edu.au/b/bentham/jeremy/morals/

Brown v. Board of Education of Topeka, 349 U.S. 294. (1955). Retrieved from https://supreme.justia.com/cases/federal/us/349/294/case.html

Cohen, E. D., & Cohen, G. S. (1999). *The virtuous therapist: Ethical practice of counseling and psychotherapy*. Belmont, CA: Wadsworth.

Feinberg, J. (1973). *Social philosophy*. Englewood Cliffs, NJ: Prentice-Hall.

Frankena, W. K. (1973). *Ethics* (2nd ed.). Englewood Cliffs, NJ: Prentice-Hall.

Fuller, L. (1964). The morality of law. *Indiana Law Journal, 40*(2), 270–279.

Gilligan, C. (1982). *In a different voice*. Cambridge, MA: Harvard University Press.

Kant, I. (1964). *Groundwork of the metaphysics of morals* (H. J. Paton, trans.). New York, NY: Harper & Row.

Kitchener, K. S. (1984). Intuition, critical evaluation and ethical principles: The foundation for ethical decisions in counseling psychology. *Counseling Psychologist, 12*(3), 43–55.

Kitchener, K. S. (1988). Dual role relationships: What makes them so problematic? *Journal of Counseling & Development, 67*(4), 217–221.

Lo, B. (2013). *Resolving ethical dilemmas*. Philadelphia, PA: Lippincott Williams & Wilkins.

Meyers, L. (2014). Advocacy in action. *Counseling Today*. Alexandria, VA: American Counseling Association. Retrieved from https://ct.counseling.org/2014/04/advocacy-in-action/

National Association of Social Workers. (2017). *Code of ethics of the National Association of Social Workers*. Retrieved from https://www.socialworkers.org/About/Ethics/Code-of-Ethics/Code-of-Ethics-English.aspx

Peterson, M. S., & Urquiza, A. J. (1993). *The role of mental health professionals in the prevention and treatment of child abuse and neglect*. Washington, DC: U.S. Department of Health and Human Services. Retrieved from https://www.childwelfare.gov/pubPDFs/mentlhlth.pdf

Rogers, C. R. (1961). *On becoming a person*. Boston, MA: Houghton Mifflin.

Rogers, C., & Skinner, B. F. (1975). *Control of human behavior*. Madison, CT: Jeffrey Norton Publishers.

Ross, W. D. (2002). *The right and the good*. New York, NY: Oxford University Press.

Seltzer, L. (2013, February). A new take on manipulation. *Psychology Today*. Retrieved from https://www.psychologytoday.com/blog/evolution-the-self/201302/new-take-manipulation

Shallcross, L. (2010). Managing resistant clients. *Counseling Today*. Alexandria, VA: American Counseling Association. Retrieved from https://ct.counseling.org/2010/02/managing-resistant-clients/

Sinnott-Armstrong, W. (2015, Winter). "Consequentialism." *The Stanford encyclopedia of philosophy* (E. N. Zalta, Ed.). Retrieved from https://plato.stanford.edu/archives/win2015/entries/consequentialism/

Soble, A. (1982). Physical attractiveness and unfair discrimination. *International Journal of Applied Philosophy, 1*, 37–64.

Szabo, L. (2014). Cost of not caring. Nowhere to go. *USA Today*. Retrieved from https://www.usatoday.com/story/news/nation/2014/05/12/mental-health-system-crisis/7746535/

Treatment Advocacy Center. (2014). How many people with serious mental illness are homeless? Arlington, VA: Treatment Advocacy Center. Retrieved from http://www.treatmentadvocacycenter.org/fixing-the-system/features-and-news/2596-how-many-people-with-serious-mental-illness-are-homeless

Whitbourne, S. K. (2012, June). The ultimate guide to body language. *Psychology Today*. Retrieved from https://www.psychologytoday.com/blog/fulfillment-any-age/201206/the-ultimate-guide-body-language

Zur, O. (2007). When is a patient's behavior unacceptable? *National Psychologist*. Retrieved from http://nationalpsychologist.com/2007/01/when-is-a-patient%E2%80%99s-behavior-unacceptable/10886.html

4

USING AN ETHICAL DECISION-MAKING PROCESS

Case Study: A Hateful Client

In Chapter 3, 10 standards for addressing moral problems were introduced. However, seeing these standards in the broader context of a decision-making process can be useful for addressing moral problems as they arise in clinical practice. Indeed, ethical decisions can be quite daunting when there is no clear, systematic way of making them. Given the oftentimes complex nature of moral problems, it is easy enough to overlook nuances and details of the case in question or to focus on some details to the exclusion of others. In many cases, the decision maker may lack a clear understanding of the moral problem itself, the relevant facts surrounding it, and precisely how and what ethical, professional, and legal standards may apply to the case at hand. As such, this chapter develops and illustrates a step-by-step decision-making process, which is intended to provide order and system to an otherwise piecemeal approach. While ethics is not science, just as a scientist would likely make little progress in scientific investigations without utilizing the methods of science, ethics can also lend itself to process and functionality, making the possibility of an enlightened and rational ethics decision more probable.

"Counselors acknowledge that resolving ethical issues is a process," states the Preamble of the ACA Code of Ethics (American Counseling Association [ACA], 2014). It also provides that when therapists confront ethical problems they apply and document, where appropriate, an ethical decision-making model that may include consultation, ethical standards and/or principles, and facility for considering alternative courses of action, their risks and benefits, and for making objective decisions that take into account the circumstances and the welfare of all stakeholders (I.1.b). A number of different models have been proposed that attempt to address all or most of the aforementioned considerations (Cottone & Clause, 2000; Deroche, Eckart, Lott, Park, & Raddler, 2015). Offered here is a five-step process based on the model proposed by Cohen & Cohen (1999) that methodically addresses the stated considerations as well as considerations included in some of the other proposed models such as the use of principle ethics

(Beauchamp & Childress, 1979; Kitchener, 1984), philosophical ethics (Hare, 1991), and "social constructivism" (Cottone, 2001). These five steps proceed as follows, but it is not unacceptable to revisit a preceding step when more information or ideas surface (Hill, Glasser, & Hardin, 1995):

1. Define the moral problem
2. Collect the morally relevant facts
3. Conduct an ethical analysis
4. Make a decision
5. Act on the decision

Using a case of a hateful client as illustration, this chapter examines each of the above steps.

A CASE OF A HATEFUL CLIENT

> Paul Gilroy has been in court-ordered counseling with Dr. Stanley Fry, which he was required to successfully complete as part of a parole agreement, after serving 6 years of an 8-year sentence in the state penitentiary for felony assault of a black man who was protesting the slaying of a young, unarmed black man by a white police officer. Paul beat the man with a baseball bat, causing permanent brain damage and partial paralysis. He is presently living in a halfway house and in search of employment. As part of his parole agreement, Paul was also required to sign a waiver of confidentiality, and Dr. Fry is required to report back to Paul's parole officer on a weekly basis about his client's progress. In prison, Paul was a "model citizen" and presented his case to the parole board, convincing the board that he was rehabilitated and no longer presented a threat to the public. Now, into his second week of counseling with Dr. Fry, Paul disclosed a side of himself that was not evident to the parole board, but which harkened back to the days prior to his incarceration. Specifically, he used the N-word to refer to blacks and said that they all needed to be "shipped back to Africa," and that they were all rapists and murderers, but fell short of threatening to harm anyone. "I did my time," he said and, referring to black people, added, "I'm not wasting any more years of my life trying to give them what they deserve." So it was not surprising that Dr. Fry, a fair skinned middle aged man who identified with being black because his father was black, felt resentment toward this client when he expressed these hateful words, not realizing that Dr. Fry himself was black! Ending his second week of counseling with Paul, Dr. Fry now was required to report back to the parole officer about his client's progress.

Indeed, in the above situation, Dr. Fry has a moral problem. However, identifying this problem in clear, non–question-begging terms, assessing it efficiently, and doing something appropriate about it require insight into the nature of the moral decision-making process itself. Accordingly, this chapter provides a systematic approach to addressing moral problems. But what is a moral problem in the first place, and why does Dr. Fry have one?

WHAT A MORAL PROBLEM IS

Whenever a therapist walks into the counseling room, she takes on a *moral problem*. This may seem somewhat paradoxical because we are accustomed to distinguishing morally problematic contexts from ones in which no such problems exist. However, the distinction may be more accurately viewed as one of degree rather than kind. To see this, it is helpful to clarify what is meant by a moral problem in the first place.

A person can properly be said to have a *problem* when he has an unanswered question to which he wants an answer. "Is there life on other planets?" can present a problem for you if you happen to want to know the answer. "Will there be a test in ethics class next week?" also presents a problem if you want an answer. However, the difference between the former and latter question is one of practicality. You may want to know the answer to the first because you are intellectually curious. On the other hand, you may want to know the answer to the second question because you want to know if you need to study. Accordingly, the former question about life on other planets raises an *intellectual problem*. You want to know for knowledge sake. The latter question about whether there will be a test in ethics class is a *practical problem*. You want to know the answer for the sake of *doing* something about it. Generally speaking, intellectual problems are problems about what to believe; whereas practical problems are problems about what to do. While answers to intellectual problems can become relevant to answering practical problems (scientists discover that a certain planet has life on it, which becomes a factor in deciding on whether to invest in exploring this planet), practical problems always raise questions about what to do.

Moral problems are a kind of practical problem. This means that the way we answer them has *moral significance*. "Is it okay to lie to my client when telling her the truth can lead her to commit suicide?" presents a moral problem *for you* because the way you answer it has moral significance. This is because the way you answer it can affect the welfare of a moral stakeholder, namely your client. In general, whenever your answer to a practical question can affect the welfare and/or interests of others, you have a moral problem. *Personal problems* exist when what you do can affect *only* your own welfare and/or interests. When the answer is thought to have repercussions for others, then you have a moral problem, not merely a personal one. Moral problems can definitely involve your own welfare and/or interests (as when a client threatens to harm you), but moral problems *always* involve others as well. As such, decisions about moral problems are always social constructs (Cottone, 2001).

A person has a serious moral problem when the potential effects are serious ones, such as serious bodily injury or death, and the probabilities of such harms are substantial. Serious moral problems do not necessarily have the potential to cause physical harm, however. They can also cause emotional harm, for example, trauma or depression. They can also be about moral damage. If I lie to my client, even if she never finds out that I have lied to her, I have still violated her, inasmuch as she had a right to be treated respectfully (as a person, not as an object manipulated).

As discussed in Chapter 3, welfare can be positive or negative. *Positive welfare* refers to states that portend happiness, pleasure, or contentment such as health (mental as well as physical), functional relationships, stress-reduction, and pain relief. *Negative welfare* refers to harms or states that portend unhappiness, pain, or suffering such as trauma, disease, physical injury, loss of a loved one, and other substantial losses. The satisfaction of *needs* is a form of positive welfare necessary for survival. A person needs a certain amount of food, clothing, and shelter to survive. One needs air to breathe and a habitable planet upon which to live. A person may need a certain life-saving, medical intervention. The deprivation of needs is a form of negative welfare. A patient who needs a kidney transplant to survive but whose health insurance plan won't cover it suffers negative welfare.

Interests are things that satisfy people's desires, respect their rights or dignity, or conduce to their goals or aspirations. A client may have an interest in being wealthy, while another may care more about forging a lasting personal relationship than having a lot of money. So what is an interest for one individual may not be for another. Still, there are common human interests such as being treated fairly, having friends, and the desire to belong or be approved of by others. Values such as sex and love are at least common human interests if not, strictly speaking, needs. Therapists seek to protect interests that do not violate other peoples' common interests, such as interests protected by criminal law.

An interest that a person may have need not conduce to the (positive) welfare of the person because the interest may be unhealthy, destructive, or otherwise harmful to the person. On the other hand, one can have, and generally does, have interests in one's own welfare. But this is not always the case. For example, a client with major depression who has suicidal ideation tends not to have an interest in his own welfare while depressed. Indeed, therapeutic interventions aim to restore or create the conditions conducive to client positive welfare, under which the client has life-affirming interests.

Clients may harbor interests which, while not damaging to their own welfare, are nevertheless damaging to others. For example, a client may have a criminal intention (say, reducing anxiety about engaging in the commission of a fraud) and seek therapy for this purpose. Virtuous therapists do not serve such unlawful interests. There are therefore limits to what a therapist may be expected to do on behalf of her clients.

Within such constraints of legitimate welfare and/or interests, a moral problem arises for a therapist when what he does can (for good or ill) affect the welfare and/or interests of his client and/or others (Cohen & Cohen, 1999). Because what therapists do in their sessions with their clients always (or almost always) has a significant potential to affect the welfare and/or interests of their clients and/or others, it should be clear why they routinely confront moral problems as soon as they take on a client. While some of these problems may be less serious than others (for example, serious injury or death is not an imminent likelihood), they are nevertheless moral problems—many of which have the capacity to evolve into more serious moral problems if not handled competently. For example, failure to properly diagnose and treat a common mental illness (such as Generalized Anxiety Disorder) can lead to comorbid disorders such as Major Depression, including the risk of suicide (American Psychiatric Association, 2013; Cohen, 2017a).

It should now be clear why Dr. Fry has a moral problem, for it is clear that what he does can have moral significance insofar as it has the potential to affect the welfare and/or interests of others, not to the exclusion of his client and himself. Obviously, if Dr. Fry is to address his moral problem, he needs to *define* it. This, then, is the first step of the moral decision-making process. Unfortunately, while an extremely important step (because it affects the disposition of an ethics case), it is often glossed over or poorly addressed (Cohen & Cohen, 1999).

THE SIX STEPS OF ETHICAL DECISION MAKING

Step 1: Define the Moral Problem

Clearly, as a *practical problem*, the formulation of a moral problem will be a question about what to do. And, as a *moral problem*, it will be a morally significant question about what to do, that is, one that has significance for the welfare and/or interests of others. Subjects whose welfare and/or interests will or might be affected are properly called *stakeholders*. Here, stakeholders can include aggregates of human beings such as communities, as well as insurance companies, agencies, and other institutions; it can also include nonhuman subjects such as dogs and cats inasmuch as they too have welfare and/or interests that may be at stake.

Accordingly, *the definition of a moral problem will be a question about what to do when there are such-and-such stakeholders with such-and-such welfare and/or interests at stake.* So Dr. Fry's moral problem is what to do when such-and-such stakeholders have such-and-such at stake. The definition of the problem then includes a list of the stakeholders and what each has at stake, depending on what he does.

The capacity to key into what is at stake, and for whom, is called *moral sensitivity* (Cohen & Cohen, 1999). This capacity involves the ability to sense what others are going through, subjectively, that is, the ability to empathize with the plights of others. In mental health practice, the client herself is ordinarily considered a stakeholder inasmuch as her welfare and/or interests depend on the success of therapy. As discussed in Chapter 2, empathetic understanding is paramount for building client trust, which leads to client self-disclosure, which, in turn, promotes client progress. Further, as illustrated in Chapter 3, the Standard of Compassionate Caring, which trades on applying empathy in being with and there for the client, can be invaluable for addressing moral problems. So applying empathy to address a moral problem and to promote therapeutic success can be mutually supportive. This appears to be true in the present case inasmuch as Paul's successful reintegration into society, which is a chief ethical concern, is also the therapeutic goal.

Compassionate caring for Paul's circumstances can also help Dr. Fry appreciate, on an emotional level, how important Paul's interest is for him in not going back to prison. Indeed, he has spent the past 6 years of his life in a state penitentiary. As a morally sensitive person, knowing how important one's freedom can be to one's happiness, Dr. Fry can emotionally appreciate what Paul might have gone through doing 6 years in a state penitentiary and how much he surely dreads the possibility of being sent back to prison. As a morally sensitive person, Dr. Fry therefore also can appreciate how important it is for his client to be successfully reintegrated into society and how important the success of his present therapy would be in attaining this goal. Further, he also realizes that the racial hatred that his client harbors is an impediment to the client's welfare and/or interests and that he must, therefore, seek to help the client address this issue in the course of therapy. Additionally, Dr. Fry is aware that his client has openly expressed his racial antipathy notwithstanding that he has signed a confidentiality waiver and has been fully informed by Dr. Fry about the required limitations of confidentiality (ACA, 2014, A.2.e). Still, Paul confides in Dr. Fry and trusts him with this information. Clearly, Paul has an interest in the therapist respecting this trust that has been reposed; conversely, Dr. Fry has an interest in not violating this trust; for to do so would likely destroy the prospects for a successful therapeutic outcome. It is also part of Paul's welfare and/or interests that his therapist is able to work with such a hateful client, and that he does not receive less than competent treatment due to any personal problem harbored by the therapist.

However, not only the client but also third parties can be, and often are, stakeholders, so the virtuous therapist seeks to be morally sensitive to the welfare and/or interests of others as well as the client. In the present case, the black community, collectively speaking, is a stakeholder because black people have an interest in their fellow citizens not having racial antipathy toward them. Further, while Paul has denied that he would ever again engage in violent behavior toward blacks, his past history of racially motivated violence against a black person along with his enduring hatred of black people raises the question of whether he still poses a significant risk to the welfare of others.

Ordinarily, the therapist herself is a stakeholder too because, as the therapist, she has an interest in the success of therapy. However, the interest of the therapist can also go beyond a professional interest to include a personal one. This is true in the case of Dr. Fry because, as a black person, he has a personal interest in not being discriminated against. In fact, he resents, on a personal emotional level, the things his client is saying about black people. So, in the present case, the therapist's own feelings are at stake and must be considered part of the moral problem.

Social and government institutions can also be stakeholders. Thus the parole board that approved Paul's parole is also a stakeholder insofar as it has an interest in the client's successful reintegration into society outside of prison, in protecting society against any potential threat he poses, and in his not becoming a repeat offender, ending up in prison again. As such, society itself can be conceived as a stakeholder inasmuch as society has a stake in decreased crime and a lower recidivism rate.

Table 4.1 summarizes the aforementioned information about the stakes of each relevant stakeholder. Such a table can provide a useful means for therapists to organize this information so that it can be utilized in the decision-making process. In effect, this table defines Dr. Fry's problem, which is *what to do when there is such an array of stakeholders and respective stakes*. Notice that this definition is *objective*. That is, it sticks to the facts about stakeholders and what is at stake. And it does not *assume* any solutions to the moral problem. A common mistake in ethical decision making is to short-circuit the process of decision making by assuming a solution in the very formation of the moral problem. For example, an assuming therapist might formulate the moral problem as being how to get around having to counsel this client. In such a case, the therapist would have failed to provide an objective assessment of the facts by assuming that the only morally significant issue was the fact that he was not comfortable with this client. In so doing, the therapist would also have assumed that the only alternative to resolving the moral problem was to withdraw from counseling this client. When there are multiple ethical considerations involved, it is important to give them all

TABLE 4.1 ■ Stakeholders/Welfare/Interests

Stakeholder	Welfare (Positive/Negative)	Interests
Client	• Reintegration into society • Overcoming racial antipathy through therapy • Not having trust betrayed • Potential for therapist's personal problem with client to affect ability to effectively counsel client	• Getting and staying out of prison • Being able to confide/trust therapist • Deceiving the parole board about his hatred for black people
Therapist	• Feeling uncomfortable about the client's hatred of black people (like him)	• Reintegration of client into society • Helping client to overcome racial antipathy • Keeping the confidences of client • Not being discriminated against • Client not posing a threat to others • Not being used by the client to perpetrate a fraud on the parole board
Parole Officer/Board		• Reintegration of client into society • Client not posing threat to others • Client not becoming a repeat offender and being re-incarcerated
Black Community	• Threat of physical violence posed by the client	• Not being racially discriminated against by others
Society	• Reduction in crime and recidivism rates	

a fair hearing instead of finding out after the fact that there were other overriding considerations that were never even taken into account. The moral problem defining stage of moral decision making is not the time for deciding what to do. That comes later, after careful, objective consideration of the welfare and/or interests at stake, inspection of the pertinent facts, and consideration of appropriate ethical and legal standards. As such, some of the identified interests at stake, such as those of the client, need not be ones that maximize the client's net positive welfare. They may even work against the client's best interest. For example, lying to the parole board might eventually land Paul in worse trouble than being honest with it. As discussed in Chapter 3, the client's best interest is that which produces a greater balance of positive welfare over negative welfare than any alternative option. Figuring out what is truly in the client's *best* interest is reserved for a later step in the decision-making process (Step 3, on conducting an ethical analysis, discussed below).

On occasions in which there is simply no time to conduct a thorough assessment such as in the case of a suicidal client who poses a clear and imminent danger to others, the most salient ethical considerations might be glaring (someone's life is in jeopardy), and the depth and breadth of the decision-making process may need to yield to the urgency of the situation. However, this should be the exception, not the rule. Unfortunately, we have found that the first inclination of many students of ethics is to look for a solution to a problem before it is objectively defined. We admonish you to resist this tendency if you are so inclined.

Step 2: Collect Relevant Information

The next step of the decision-making process is to collect further information that is *morally relevant.* Such information is that which is relevant to the welfare and/or interests identified as being at stake. Here, relevance means providing *empirical support* for conclusions about what is, or might be, at stake. For example, Paul's past history includes a racially motivated assault on a young black man. This fact is relevant to whether Paul presents a threat to others; so too is the fact that he still expresses hatred for black people. These facts are morally relevant because they increase the probability that he is still a threat. On the other hand, the facts that Paul has served 6 years in prison, his parole has been approved by the parole board, and he has denied that he would harm anyone again are relevant because they lower the probability that the client presents a threat to others. Similarly, the fact that Paul trusts and confides in Dr. Fry is relevant to whether he will accomplish his therapeutic goals since it increases the chances of this happening. Table 4.2 provides a list of some general types of information that can be morally relevant to the welfare and/or interests of clients.

Clearly, client information such as diagnosis can be significant in considering whether Paul presents a danger to others in the future. If his diagnosis is Anti-Social Personality

TABLE 4.2 ■ Some Common Types of Morally Relevant Client Information

Potentially Morally Relevant Client Information

- Presenting problem (original problem for which therapy is sought)
- Diagnosis (*DSM-5* classification)
- Personal disclosures (information acquired in course of therapy)
- Functionality (impulse control, memory, attention span, suicidal ideation, logical thinking ability, alertness, etc.)
- Background (employment, education, family, religion, race, etc.)
- History (drug or alcohol addiction, attempted suicide, victim of sexual abuse, criminal convictions, etc.)
- Family dynamics (domestic violence, sexual abuse, enabling, etc.)
- Living arrangement (lives alone, with partner, with friends, in shelter, etc.)

Disorder, this could support a concern about the potential of Paul to behave aggressively in the future; whereas a diagnosis of General Anxiety Disorder would not equally support such a concern. If Paul has a drug or alcohol problem, this could contribute to his aggressive tendencies. The client's signing of a confidentiality waiver is relevant insofar as this can entitle the board to request and examine Paul's counseling records. This could increase the chances of its protecting the public. On the other hand, this could also adversely affect the therapist's interest in maintaining client trust through confidentiality and in helping the client reintegrate into society. Dr. Fry's discomfort about counseling a hateful client like Paul might be helped through an empathetic understanding of this client's history, for example, his having been sexually and physically abused and orphaned as a young child. Emotionally appreciating how a young black male might feel when he is targeted by a hateful individual such as Paul can help Dr. Fry see the importance, if not the urgency, of working diligently with his client.

As the ethical decision maker continues to collect morally relevant information, Dr. Fry will invariably reach a point where he has a sense (albeit an imperfect one) that a reasonable job has been done in collecting the facts surrounding the case. Of course, there are an infinite number of facts one can collect, so there are also practical limits. Generally, the decision maker will gain some sense that adding new facts to the existing facts will be redundant. At this point, he will inevitably start to analyze possible options. This is the time in the decision making process wherein focus should shift to the third step, which is the ethical analysis itself.

Step 3: Conduct an Ethical Analysis

In conducting an ethical analysis, the ethical decision maker begins to inspect possible ways to address the moral problem defined in Step 1. There are four resources generally used to conduct such an analyses: (1) ethical standards, (2) professional codes of ethics, (3) legal standards such as statutes and case law, and (4) self-inventories. Ethical standards, such as the ones discussed in the previous chapter, tend to be the basis of many rules contained in codes of ethics. For example, the standard of Client Autonomy, which enjoins that therapists treat clients as self-determining agents, provides a basis for rules telling therapists to give clients informed consent to therapy, tell them the truth, and keep their confidences. Legal standards set minimum conditions for ethical conduct, for example, requiring therapists to avoid sexual relationships with clients. Such legal requirements are also typically reflected in codes of ethics (ACA, 2014; American Psychological Association [APA], 2016; National Association of Social Workers, 2017). Last, therapists themselves may harbor irrational thinking that prevents them from adequately addressing their moral problems (Cohen & Cohen, 1999). To be complete, a therapist's ethical analysis should include a self-assessment of her own thinking to avoid personal biases, imposing her own values on the client, or otherwise losing objectivity in conducting the analysis.

Effectively, in the first step of the decision-making process (defining the problem), one will have already begun to apply an ethical standard, namely, the Standard of Compassionate Caring. This enables the therapist to attain an empathetic understanding of the client's welfare and/or interests. Indeed, an empathetic therapist will have already practiced this standard beginning with the first therapist-client encounter. And such a

TABLE 4.3 ■ Inventory for Ethical Analysis of a Moral Problem

INVENTORY QUESTIONS

1. **What possible courses of action might be taken to address the moral problem?**

2. **Which of these courses of action best supports the *Primary Responsibilities* to the client?**

    a. In light of the facts identified in Step 2 of the ethical decision-making process, which of the aforementioned options is in the *best interest* of the client (that is, maximizes net positive client welfare)?

    (In answering this question, consider the items listed in the Client line, Welfare column, of the Stakeholders/Welfare/Interests Table created in Step 1.)

    b. Does the course of action, identified in Question 2, conflict with *client autonomy*?

    (In answering this question, consider whether there is (or might be) any client interest(s) listed in the Client line, Interests column, of the Stakeholders/Welfare/Interests Table that is inconsistent with this action.)

    c. Does it conflict with any *basic responsibility* to the client (needlessly harming the client or not being equitable or fair)?

3. **Does there appear to be any *self-regarding* conflicts?**

    a. Does the action identified, in Question 2, as the client's best interest conflict with the therapist's interest in respecting his own rational self-determination? (See Therapist Line, Interests column, of the Stakeholders/Welfare/Interests Table.)

    b. Does the action identified, in Question 2, have a likelihood of causing serious harm to the therapist? (See Therapist Line, Welfare column, of the Stakeholders/Welfare/Interests Table.)

4. **Does there appear to be any *other-regarding* conflicts?**

    a. Does the action identified as being in the client's best interest conflict with any other-regarding responsibilities (that is, not harming others, respecting others' self-determination, or advancing the good of society)? (See Third Party Lines, Welfare and Interests columns, of the Stakeholders/Welfare/Interests Table.)

5. **Is there any self- or other-regarding conflicts that have been identified (in Questions 3 or 4) that *override* the course of action identified in Question 2 as the client's best interest?**

therapist will continue to practice it throughout the course of therapy by being with and there for the client.

The primary client responsibilities, namely Client Welfare and Client Autonomy, are generally the main focal point of an ethical analysis. As discussed in Chapter 3, these standards are themselves supported by the Compassionate Caring Standard. The latter standard provides the emotional insight and empathetic regard necessary for building a therapeutic and empowering bond of therapist-client trust. Such moral sensitivity, in turn, helps the therapist glean the welfare and/or interests of the client, which is requisite to identifying the client's *best* interest. As suggested earlier, while the best interest of the client may align with the actual interests of the client, this is not necessarily the case. Thus, Paul has an interest in not going back to prison. However, if he is not capable of living on the outside, then this may not be in his *best* interest, for he may get into even worse trouble.

Accordingly, the ethical analysis proceeds by asking certain key questions that can help the therapist fulfill her primary client responsibilities and to address any potential conflicts. These guiding questions are formulated in Table 4.3.

Identifying Possible Courses of Action

In the case of Paul Gilroy, possible courses of action might include Dr. Fry's informing Paul's parole officer that he wishes to terminate Paul's counseling due to a personal problem and communicates the same to the client. (It is assumed that Dr. Fry is *court ordered* but not *court appointed*, which means that the court order did not specify Dr. Fry as the counselor, thereby making it possible for a different therapist to counsel Paul.) Alternatively, Dr. Fry could inform the officer about the nature of the personal problem, which would involve disclosing to the officer that Paul has expressed strong hatred of blacks. The latter alternative may include also telling Paul about the nature of his personal problem, or he could simply tell Paul that he has a personal problem but provide no further details about the nature of the problem. Alternatively, Dr. Fry could just inform the parole officer but say nothing to the client, who will then find out from the officer that he has asked to withdraw from counseling Paul. Another option would be simply to continue counseling Paul and say nothing to either the parole officer or to Paul about his personal problem or about Paul's hateful remarks. Another option would be to continue counseling Paul, say nothing to the officer about his personal problem or hateful remarks while seeking professional consultation or assistance from a colleague for his personal problem. A further option would be for Dr. Fry to continue counseling Paul, say nothing to the officer, seek professional assistance, and disclose to Paul that he is black. In this manner, Dr. Fry can brainstorm about possible approaches until he has generated a number of possibilities to consider. (Indeed, while other permutations of possible options appear to be possible, they tend to raise similar issues as the ones already mentioned.) Here the purpose is to creatively and comprehensively generate possible courses of action, not evaluate them for their conduciveness to the client's welfare and/or interests. This comes next.

Identifying the Course of Action That Is in the Client's Best Interest

So which of the cited options is in Paul's best interest? This will be the course of action that promotes the greatest balance of positive welfare over negative welfare than any alternative option. This would be the option that promotes positive welfare Considerations 1 through 4 in the Client's Welfare (Positive/Negative) column of Table 4.1; and which avoids or reduces the negative welfare consideration raised in 4 (namely, the potential for the therapist's personal problem to adversely affect counseling his client).

Arguably, each of the courses of action that involve disclosure to Paul's parole officer fail to support client welfare Consideration 3 (not having his trust betrayed), since disclosure to the parole officer would almost definitely be seen by Paul as a violation of his trust and as a reason never to trust him again. Further, this may also signal to Paul that he should never trust any *other* therapist again, which would adversely affect his ability to overcome his racial antipathy through therapy (client welfare Consideration 2).

This could, in turn, adversely affect his prospects for being reintegrated into society (client welfare Consideration 1).

Dr. Fry's garnering of facts about Paul's history of handling disappointment could be helpful in exploring the implications of requesting withdrawal from counseling. Does he, for example, have a history of attempted suicide? Dr. Fry's knowledge about this particular parole officer's disposition would also be helpful. How understanding is he about the process of therapy? How has he responded in cases similar to the present one where a therapist has had a problem counseling a client? Is this parole officer likely to opt for sending Paul back to prison? Are clients afforded other counselors in such cases? In the end, answers to at least some of these questions may be tentative and uncertain, thereby making courses involving withdrawal quite risky for the client.

In contrast to options that include withdrawal, the options in which Dr. Fry says nothing to the parole officer about his personal problem or Paul's hateful remarks seem to serve the client's best interest better than those options in which Dr. Fry discloses to the parole officer. One concern, however, is whether Paul would receive competent therapy from Fry given his personal problem in counseling Paul. Clearly, the two possible courses of action that include Fry's seeking consultation or assistance best address this problem. In fact, professional codes of ethics would advise such action in situations such as Dr. Fry's where a personal problem may impair a practitioner's ability to provide competent mental health services. For example, according to the American Psychological Association's *Ethical Principles of Psychologists and Code of Conduct* (2016, 2.06.b), "When psychologists become aware of personal problems that may interfere with their performing work-related duties adequately, they take appropriate measures, such as obtaining professional consultation or assistance and determine whether they should limit, suspend or terminate their work-related duties."

Accordingly, if Dr. Fry believes that his personal problem is adversely affecting his counseling, he has a professional responsibility to address this problem. So it would, arguably, be in Paul's best interest for Dr. Fry to continue counseling Paul, saying nothing to the officer about his personal problem, so long as he also seeks professional consultation or assistance. But what about the option that also involves Dr. Fry's disclosing to Paul that he is black?

As an authentic counselor, Fry would be inclined to disclose this fact. In doing so, there would be transparency, so the discomfort would no longer include hiding who he truly is from his client. The proverbial cat would be out of the bag and the client could now confront the fact that the therapist he has confided and trusted in, who was there to help him, is actually a member of the racial group he has been reeling against. But therapy is not about the therapist, it is about the client; and the question is whether such disclosure would be in this client's best interest.

There is the possibility that self-disclosure could backfire and create a wedge between client and therapist rather than helping the client work through his problem. There is the possibility that the disclosure would make therapy more about the therapist's working through his problem than that of the client working through his problem. Timing too is important, and the disclosure may work better at one point in therapy than another; perhaps better when the client has already attained an insight that his racism rests on shaky ground. Such ambiguity underscores the nature of ethical choices and, by implication, mental health practice. As in the present case, there is clarity about what general course of action to follow (namely, continuation of counseling while seeking help from a professional consultant) but still need for discretion about other aspects such as whether self-disclosure would help the client rather than cause unnecessary harm.

Does continuation of counseling while seeking consultation conflict with client autonomy or any other responsibility to the client? This question can be answered by looking at the client's interests (Client line, Interests column, Table 4.1). These interests are (a) getting and staying out of prison, (b) being able to confide/trust therapist, and (c) deceiving the parole board about his hatred for black people. Indeed, continuing with counseling, while seeking consultation, saying nothing about his personal problem to the parole officer, may be the most effective way for Paul to get and stay out of prison insofar as it can lead to constructive change. This, of course, assumes that the consultation helps Dr. Fry effectively counsel Paul in spite of his personal problem with him. It is also supportive of Paul's interest in being able to confide and trust his therapist. It is also consistent with permitting Paul to keep the parole board uninformed about his hatred for black people so long as Dr. Fry continues to be non-disclosing about Paul's hatred for blacks. As such, the course of action in question does not conflict with any of Paul's three interests given above. This would be in contrast, for example, to a course of action such as Dr. Fry's seeking to withdraw from the case due to Paul's hatred for blacks; since the latter action could not treat the client as an autonomous person by betraying his trust.

Identifying Any Apparent Self-Regarding Conflict

However, there is an apparent self-regarding conflict. Because Dr. Fry has an interest in not being used by the client to perpetrate a fraud on the parole board (Therapist line, interests, Table 4.1), continuing to counsel him and saying nothing to the parole officer about Paul's enduring hatred of blacks, places him in the situation of having his autonomy subverted. Indeed, the therapist effectively becomes an accessory to the client's attempt to keep secret the fact that he has not really changed his hateful attitude.

There is also the question of legal risk for the therapist if he fails to disclose to the parole officer Paul's hatred for black people, especially if the client subsequently commits an act of violence against another black person. However, the assignment of liability in cases involving court-ordered counseling and potential harm to others is not black or white and may depend on interpretation of case law. For example, in *Division of Corrections v. Neakok* (1986), the Alaska Supreme Court declared that the state has a duty to protect society against dangerous parolees. This case involved a parolee who, when released back into his community, killed three people. However, it is not clear whether this decision would be applied by the courts to a mental health provider who failed to inform his client's parole officer about racist comments that did not amount to a threat (Wilde, 2003). In fact, in *Fredericks v. Jonsson* (2010), a U.S. district court case for Colorado, a mental health provider who was providing counseling services for a client as a condition of probation for stalking, failed to inform the client's probation officer about violent sexual fantasies the client said he used to have about the Fredericks. Two weeks later, the client got drunk and attempted to break into the Fredericks' home. The court found that, because the client made no direct threat, there was no actionable cause pursuant to Colorado statute. So, amid such ambiguity about legal risk, a therapist in Dr. Fry's position may find it difficult to reasonably conclude that such potential self-harm takes priority over promoting the client's welfare and dignity. True, if Dr. Fry wanted to play it safe, he could make full disclosure to the parole officer. However, such a practice posture is less likely to serve client welfare than to serve oneself; and it is even less likely to foster the courage, compassion, and trustworthiness that is emblematic of virtuous practice.

Identifying Any Apparent Other-Regarding Conflicts

The client has clearly sought to "put it over" on the parole board by concealing his hatefulness. As such, in not disclosing this fact to the client's parole officer, Dr. Fry would effectively also not be treating this officer as an autonomous agent. But the most serious other-regarding conflict in this case may be that arising out of the threat posed by the client to the black community while released from prison without truly being rehabilitated.

Do any of the stated conflicts *override* the course of action in question, namely continuing to counsel Paul, saying nothing to the officer about his personal problem, while receiving professional consultation or assistance?

Identifying and Weighing Potentially Overriding Conditions

Table 4.4 provides a set of questions that enables a therapist to check for conditions that might *override* pursuing the course of action that appears to be in the client's best interest (that is, the act that promotes the greater balance of positive client welfare over negative client welfare than any alternative course of action that is available). Table 4.4 allows for a response to each question. As such, responses to these questions for the case at hand have been included in the response section for purposes of illustration. These responses can all be gleaned from Table 4.1 prepared in Step 1.

The weighing of the conditions identified in Table 4.4 against seeking the course of action that best optimizes client welfare may vary from different perspectives, and it is not our intention to provide a calculus for such determinations. Indeed, there is considerable latitude for rational professionals to agree to disagree. Recall Aristotle's (2015) admonition that we must be content with as much objectivity as our subject allows. This said, some weights are *un*reasonable by most people's standards. For example, most of us would not need to think twice about the wrongheadedness of using state funds to build an amusement park instead of spending the money to pay for vaccines effective against a disease threatening to kill thousands of people. The illustration here is admittedly a stark one, but the point is that not just any moral balancing of competing alternatives can pass ethical muster.

In her well-known book, *Lying*, Sissela Bok (1999) argues that subjecting an ethical evaluation to public inspection is a necessary part of justifying or defending a moral judgment such as the weighing of alternatives. "Moral justification," she states, "cannot be exclusive or hidden; it has to be capable of being made public." In attempting to subject a moral judgment to public scrutiny, we can go beyond what is merely subjective by looking at an ethical issue from the perspective of a reasonable person. According to Bok, this is possible, to an extent, by looking at the matter at hand from

TABLE 4.4 ■ Checking for Possible Overriding Conditions

Question (to check for possible overriding conditions)	Response
1. Will the course of action that is in the client's best interest, as determined, disrespect the client as a self-determining agent?	No. It does not deceive, manipulate, or otherwise disrespect the client as a self-determining agent.
2. Is it unfair to the client according to the Standard of Justice?	No. There is no evidence that the therapist is treating the client any differently than any other client who is in a similar situation.
3. Will the therapist be disrespecting his own dignity as a self-determining agent?	Yes. The therapist allows himself to be used by the client to perpetuate the deception that the client is rehabilitated.
4. Will it pose any harm or risk of harm to the therapist?	Yes. The therapist is uncomfortable with counseling this client and may risk legal liability for failure to disclose.
5. Will it pose any harm or risk of harm to others?	Yes. It can pose a risk to the black community if the client is not behind bars.
6. Does it manipulate, deceive, or otherwise fail to respect all third parties as autonomous agents?	Yes. It helps perpetuate the client's deception on the parole board.
7. Does it have any broader negative implications for mental health practice itself or for society?	No. The therapist best serves the profession and society by affectively treating the client, which is what the therapist is attempting to do.

the perspective of a reasonable person who may be affected by the action in question. This can be done, she maintains, by applying the Golden Rule, which, in its negative form, says "Do not do to others what you would [reasonably] not want others to do to you" (Bok, 1999, p. 93).

So, in the case at hand, Dr. Fry would need to take the perspective of a reasonable person who may be affected by not letting the officer know about Paul's hateful remarks. The relevant and most significant welfare and/or interest consideration in this case is the potential threat of physical violence posed by the client to black people as long as he is not behind bars. Indeed, inasmuch as Paul continues to harbor the same hateful attitude that led him to assault a black man, it would be reasonable for a black person in the community to be concerned about the danger posed by Paul if not kept behind bars. So, looking rationally at the situation from the perspective of a black person who resides in the community in which Paul resides, one can see that the threat posed by the client should be taken seriously. But is it an overriding reason for Dr. Fry *not* to do what is in the best interest of his client, namely continuing to counsel Paul without reporting the potential danger to the parole officer?

As a black person, Dr. Fry may still not be in the best position to answer this question, perhaps because he is, in fact, also black. The conflict he experiences between his role as a therapist and his being a black man who has strong feelings about racial hatred and bigotry of the sort espoused by his client may make it difficult for him to take a rational perspective, especially without help from other qualified professionals. Thus another level of publicity that Bok (1999) suggests is to consult with others. Accordingly, the ACA Code of Ethics (2014) states, "Counselors take reasonable steps to consult with other counselors, the ACA Ethics and Professional Standards Department, or related professionals when they have questions regarding their ethical obligations or professional practice" (C.2.e). As such, Dr. Fry can take reasonable steps to get the perspective of another counselor who is not in the same conflicted situation as he.

Checking for Faulty Thinking

The conflicted situation of Dr. Fry underscores the importance of therapists taking stock of their own faulty thinking, which can impair their ethical judgment. Table 4.5 provides a self-inventory that therapists can use for this purpose (Cohen, 1993, 2007, 2017b).

TABLE 4.5 ■ Faulty Thinking Self-Inventory

Fallacy	Definition	Example
Stereotyping Others	Classifying human beings into fixed, rigid categories without respect to individual differences.	Is Dr. Fry stereotyping all whites as being like Paul in being racially bigoted against blacks?
Hasty Generalization	Generalizing from an insufficient number of individuals too small to be representative.	Is Fry generalizing about all whites from his negative experiences with just some of them?
Catastrophic Reasoning	Magnifying the risks of serious negative consequences.	Is Fry's past experience with racism affecting his ability to make rational predictions about dangerousness?
Cultural Blinders	Perceiving reality through a culturally conditioned mindset that is impervious to evidence to the contrary.	Is Fry seeing his current situation exclusively from the perspective of an oppressed minority; for example, seeing all whites as untrustworthy?
Demanding Perfection	Making absolutistic, perfectionistic, and unrealistic demands about the way things must or should be.	Is Fry demanding that others always treat him justly or that evils, such as racism, not exist?
Bandwagon Reasoning	Thinking or acting a certain way based merely on what others think or do.	Is Fry inclined to withdraw from his case because he thinks that other black men in his position would not counsel such a racist?
Damnation of Self or Others	Damning the doer rather than the deed.	Is Fry damning Paul as totally worthless and no good because he hates blacks?
Low Frustration Tolerance	Under-assessing one's ability to tolerate or stand what one finds difficult or challenging.	Is Fry telling himself that he *can't stand* to counsel Paul because he finds it difficult?

Indeed, in asking the above questions, Dr. Fry can take due precautions against making ethical judgments based on faulty thinking, which can lead him to draw self-defeating and regrettable judgments about how he should proceed.

Step 4: Make a Decision

So what should Dr. Fry do? An ethical analysis does not decide the problem for you. As existential philosopher Jean-Paul Sartre admonished, ethical analysis can take a person so far, and then one still must decide. "No rule of general morality can show you what you ought to do: no signs are vouchsafed in this world" (Sartre, 1989, para. 13). How much weight should ultimately be given to other-regarding responsibilities in the face of one's primary responsibility to the client? For example, Bok's ideas about publicity and applying the Golden Rule provide useful perspectives from which to decide this question, but they do not themselves make the decision. In the end, there may be tweaking to negotiate the terms of the decision, and compromise is often a useful approach. In the present case, unless counseling is given a chance to work, this could effectively preclude Paul from getting the therapy he needs to be reintegrated into society. So a possible compromise might be to reassess the danger posed by Paul to the black community after Paul has been in counseling for a period of time sufficient for counseling to work. At this later time, if counseling has helped the client work through his hostility, then Dr. Fry could report to the parole officer that Paul has successfully completed counseling. This could somewhat address the issue of not having been forthright with the parole board as well as the potential danger posed by his client to the black community. On the other hand, after giving the counseling time to work (and how much time is sufficient for counseling to work is itself not formulaic), if Paul still continued to harbor such intense hatred for blacks, then he could then alert the officer, in which case his client would not satisfy the conditions of parole. As such, this would reduce the amount of time the black community would be exposed to the potential threat.

This is still not a perfect decision because perfection is too much to ask in this imperfect world. Arguably, the courageous therapist would be willing to assume any potential legal risk for the interim period in which counseling is conducted. After all, the primary responsibility of a therapist is to do what is in the best interest of the client. However, if counseling is ineffective after the given period, then one could reasonably argue that the best interest of the client has been overridden by the threat posed to the welfare of others. This would be regrettable because the client would probably never trust another therapist. Unfortunately, the right choice is not necessarily one that *feels* good and has a happy ending (Cohen & Cohen, 1999).

In the end, the final decision in an ethics case can involve compromise and adjustment between competing ethical responsibilities. In this manner, other and self-regarding responsibilities may be balanced carefully against client welfare in an effort to seek the latter within the constraints of due regard for the former. However, the decision finally reached by Dr. Fry may not necessarily be the one that another therapist may reach (Forester-Miller & Davis, 1996). For example, another therapist may come to the conclusion that the other-regarding responsibilities are overriding in the present context. Nevertheless, while each such decision may pull in opposite directions, each can still be a rational choice as long as all relevant considerations—such as the best interest of the client, respect for client autonomy, the autonomy of others, potential harm to self or others, significant therapist biases, and possible precedents or implications for mental health practice—are given due consideration.

Step 5: Act on the Decision

Further, it is one thing to decide what to do, and another to actually do it. In many instances, people fail to do what they decide. This may be due to procrastination, weakness of will, demanding certainty, being distracted by other problems or issues, and a host of other things. The significant feature of such a result is that the failure to act still has consequences, and these consequences are often regrettable. For example, part of Fry's decision was to seek assistance with his personal problem and with the ethical decision itself. While Fry may know, on a rational level, that he should do these things he may still not do them. As a result, his personal problem may thwart the success of therapy and the client may be needlessly harmed, not ever having had the opportunity to transition to the world outside the prison gates. When something of this magnitude happens in counseling, the therapist will have violated a cardinal client responsibility, that of Nonmaleficence, the standard that enjoins that mental health practitioners not do avoidable harm to their clients.

A rational decision does not have to be a certain decision. Waiting until one is certain that one is doing the right thing is a recipe for inaction because in ethics there is seldom, if ever, a decision about which one can be certain one is doing the right thing. Instead, it is a matter of making a reasonable effort to do the right thing. This can be accomplished by following the five-step process illustrated in this chapter. This does not mean that deciding and acting according to this decision-making process will be without regrets. As you can see from the many tentacles of a moral problem that can arise in a carefully considered ethics problem, there are likely to be some regrets. For example, Fry may regret not being able to entirely overcome his personal problem, even with seeking help from a qualified professional. He may wish that he could have helped the client more, or that he was able to be completely forthright, transparent, and authentic with the client about his own resentment. However, the Aristotelian mean between excess and deficiency is typically a balancing act between such excesses and deficiencies, where the reasonable response lies somewhere in the middle.

Questions for Review and Reflection

1. Why is it useful to have a decision-making process in ethics?

2. What are the five steps of the ethical decision-making process proposed in this chapter?

3. What does it mean to have a problem? What is the difference between a practical problem and an intellectual problem?

4. What does it mean to have a moral problem? Is a moral problem an intellectual or a practical problem? Explain.

5. Why might a therapist be said to have a moral problem every time he or she walks into the counseling room to counsel a client?

6. What is the difference between a personal problem and a moral problem?

7. When does a person have a serious moral problem in contrast to a minor one?
8. What is the difference between positive welfare and negative welfare?
9. What is an interest? Are there common human interests? Explain.
10. What is a need? Are there emotional needs in your estimation? Explain.
11. Do therapists serve all client interests or are there limits? Explain.
12. Does Dr. Fry in the case introduced in this chapter have a moral problem? Explain.
13. What does the definition of a moral problem consist of?
14. What is moral sensitivity, and why is it important to defining a moral problem? Is Dr. Fry morally sensitive in your estimation? Explain.
15. Are therapists themselves ordinarily stakeholders in their moral problems? Explain. Who are the stakeholders in Dr. Fry's moral problem?
16. What mistake is commonly made in defining a moral problem, and why should it be avoided?
17. When is information morally relevant in addressing a moral problem? What would be an example of a morally relevant fact in addressing Fry's moral problem? Why is this fact morally relevant?
18. Provide at least three examples of different types of potentially morally relevant client information, and briefly explain how each type might be morally relevant to a particular stakeholder in Fry's moral problem.
19. What is the purpose of an ethical analysis (Step 3 of the decision-making process), and what resources are commonly used in conducting it?
20. Using Tables 4.3 and 4.4 as your guide, what course of action do you think is in Paul's best interest? Are there any overriding other- or self-regarding responsibilities in your estimation? Explain.
21. What is Sissela Bok's approach to determining the weight of competing self- and other-regarding responsibilities? Provide an example of how her approach applies in the case of Paul.
22. Does Bok's approach, in your estimation, help provide some measure of objectivity in weighing competing responsibilities? Does it make the decision for you? Explain.
23. Table 4.5 provides eight types of biased or irrational thinking that may adversely affect an ethical decision. Which, if any, of these thinking errors do you think Dr. Fry might have been especially vulnerable to in making his ethical decision regarding Paul?
24. Can the ethical analysis (Step 3) make the decision (Step 4) for a therapist? Explain.
25. Are perfect ethical decisions likely? Explain.
26. What role can compromise play in addressing competing ethical responsibilities in ethical decision making?
27. Is there just one acceptable ethical decision that is possible? Explain.
28. Does making a decision (Step 4) ensure acting on the decision (Step 5)? Explain. What danger is there in waiting to be certain before a decision is acted on?

Cases for Analysis

Use the information in this chapter to analyze each of the below cases. In particular, apply the five-step decision-making process developed in this chapter using the appropriate tools (for example, Stakeholder Table; Table to Check for Possible Overriding Conditions; Faulty Thinking Self-Inventory, etc.).

1. Bartholomew Harrington, age 30, is in therapy with Dr. Phillipa Edelman, a clinical social worker, for problems related to lack of productivity at work. Harrington also has a history of voyeurism, but initially contends that he has not engaged in this practice for about 5 years. During the course of treatment, Harrington hesitantly reveals to Edelman that he has been reexperiencing urges to engage in voyeurism and has purchased high power binoculars so that he can gaze into his neighbor's windows. In fact, he relates that he has also taken pictures of his neighbor undressing and is now contemplating taking videos of her. Since Edelman does not specialize in treating paraphilias, she informs Harrington that she will need to refer him to another therapist. Harrington tells her that he will never reveal to another therapist what he revealed to Edelman and pleads with her to continue to counsel him regardless of her lack of expertise in this area. Define an ethical problem Edelman has in this situation. That is, who are the stakeholders and what welfare and/or interests are at stake? What is in the best interest of Edelman's client? Are there any basic responsibilities to Harrington that may be violated? Are there any overriding self-regarding responsibilities (needlessly harming the client or not being equitable or fair to him)? Are there any overriding other-regarding responsibilities? What decision do you think would be justified based on your analysis?

2. Lana Michaels is a 32-year-old clerical worker who has been diagnosed with histrionic personality disorder. She has been in therapy with Roberto Snellings, a male clinical psychologist, for 4 months after her fiancé broke off the engagement due to Michaels' excessive flirting with other men. Snellings is a solo practitioner; however, he does share office space with another psychologist, Sampson Brubaker. Lana Michaels usually comes to sessions with low-cut necklines, short skirts, and brightly colored eye shadow. She has, on several occasions, made it clear that she finds Snellings sexually attractive; however, Snellings informs her that he is interested in her only as a client and that boundaries must be observed. Recently, Snellings observes Michaels talking to Brubaker after Michaels' session. Michaels is standing very close to Brubaker and running her hands through his hair. Although Michaels is not a client of Brubaker, she is a client in the same office suite, and it should be apparent to Brubaker that she is a client. Upset about what he sees, Snellings confronts Brubaker with his concerns about his conduct with Michaels. Brubaker responds that Michaels is "hot" and states that there's no problem because she is not his client. Since Snellings and Brubaker only share office suite space, but do not work in the same practice, Snellings cannot legally disclose any information about Michaels to him without Michaels' consent. Snellings is very concerned about what he considers to be the exploitive nature of Brubaker's possible relationship with Michaels and is exploring what to do next. Define an ethical problem that Snellings has in this situation. That is, who are the stakeholders and what welfare and/or interests are at stake? What is in the best interest of Snellings' client? Are there any basic

responsibilities to Michaels that may be violated (that is, needlessly harming the client or not being equitable or fair to her)? Are there any overriding self-regarding responsibilities? Are there any overriding other-regarding responsibilities? What decision do you think would be justified based on your analysis?

3. Dalma Norman is a 16-year-old female who is seeing Sasha Turnbull, a mental health counselor who provides counseling services once weekly at Dalma's high school. Dalma's presenting problem is poor grades, but, after only two sessions, she reveals to Turnbull that she is 2 months pregnant and wants to get an abortion. She contends that her parents are very religious and that they would not approve of her decision. She reveals that she has already identified a facility where her abortion can be done and that she has saved up money to pay for the procedure.

Parental consent is not required in Dalma's state; however, Turnbull is concerned that Dalma might need family support in making the decision. Although Turnbull attempts to remain objective and neutral about Dalma's decision, she is having difficulty because she regrets having had an abortion herself at age 17. She debates whether she has a responsibility to Dalma to disclose this information to her parents or whether that would violate the trust of her client. Define a moral problem that Turnbull has in this situation. Who are the stakeholders, and what welfare and/or interests are at stake? What is in the best interest of Dalma? Are there any basic responsibilities to Dalma that may be violated (that is, needlessly harming the client or not being equal or fair to her)? Are there any overriding self-regarding responsibilities? Are there any overriding other-regarding responsibilities? What decision do you think would be justified based on your analysis?

References

American Counseling Association. (2014). *ACA Code of Ethics.* Alexandria, VA: Author. Retrieved from counseling.org/resources/aca-code-of-ethics.pdf

American Psychiatric Association. (2013). *Diagnostic and statistical manual of mental disorders: DSM-5.* Washington, DC: Author.

American Psychological Association. (2016). *Ethical principles of psychologists and code of conduct.* Washington, DC: Author. Retrieved from http://www.apa.org/ethics/code/?item=11#805

Aristotle. (2015). *Nicomachean ethics* (W. D. Ross, trans.). eBooks@Adelaide. Retrieved from https://ebooks.adelaide.edu.au/a/aristotle/nicomachean/

Beauchamp, T., & Childress, J. (1979). *Principles of biomedical ethics.* New York, NY: Oxford University Press.

Bok, S. (1999). *Lying: Moral choice in public and private life.* New York, NY: Vintage Books.

Cohen, E. D. (1993). *Caution: Faulty thinking can be harmful to your happiness.* Fort Pierce, FL: Trace-Wilco.

Cohen, E. D. (2007). *The new rational therapy: Thinking your way to serenity, success, and profound happiness*. Lanham, MD: Rowman & Littlefield.

Cohen, E. D. (2017a, June). Anxiety as depression waiting to happen: The comorbidity of anxiety and depression explained using a logic-based model. *Psychology Today*. Retrieved from https://www.psychologytoday.com/blog/what-would-aristotle-do/201706/anxiety-depression-waiting-happen

Cohen, E. D. (2017b). *Logic-based therapy and everyday emotions*. Lanham, MD: Rowman & Littlefield.

Cohen, E. D., & Cohen, G. S. (1999). *The virtuous therapist : Ethical practice of counseling and psychotherapy*. Belmont, CA: Wadsworth.

Cottone, R. R. (2001). A social constructivism model of ethical decision-making in counseling. *Journal of Counseling & Development, 79*, 39–45.

Cottone, R. R., & Clause, R. E. (2000). Ethical decision-making models: A review of the literature. *Journal of Counseling & Development, 78*(3), 275–283.

Deroche, M. D., Eckart, E., Lott, E., Park, C.N., & Raddler, L. (2015). A review of ethical decision-making models. In B. Herlihy and G. Corey (7th ed.). *ACA Ethical Standards Casebook*. Alexandria, VA: American Counseling Association.

Division of Corrections v. Neakok, 721 P.2d 1121. (Alaska 1986).

Forester-Miller, H., & Davis, T. E. (1996). *A practitioner's guide to ethical decision-making*. Alexandria, VA: American Counseling Association.

Fredericks v. Jonsson 609 F. 3d 1096 (2010). Retrieved from http://cases.justia.com/federal/appellate-courts/ca10/09-1169/09-1169-2011-03-14.pdf?ts=1411089865

Hare, R. M. (1991). The philosophical basis of psychiatric ethics. In S. Block & P. Chodoff (Eds.), *Psychiatric ethics* (pp. 31–45). New York, NY: Oxford University Press.

Hill, M., Glasser, K., & Hardin, J. (1995). A feminist model for ethical decision-making. In E. J. Rave & C. C. Larsen (Eds.), *Ethical decision-making in therapy: Feminist perspectives* (pp. 18–37). New York, NY: Guilford Press.

Kitchener, K. S. (1984). Intuition, critical evaluation and ethical principles: The foundation for ethical decisions in counseling psychology. *Counseling Psychologist, 12*(3), 43–55.

National Association of Social Workers. (2017). *Code of ethics of the National Association of Social Workers*. Retrieved from https://www.socialworkers.org/About/Ethics/Code-of-Ethics/Code-of-Ethics-English.aspx

Sartre, J. P. (1989). Existentialism is a humanism. In W. Kaufman (Ed.), *Existentialism from Dostoyevsky to Sartre*. New York, NY: Meridian. Retrieved from https://www.marxists.org/reference/archive/sartre/works/exist/sartre.htm

Wilde, M. L. (2003). The liability of Alaska mental health providers for mandated treatment. *Alaska Law Review, 20*(2), 271–303. Retrieved from http://scholarship.law.duke.edu/cgi/viewcontent.cgi?article=1112&context=alr

NAVIGATING KEY CONCEPTS
Confidentiality and Informed Consent

PART III

5

EXERCISING DISCRETION

Case Study: A Dangerous Client

As discussed in Chapters 3 and 4, the primary responsibility of the therapist is to advance the positive net welfare of the client qualified by consideration of Client Autonomy. Further, as discussed in Chapter 2, to promote a client's best interest the therapist needs to be trustworthy. Clients who do not trust their therapists are not likely to be self-disclosing; and, without disclosure of such personal information, therapists are not likely to act in their clients' best interest. As such, being trustworthy is no small matter for a therapist. It can make the difference between competent treatment and treatment that portends serious harm to the client or others. This is particularly the case in situations in which the client is suicidal or poses a threat to others.

In such situations, technical training may not be enough to avert regrettable consequences, including serious bodily harm or death. Here, of utmost importance is being the sort of *person* to whom the client feels comfortable disclosing his private, personal information, and deepest secrets. This tends to be a person who presents as one worthy of being trusted. As discussed in Chapter 1, this is a person who is kind, empathetic, genuine, courageous, honest, respectful, candid, discreet, diligent, empowering, loyal, competent, and fair.

In turn, this chapter examines the challenges such practitioners may confront in counseling clients who threaten harm to others. It looks carefully at some pertinent professional and legal standards of therapist-client confidentiality in such contexts and offers guidance in making rational predictions about dangerousness and exercising discretion in disclosing confidential client information.

Indeed, without reasonable assurance that their disclosures will remain confidential, most, if not all, clients would be reticent to share very personal information with their therapists, and, consequently, the therapists would not be able to help their clients satisfactorily address their issues. Further, therapists who fail to exercise discretion in keeping clients' confidences betray their clients by treating them as objects manipulated rather than as rational self-determining persons and are therefore not worthy of their clients' trust. Nonetheless, cases where clients threaten the welfare of others may test the rational limits of the therapist-client bond of confidentiality.

A CASE OF A DANGEROUS CLIENT

Consider the case of Arty Derwood, a 32-year-old, recently divorced man, who has been in therapy for 6 months with Dr. Molly Morgan, a licensed mental health counselor. Arty worked as a cashier in a supermarket. Diagnosed with Borderline Personality Disorder, he was making substantial progress. When he first came to Dr. Morgan after his divorce, he was contemplating suicide but had since become increasingly optimistic about his future. So, when he encountered some bad news, he became very angry and distraught.

"Good morning, Arty," said Dr. Morgan, as he entered her office.

"Hi, Doctor," he responded in a stilted tone.

"Have a seat Arty. How are you doing?" said Dr. Morgan as she and Arty took their respective seats facing each other.

"Not good. That son-of-a-bitch fired me yesterday!"

"Your manager?"

"Yeah, Johnny Harmon, that fat bastard!"

"What happened?"

"He told me that he had received complaints about the way I was treating customers. I have worked there for 2 years, and this is the first time anyone ever complained about me. There was some woman last week who accused me of ringing things up too slowly, and I told her where to go. I bet it was her, that piece of crap. But she had it coming. He had no right to fire me."

"Sounds like you are taking this news very hard."

"I thought that guy liked me, and now he turns out to be a traitor. I have bills to pay. That rotten bastard screwed me, and he's gonna pay dearly."

"Tell me what you mean when you say 'he's going to pay dearly'?"

"I mean I have been thinking about killing him."

"Do you have a plan?"

[There is a momentary silence] "No, not yet, but maybe shoot him between the eyes or strangle him with my bare hands. I'd love to see his face just before he stops breathing!"

"Do you own a gun?"

"Yes. I also have a permit to carry a concealed weapon."

Clearly, Arty appears to be comfortable speaking candidly to Dr. Morgan about his feelings. Morgan has forged a bond of trust with Arty, which has allowed her to find out information about the potential danger he may pose to his former manager and/or to other coworkers and customers. Arty has trusted Morgan enough to confide these things in her. So is it now ethical for Morgan to use this information acquired in confidence against Arty to protect the life of another?

ETHICAL LIMITS OF CONFIDENTIALITY: PROFESSIONAL CODES OF ETHICS

According to the prevailing professional codes of ethics the answer is a qualified yes. For example, Paragraph B1(c) of the American Counseling Association (ACA; 2014) provides that counselors "protect the confidential information of prospective and current clients" and "disclose information only with appropriate consent or with sound legal or ethical justification." B2(a) of the ACA Code permits counselors to disclose confidential information when necessary "to protect clients or identified others from serious and foreseeable harm," or when legally required. Similarly, Paragraph 1.07(c) of the National Association of Social Workers (NASW; 2017) Code of Ethics, tells social workers to "protect the confidentiality of all information obtained in the course of professional service, except for compelling professional reasons," such as "when disclosure is necessary to prevent serious, foreseeable, and imminent harm to a client or other identifiable person."

These codes, however, do not themselves mandate disclosure of confidential information to prevent harm to another person. Instead they *permit* such disclosure. So is Dr. Morgan *legally required* to disclose confidential information to prevent harm to Johnny, his coworkers, or others who might be in the store should Arty show up with a loaded, concealed firearm?

THE LEGAL LIMITS OF CONFIDENTIALITY

In 1976, the California Supreme Court, in *Tarasoff v. the Regents of the University of California*, set a landmark legal precedent for addressing cases like that of Arty. In *Tarasoff*, Prosenjit Poddar confided in Dr. Lawrence Moore, a psychologist at the counseling center of the University of California at Berkeley. Poddar told Moore that he intended to kill a young woman, Tatiana Tarasoff. Responding to the threat, Moore requested that the campus police detain Poddar, but the campus police questioned Poddar, concluded that he posed no threat, and released him. Subsequently, Moore's superior, Dr. Harvey Powelson, requested that the police return Moore's letter, directed that all copies of the letter, and even Moore's clinical case notes, be destroyed, and ordered that no further action be taken to involuntarily detain Poddar for psychiatric evaluation. Sadly, 2 months later Poddar killed Tarasoff. The court concluded, "the public policy favoring protection of the confidential character of patient-psychotherapist communications must yield to the extent to which disclosure is essential to avert danger to others. The protective privilege ends where the public peril begins." Accordingly, it declared that, in such cases, therapists incur a "duty" or "obligation" to protect:

> When a therapist determines, or pursuant to the standards of his profession should determine, that his patient presents a serious danger of violence to another, he incurs an obligation to use reasonable care to protect the intended victim against such danger. The discharge of this duty may require the therapist to take one or more of various steps, depending upon the nature of the case. Thus it may call for him to warn the intended victim or others likely to apprise the victim of the danger, to notify the police, or to take whatever other steps are reasonably necessary under the circumstances. (Opinion)

The case was originally decided in 1974, but was reheard in 1976 (Berger & Berger, 2009). The 1974 decision announced a duty to warn; however, the 1976 decision, as cited above, changed the duty to warn to the broader duty to protect. While warning the potential victim or her family is one way to protect an endangered person, there are other ways also, such as notifying the police or detaining an individual for observation and/or evaluation.

Prior to the *Tarasoff* ruling, there was no legal precedent in mental health practice to override confidentiality to prevent danger to others. While in the years following the *Tarasoff* ruling many states in addition to California adopted a legal duty to protect, there are currently several states that allow therapists to exercise discretion in deciding whether or not to disclose confidential information to protect identifiable third parties against potentially dangerous clients (National Conference of State Legislatures [NCSL], 2015). For example, Florida Statute 491.0147 allows therapists to make the determination of whether or not to disclose, and they are, as such, protected both civilly and criminally regardless of how they decide. There are also still some states that do not have clear case law or statutes on the duty to protect or warn. These include Maine, Nevada, North Carolina, and North Dakota (NCSL, 2015). Meanwhile, some states, such as New York, have gone from a permissive rule to a duty to protect amid an increase in domestic terrorism. Enacted in 2013, the New York state law, which is part of the Secure Ammunitions and Firearms Enforcement Act, adds a new provision to the Mental Hygiene Law, which requires mental health professionals (broadly interpreted to include registered nurses, physicians, licensed clinical social workers, and psychologists) who reasonably conclude that a client is "likely to engage in conduct that will cause serious harm to self or others" to report the potentially dangerous client to county mental health officials who will, in turn, determine if "non-clinical, identifying information" should be reported to the New York State Division of Criminal Justice Services (DCJS). The DCJS will then determine if the individual possesses a fire arms license. If so, the person will then be required to surrender the license together with all fire arms (New York Code, 2013). So if Dr. Morgan concludes that Arty does indeed present an imminent threat of serious harm to Johnny, whether she is *legally required* to disclose confidential information to the authorities, or otherwise take protective measures, will depend on the laws of the state in which she practices.

DECISION MAKING IN THE CASE OF ARTY

As emphasized in Chapter 4, the first step in making a decision is defining the problem. Without taking this step seriously, a therapist may overlook genuine possibilities and regret it in the end. For example, the problem at hand may not be simply to protect others from Arty, but also Arty from himself. Without carefully considering all the stakeholders and the welfare and/or interests at stake, there is significant risk that the problem will be inappropriately defined, for example, too narrowly without due consideration for the welfare of the client. So what is at stake in the present case, and for whom?

As illustrated in Table 5.1, there are a number of stakeholders whose welfare and/or interests are at stake. Thus, it is not just Johnny whose physical welfare may be threatened if Arty shows up at the supermarket with a loaded gun. Customers as well as other employees may end up in the line of fire. As reasonable persons, it is also quite clear that these potential victims would want to be informed about the threat. So if you were Johnny, or a customer or an employee at the supermarket, wouldn't you want to be given a heads up?

Arty's interest in having Johnny "pay dearly" for firing him is also an important consideration because it provides a motive for his carrying out his threat. Dr. Morgan is also

TABLE 5.1 ■ Stakeholders/Welfare/Interests

Stakeholder	Welfare	Interests
Arty	• Getting through a difficult period • Continuing to make progress in therapy • Not harming himself	• Having his confidences respected • Getting back at Johnny • Being gainfully employed • Being informed about the limits of confidentiality
Johnny	• Avoiding serious bodily injury or death	• Being informed about the potential threat
Dr. Morgan	• Avoiding legal harms (fines, loss of license, law suits, etc.)	• Acting in the best interest of Arty • Protecting Arty's confidentiality • Obeying the law • Preventing serious bodily injury or death of others by her client
Customers at the Supermarket	• Avoiding serious bodily injury or death	• Being informed about the • potential threat
Other Employees	• Avoiding serious bodily injury or death	• Being informed about the potential threat
Law Enforcement		• Protecting the public against an imminent threat of death or serious bodily injury

justified in being concerned about avoiding legal harms such as being sued or losing her license; so she is obviously motivated to act in accordance with state law and professional codes of ethics. And law enforcement authorities can be reasonably presumed to have an interest in protecting public welfare.

Importantly, Arty has confided in Morgan because he trusts her. As such, he has a serious interest in having his confidentiality protected, and disclosure of such confidences for the purpose of protecting others would militate against such protection. Further, in light of the latter, Arty would reasonably want to know the limits of confidentiality. As discussed in Chapter 7, as part of a client's informed consent to therapy, a therapist has a responsibility to inform the client of exceptions to confidentiality, notably disclosure of confidential information to prevent harm to the client or to others. Moreover, given Arty's past attempt at committing suicide when his wife divorced him, the disclosure may raise the likelihood that he might attempt suicide again. So Dr. Morgan has an especially strong interest in protecting Arty's confidentiality and his welfare, but she clearly also has a serious interest in preventing Arty from inflicting serious bodily injury or death on others.

Amid such a conflicting set of welfare and/or interests, what should Morgan do? Here, the second step of the decision-making process, collecting morally relevant information, is crucial. For instance, in the state where Dr. Morgan practices, is she legally required to disclose the threat? Is disclosure permissible, but not required? Is disclosure and nondisclosure civilly protected? These questions are less daunting than others, however. Except for the exceptions previously noted, state statutes are generally clear about whether there is a duty to warn or protect. Determining whether the statute applies to a particular case is less clear-cut. Moreover, settling the legal issue may only address the therapist's interest in avoiding a legal penalty, and not the *moral* problem at hand. This is why it is very important to define the problem carefully in terms of the various stakeholders and what is at stake for each. A narrow concern, even preoccupation, with the legal consequences, falls sorrowfully short of such an analysis.

The inherent ambiguity of Morgan's situation is typical of situations in which the question arises about whether to disclose confidential information to prevent serious, imminent harm to others. On the one hand, therapist-client confidentiality is essential to the working relationship, and therefore to acting in the best interest of the client. On the other hand, when death or serious, imminent harm to others hangs in the balance, keeping confidences needs to be weighed against such potential harm. In this weighing up of competing welfare and/or interests, the probability of the risk is a major factor. A remote risk is more readily overridden by client welfare and/or interests than one that can be reasonably assessed with high probability. As discussed in Chapter 1, while there is no calculus for balancing these competing considerations, the discreet and loyal therapist avoids the extremes of client betrayal and blind client allegiance. Supposing that Morgan is such a therapist, she will seek the mean, or point of moderation, between these extremes. This decision will involve giving due consideration to the welfare and/or interests of the client and the potentially endangered third parties, as well as the legal risks. This balancing of competing factors can be daunting inasmuch as the future is uncertain, and even quite rational decisions can lead to regrettable outcomes. For example, disclosure could lead Arty to attempt suicide again or to vow never to seek much needed therapy.

As such, the virtuous therapist also exercises courage to act in the face of uncertainty and lack of absolute assurance and understands that it is generally better to act according to a *reasonable* judgment than to procrastinate and fail to act at all. In fact, pursuant to *Tarasoff*, a therapist is not expected to "render a perfect performance" but "need only exercise 'that reasonable degree of skill, knowledge, and care ordinarily possessed and exercised by members of [the given professional specialty] under similar circumstances'" (*Tarasoff*, 1976, Section 2). Indeed, there are generally more ways for things to go wrong than right, more ways to miss the target than to hit it. As such, by relinquishing the opportunity to rationally influence the outcome through calculated action, one also increases the odds of things going wrong. Hence, "Shall we not, like archers who have a mark to aim at, be more likely to hit upon what is right?" (Aristotle, 2015, Bk. 1, Ch. 2).

So when is a judgment about risk to others a *reasonable* one? Generally speaking, reasonable judgments are based on evidence; there needs to be sufficient evidence to suggest a high probability of imminent harm to another. While there is no probability calculus to predict dangerousness, based on the current literature, there are certain evidentiary questions that can be posed to guide a reasonable judgment. Table 5.2 provides a list of relevant questions (American Psychiatric Association, 2013; McSherry, 2004; Merrill, 2013; Ministry of Health, 1998; National Collaborating Centre for Mental Health, n.d.; National Council on Alcoholism and Drug Dependence, 2017; Szalavitz, 2013).

TABLE 5.2 ■ Guidelines for Predicting Violence

Does the client have	Yes (Y)	No (N)
1. A psychiatric diagnosis such as Antisocial Personality Disorder associated with a high incidence of violent or aggressive behavior?		N
2. A psychosis (delusion or hallucination) disposing the client to violent or aggressive behavior such as a paranoid psychosis?		N
3. A history of violence toward others?		N
4. A clearly articulated, feasible plan to commit a violent act?		N
5. An intended, specific victim?	Y	
6. The means to execute a contemplated violent act?	Y	
7. A situational trigger that can provide a motive to behave in a violent or aggressive way (job loss, relationship problems such as a breakup, rejection by others)?	Y	
8. A substance abuse problem?		N

Table 5.2 includes Yes and No responses to the eight questions, which (presumably) apply to Arty. Regarding Question 1, if Arty's diagnosis were Antisocial Personality Disorder, the probabilities of his posing a danger to others would be substantially higher than that which he poses relative to his present diagnosis of Borderline Personality Disorder. This is because the latter diagnosis is generally associated more with harm to self than to others, a fact that, taken along with Arty's past history of attempted suicide, may increase the probability of self-harm if disclosure is made. True, aggression toward others, even murder, does occur in the population of clients with Borderline Personality Disorder (Sansone & Sansone, 2012), but this is also the case in populations who do not have mental illness. In fact, there is evidence to suggest that most people who commit violent acts do not suffer from a mental illness (Phillips, 2012). As such, adding to the problematic nature of predicting dangerousness is the fact that it is not always clear whether acts of aggression are a result of a client's diagnosed mental disorder or some other aspect of the client's profile (Lakeman, 1996). Indeed, inasmuch as the social and behavioral sciences have not advanced to the level of predictability found in the physical sciences, we must accept the inevitable fallibility of even the most thorough and cautious prognostications.

Regarding Question 2, it is important to note that client populations with mental illnesses such as Schizophrenia, which are associated with delusions, have a relatively low percentage of violence. It is rather a relatively small subset of such populations, which have specific types of psychotic disorders such as paranoid delusions or command hallucinations to commit violent acts, which are associated with a significant increase in violence. Indeed, most people with Schizophrenia do not present a greater risk of dangerousness as a result of their mental illness ("Living With Schizophrenia," n.d.). Inasmuch as Arty does not suffer from delusions associated with violence, he does not carry such increased risk of committing a violent act.

Arty's more usual response to stress would also be a major consideration in making such imperfect but rational predictions of dangerousness to others. For example, after his former wife divorced him, he attempted suicide. This suggests that, in his distraught state of mind, Arty may more likely present a danger to himself than to others. Still this client has made a threat against an identifiable person and, while he does not have a clearly articulated plan, he has contemplated killing this person using a firearm, and he does have the means to carry out the threat, along with a concealed weapons permit to carry the weapon into the grocery store.

Still, Arty does not have a history of violence, which would have made a prediction of future violence more likely. If Arty had served time in prison for violent crimes such as armed robbery, rape, or homicide, the probabilities that he would repeat such an act are increased (Dvoskin, 1990). However, even in such as case, there may have been factors present in the past that are no longer present. For example, the client may have had a drug or alcohol dependency problem but is now in recovery.

Regarding Question 4, Arty has speculated about how he might kill Johnny, but he has not articulated a clear and definite plan about how he was going to kill him. He says that he might kill him by shooting him or maybe by strangling him to death. He has not given the issue careful thought, planning out exactly when and how he would perpetrate the violent act. Further, while Arty does have a gun and an identified victim, he has not connected the use of the weapon to a clearly articulated plan to harm this person.

Arty does have a potential trigger to motivate him to commit the violent act, namely, having been fired by the intended victim. However, if a therapist were to breach confidentiality to report every client who has had such motivation, then there would be a high proportion of the therapist's case load whose confidentiality would be breached for such purposes. Indeed, many of us, inside and outside the counseling room, have expressed anger in the form of empty threats. A therapist needs more than such potential motives to make a reasonable judgment of dangerousness.

Drug or alcohol abuse appears to substantially increase probability of violent action, especially in combination with other psychosocial factors including those discussed above. For example, intoxication or withdrawal from substances such as alcohol, sedatives, cocaine, amphetamines, and opiates can increase the chances of violent behavior, with or without comorbid mental illness (Rueve & Welton, 2008). According to one study, alcoholism comorbid with antisocial personality disorder increased the probability of women committing homicide 40 to 50 times; and, with schizophrenia, 5 to 6 times (Eronen, Hakola, & Tiihonen, 1996).

If Arty had a substance abuse problem and a history of violence and made such a threat, then there would potentially be a rationale for disclosing the threat to protect the prospective victim(s). If he had a substance abuse problem and no history of violence toward others and made such a threat, then the argument for disclosure to protect others would be weaker but more arguable than the present case in which there is (presumptively) no known substance abuse disorder. In fact, in the present case, Arty has a history of attempted suicide. Supposing a substance abuse problem, this would be more of an argument for disclosure for purposes of client protection than for disclosure to protect others.

Dr. Morgan, of course, needs to consider the viewpoint of the potential victim. Would Morgan not want to know if someone made a threat on her life? However, Morgan's primary responsibility is the welfare of her client, and there is a professional bond of confidentiality that cannot ethically be overridden without probable, imminent danger to others. This does not appear to be true in the present case. This does not mean that situational variables will remain constant in the future. For example, Arty may later carefully articulate his plan to kill Johnny. As such, Morgan can take steps to lessen the probability that Arty will act on his threat. For example, in the interim, she can ask Arty to sign a unilateral no-harm "contract," which means that he agrees not to harm himself or others ("Conducting a safety assessment," n.d.; Hyldahl & Richardson, 2011); and she can schedule a follow-up session (for instance, the following day) to monitor the client's progress. Indeed, a key factor in the efficacy of such measures is, arguably, the extent to which the therapist-client relationship is a trusting and respectful one; which, as emphasized in this book, largely depends on whether the therapist demonstrates a trustworthy character.

In the end, Dr. Morgan will need to weigh the welfare of her client against the potential for harm to others and strike a balance. Without a reasonable assessment of high probability and imminence of harm to others, based on careful consideration of the evidence before her (specifically, the responses to questions posed in Table 5.2), Morgan's primary responsibility remains to her client. This means protecting Arty's confidentiality and acting mindful of his welfare and interests.

CONFIDENTIALITY AND PRIVILEGED COMMUNICATION

The key note of protecting Arty's welfare and interests is the bond of trust generated between client and therapist. Because this factor, perhaps more than any other single factor, facilitates clients' ability to derive benefit from therapy, the state has perceived it as falling within its purview of protecting public welfare. One of the strongest expressions of such legal recognition was announced in a medical case, *Hammonds v. Aetna Casualty and Surety Company* (1964, § 1):

> To foster the best interest of the patient and to insure a climate most favorable to a complete recovery, men of medicine have urged that patients be totally frank in their discussions with their physicians. To encourage the desired candor, men of law have formulated a strong policy of confidentiality to assure patients that only they themselves may unlock the doctor's silence in regard to those private disclosures.

As such, based on the stated rationale, all or most states in the United States have statutes that legally protect, as confidential, information disclosed by a client in the course of therapy. These statutes, with some exceptions, forbid the therapist to disclose this information to third parties not involved in the administration of the therapy. Exceptions commonly include cases in which (1) the specific information is needed by therapists to defend themselves in civil, criminal, or disciplinary proceedings; (2) when the client signs a written release; and, as discussed earlier, (3) when there is imminent danger of physical harm to the client or another (Grabois, 1997).

Further, all but a few states in the United States (Legal Momentum, n.d.) now recognize *privileged communication* between therapists and their clients. This is a more specialized form of protection afforded to clients, which is granted only by statute. It means that, as in other legally recognized fiduciary relationships (for example, the attorney-client, clergy-penitent, and husband-wife relationships), information acquired in the course of therapy is, with some exceptions, legally exempt from having to be disclosed to a court or other legal proceeding. Typically, this provision is included in the state's code of evidence, which provides a state's rules of admissible evidence for legal proceedings. For example, according to the Florida Evidence Code (2016), Statute 90.503(2),

> a patient has a privilege to refuse to disclose, and to prevent any other person from disclosing, confidential communications or records made for the purpose of diagnosis or treatment of the patient's mental or emotional condition, including alcoholism and other drug addiction, between the patient and the psychotherapist, or persons who are participating in the diagnosis or treatment under the direction of the psychotherapist. This privilege includes any diagnosis made, and advice given, by the psychotherapist in the course of that relationship. ("Psychotherapist-patient privilege," 2016)

While there is some variability between states that recognize privileged communication in the therapist-client relationship, some common exceptions may include a communication (1) necessary to compel involuntary hospitalization if the therapist has reasonable belief that the client requires it; (2) made in the course of a court-ordered examination of the client's mental or emotional condition; (3) relevant to a claim or defense in a legal proceeding, which a client is making about the client's own mental condition; (4) relevant to a claim or defense being made in a proceeding about a deceased client; (5) made in the course of services obtained to commit a crime or tort, or to avoid detection of a crime or tort; (6) requested by a defendant in a criminal action to determine his sanity; (7) needed to show the client is in a mental or emotional state to be a danger to self or others to prevent the danger; and (8) needed to protect the welfare of a child reasonably believed by the therapist to have been a victim of a crime including child abuse (Psychotherapist-patient privilege [CA], 2007; Psychotherapist-patient privilege [FL], 2016; Stone, 2013).

Further, a communication can be treated as privileged only if it is confidentially disclosed to the therapist, that is, only to the therapist in the course of therapy, and not also to a third party such as a friend or family member. Inasmuch as the information in question is shared with others outside the professional relationship, the evidence is no longer considered confidential and is not legally entitled to be treated as privileged (NASW, 1991).

In addition to state recognition, federal courts now also enjoy privileged communication between therapists and clients pursuant to *Jaffee v. Redmond* (1996). In this case, Karen Beyer, a Licensed Clinical Social Worker, refused to comply with a judge's order to turn over the counseling records of her client, Mary Lu Redmond, an Illinois police officer who was in therapy with Beyer after having shot and killed a man in line of duty. Beyer contended that the information was privileged. The lower court found in favor of the petitioner; on appeal the decision was reversed. The Supreme Court affirmed. According to the court,

Like the spousal and attorney client privileges, the psychotherapist patient privilege is "rooted in the imperative need for confidence and trust." . . . Effective psychotherapy . . . depends upon an atmosphere of confidence and trust in which the patient is willing to make a frank and complete disclosure of facts, emotions, memories, and fears. Because of the sensitive nature of the problems for which individuals consult psychotherapists, disclosure of confidential communications made during counseling sessions may cause embarrassment or disgrace. For this reason, the mere possibility of disclosure may impede development of the confidential relationship necessary for successful treatment. (Opinion)

A further layer of *federal* protection of therapist-client confidentiality is contained in the Health Insurance Portability and Accountability Act of 1996 (HIPAA), according to which "psychotherapy notes" may not be shared by "covered entities" for any purpose without written authorization from the client. A covered entity, according to the Act, is any individual or institution involved in electronically transmitting health information for purposes of billing and payment for services or insurance coverage. "Psychotherapy notes" are "notes recorded (in any medium) by a health care provider who is a mental health professional documenting or analyzing the contents of conversation during a private counseling session or a group, joint, or family counseling session and that are separated from the rest of the individual's medical record." Such notes do not include information that would ordinarily be needed for "billing, payment, or healthcare operations" such as medication prescriptions, counseling session times, counseling modality used, clinical test results, diagnosis, treatment plan, prognosis, and progress (HIPAA, 1996, §164.501). However, exceptions (HIPAA, 1996, §164.508[2][i]) in which the client's authorization is not required include use or disclosure by the covered entity for its own training programs, to defend itself in a legal action or proceeding brought by the client, or which is required or permitted by law such as to prevent probable and imminent harm to the client or another, or to report child abuse. While the provisions of HIPAA preempt state law in case of conflict (HIPAA, 1996, §160.203), state laws can set stricter limits on what can be disclosed (HIPAA, 1996, §160.203[2][b]). For example, a state may require disclosure of information to prevent imminent serious harm to a third party whereas HIPPA only permits such disclosure consistent with state law (§164.512[c][iii]A).

Confidentiality and Respect for Privacy

As has been stressed in this chapter, therapist-client confidentiality, protected by both state and federal law, is necessary for the promotion of client welfare. Moreover, as mentioned, this protection also supports the ethical standard of *Client Autonomy*. In respecting the confidences reposed by clients, therapists treat clients as persons rather than as objects manipulated. Indeed, to guard clients' deepest and often darkest secrets against unjustified intrusions by others including legal authorities sends the message to clients that their therapists respect their personal privacy and do not seek to use them as mere means to the promotion of the welfare of others. Accordingly, when a court of law or other legal authority orders a therapist to disclose confidential or privileged information that could be damaging to the client or to the therapist-client relationship, the therapist should request that the court withdraw the order, limit it to the least information possible, or have the record sealed so that it unavailable to the public (NASW, 2017, 107.j). In exceptional situations in which therapists conclude that, unless confidential client information is disclosed, there is a high probability of imminent, serious harm to others, the therapists should do what they can to avoid wholesale sacrifice of client confidentiality. Thus, "when circumstances require the disclosure of confidential information, only essential information is revealed" (ACA, 2014, B.2.e). "[O]nly information that is directly relevant to the purpose for which the disclosure is made should be revealed" (NASW, 2017, 1.07[c]). In the case of preventing serious, imminent harm to another, this would be restricted only to information necessary to prevent the harm in question to an identifiable person. For example, if disclosure were warranted in Arty's case, this would include the name and contact information of the endangered person, Johnny Harmon, but it would not include that Johnny recently fired Arty, since the latter fact is not essential to preventing the potential harm. A more general statement such as "There is reason to believe that Arty presents a serious threat" may suffice.

It should be evident from the foregoing discussion of (state and federal) laws and codes of ethics regarding therapist-client confidentiality that the present legal and professional climate in the United States supports promotion of trust among therapists and their clients. As in the case of Arty, knowing when it is appropriate to disclose confidential information in instances of potential harm to others requires such a trusting environment. Without trust, clients would not venture to discuss their irrational inclinations with their therapists and therapists would miss the opportunity to help their clients deal satisfactorily with their issues or stave off dangerous, lamentable actions arising from such inclinations.

The next chapter raises another aspect of the therapist-client relationship that is also essential to the maintenance of trust. This aspect is therapists' ongoing provision to their clients of sufficiently informed, uncoerced consent to therapy.

Questions for Review and Reflection

1. Why should client confidentiality be treated by therapists as an essential part of the therapist-client relationship?

2. What ethic codes mentioned in this chapter treat harm to self or others as possible exceptions to therapist-client confidentiality? Do these codes of ethics *require* disclosure in such cases? Explain.

3. Briefly describe the facts in the 1976 California Supreme Court case *Tarasoff v. the Regents of the University of California*. What landmark conclusion did the court reach?

4. What is the difference between the duty to protect and the duty to warn?

5. In the case of Arty, suppose that Dr. Morgan practices in New Jersey where there is a duty to warn and/or protect if the client communicates a threat of serious physical harm to him- or herself or to an identifiable third party, and it would be reasonable for a therapist to believe that the client will carry out the threat (N.J. Rev. Stat. 2A:62A-16). If you were in Morgan's position would you believe you had a duty to warn or protect? If not, why not? If so, given the significant number of stakeholders, to whom would this

duty be owed? On what basis would you make this determination?

6. What if the applicable state law was that of Florida where there is no duty to warn or protect and the therapist is protected civilly and criminally whether or not disclosure is made when the decision is made in good faith? Would this law affect the manner in which you handled the ethical decision whether or not to disclose? Explain.

7. What if Arty did not have a history of any violent actions or a mental illness that disposed him toward violence? Would this affect your decision if you were Morgan? Explain. What if he did have such a history or such an illness?

8. How might Morgan lessen the probability that Arty might follow through on his threat?

9. What exceptions to client confidentiality do state laws commonly recognize?

10. What is privileged communication, and what is the difference between legally recognized client confidentiality and privileged communication?

11. Is privileged communication absolute or does it have exceptions? Explain.

12. What was the significance of the legal case of *Jaffee v. Redmond*?

13. How does the Health Insurance Portability and Accountability Act of 1996 (HIPAA) protect client confidentiality?

14. If state laws protecting client confidentiality conflict with HIPPA, which would apply: the state law in question or HIPPA?

15. According to the professional codes of ethics such as the American Counseling Association Code of Ethics or the National Association of Social Workers Code of Ethics, what should a therapist do if a court orders confidential client information?

Cases for Analysis

Using concepts discussed in this chapter, discuss and reflect on virtuous practice in the following scenarios.

1. Sasha is a 58-year-old divorced male who is in therapy with Minerva Gatsby, a clinical social worker for a community mental health clinic. Sasha has recently disclosed to Gatsby that he is very low on funds, in danger of losing his home, and has been contemplating robbing a bank. He states that he does not own a gun and does not want to "harm anybody" but that he "will pretend" that he has one for purposes of accomplishing the robbery. How should Gatsby handle this situation?

2. Victor Vale is a middle-aged male who is in treatment with Dr. Suzie Sturgeon. Victor's primary goal is to learn to lessen his angry outbursts at his wife and coworkers. Recently, he discovered that a friend of his wife, Arlene, had told his wife that she saw Victor at a motel with another woman. Victor conceded to Sturgeon that he is in fact having an extramarital affair, but that he has no intention of leaving his spouse. He expressed intense anger at Arlene and stated that "she will wish that she never opened her mouth." When asked to explain what he meant by this, Victor replied, "Never mind." He stated that if Sturgeon brings up this topic again, he will

terminate therapy. What options does Sturgeon have in dealing with this case?

3. Rita Blumson, a 75-year-old female has been in therapy for 6 months with Dr. Andrea Davinci, a psychologist. Last night, Rita confided to Davinci that she is exhausted and overwhelmed from taking care of her elderly spouse who is suffering from dementia. She states that she wants "no strings attached to him" any longer and is contemplating abandoning him at a crowded football stadium without leaving any identification on him. She has begged Davinci not to tell anyone about her plan. What are Davinci's ethical and legal responsibilities?

References

American Counseling Association. (2014). *ACA code of ethics.* Alexandria, VA: Author. Retrieved from counseling.org/resources/aca-code-of-ethics.pdf

American Psychiatric Association. (2013). *Diagnostic and statistical manual of mental disorders: DSM-5.* Washington, DC Author.

Aristotle. (2015). *Nicomachean ethics* (W. D. Ross, trans.). eBooks@Adelaide. Retrieved from https://ebooks.adelaide.edu.au/a/aristotle/nicomachean/

Berger, S. E., & Berger, M. A. (2009). Tarasoff "duty to warn" clarified. *National Psychologist.* Retrieved from http://nationalpsychologist.com/2009/03/tarasoff-%E2%80%9Cduty-to-warn%E2%80%9D-clarified/101056.html

Conducting a safety assessment. (n.d.). Become-An-Effective-Therapist.com. Retrieved from http://www.become-an-effective-psychotherapist.com/Conducting-A-Safety-Assessment.html

Dvoskin, J. A. (1990) What are the odds on predicting violent behavior? *Journal of California AMI, 2*(1). Retrieved from http://www.joeldvoskin.com/Dvoskin_1990.pdf

Eronen, M., Hakola, P., & Tiihonen, J. (1996). Mental disorders and homicidal behavior in Finland. *Arch Gen Psychiatry, 53*(6), 497–501.

Grabois, E. W. (1997). The liability of psychotherapists for breach of confidentiality. *Journal of Law and Health, 12*(39), 39–84.

Hammonds v. Aetna Casualty & Surety Company. 243 F.Supp. 793. (1965). Retrieved from http://law.justia.com/cases/federal/district-courts/FSupp/243/793/2386187/

The Health Insurance Portability and Accountability Act of 1996 (HIPAA). Pub.L. No. 104–191, 110 Stat. 1938. (1996). Retrieved from https://www.hhs.gov/sites/default/files/ocr/privacy/hipaa/administrative/combined/hipaa-simplification-201303.pdf

Hyldahl, R. S., & Richardson, B. (2011). Key considerations for using no-harm contracts with clients who self-injure. *Journal of Counseling and Development, 89*(1), 121–127.

Jaffee v. Redmond (95–266), 518 U.S. 1. (1996).

Lakeman, R. (1996). Dangerousness and mental illness: The research and implications for nursing practice. *Hawke's Bay Nurses Forum.*

Retrieved from http://www.testandcalc.com/Richard/resources/archive_papers/danger.htm

Legal Momentum. (n.d.). State confidentiality statutes. Washington, DC: Author. Retrieved from https://www.lsc.gov/sites/default/files/LSC/pdfs/8.%20%20Appendix%20VI%20%20Handout%2030%20State%20Confidentiality%20Chart%207-20.pdf

Living with schizophrenia. (n.d.). *Schizophrenia and dangerous behaviour.* Plymouth, Devon, UK: Author. Retrieved from https://www.livingwithschizopreniauk.org/advice-sheets/schizophrenia-and-dangerous-behaviour/

McSherry, B. (2004). Risk assessment by mental health professionals and the prevention of future violent behavior. Retrieved from http://www.aic.gov.au/media_library/publications/tandi_pdf/tandi281.pdf

Merrill, G. (2013). *Assessing client dangerousness to self and others: Stratified risk management approaches.* Berkeley, CA: Berkeley Social Welfare. Retrieved from http://socialwelfare.berkeley.edu/sites/default/files/users/gregmerrill/Assessing%20client%20dangerousness%20to%20self%20and%20others,%20stratified%20risk%20management%20approaches,%20Fall%202013.pdf

Ministry of Health, New Zealand. (1998). Guidelines for clinical risk assessment and management in mental health services. Retrieved from http://www.moh.govt.nz/notebook/nbbooks.nsf/0/2fe380c25ed2f1b34c25668600741eba/$FILE/mentalra.pdf

National Association of Social Workers. (1991). *NASW commission on education position statement: The school social worker and confidentiality.* Washington, DC: Author.

National Association of Social Workers. (2017). *Code of ethics of the National Association of Social Workers.* Washington, DC: Author. Retrieved from https://www.socialworkers.org/About/Ethics/Code-of-Ethics/Code-of-Ethics-English.aspx

National Collaborating Centre for Mental Health (UK). (n.d.). *Antisocial personality disorder: Treatment, management and prevention.* London, UK: National Institutes of Health. Retrieved from https://www.ncbi.nlm.nih.gov/books/NBK55331/

National Conference of State Legislatures. (2015). *Mental health professional's duty to warn.* Washington, DC: Authors. Retrieved from http://www.ncsl.org/research/health/mental-health-professionals-duty-to-warn.aspx

National Council on Alcoholism and Drug Dependence. (2017). *Alcohol, drugs, and crime.* New York, NY: Author. Retrieved from https://www.ncadd.org/about-addiction/alcohol-drugs-and-crime

New York Code § 9.46 (2013). Mental Hygiene Law. Reports of substantial risk or threat of harm by mental health professionals. Retrieved from http://codes.findlaw.com/ny/mental-hygiene-law/mhy-sect-9-46.html

Phillips, R. T. M. (2012). Predicting the risk of future dangerousness. *AMA Journal of Ethics, 14*(6), 472–476. Retrieved from http://journalofethics.ama-assn.org/2012/06/hlaw1-1206.html

Psychotherapist-patient privilege. (2007). California evidence code. Article 7, Section 110-1027. Retrieved from http://law.justia.com/codes/california/2007/evid/1010-1027.html

Psychotherapist-patient privilege. (2016). Florida evidence code. 90.503. Retrieved from http://law.justia.com/codes/california/2007/evid/1010-1027.html

Rueve, M. E., & Welton, R. S. (2008). Violence and mental illness. *Psychiatry*, *5*(5), 34–48. Retrieved from https://www.ncbi.nlm.nih.gov/pmc/articles/PMC2686644/

Sansone, R. A., & Sansone, L. A. (2012). Borderline personality and externalized aggression. *Innovations in Clinical Neuroscience*, *9*(3), 23–26. Retrieved from https://www.ncbi.nlm.nih.gov/pmc/articles/PMC3342993/

Stone, C. (2013). *State statutes regarding confidentiality and privilege for the students of school counselors.* Lake Havasu City, AZ: Alaska School Counselor Association. Retrieved from http://www.alaskaschoolcounselor.org/uploads/files/x/000/07a/4dd/privilege-state-by-state.pdf

Szalavitz, M. (2013). What really causes violence in psychosis? *Time*. Retrieved from http://healthland.time.com/2013/03/18/what-really-causes-violence-in-psychosis/

Tarasoff v. Regents of the University of California. (1976). California Supreme Court. 17 *California Reporter*, 3rd Series, 425. Retrieved from http://scocal.stanford.edu/opinion/tarasoff-v-regents-university-california-30278

6

BEING CANDID AND HONEST

Case Study: Withholding Information From a Depressed Client

Respect for client autonomy requires that clients be kept informed by therapists about the process of therapy. Without such a general provision clients would be subject to unjust manipulation and deception. Inasmuch as a primary reason why clients seek therapy in the first place is often because they feel nonautonomous (incapable of exercising rational, self-determination over their personal circumstances, emotions, thoughts, and deeds), therapists who fail to adequately involve clients in the therapeutic decision-making process by keeping them sufficiently informed defeat the very point of therapy (McWhirter, 1991). Accordingly, this chapter examines the nature of informed consent, its ethical and legal parameters, including exceptions and challenges to its provision. It begins with a case of suspected child abuse, and, in this context, shows how providing a client with informed consent can mean the difference between a client's trust in her therapist and a sense of unmitigated betrayal.

A CASE OF SUSPECTED CHILD ABUSE

The client in this case is Diana Dillinger, a 25-year-old, married woman with two children, a 4-year-old girl and a 7-year-old boy. Diana was in therapy with Carla George, LCSW, practicing in Georgia.

At the inception of therapy, Carla gave Diana an informed consent form to sign and carefully discussed the provisions of the form with the client to insure that she clearly understood these provisions before signing it. She was careful to point out that while what Diana disclosed in the course of therapy would be treated as confidential there were some exceptional circumstances under which such information might be disclosed without her authorization. For example, she explained that she was a mandatory reporter of child abuse, and therefore she was required to report suspected child abuse. As therapy progressed, Diana disclosed to Carla that when she was a small child, her mother, who was single, used to bring men home who would sexually abuse her. The abuse continued until she was 15, when she was taken out of the home and put into foster care. In foster care, she was both physically and sexually abused by her foster parents. At the age of 18, she had her two children out of wedlock and worked two jobs to support the children. Then, she met Bob, who was a wealthy real estate investor. Bob, she said, was "crazy" about her children and "provided a good home for all three of them." However, she added, "Bob's a really good guy and means well and all but sometimes he can get a bit rough with my son."

"Can you tell me about that?" asked Carla.

"He smacks him pretty hard sometimes when he does something wrong."

"Smacks him?"

"Yes, he's a big guy, and my son's small for his age. He does it with an open hand and all."

"Where does he hit him?"

"Once did it on his face. Left a nasty bruise on his cheek!"

"How often does he hit him?"

"Only when my son talks back to him, doesn't do his chores or do what he's told. He says he wants my son to grow up to be a man."

Carla, in turn, reminded Diana that she had a legal requirement to report suspected cases of child abuse, and Diana pleaded with her not to do so.

"Is this really child abuse, even though Bob means well?"

"Yes, according to Georgia law, if Bob hits hard enough to leave a bruise, then it's physical abuse, regardless of his motives."

"Oh please don't turn him in! I don't know what we would do without him!"

Notwithstanding Diana's pleas, Carla informed Child Protective Services (CPS) of the suspected child abuse, and the state launched an investigation. Bob, in turn, separated from Diana and sued for divorce and full custody of both children on the grounds that Diana was an unfit mother. However, Diana continued to see Carla through this difficult time. Allegations of abuse came back unfounded (which only meant that the abuse was not proven, not that it didn't occur). The judge hearing the custody case ordered Carla to produce her mental health records since Diana's suitability as a parent was called into question by one of the parties (Comment, 2001). Diana became increasingly despondent about the possible loss of her two children, and she began to contemplate suicide. Further, in Diana's counseling records was a diagnosis of Borderline Personality Disorder (BPD), of which Diana herself was unaware. Since Carla was convinced that disclosure of this information to the court presented a probable and imminent danger to her client's welfare, she filed a motion to protect this information, and the judge responded by ordering an independent psychological evaluation so as not to pierce the therapist-client privilege (Comment, 2001). At the same time, however, Diana began asking Carla for a copy of her counseling records since she wanted to know what would have been revealed about her.

Diana's case clearly underscores the importance of providing informed consent to clients who enter into therapy. Indeed, if, contrary to fact, Carla had not disclosed, at the outset of therapy, that she was a mandatory reporter of suspected child abuse, then Carla's having been informed by Diana about the apparent physical abuse of her son by Bob would have presented a more daunting moral problem for Carla. For this would have been a clear violation of respect for client autonomy as it would have been to treat Diana like an object manipulated. This is because Diana would have had a reasonable expectation that such a disclosure would be protected by her therapist. True, Diana did not seem to be clear enough about Georgia's definition of child abuse, which underscores the need for therapists to be clear about exceptions to confidentiality. In particular, she could have provided some examples of physical abuse.

Candor is, as such, an essential aspect of virtuous practice. In the present case, Carla's not having shared Diana's diagnosis of BPD with her in advance could have been utterly destructive to Diana had she ended up finding this out in court. Even if Carla was led to disclose the information to Diana as a result of the court order, the client would likely have felt betrayed by her therapist for not having been informed sooner. Thus, keeping the client informed in a timely way is ethically important. A client should not have to find out about such things as her diagnosis accidentally. Informed consent is accordingly not a moment in time. It is not transacted exclusively at the beginning of therapy, as though it was something to get out of the way to proceed with therapy. Instead, ethically, informed consent is a *process that proceeds in a timely fashion throughout the course of therapy as new, pertinent information becomes available.* (What information, in particular, is pertinent is discussed below.) Without such a policy of ongoing, timely informed consent, the idea that the relationship is a joint venture between therapist and client, based on trust, is empty pretense.

However, informed consent also has rational limits. In some cases, respect for client autonomy may be overridden by client welfare. In the case at hand, Diana appeared to be clinically depressed and had suicidal ideation. Moreover, Carla believed that disclosing to her that she had BPD might lead her to seriously harm or kill herself. So should she have shared this information with her client under these circumstances?

LEGAL LIMITS OF INFORMED CONSENT

State laws typically require therapists to provide copies, or at least a report, of a client's mental health records upon written request by the client. For example, Florida Statute (FS) 456.057 (2016) requires that mental health practitioners provide "copies of all reports and records relating to such [mental] examination or treatment including . . . insurance information." However, according to the statute, a mental health practitioner "may provide a report of examination and treatment in lieu of copies of records." Still, there are also limits to access. For example, according to the New York Mental Hygiene Law (2013), Access to Clinical Records 33.16(c)3,

> If, after consideration of all the attendant facts and circumstances, the practitioner or treating practitioner determines that the requested review of all or part of the clinical record can reasonably be expected to cause substantial and identifiable harm to the patient or client or others . . . the facility may accordingly deny access to all or a part of the record and may grant access to a prepared summary of the record.

Case law has also established precedent for limiting a client's access to records in cases where such access could be harmful or detrimental to the client. In *Canterbury v. Spence* (1972), the United States Court of Appeals for the District of Columbia Circuit maintained that a medical practitioner can withhold information from the patient if the practitioner believes that disclosing it to the patient may cause bodily or psychological harm to the patient. However, the court makes clear that this exception to informed consent "must be carefully circumscribed . . . for otherwise it might devour the disclosure rule itself" (Section VI, para. 49). As such, in Diana's case, consistent with state law, Carla may have had legal as well as ethical grounds to withhold information from Diana about her diagnosis of BPD, or other parts of her counseling records that might have caused substantial harm to her if they had been revealed.

As a virtuous therapist, Carla would regret such a decision and would do her utmost to rectify the situation as much and as soon as possible. For example, as soon as she determined that Diana was capable of receiving the previously withheld information with negligible risk of harm, it would then have been incumbent on her to provide the information to her client. In this way, a therapist can preserve the trust on which both respect for client autonomy and promotion of client welfare depend.

WHEN IS INFORMED CONSENT INFORMED?

Clearly, there may be some information that is pertinent to disclose to a client yet other information that may be unnecessary to disclose. For example, Diana would not ordinarily need to know the history of the modality Carla intends to use (the name of the person who developed it, the year it was conceived, etc.); but she may reasonably want to know some facts about the approach itself, for example, that it tries to correct irrational beliefs, change behavior, help the client take responsibility, confront emotions in the here and now, reclaim personal autonomy, relieve stress using biofeedback, and so on. The ethical and legal standard for what a therapist should disclose to a client can be gleaned from the earlier cited case of *Canterbury v. Spence*. This case involved a patient who received lumbar surgery to relieve low back pain (laminectomy) without having been told by his physician that there was a 1% risk of paralysis from the surgery. Citing Waltz and Scheuneman, the court declared that a risk is "material when a reasonable person, in what the physician knows or should know to be the patient's position, would be likely to attach significance to the risk or cluster of risks in deciding whether or not to forego the proposed therapy" (Section 5, para. 44). And more generally, it declared,

> True consent to what happens to one's self is the informed exercise of a choice, and that entails an opportunity to evaluate knowledgeably the options available and the risks attendant upon each. The average patient has little or no understanding of the medical arts, and ordinarily has only his physician to whom he can look for enlightenment with which to reach an intelligent decision. From these almost axiomatic considerations springs the need, and in turn the requirement, of a reasonable divulgence by physician to patient to make such a decision possible. (Section III, para. 28)

Pursuant to *Canterbury*, the stated standard of what a *reasonable person* would want to know can set both an ethical as well as legal guideline for the provision of informed consent in psychotherapy as well as medicine. Clearly, as a reasonable person, a client in therapy would want to know the therapeutic options available as well as the risks and effectiveness of each option. Thus, a client with Panic Disorder, presumed to be reasonable, would want to know the alternative treatments available and the risks and efficacy of each, for example, the use of cognitive-behavioral therapy versus antianxiety medication. Perhaps the therapist in question is not legally permitted to prescribe antianxiety medications; or she is not otherwise competent to practice an alternative treatment. Nevertheless, the client is entitled to know about the treatment in question, its risks (side effects, contraindications, etc.), and how comparatively effective it is. This is not a decision that the therapist should make for the client; nor should the therapist attempt to pressure, intimidate, cajole, or otherwise manipulate the client's choice. Informed consent aims at empowering the client to act autonomously. It is therefore inconsistent with the point of providing informed consent, in the first place, to prevent the client from autonomously deciding.

A reasonable person in therapy would want to know if a treatment in question is conventional (generally accepted) or experimental (American Counseling Association [ACA], 2014, G.2.a). Thus, clients have both a legal and ethical right not be used as guinea pigs in trying out new approaches. This does not mean that a therapist who has carefully researched a new counseling technique should not be permitted to use it. Instead, this information needs to be part of the client's informed consent. For example, some relatively new therapies, such as eye movement desensitization and reprocessing (EMDR) used to alleviate the effects of traumas, have had controversial histories, and therapists who employ them have an ethical responsibility to inform the client about the controversy (Carroll, n.d.). "When counselors use developing or innovative techniques/procedures/modalities, they explain the potential risks, benefits, and ethical considerations of using such techniques/procedures/modalities" and they "work to minimize any potential risks or harm when using these techniques/procedures/modalities" (ACA, 2014, C.7.b).

Clients would also reasonably want to know what sort of technologies might be used in the therapy. For example, while biofeedback is relatively safe, some patients may not want to have sensors hooked up to various parts of their bodies. Moreover, they would want to know the qualifications the therapist has in utilizing the technology in question, as well as in utilizing any other intended technique, modality, approach, or technology (ACA, 2014, A.2.b).

More generally, a reasonable person in therapy would also want to know the qualifications of the therapist, including how long the therapist has been practicing, their credentials and/or degrees, and whether they hold a valid state license to practice in their field of mental health (ACA, 2014, C.4). Honest practitioners also do not mislead about their credentials. For example, a practitioner who holds a master's degree in mental health counseling and a doctorate in educational leadership does not represent himself as a doctor in the context of providing therapy (ACA, 2014, C.4.d). Further, candid and honest practitioners also disclose their *lack* of qualifications. Therapists who are not competent to treat a particular type of problem, or who do not have certain credentials, do not allow clients to believe that they do hold such qualifications or credentials by remaining silent. Thus, an ethical practitioner does not permit a client to refer to him as "Dr." when the therapist lacks the qualification; or to believe that the therapist is a specialist in a certain therapeutic modality when the therapist lacks the requisite training. Instead, the virtuous therapist dispels the false belief by informing the client that she does not have the supposed qualification or credential.

A client would reasonably want to know with whom the information disclosed in therapy is to be shared. As discussed previously, this includes possible exceptions to confidentiality where information may be shared with endangered third parties, government agencies, or law enforcement. However, others with whom the information is shared may include supervisors, consultants, other therapists, and office staff. Clients therefore have a right to be informed about the sharing of the personal information with such other individuals. In addition, certain types of client information may be shared with *third party payers* such as insurance, HMOs, and managed care companies. Inasmuch as these organizations require specific types of client information to provide reimbursement for services rendered, clients would reasonably want to know what information would be shared with them. In particular, therapists inform clients that, for purpose of reimbursement, third party payers may require information regarding

> medication prescription and monitoring, counseling session start and stop times, the modalities and frequencies of treatment furnished, results of clinical tests, and any summary of the following items: Diagnosis, functional status, the treatment plan, symptoms, prognosis, and progress to date. (Health Insurance Portability and Accountability Act [HIPAA], 1996, § 164.501)

In some cases, a client may not want a third party payer to know her clinical diagnosis or other required information and may prefer to pay out of pocket. In informing the client, as close to the inception of therapy as possible, about the kinds of information that may be shared, and with whom it may be shared, the client is afforded maximum autonomy to decide whether to consent to such disclosures or to pursue a different course of action.

Clients would reasonably want to know about the fee for counseling, possible arrangements for paying the fee, and how nonpayment of the fee is to be handled (ACA, 2014, A.2.b). They would also want to know about the length of treatment, how often sessions are, and how long each session lasts. Indeed, treatment length is a variable that often depends on the type and severity of the client's problem. Accordingly, it may not be possible to provide an accurate estimate of how much time it may take to successfully complete therapy. As such, the therapist explains to her client that the time can vary and provides a reasonable estimate of the range of time it may generally take to treat the problem, consistent with the type of problem (when diagnosed), and modality being used. For example, cognitive-behavior therapy may take in the range of 10 to 15 or 50 to 60 minute sessions but can be longer or shorter depending on the type of problem and severity (Cognitive Behavioural Therapy, n.d.). Because specific information about the nature of the problem may not be evident at the inception of therapy, or may be reassessed as therapy progresses, informed consent about the length of treatment can be ongoing and in need of periodic updating.

Clients as reasonable persons would want to know their role in the therapeutic process, in particular, that they will be participating in constructing a therapeutic plan, and that they may refuse to participate in any aspect of therapy with which they do not feel comfortable. For example, a client may not want to engage in exposure therapy and may prefer a different approach. Virtuous therapists are flexible within reason and do what they can to work within the client's sets of preferences and beliefs. Still, there are limits to accommodating clients who make unreasonable requests; and the therapist may refuse to accommodate a client when doing so lacks therapeutic value or poses a significant risk of harm to the client. As such, therapists inform clients of the consequences of refusing to make reasonable cooperative efforts to participate in a therapeutic plan (ACA, 2014, A.2.b).

Reasonable clients would also want to know what information about them has been placed in their files; and therapists should therefore inform clients of their right to such information. Indeed, this information belongs to the client, it is his property, and, therefore, should have access to it. "Courts have established the patient's common law property right to the information in their records, so the transfer of this 'property' is only just if it is freely chosen by the patient" (Borkosky, 2013). Federal law also entitles clients to inspect and receive a copy of the information in their records (HIPAA, 1996, §164.524). (This does not include "psychotherapy notes," however. See also Chapter 11.) True, as in Carla's case, there may be occasions in which the therapist justifiably refuses to permit the client access to this information, or to part of it, due to concern for client welfare. However, as the *Canterbury* court (1972) admonished, such circumstances are exceptional and must not be permitted to "devour the disclosure rule" (Section VI, para. 49).

Clients who are reasonable would also want to know if their sessions are being electronically recorded or otherwise observed (ACA, 2014, B.6.c). Indeed, to do so without first obtaining the client's informed consent is to violate the client's autonomy, to treat him as an object manipulated. As stated, the information disclosed by the client in the course of therapy belongs to the client. "To duplicate this information electronically or otherwise share it without the client's express, advance permission is to deprive the client of her autonomous control over her own property" (Cohen & Cohen, 1999, pp. 80–81).

It cannot be assumed that clients understand the nature of therapy itself, regardless of what modality is used. It is commonly assumed by clients who have not previously been in therapy that counseling is advice giving and that therapists' primary purpose is to listen to the problems clients are having and to provide advice about how to remedy them. The client often does not understand that he needs to solve his own problem(s) and that the therapist is there to facilitate such constructive change. Clients often come to therapy feeling powerless over their own lives and think that the therapist will tell them what to do and that the problems will be solved. They often do not understand that their problems are often (although not always) a result, not primarily of external factors, but rather the manner in which they frame them. They think that the therapist is there to show them what to do to change the external or "objective" reality where it is rather than their "subjective" reality or psychological processes that are primarily the problem. For example, a client may believe that her problem is that nothing ever goes her way and thus blames others or the world for her plight, failing to understand that her interpretation of reality is contributing to her depression. Therapists therefore need to make clear to clients that they will need to work to make constructive changes *in themselves* and that counseling will not work unless they are willing to expend the effort. Without this admonition, consent to therapy is not informed and clients may be wasting their time and money as well as that of their therapists.

As previously discussed, as a reasonable person, a client would also want to know the nature and limits of confidentiality of client information. In therapy, clients may reveal the deepest secrets about themselves to their therapists. Knowledge of how this information is to be treated can be crucial to the establishing of a bond of trust between client and therapist. Without reasonable assurance that the client's privacy will be respected, a reasonable client would not venture to disclose information that could subsequently prove embarrassing or harmful to the client if made public. At the same time, the candid therapist does not misrepresent the boundaries of confidentiality. "Everything you tell me is confidential" may entice the client to disclose her personal and private information, but it is deceitful and manipulative. As gleaned from the case of Diana, it is essential that clients also be informed about possible exceptions to confidentiality (see Chapter 5).

It is, indeed, remarkable that Diana continued with therapy even after Carla disclosed the suspected child abuse and even after her husband left her as a result of the disclosure. Such commitment is not likely when the therapist fails to treat the client with the dignity and respect of an autonomous agent. This requires perceiving her as a reasonable person worthy of being kept reasonably informed, that is, in the manner described in this chapter.

CIRCUMSTANTIAL INFORMATION AS PART OF INFORMED CONSENT

Still, the extent of information that a client may reasonably want to know is also a function of the variable and often changing context or circumstances of counseling. For example, as a part of ongoing informed consent, a client who suggests that the therapist and the client enter into a social or business relationship needs to be informed about the problematic nature of forming personal relationships outside the counseling relationship. A therapist who resides in a small urban town and is therefore likely to have interactions with his clients outside the counseling room needs to discuss the potential problems raised by such outside interactions. A therapist who teaches may need to inform a potential client that he will not continue to counsel him if he enrolls in one of his classes. The challenges raised by such dual or multiple role relationships are discussed in Chapter 9.

Providing informed consent can also be affected by whether the counseling relationship is to be conducted face-to-face or online. In fact, some states have adopted legal standards of informed consent that must be satisfied in conducting online counseling. This aspect of informed consent is discussed in Chapter 12.

Inasmuch as counseling records are now often being stored in an online environment, clients may reasonably want to know this information and what safety precautions are being taken to ensure that their confidential information is being adequately protected against unauthorized access. Likewise, a client may also reasonably want to know what measures are being taken to protect their counseling records even if they are not being stored online. This aspect of the counseling context is addressed in Chapter 11.

CAPACITY AS A CONDITION OF INFORMED CONSENT

The foregoing informational requirements of informed client consent assume that the client is capable of providing informed consent in the first place. However, a client may not, in fact, be able to be reasonably informed and hence able to provide informed consent. Clearly, a precondition is the *capacity* of the client to give informed consent. "A person is capable with respect to a treatment . . . if the person is able to understand the information that is relevant to making a decision about the treatment . . . and able to appreciate the reasonably foreseeable consequences of a decision or lack of decision" (Health Care Consent Act [Ontario], 1996). Although state law varies regarding when a person possesses decision-making capacity, there are some necessary conditions: (1) ability to make a choice, (2) ability to understand information relevant to the decision at hand such as diagnosis and proposed treatment plan, (3) ability to appreciate the consequences of the situation such as the nature of the illness, alternative treatments and their consequences, and the implications of foregoing treatment, and (4) the ability to think rationally, that is, the ability to think logically in reaching a decision (Leo, 1999). For example, according to California statute (Probate Code, 1999, Section 811[a]):

> A determination that a person is of unsound mind or lacks the capacity . . . to make medical decisions . . . shall be supported by evidence of a deficit in at least one of the following mental functions, subject to . . . evidence of a correlation between the deficit or deficits and the decision or acts in question:
>
> 1. Alertness and attention, including, but not limited to, the following:
>
>   (A) Level of arousal or consciousness.
>
>   (B) Orientation to time, place, person, and situation.
>
>   (C) Ability to attend and concentrate.
>
> 2. Information processing, including, but not limited to, the following:
>
>   (A) Short- and long-term memory, including immediate recall.
>
>   (B) Ability to understand or communicate with others, either verbally or otherwise.
>
>   (C) Recognition of familiar objects and familiar persons.
>
>   (D) Ability to understand and appreciate quantities.
>
>   (E) Ability to reason using abstract concepts.

(F) Ability to plan, organize, and carry out actions in one's own rational self-interest.

(G) Ability to reason logically.

3. Thought processes. Deficits in these functions may be demonstrated by the presence of the following:

(A) Severely disorganized thinking.

(B) Hallucinations.

(C) Delusions.

(D) Uncontrollable, repetitive, or intrusive thoughts.

4. Ability to modulate mood and affect. Deficits in this ability may be demonstrated by the presence of a pervasive and persistent or recurrent state of euphoria, anger, anxiety, fear, panic, depression, hopelessness or despair, helplessness, apathy or indifference, that is inappropriate in degree to the individual's circumstances.

Legal provisions such as (3) and (4) above do not mean that clients such as Diana who have serious mental disorders lack the capacity to give informed consent, although this can be the case when, due to the mental disorder (for example, Schizophrenia or Major Depression), the client lacks the capacity to comprehend and appreciate the information reposed, especially information about the nature of the treatment, alternatives treatments, and the risks and benefits of each. In cases in which a client lacks decision-making capacity, a surrogate is necessary to provide informed consent. In such cases, the decision should be made consistent with what the client would likely have wanted. If this cannot be determined, then the surrogate should decide according to what is in the best interest of the client. It is important to emphasize that clients who lack decision-making capacity are still persons and are entitled to be treated as such. This includes respecting the confidentiality of the client.

> When counseling minor clients or adult clients who lack the capacity to give voluntary, informed consent, counselors protect the confidentiality of information received—in any medium—in the counseling relationship as specified by federal and state laws, written policies, and applicable ethical standards. (ACA, 2014, B.5.a)

Lack of capacity may also be temporary. Thus, a client may be treated (for example, medicated) and, consequently, regain the capacity to make informed health care decisions. In such cases, a client should be treated no differently than any other self-determining client. It is also important to mention that a client who lacks decision-making capacity is not necessarily *incompetent*. The latter is a legal determination that requires declaration by a court of law. In contrast, a therapist can determine whether or not a client lacks capacity.

In some cases a court can determine that a person is incompetent to make specific decisions such as financial ones. In other cases, a person can be declared incompetent to make personal decisions, including health care decisions. In the latter case, the court appoints a guardian to make such decisions on behalf of the person. Such legal declarations of incompetence are not rendered unless the client can be shown to be incapable of safely taking care of himself or managing his own affairs (Leo, 1999).

In any event, whether or not a client who lacks decision-making capacity is declared incompetent by a court, this does not mean that the client is incapable of making decisions within her capacity. "When counseling minors, incapacitated adults, or other persons unable to give voluntary consent, counselors seek the assent of clients to services and include them in decision making as appropriate" (ACA, 2014, A.2.d). Thus, the therapist explains the nature of the therapy to the client in language appropriate to the client's level of understanding and respects her wishes as appropriate. For example, the client may object to certain types of behavioral exercises. Clearly, building trust and cooperation is not possible when the client is cajoled, forced, tricked, or otherwise manipulated into doing things she does not want to do. Such tactics are likely to prove to be self-defeating. In contrast, adjusting therapy in a manner that enlists the client's assent is more likely to lead to constructive change. This may include holding off on the assignment until the client is ready to undertake it or substituting a more congenial one instead.

As persons, all clients must not be manipulated or forced to undergo treatment. Consent that is not voluntary is legally as well as morally invalid. A patient who is manipulated or forced to undergo treatment is treated like a mere object, not a person. This is a blatant violation of the Standard of Client Autonomy. Legally, unless declared personally incompetent by a court of law (Menninger, n.d.), even a person who is involuntarily hospitalized has (in the absence of an emergency situation) a constitutional right to refuse treatment based on the due process clause of the Fourteenth Amendment (*Rennie v. Klein*, 1978). State statutes follow suit. For example, according to Florida's Patient's Bill of Rights, "A patient has the right to be given by his or her health care provider information concerning diagnosis, planned course of treatment, alternatives, risks, and prognosis . . ."; and "has the right to refuse any treatment based on information required by this paragraph . . ." (FS 381.026, 2016). Coercive means of affecting client cooperation in therapy is an affront to, and abridgment of, this constitutionally protected sphere of privacy.

INFORMED CONSENT AND THE TERMINATION OF THERAPY

Inasmuch as informed consent is an ongoing process, it is also an essential aspect of the termination of therapy. Therapy must therefore not be terminated in the absence of the client's informed understanding of the nature and purposes of termination. In the event a therapist anticipates that therapy will be prematurely terminated, discontinued, or disrupted, the therapist "should notify clients promptly and seek the transfer, referral, or continuation of services in relation to the clients' needs and preferences" (National Association of Social Workers [NASW], 2017, 1.17.e). In the event that the therapist anticipates leaving an employment setting, he "should inform clients of appropriate options for the continuation of services and of the benefits and risks of the options" (NASW, 2017, 1.17.f).

When a client is no longer benefitting from counseling, but the client's problems persist, the honest therapist informs the client of the same and makes an appropriate referral. The honest therapist neither misrepresents to himself nor to the client about the efficacy of therapy. If the therapist is unable to help the client, then it is time to refer. On the other hand, if counseling appears to have been reasonably successful and therapy is no longer indicated, then the therapist provides pretermination therapy (ACA, 2014, 11.c), which prepares the client to apply what he has learned in course of therapy without reliance on therapy sessions on a regular basis. In this context, the therapist works cooperatively with the client to establish a mutually agreed on schedule of remaining sessions. For example, there may be a session scheduled every other week until therapy is terminated. Here, the client should be informed that the therapist is not abandoning him and that if he should want to come in for an occasional "checkup," even after the termination of therapy is reached, then he may do so (Corey, 2005, p. 525). Such assurance that therapy is still available if the client deems appropriate respects client's self-determination, whereas cutting the client off without recourse undermines client autonomy.

INFORMED CONSENT IN COUPLES AND FAMILY COUNSELING

Respect for client autonomy also requires defining carefully who the client is. The client is the one to whom the therapist owes primary responsibilities. However, in the case of couples or family counseling, there are several possibilities: The couple or family is the client, and/or each partner or family member is a separate client (Pukay-Martin, 2008). For example, the ACA asserts,

> In couples and family counseling, counselors clearly define who is considered "the client" and discuss expectations and limitations of confidentiality. . . . In the absence of an agreement to the contrary, the couple or family is considered to be the client. (2014, B.4.b)

However, since what is true of the whole is not necessarily true of the part, it is possible for something to be good for the couple or family and harmful to a partner or family member. For example, it could be good for a couple for both partners to know that one of the partners has erectile dysfunction and is avoiding having sex because of it; but it can also be emotionally destructive for the partner who has the problem and refuses to disclose this information on his own. In the therapeutic context of family and couples counseling, we therefore recommend that the individual family members or partners, not the relationship itself (familial unit or partnership), be regarded as the clients. Indeed, in some cases, as in cases of abusive relationships and child sexual abuse, perceiving the couple or the family as the client to whom the therapist owes a primary responsibility may miss the point that some relationships are not worth preserving. Accordingly, respecting confidentiality is as important in couples and family counseling as it is other areas of counseling; for it respects the dignity of each individual member of the relationship, which is a primary responsibility of the therapist to the client. As Standard 2 of the American Association of Marriage and Family Therapists (AAMFT) Code of Ethics succinctly states, "*Marriage and family therapists have unique confidentiality concerns because the client in a therapeutic relationship may be more than one person. Therapists respect and guard the confidences of each individual client*" (AAMFT, 2015, emphasis in original). As such "the therapist may not reveal any individual's confidences to others in the client unit without the prior written permission of that individual" (AAMFT, 2015, 2.2).

Nevertheless, if a therapist wishes to define the client as the couple or family, and to limit what information is kept confidential based on what is best for the client, so defined, then the therapist needs to include this information as part of the couple's or family's informed consent agreement, and each partner or family member needs to be apprised and in agreement (NASW, 2017, 1.07.g). Otherwise, the therapist fails to respect the dignity and self-determination of the parties to the relationship and therefore treats them as objects manipulated. This, in turn, destroys the therapist-client trust on which successful therapy depends.

INFORMED CONSENT AND THERAPIST-CLIENT TRUST

It should be clear from this chapter that informed consent, along with confidentiality, is key to promoting a trusting relationship between therapist and client. As evident in Carla's case, a therapist cannot always anticipate what may arise in the course of therapy to strain the bond of trust. Therapists who take care to keep their clients informed on an ongoing basis are likely to keep the client's trust through turbulent times. As such, Diana continued to see Carla even after she disclosed the suspected child abuse in accordance with her legal obligation. Further, when the court asked that Diana's counseling records be produced, Carla sought to protect this information on the grounds that its disclosure posed a probable and imminent danger to her client. Indeed, had the judge refused to order an independent mental evaluation, and insisted on disclosure of the information in the counseling records, particularly the diagnosis of BPD, this could have been devastating to her client. This underscores the importance of providing clients with informed consent on an ongoing basis. Carla's failure to inform her client of this information in a timely fashion might have otherwise been a misjudgment with dangerous repercussions for her client. Hindsight is, of course, always better than foresight. Still, a virtuous therapist is aware of the potential vicissitudes that could undermine client trust and acts responsibly to keep the client informed. Legal parameters of this ongoing responsibility to keep the client informed include the exercise of discretion when disclosure of certain information portends serious harm to a client. But such circumstances are the exception, not the rule. However, as in Carla's case, nondisclosure of such information is only temporary until the therapist deems the client capable of safely receiving the withheld information. Otherwise, the therapist-client trust on which successful therapy depends can be undermined.

Questions for Review and Reflection

1. Why is providing informed client consent to therapy necessary?

2. In the case of Diana, why was it important for Carla to include exceptions to confidentiality as part of Diana's informed consent? Was the information Diana received about the reporting of physical abuse adequate?

3. In your estimation, was Carla a candid therapist? Explain.

4. Is informed consent a moment in time or a process? Explain.

5. Was it appropriate for Carla not to have shared Diana's diagnosis with her? Explain.

6. Would Carla *ordinarily* have had a legal right to see what her diagnosis was? Explain.

7. What measure might a candid therapist take to ensure that the therapist-client trust is not weakened after information in the client's records had been intentionally withheld from the client?

8. In the legal case of *Canterbury v. Spence*, what precedent (legal rule) did the court establish with regard to providing a patient informed consent? What possible exception to informed consent did the court make? What standard did the court adopt for determining whether particular information should be disclosed to a patient?

9. Based on the standard of disclosure set in *Canterbury v. Spence*, list 11 sorts of information that should be provided to a client for the client to give informed consent to therapy?

10. As discussed in this chapter, some information included in informed consent may depend on the context or circumstances of therapy. Provide at least one example of your own, other than the ones provided in the chapter.

11. What conditions are necessary for a client to possess capacity to make decisions about their treatment?

12. Carla did not disclose Diana's diagnosis of Borderline Personality Disorder to Diana because of her state of mind. In your estimation, did Diana have capacity to make her own treatment decisions? Apply the legal standards discussed in this chapter to respond to this question. Would it have been appropriate for Diana to have a surrogate to make her treatment decisions? Explain.

13. What does it mean to be "incompetent"? Is incompetence all or nothing, or can a person be incompetent in some respects but not in others? Explain. Who has the authority to render a judgment of incompetence? Who decides whether a client lacks capacity?

14. Do the fact that young children lack capacity to make their own treatment decisions mean that therapists do not need to get their informed consent? Explain.

15. What information should be addressed with the client in terminating the counseling relationship? What if the therapist intends to leave the practice?

16. In couples or family counseling, who is the client, in your estimation? What implications does this have for confidentiality and informed consent?

Cases for Analysis

Using concepts discussed in this chapter, discuss and reflect on virtuous practice in the following situations.

1. Dr. Amelia Armstrong, an 80-year-old retired physician, has been in therapy for issues related to loneliness after the death of her husband. Her psychologist is 45-year-old Dr. Calhoun Winters. Armstrong, a prominent former physician in her city, prides herself on her intellectual acumen and still keeps abreast of trends in her field. Recently, Winters has begun to strongly suspect that Armstrong has the beginning symptoms of dementia; however, he wants to rule out any other physical ailments that might be causing her apparent short-term memory loss. When he broaches the topic of Armstrong's memory possibly not being as good as it formerly was (but never mentioning dementia), she becomes angry and leaves the session early. Winters follows up with a phone call to Armstrong who admonishes him for being ageist and states that she will not continue with the sessions unless he "stops this crap." How should Winters proceed?

2. Fiona, a 36-year-old mother of two, is in counseling with Cheryl Manning, a mental health counselor. Her sister, Renata, age 40, is also in treatment for similar issues. Both suffer from flashbacks related to sexual abuse by a close family member who is now deceased. Fiona believes that this abuse stopped when she was 8 years old when she "ordered" the perpetrator to "stop." However, Renata recently disclosed to Manning that she witnessed her sister being abused on one occasion when Fiona was 12 years old. Renata has asked that Manning not disclose this information to Fiona because "this will destroy her." What should Manning do? Can she justify not disclosing this information to Fiona and still remain a candid and honest therapist?

3. Brigham Hall, a 25-year-old male, is in treatment with Rona Farmer, a mental health counselor, in a small town clinical practice. Hall recently discovered that he was adopted as an infant and is struggling with issues of betrayal and anger. He no longer speaks to members of his family and states that he "can't believe that they all lied to me for my entire life." He has become estranged even from his friend and has searched extensively to find his birth mother, albeit unsuccessfully. Both Farmer and Hall have lived in the same small town since childhood, and Farmer believes that she knows someone who probably has knowledge of Hall's parentage, a former county clerk. There are potential legal, ethical, and therapeutic implications, including privacy issues of Farmer disclosing the name of this individual. What would you do in this case?

References

American Association of Marriage and Family Therapists. (2015). *Code of ethics.* Alexandria, VA: Author. Retrieved from http://www.aamft.org/iMIS15/AAMFT/Content/Legal_Ethics/Code_of_Ethics.aspx

American Counseling Association. (2014). *ACA code of ethics.* Alexandria, VA: Author. Retrieved from counseling.org/resources/aca-code-of-ethics.pdf

Borkosky, B. G. (2013). Patient access to records: The invisible confidentiality right. *National Psychologist*. Retrieved from http://nationalpsychologist.com/2013/11/patient-access-to-records-the-invisible-confidentiality-right/102340.html

Canterbury v. Spence, 464 F.2d 772. (D.C. Cir. 1972). Retrieved from http://biotech.law.lsu.edu/cases/consent/canterbury_v_spence.htm

Carroll, R. T. (n.d.). Eye movement desensitization and reprocessing (EMDR). *The Skeptics Dictionary*. Retrieved from http://skepdic.com/emdr.html

Cognitive Behavioural Therapy (CBT). (n.d.). Patient. Retrieved from http://patient.info/health/cognitive-behavioural-therapy-cbt-leaflet

Cohen, E. D., & Cohen, G. S. (1999). *The virtuous therapist: Ethical practice of counseling and psychotherapy*. Belmont, CA: Wadsworth.

Comment. (2001). The use of mental health records in child custody proceedings. *Journal of the American Academy of Matrimonial Lawyers*, *17*, 159–181. Retrieved from http://www.aaml.org/sites/default/files/use%20of%20mental%20health%20records-article.pdf

Corey, G. (2005). *Theory and practice of counseling and psychotherapy*. Belmont, CA: Brooks/Cole.

Health Care Consent Act, S.O. 1996, c. 2, Sched. A. (1996). Retrieved from https://www.ontario.ca/laws/statute/96h02

The Health Insurance Portability and Accountability Act of 1996 (HIPAA). Pub.L. No. 104-191, 110 Stat. 1938. (1996). Retrieved from https://www.hhs.gov/sites/default/files/ocr/privacy/hipaa/administrative/combined/hipaa-simplification-201303.pdf

Leo, R. J. (1999). Competency and the capacity to make treatment decisions: A primer for primary care physicians. *Primary Care Companion Journal of Clinical Psychiatry*, *1*(5), 131–141.

McWhirter, E. H. (1991) Empowerment in counseling. *Journal of Counseling & Development*, *69*(3), 222–227.

Menninger, J. A. (n.d.). *Involuntary treatment: hospitalization and medications*. Providence, RI: Brown University. Retrieved from http://www.brown.edu/Courses/BI_278/Other/Clerkship/Didactics/Readings/INVOLUNTARY%20TREATMENT.pdf

Mental Hygiene Law. (2013). Access to clinical records. New York Code § 33.16. Retrieved from http://codes.findlaw.com/ny/mental-hygiene-law/mhy-sect-33-16.html

National Association of Social Workers. (2017). *Code of ethics of the National Association of Social Workers*. Retrieved from https://www.socialworkers.org/About/Ethics/Code-of-Ethics/Code-of-Ethics-English.aspx

Pukay-Martin, N. D. (2008). *Ethical considerations in working with couples: Confidentiality within the couple*. New York, NY: National Register of Health Service Psychologists. Retrieved from https://www.nationalregister.org/pub/the-national-register-report-pub/the-register-report-fall-2008/ethical-considerations-in-working-with-couples-confidentiality-within-the-couple/

Rennie v. Klein, 462 F. Supp. 1131. (D.N.J., 1978). Retrieved from http://law.justia.com/cases/federal/district-courts/FSupp/462/1131/2142341/

EMPOWERING AND ADVOCATING FOR VULNERABLE POPULATIONS

PART IV

7

EMPOWERING ADULT VICTIMS OF DOMESTIC ABUSE

Case Studies: Physical and Emotional Abuse

As discussed in the last chapter, providing a client with informed consent fosters the autonomy and dignity of the client. As such, client empowerment appears to be particularly critical when counseling abused, battered, and victimized populations (Wood, 2015). Acts of abuse or victimization, particularly those of a repetitive nature tend to foment feelings of disempowerment, low self-esteem, low self-efficacy, and depression (Anczewska, Roszczynska-Michta, Waszkiewicz, Charzynska, & Czabala, 2012). Counselor virtues can serve to help facilitate disclosure and, subsequently, exploration and processing of client issues. This chapter focuses on ways in which empowerment and supportive virtues of authenticity, empathy, and courage can facilitate and fortify client autonomy and welfare in adult victims of domestic abuse. Two case studies are examined. The first involves physical domestic abuse, control, and isolation. The second involves spousal emotional abuse, manipulation, and infidelity. In both cases, counselors face challenges and dilemmas as they work to provide virtuous counseling to their respective clients.

A PHYSICALLY ABUSED CLIENT

The first of these cases involves Tabitha, a 46-year-old professional female seeking therapy for difficulties related to getting along with her peers in the workplace as well as for feelings of loneliness. Tabitha attributed the latter issues to not having any friends or close relatives. She and Dr. Jennifer Langmore, a licensed mental health counselor, explored a wide array of issues during several months of therapy including the aforementioned presenting problems. During the fifth session, new revelations began to emerge.

"I always seem to attract the same kind of guy," stated Tabitha. "I just don't know how to break the pattern."

"Tell me more about that," asked Langmore.

"Well, my last two boyfriends and now, my husband, all have drinking problems."

"Can you give me more details?"

"All alcoholics and very controlling."

"Explain what you mean by 'controlling.'"

"Not letting me go out without permission and regulating whom I talk to."

Langmore lowered her voice slightly. "It sounds as if you're pretty uncomfortable with this pattern of behavior."

"Yes, and I want to change it now! I feel like a robot or a machine that's being programmed."

"You're yearning for more control over your life."

"Yes. I really NEED more control."

As the counseling relationship unfolded, Tabitha revealed to Langmore that her present husband, Gus, had pushed and shoved her frequently, once knocking her to the floor.

"It doesn't take much to get Gus angry."

"Tell me about that."

"Well, if I don't say or do what he thinks I should, he usually pushes or shoves me," said Tabitha sobbing softly. "A few months ago, he did it so hard that I fell and broke a tooth."

Langmore reflected Tabitha's feelings. "It sounds as if you're experiencing both physical as well as emotional pain from this behavior."

"Yes, and the emotional may even be worse than the physical."

"Let's discuss the physical part first. Tell me more about that."

"Well, he doesn't get physical that often, but it is sometimes scary. He usually pushes or shoves me and then runs out the door and drives away. I don't really feel unsafe."

"What Gus does is considered to be domestic abuse. There are shelters and resources available if you decide you want to explore your options. If you'd like, I can provide you with a list of agencies and programs."

"Thanks for the information. I'll keep it, just in case. Actually, what I'd like to continue talking about now is the emotional part."

"Tell me more about that."

"Mom and I don't really talk anymore. We used to, but we don't now."

"What has changed?"

"I married Gus. He hates Mom because she used to call me every week. He said she should stay out of our lives."

The above mentioned estrangement with her mother was part of a pattern of isolation experienced by Tabitha. She also disclosed that although she worked as a business professional, she had very little conversation with her associates and attributed this to her fear of being rejected by them.

In addition to this sense of estrangement from others, Tabitha's feelings of independence were appreciably contributing to her unhappiness. At her husband's insistence, her entire salary was automatically deposited into his individual bank account, which only he managed. He had been unemployed for the last 4 years, and the couple lived well due only to Tabitha's income.

As therapy progressed, Tabitha started to recognize that she could manage her own finances and began to actualize several of her mutually agreed on therapeutic goals. This included beginning to make a few new friends and speaking more often to coworkers. Using cognitive-behavioral tools, Langmore was able to challenge Tabitha's self-defeating beliefs about her social prowess and her inability to develop social connections. Tabitha was also able to rehearse mutually agreed on new behaviors in vivo. These goals and behavioral strategies were jointly formulated and illustrated a mutually collaborative relationship. Eventually, Tabitha began to report that she was feeling more self-confident and less isolated. The subject of her husband soon began to take up most of her sessions. Finally, she declared her intention to leave Gus. She expressed some concern that he might escalate his violence to a dangerous level if she actually left and stated that she had decided to temporarily live in a shelter until she could find appropriate housing and a restraining order. Langmore made certain that Tabitha had appropriate agency names and contacts, including the updated contact name for one of the agencies and worked with her to craft a safety plan intended to lessen the chances that a physically dangerous confrontation would occur as Tabitha attempted to leave. In cases of interpersonal violence, it is vital to maintain focus on potential changes to the safety status of the victim (Murray, 2016).

Tabitha stated that this planning and attention to her evolving needs added to her comfort level and expressed that she felt more assured that her decision to leave was in her best interest. She also shared that one of her new friends was offering her a lot of emotional support. She asked if Langmore would still be available for her as well. Langmore assured her that she would.

EMPOWERING A PHYSICALLY ABUSED CLIENT

At the start of therapy, Langmore displays her empathy for Tabitha by accurately reflecting her client's rather raw emotions. In this regard, she is able to demonstrate that she understands that her client is struggling with issues of autonomy and feels lost and alone. Also, she does not attempt to lead or to persuade Tabitha in one direction or another. She does offer names of resources and possible sources of information but in no way attempts to direct or cajole her client. Instead, Langmore shows warm regard and empathy as she tries to enter her client's subjective world. This continues as Tabitha shares additional details about her relationship.

Langmore, an empathetic therapist, attempts to enter Tabitha's inner world as if she were Tabitha. Although Langmore has never been in an abusive relationship, she has experienced feelings of loneliness, betrayal, confusion, and discomfort in her own life. It is this ability to hone into the commonality of feelings, irrespective of actual individual life experiences, that allows empathetic counselors to understand their clients' experiences from the clients' perspectives.

Langmore's ability to enter into Tabitha's world empathetically is more likely to be successful because Langmore is in the "habit" of being empathetic. She does not simply don the hat of empathy when she enters her sessions, only to remove it in her personal life. She is able to sense the feelings that others in her life experience, not only in her role as therapist, but also in her roles as friend, partner, and family member. Indeed, virtues or habits of behaving virtuously involve deeply imbedded inclinations to act in certain ways. Such behaviors are practiced and exercised regularly and become inclinations that are second nature. The ability to care for one's clients, and to do so unconditionally, thus becomes, in Carl Rogers' (1975) words, "a way of being." This way of being allows Tabitha to feel connected to Langmore and to see that she understands what the client is feeling. Reflection, as discussed in previous chapters, is the art of saying back in new language the essence of the feelings that the client is experiencing.

This empathy, coupled with Langmore's genuineness, as illustrated (e.g., as she lowers her voice as she resonates with her client's sadness), contributes to Langmore's empowering nature. In addition, as an empowering and competent therapist, Langmore, at no point, attempts to coax or cajole Tabitha into leaving her spouse. Since she, as previously noted, does not have reason to suspect that Tabitha is in imminent danger, empowering her toward autonomy and self-determination is not clouded by the question of whether to be more directive with Tabitha about safety concerns. On the other hand, if Langmore had, at any time, suspected that Tabitha was in imminent danger, then, as a competent therapist, she would have had to take measures to help protect her client. This could include reporting any imminent threats to law enforcement or being highly directive in advising Tabitha to go to a shelter.

This is a critical point for, as discussed earlier, serially and chronically abused and maltreated persons often experience chronic feelings of disempowerment and loss of self-determination (Anczewska et al., 2012). Competent therapists seek to foster re-empowerment through the use of more nondirective styles whenever feasible. As a result of Langmore's nondirective approach, Tabitha is able to more fully develop feelings of autonomy and self-determination. She feels more capable and comfortable with formulating her own decisions. Thus, Langmore's personal virtues of empowerment and benevolence allow her to ably facilitate the self-determination of her client. When a decision to leave her spouse is ultimately reached, it is Tabitha's alone.

Although Tabitha eventually chooses to go to a shelter, this does not mean that the counseling relationship will necessarily end. On the contrary, it is incumbent on Langmore at this juncture to make certain that Tabitha has retained the necessary information regarding shelter contact information and availability. Although she presented such information to the client earlier on in the session, diligence requires that she make certain that Tabitha not only has all this material, but that she also is presented with any important updates to that information as well.

In addition to the transmission of shelter information, Langmore must also try to ensure continued client safety and welfare. According to Dudley, McCloskey, and Kustron (2008), "[T]herapists must be aware of the risk factors which indicate imminent danger for women involved in relationships where they are victims of IPV in order to intervene to decrease victims' risk of lethality." Adhering to the standard of beneficence,

Langmore will work with her client regarding her concerns and discuss creating a safety plan, which may be necessary if Tabitha's situation takes a turn for the worse or if the client has any doubts that she will be able to safely leave the marital home and arrive at the shelter.

Although counseling services may be provided at the shelter, they may be short-term or insufficient for Tabitha's needs. Langmore, a benevolent therapist, has intrinsic regard for the welfare of her client. She will continue to make herself available as needed either in person or via phone (especially if the client's safety needs dictate this) until the client and the therapist concur that goals have been sufficiently met and the client appears to be safe.

AN EMOTIONALLY ABUSED CLIENT

In Tabitha's case, the abuse had a distinctive physical nature. This dimension sometimes allows the victim to be more amenable to labeling maltreatment as abusive. When spousal abuse does not, however, have any physical dimensions, but instead is of a psychological or emotional nature, it may be more perplexing for victims to identify. As is illustrated in the case to follow, a client may be confused about what constitutes abuse and may blame herself for her own maltreatment. This is illustrated in the case of Thea, a 36-year-old female and mother of three and a client of Bart Montego, a licensed mental health counselor.

> Thea has a master's degree in elementary education and had worked as a teacher for 5 years before marrying Lyndon, age 40. Lyndon is a talent agent with ties to major network television. His six-figure income dwarfed Thea's $50,000 a year salary. According to Thea, Lyndon convinced her to "retire early" and to "live the comfortable life of wife and mother."
>
> Thea reported that over the last several years she had wrestled with feelings of low self-esteem, sadness, and anger. She maintained that Lyndon frequently arrived home from work as late as 10 or 11 PM usually smelling of perfume and that, when confronted by Thea, he usually insisted that he was merely working late with clients. According to Thea, Lyndon often accused her of being pathologically jealous and in need of intensive therapy for her "craziness." Thea recounted that on one occasion, when Lyndon returned home at two o'clock AM, she locked him out from the home. Lyndon called law enforcement and a humiliated Thea was forced to open the door.
>
> As time went on, Thea continued to feel embarrassed and demeaned by Lyndon. He began to ridicule her appearance in public and to tell friends that she was a "nut job." In session four, after establishing rapport and beginning to cultivate a feeling of trust, Montego began to see increased openness and disclosures from Thea.
>
> "Lyndon is a real bully and probably a cheat as well," exclaimed Thea.
>
> "Tell me about that."
>
> "Well, he always thinks that he's right, and if I disagree with him, he tells me I'm a stupid bitch."
>
> "How do you feel about that?"

"Demeaned and degraded, but I'm beginning to believe that I may actually be stupid."

"How so?"

"He's said it so many times for so many years that it almost seems to make sense."

"So you're starting to doubt yourself."

"Yes, and I'm starting to think that I'm crazy as well."

"Crazy?"

"Yes, crazy. He always calls me a nut job because I'm suspicious that he comes home late smelling like women's perfume. He says that it's from standing close to his clients. He says that if I'm not careful, he'll cut me off financially and take the children."

"How do you respond to that?"

"Now, I usually just walk away, but I've contemplated getting drunk just to feel normal again. I'm afraid to drink though, because I need to take care of my kids."

Montego and Thea explored her confusion and pain surrounding the abuse and her feelings of loneliness and low self-esteem at length. Thea reported feeling trapped in her marriage primarily because of her children. She acknowledged that Lyndon's behavior was beginning to "rub off" on her children because they too had begun to call her "stupid" and "nuts." Montego reflected how embarrassed and upset Thea must feel about this. The two decided to re-prioritize Thea's original goals. The first goal had been for Thea to find a part-time job to give her a sense of autonomy and self-respect. The second had been to return to school for training in fashion design, a career that had always fascinated her. Now, with knowledge that Lyndon's abuse was not only affecting her, but was impacting her children as well, Thea decided that she wanted to leave Lyndon and begin a new life.

Thea talked about feeling degraded beyond words now that her own children were joining in and echoing her husband's disparaging rants. When she asked Montego if she was the victim of "actual" emotional abuse Montego responded in the affirmative. Thea then asked if all her mistreatment was considered to be abuse or if abuse was limited to being called names. Montego carefully explained the dynamics of emotional abuse by providing factual information and objective educational material.

As sessions continued, the question of Thea returning to work immediately arose. Her search for part-time work had not yielded any viable prospects, and she spoke of feeling unfulfilled and worthless.

"I feel torn between my upscale at-home lifestyle, on the one hand, and the loneliness and sadness, on the other."

"I see what you are saying," stated Montego. "You staying home gives you some comforts that you'd miss out on if you worked full time, but you're not sure that it's worth the trade off."

"So what do you think that I should do?" queried Thea.

"I don't know the answer to that question, Thea, but let's brainstorm," responded Montego in a frank tone. "Why don't we list all of the possible alternatives you could take and then consider the pros and cons of each. You can decide which choice you should try first, and then make a plan of action."

Over time, Thea vacillated between deciding to teach again and remain at home. As sessions progressed, she became increasingly more disturbed by her spouse's late-night hours. One day, at midnight, Montego received a call from his answering service stating that Thea had an emergency. Sensing a serious problem, Montego quickly returned the call.

"Lyndon is still not home from work and it's after midnight. I am very lonely," stated Thea in a distressed tone.

"It sounds like you're very distraught by this."

"Yes! What can I do about this situation?"

"What if you practice some of the relaxation exercises that you practiced in sessions?"

"Could you just talk to me?"

"We can schedule an appointment for tomorrow, but I think that you can handle this for now."

"I really want to talk."

"Whom else could you call tonight to talk? I have confidence in your ability to hold out until tomorrow. This is not an actual emergency."

"I think my sister would probably be willing to talk. I'll give her a call."

"That sounds like a plan. I'll see you tomorrow."

At their session the next afternoon, Thea appeared to be calmer and more self-assured.

"Thank you for being so honest and upfront with me last night. I can really trust you to be upfront with me. That's so different than it is with most people in my life."

After 6 months of therapy, Thea announced that Lyndon had left her for a much younger woman with whom he worked and had asked her for a divorce. He told her that he did not want custody of the children but would provide for them financially. Thea decided to move across the country to be with her sister. Lyndon did not object to this. Thea terminated therapy and Montego provided her with a referral in her new state. He scheduled a follow-up phone call with her for 3 months later. At that time, she reported that she was now teaching, taking fashion design classes part time, and living in a small apartment with her children. Her sister was assisting her by providing babysitting for the children.

EMPOWERING AN EMOTIONALLY ABUSED CLIENT

Throughout the aforementioned interaction, Montego's active listening style facilitates Thea's continued and increasingly descriptive disclosures. Montego is nonjudgmental and nondirective. He asks for clarification when Thea uses terminology for which multiple interpretations are possible. For instance, when Thea reports that she's beginning to think that she's "crazy," Montego asks, "Crazy?" so that she can explain exactly what that means to her. Montego asks open questions (e.g., "How do you respond to that?") to promote client welfare and autonomy. His nondirective style allows the client to feel empowered and begin to explore her increasingly ambivalent feelings about herself and her spouse.

This nondirective style is operational again when Thea contemplates whether she should return to teaching or remain a housewife. Montego suggests that the two brainstorm to come up with some viable options. This brainstorming and decision making places the responsibility of the decision squarely on the client, consonant with the standard of promoting client autonomy and self-determination. Efforts at promoting such self-determination are usually part of a continuous process.

Also illustrative of this point is the phone call that Thea makes to Montego's answering service during the wee hours of the night; stating that she has an emergency, Thea requests that Montego return her call immediately, and Montego quickly calls back his client.

Although Montego is there for his client in what appears to be an emotionally charged situation, he senses that Thea's late-night call may breach therapist-client professional boundaries. The client appears to be acting as though she were calling a friend or a romantic intimate rather than her therapist. Continuing to return these calls might very well reinforce such behavior, thus disempowering Thea and creating an enduring dependency on Montego. As also mentioned, the call also seemed to be potentially breaching therapeutic boundaries, and reinforcing this type of behavior might well be counterproductive and contrary to what Montego has accomplished with his client.

Montego in no way wants to abridge the rapport and trust that has developed during the counseling relationship. If he confronts Thea about the call, she may feel demeaned, just as she feels with her spouse; but, if he fails to confront her, he is not being candid with his client, when, in fact, he believes that candor is needed.

As an authentic therapist, Montego follows his ethical lights and decides to gently explain to Thea that he will be there for her if she were ever in crisis, but that calling late at night just to talk is not part of a professional counseling relationship. Using reflection, Montego tries to enter Thea's subjective world and understand the feelings of distress and betrayal that she was experiencing over her spouse's suspected infidelity. The empathy exhibited by Montego demonstrates care, compassion, and respectfulness. Although Montego takes a risk in confronting Thea, he acts in a congruent and genuine manner. He is not sure that Thea will return for counseling; however, he is steadfast and courageous in holding to his decision. Indeed, exercising the strength of will, congruence, and courageousness sets the stage for emulation by one's clients.

In addition to aforementioned virtues, Montego also demonstrates candor with his client. When Thea questions him about the definition of emotional abuse, he is both candid and informative. His competence as a practicing therapist is also evident. For example, according to FL Statute 491, Sections (7), (8), and (9), the practice of clinical social workers, marriage and family therapists, and licensed mental health counselors include "the provision of needed information and education to clients." Montego accomplished this in an objective and factual manner. He does not attempt to influence or coerce Thea into any decisions based on this information. Thea thus trusts that Montego will be upfront with her without imposing his own values.

As stressed in this book, such trust is vital to client success. Indeed, Montego's courage to stand on principle, along with his ongoing empathy, candor, honesty, and benevolence make it more likely that trust will flourish. Because he is a benevolent therapist, focused on his client's best interest, Montego diligently endeavors to work with Thea in achieving the goals that the two have mutually agreed on.

Although therapy is terminated prematurely due to Lyndon leaving his wife for another woman, Montego diligently makes a referral for her to receive counseling in her new state and also follows up with her 3 months later. In fact, at the 3-month phone call, it is revealed that Thea actually does realize her goal of returning to teaching and has begun classes for fashion design.

This chapter has discussed the empowerment of adult clients who are victims of domestic abuse. As demonstrated, empowering such clients involves facilitating their rational self-determination to make their own decisions on their own. But what happens when the clients are not adults, but rather children who have neither the freedom nor the capacity to make their own life-altering decisions? In such cases, the role of the therapist takes on a different dimension, one of advocate that may, not infrequently, call for the exercise of courage in promoting the welfare and dignity of these vulnerable clients. In the next chapter, this often daunting and emotionally charged challenge is explored.

Questions for Review and Reflection

1. How can a therapist accurately empathize with a client who has experienced problems that the therapist has not herself experienced? What virtue(s) might this involve?

2. How can Langmore's virtue of empowerment help facilitate the development of Tabitha's sense of self-determination and autonomy?

3. Langmore eventually creates an escape plan with Tabitha. Might any ethical standards have been violated if Langmore had insisted earlier that such a plan be created?

4. When Montego is candid and courageous with Thea regarding her late-night phone call, he is taking a risk of alienating her. If Thea had reacted in a dejected way and threatened to terminate therapy, how could Montego have handled this without violating his values and standards?

5. In trying to foster self-determination, Montego does not try to persuade Thea to leave her husband. In what types of similar situations might it be unethical to not try to persuade the client to leave?

6. In what ways are Montego's benevolence apparent in his relationship with Thea?

7. Part of a therapist's role is to provide appropriate information or materials to clients. Did Langmore and Montego succeed in carrying out this obligation? Could either of them have accomplished this more successfully?

8. Although Thea moves out of state and Montego refers her to a new therapist, he still follows up with a 3-month phone call. What virtue(s) does this exemplify?

9. How does Langmore's genuineness with Tabitha contribute to her achieving her goals?

10. How does acting in a nonjudgmental manner with their clients allow both Langmore and Montego to develop deep rapport with their clients?

11. In what ways might psychological or emotional abuse be more difficult for victims to label and identify as compared to physical abuse?

Cases for Analysis

Using the concepts discussed in this chapter, discuss and reflect on virtuous practice in the following scenarios.

1. Renata, a 42-year-old department store clerk, has been in therapy for 2 weeks with Myra Nelson because of problems she is experiencing at work. Although she has been employed in her present position for over 10 years, she has not been promoted to manager, often being passed over for others with far less experience. Renata tells Nelson that she doesn't like to get others angry by complaining, but that she "really deserves" a promotion. She states that maybe she isn't pretty enough to be promoted or that maybe she is "destined" to never move up the ladder. What can Nelson do to empower her client?

2. Derrick, a 22-year-old college student, has been in therapy with his university counselor, Dean Dixon, for 3 weeks. Derrick presents to Dixon with failing grades and low self-esteem. He states that his mother has always told him that he was "stupid" so he rarely really tries to get good grades as he believes that it's probably a waste of time. In fact, he relates that he didn't even purchase books for the current semester because it would likely be a waste of money. What steps can Dixon take to begin to help facilitate a feeling of empowerment in his client?

3. Kathy is a 50-year-old woman who is contemplating entering the workplace after raising three children. She is in therapy with Dr. Seymour. Over the last 15 years, Kathy has gained 15 pounds and reports that her husband is upset with her about this. Kathy states that she is really bored and lonely staying home alone all day and wants to begin a job search; however, she says that she probably won't get a job until she loses weight. How can Dr. Seymour help empower Kathy?

References

Anczewska, M., Roszczynska-Michta, J., Waszkiewicz, J., Charzynska, K., & Czabala, C. (2012). Empowering women with domestic violence experience [Abstract]. *Part 4: Higher education, lifelong learning and social inclusion* (pp. 250–256). Retrieved from http://files.eric.ed.gov/fulltext/ED567107.pdf

Dudley, D. R., McCloskey, K., & Kustron, D. A. (2008). Therapist perceptions of intimate partner violence: A replication of Harway and Hansen's study after more than a decade. *Journal of Aggression, Maltreatment & Trauma, 17*(1), 80–102. Retrieved from https://www.ncbi.nlm.nih.gov/pmc/articles/PMC3981103/#R6

Murray, C. (2016). *Intimate partner violence—Treating victims practice brief.* Alexandria, VA: American Counseling Association. Retrieved from https://www.counseling.org/knowledge-center/practice-briefs/articles/treating-victims

Rogers, C. R. (1975). Empathetic: An unappreciated way of being. *Counseling Psychologist, 5*(2), 2–10.

Wood, L. (2015). Hoping, empowering, strengthening: Theories used in intimate partner violence advocacy. *Journal of Women and Social Work, 30*(3), 286–301. Retrieved from https://www.researchgate.net/publication/281981812_Hoping_Empowering_Strengthening_Theories_Used_in_Intimate_Partner_Violence_Advocacy

8

EXERCISING COURAGE IN PROTECTING CHILDREN

Case Study: Child Sexual Abuse

Empowering clients can be quite challenging when the identified client is a minor. When working with children, the virtuous therapist must be extraordinarily diligent in fostering an atmosphere where not only legal and potentially life protecting statutes and standards are followed, but also where the ethical standards of beneficence, nonmaleficence, and justice are scrupulously woven into multifaceted and complex decision-making processes. In cases of child abuse, these processes, of necessity, involve deciding how, to whom, and the extent to which information related to the abuse is disclosed.

This can be particularly daunting to therapists working with sexually abused children. The perpetrators in most reported sexual abuse of children appear to be those who know the child (RAINN, n.d.). Disclosure by the victim, if it occurs, is usually delayed (London, Bruck, Ceci, & Shuman, 2005).

Children are prone to experience guilt, self-blame, and shame related to their abuse (Sinanan, 2015). In such an environment, therapists must be particularly sensitive to sustaining the dignity of child clients and their families, and must strive to be courageous in their willingness to make often difficult and complex decisions on behalf of the child and the family. Such decisions may be particularly challenging when they involve balancing client welfare and autonomy and third party nonmaleficence and autonomy.

In fact, the therapist often needs to step forward to assume responsibility to protect the welfare and dignity of the vulnerable child and to emerge as his advocate (Miller, Dove, & Miller, 2007). The virtuous therapist must thus navigate the headwaters of a dysfunctional, sometimes hostile, family dynamic, contentious court battles, and/or detrimental agency policies to protect the child. This advocacy role may incur personal as well as professional risks and, therefore, requires the exercise of courage. As explained in Chapter 1, courage involves doing what you think is morally right even when this involves risking incurring a substantial loss such as that of time, money, reputation, friendship, popularity, or other personal or professional resources. This chapter discusses the exercise of courage in the context of the therapist's advocacy role in the case of suspected child abuse.

A CASE OF ADVOCACY FOR VICTIMS AND THEIR FAMILIES

Brooke Martin, a 7-year-old female, had been recently referred to Allright Counseling Agency and was assigned to Dr. Carolina Flowers, a child and family counselor with a specialization in child abuse. A second grader, Brooke had begun to experience declining grades in school. Her teacher, Dan Major, began to notice that she appeared to be distracted on several occasions and was interacting with her peers in an usually aggressive manner. In addition, Brooke was uncharacteristically failing to complete her classwork. That these behaviors were inconsistent with what Major had previously observed in this student was particularly troublesome to him. He decided to refer the student to the school guidance counselor who subsequently discussed counseling referrals with Brooke's mother, Audrey Martin. Audrey subsequently contacted Dr. Flowers, a therapist who had been on the school's referral list, to set up counseling. Flowers, in accordance with the ACA Code of Ethics (American Counseling Association [ACA], 2014, A.2.b.), explained in both oral as well as written form a plethora of information including the types of services provided, her professional qualifications, approaches to counseling that may be used, records, diagnosing, fees, and limits of confidentiality. She informed Audrey that it would be counter therapeutic to reveal the contents of Brooke's sessions with her, but that she would inform Audrey if Brooke was in imminent danger. Although Brook was 7 years old, and not legally required to sign a treatment consent form on her own behalf, Flowers also informed her of the aforementioned information in language that was understandable to a child of that age. It is significant to note, that although the age of majority in most states is 18, there are several states where this is not the case. As Polowy and Felton (2014) explain, there are five states where the age to consent to treatment is older than 18. They are Alabama, Colorado, Mississippi, Nebraska, and Pennsylvania. In addition, the state of Maryland allows 16-year-olds to consent to treatment, and the therapist is allowed the discretion of whether or not to notify parents or guardians of these services. In Illinois, a child who is 12 years old or older can receive up to five sessions of outpatient therapy without parental consent, although parents are not responsible for payment for these services (Polowy & Felton, 2014). Since Brooke and Audrey reside in a state where the legal age of consent to treatment is 18, Flowers was not legally required to obtain her consent.

During her second session with Flowers, Brooke related that she had been molested by an adult male cousin:

"He does it whenever he babysits for me. He told me that I can't tell Mom because she'll get very angry at me. She may even send me away. I shouldn't be telling you either, because Mom will find out and get upset."

"Tell me about him being angry."

"He said that very bad things will happen if I tell anybody about this."

Although Brooke had already been informed that allegations of abuse needed to be reported, Flowers believed this should be emphasized again. She reminded Brooke of her duty to report explaining that by so doing she was also trying to protect her. Flowers emphasized that reporting the allegation was the best way to accomplish this and emphasized that Brooke was in no way responsible for the abuse. The next question that Flowers pondered was whether or not to inform Audrey beforehand of her intent to report. Ultimately, Flowers decided it was best to share Brooke's allegations with Audrey so that she also would be better equipped to assist Brooke. She asked Brooke's permission to do this although she sensed the child's fear and confusion about the entire situation. Flowers tried to reassure Brooke that she did the right thing by disclosing the abuse and reflected that Brooke might be experiencing confusion and uncertainty about having made the disclosure. Brooke corroborated these reflections and shared that she felt troubled that she had not come forward with her allegations earlier as had other children in the family.

When Audrey was informed of the aforementioned allegations, she seemed shocked, but then told Flowers that other children in the extended family had previously made similar allegations about this relative. She explained that, when asked, Brooke had maintained that she had not been abused in any way. Nonetheless, she stated that she would be supportive of her child. Flowers emphasized how important such parental support would be to Brooke's treatment and recovery.

Because of these previous abuse allegations, an abuse investigation into Brooke's cousin had already been opened, and now, based on Brooke's allegations and Flowers's report, a new investigation was also initiated. This investigation spurred the questioning of the child, her parents, and her siblings. Audrey reported that in the wake of this questioning, she noticed an increase in acting out behaviors by Brooke.

She also related that she herself felt unprepared to handle the emotional turmoil and the legal entanglements that ensued from the report and wondered if she could begin treatment with Flowers as well. Since Flowers's practice included a family sexual abuse treatment program, it seemed reasonable that she agree to accept Audrey as a client.

Brooke's progress in therapy was encouraging. She was open and disclosing. She related having difficulty concentrating in school due to intrusive thoughts and images related to the sexual abuse. The use of imaging and behavior modification appeared to work well for these issues because Brooke's grades began to appreciably rise and her conduct to improve as reported to Audrey by Brooke's teacher.

Audrey also appeared to be making inroads in treatment. She had begun therapy with the presenting problem of having difficulty dealing with Brooke's abuse. As counseling progressed, she hinted at and then revealed that she too had been sexually abused. Brooke's revelation had seemingly reopened the never sufficiently healed wounds from Audrey's past. Although many in the family knew of her abuse, she had been encouraged to not talk about it and to "let it go." Her abuser was dead, and she had rationalized that this fact would make it easier for her to move on. She was now, however, having flashbacks of her own abuse and was struggling to remain supportive for Brooke.

Audrey's attempts to support Brooke were evident to Flowers. She transported Brooke to weekly sessions and attended her own weekly sessions as well. Neither of the two missed a session for the first 8 months of treatment. At that point in time, Audrey became ill and was told that she required surgery. The surgery and recuperation would take about 3 weeks' time. During those 3 weeks, Audrey would be homebound and would not be able to transport either herself or Brooke to sessions.

Distressed, Audrey tearfully informed Flowers of this development. She expressed fear about both Brooke as well as herself losing ground in therapy and made a point of informing Flowers that she had made every effort to find someone to take Brooke to sessions in her absence. She implored Flowers to allow her to continue with her treatment. Flowers assured Audrey that she could continue; that it might take a while for the two to become fully reengaged on their return, but that she had confidence in them both.

Several days after this conversation, Flowers's agency adopted a new policy related to sequential missing of therapy appointments. The new policy stated that any client who missed three consecutive sessions would be automatically terminated from therapy. At the next agency meeting, all therapists were instructed that this new policy was to be vigorously instituted. Several therapists were told to terminate their clients who had already missed sessions, and they agreed to do so. Flowers's situation was a bit different from the others, however. Her clients had only missed one session each so far and had informed Flowers ahead of time. In addition, the absence that had already occurred and the two that would subsequently follow were due to health issues beyond the control of the clients. In addition, Flowers had promised Audrey without consultation with her supervisor that she could remain in counseling because the three session rule had not yet been proposed at that point in time.

After Flowers shared the details of her cases with her clinical supervisor she was, nonetheless, instructed to immediately terminate these clients. Flowers attempted to explain how this situation was different from the other cases and that Brooke and Audrey had made good progress in treatment and should not be penalized for becoming ill. Unfazed by her pleadings, the supervisor remained intractable. Subsequently, Flowers requested a private meeting with her supervisor. At this time, she maintained that it would be unethical for her to terminate her clients and argued that such actions would actually amount to client abandonment. She stated that child sexual abuse victims are vulnerable and disenfranchised and that termination of services would compound Brooke's trauma. Brooke had established trust and rapport with Flowers and was showing objective improvement both in school and at home. Refusing her services might well cause her to regress and lose any milestones she may have reached. If, in fact, she were to begin working with another therapist, she would have to develop a relationship from scratch and might well feel betrayed and violated. Flowers maintained that Audrey had as well made significant progress and that terminating her would not only violate her trust, but might also create a situation which left Audrey unprepared to emotionally support Brooke because her own issues might become overwhelming.

Although she diligently tried to convincingly share these concerns with her supervisor, Flowers was instructed, nonetheless, to terminate her clients. When Flowers refused to comply on ethical grounds, her supervisor informed her that this action would likely result in her losing her job and that she was referring the situation to the executive director. Flowers was admonished not to discuss the situation with her colleagues in the meantime. During this interim, two fellow therapists who had been in the initial meeting approached Flowers and commented that she was violating agency policy and that although some people might be hurt by the rules, in the long run, these rules would be helpful. One therapist told Flowers that she had heard that she was going to be fired in a few days. Flowers remained steadfast, and she was prepared to uphold her decision. She recoiled emotionally at the thought of abandoning her clients or violating the trust that they had in her.

Flowers, was, in effect, prepared to face this seemingly mounting challenge head on. At her meeting with Morgan Michaels, Executive Director, 3 days later, the director eventually concluded that although she had, at first, been taken aback by Flowers's actions, upon thorough consideration of the situation, and persuaded by Flowers's arguments, she would agree to allow both Brooke and Audrey to continue therapy. Flowers privately rejoiced at this apparent moral victory; however, she chose to never share with Brooke and Audrey the potential jeopardy that had surrounded their status as clients because this might have caused them to feel inconsequential to the agency and uncertain and insecure about their future statuses as clients.

Brooke and Audrey continued as clients for another year with successful resolution of the majority of issues they both had. Follow-up at 3 and 6 months confirmed that the two were still doing well.

In the above case, Flowers is faced with what she perceives as a critical ethical dilemma involving her supervisor and the decision not to terminate her clients. She prepares an ethical analysis to gain some clarity regarding the decisions she makes. Flowers defines her moral problem according to the process discussed in Chapter 4, by identifying the welfare and interests of all stakeholders. Her considerations are summarized in Table 8.1.

TABLE 8.1 ■ Stakeholders/Welfare/Interests

Stakeholder	Welfare (Positive/Negative)	Interests
Brooke	• Working through her issues in therapy • Not having trust betrayed • Protection from further abuse	• Being able to confide in/trust therapist • Having support of mother
Audrey	• Working through her issues in therapy	• Maintaining her relationship with Brooke • Helping Brooke improve her behavior • Supporting and protecting Brooke
Dr. Flowers	• Not losing her job	• Helping Brooke and Audrey continue counseling sessions • Helping Brooke recover from trauma and empower her • Demonstrating moral courage in the workplace • Providing equitable counseling services to Brooke and Audrey • Demonstrating trustworthiness to Brooke and Audrey

Flowers's decision to challenge her agency's mandate to terminate her clients in advance of their missing three consecutive sessions is, for her, rooted in her reverence for honesty and fairness in the delivery of services. She has promised Audrey that she can continue treatment following her recovery from surgery and makes potential career sacrifices to keep that promise. Flowers is accustomed to acting honestly (i.e., keeping her word even when doing so may put her in jeopardy). Such attitudes and actions are also demonstrative of courage.

This courageousness is inextricably bolstered by her inherent virtue of benevolence because Flowers seeks to lessen clients' pain and suffering and to advance their net positive welfare. For both Brooke and Audrey, this welfare is rooted in receiving ongoing competent therapy. Brooke's net positive welfare is also enhanced by not having her trust breached and being protected from further sexual abuse, while Audrey's is enhanced by her becoming more supportive and protective of her daughter. Flowers is aware that the aforementioned welfare of her clients would be abrogated by her superiors if she does not remain steadfast and courageous in her decision to prevent her clients from being terminated.

By courageously trying to promote the net positive welfare of Brooke and Audrey by protecting their statuses as clients, Flowers is also helping insure that their interests will be met. Brooke's interests are heavily grounded in being able to trust her therapist and in having the support of Audrey. Audrey's interests are best met if she can successfully maintain her relationship with Brooke and help her improve her acting out behaviors.

As discussed, Flowers's goal, at first, does not appear to be readily attainable. However, it is in her interest as a virtuous therapist to provide equitable and ongoing counseling to her clients, to maintain her own trustworthiness, and to empower Brooke. Although it is certainly not in Flowers's best interest to lose her own job, she is courageously prepared to take such a risk to fulfill both her other interests as a counselor as well as those of her clients.

As such, Flowers does not blindly adhere to an agency policy that fails to take into account relevant differences in client circumstances. These circumstances include the fact that Audrey and Brooke do not plan to miss sessions due to capriciousness or lack of diligence or dedication to the therapeutic process. Rather, they are going to be sidelined due to an unforeseen circumstance, Audrey's surgery. In fact, Audrey shares with Flowers that she has attempted to find transportation for her daughter during her period of recuperation but that arrangements could not be made. In addition, Audrey is obviously committed to her treatment as evidenced by the fact that both she and Brooke attended every weekly session for the prior 8 months.

Because her clients are obviously dedicated to their treatment, Flowers resists pressure that is exerted on her by her colleagues as well as her clinical supervisor and refuses to terminate them even after threats of dismissal. This further illustrates the very depths of Flowers's courage in the face of professional adversity. She does not succumb to the "herd" mentality of her coworkers. Instead, Flowers displays independence of judgment and acts courageously in maintaining that loyalty. As discussed above, Flowers conceptualizes her "victory" as a moral "win." This is premised on the idea that she successfully is able to advocate and to prevail in having her clients treated as ends in and of themselves (i.e., important for their own worth, and not merely means by which the counseling agency achieves more revenue or other extrinsic rewards).

Flowers's dedication to her clients as ends and not merely means is further exemplified because she demonstrates her regard for their primacy. Her candor and respectfulness are at the forefront of many of her decisions. For instance, Flowers, at the onset of Brooke's first therapy session, in accordance with ACA Code of Ethics (2014, A.2.b.), explains in both oral as well as written form a plethora of information including the types of services provided, her professional qualifications, approaches to counseling that may be used, records, diagnosing, fees, and limits of confidentiality. Although Brook is a minor and not legally required to sign a treatment consent form on her own behalf, Flowers also informs her of the aforementioned information in language that is understandable to a 7-year-old child. This conduct is paradigmatic of therapist virtues of candor and respectfulness. Along with Brooke's mother obtaining full informed consent, Flowers is scrupulous about also extending this to the 7-year-old child, whose confidences and disclosures are most central to this therapeutic relationship.

Indeed, for the virtuous therapist, empowering clients is an essential dynamic of the therapeutic process and demonstrates a confidence in the self-determination and respect for the client. Insomuch as Brooke is a minor, such empowerment may in fact feel unusual to her because she may not be accustomed to being treated in an equitable manner.

The possible newness of being empowered notwithstanding, Brooke and Audrey are, therefore, better prepared when Flowers informs them that she must report Brooke's allegations of sexual abuse. However, Flowers is still concerned about the possibility of Brooke feeling betrayed and helpless when informed that a report will be made. She has already been threatened by an alleged perpetrator and has denied to Audrey that she has been abused. She has probably been feeling helpless, as most victims of child sexual abuse experience such feelings (Kelley, 1986). Sexual abuse is usually shrouded in secrecy, and child victims often feel as if they are on their own. Flowers is cognizant of her responsibility to avoid possible harm to her client. She appropriately tries to reassure her that she has done the right thing by making her disclosure and emphasizes that the child has no culpability for the abuse.

As a benevolent therapist, Flowers is deeply committed to Brooke's best interest and hopes that such reassurances help bolster her client's feelings of empowerment. Reporting the allegations without first reminding Brooke of her duty to report or without reassuring her may sabotage the nascent therapeutic relationship and cause Brooke further emotional trauma.

Since Flowers strives to consistently provide her clients with beneficent and compassionate care, she genuinely attempts to enter Brooke's subjective world and understand how isolated, afraid, helpless, and alone she must be feeling. As she tries to put herself in Brooke's place, she senses that to report the abuse without first informing Brooke of her intention to do so might contribute to her client feeling further betrayed, hopeless, and disempowered.

Not only does Flowers sense the emotional toll on Brooke that Flowers's unilateral actions might take, but also her decision is further complicated by consideration of whether to inform Audrey of her child's allegations prior to the actual report being made. This decision is also fraught with an ethical dilemma that has the potential for polarization. Since both Brooke and Audrey are clients, and Audrey is a stakeholder in Brooke's therapeutic process, Flowers also has an allegiance to Audrey. She consents to her daughter participating in therapy with the understanding that she will be notified if Brooke is in imminent danger. Although it is not entirely clear whether Audrey previously suspects the alleged abuse, she does, nonetheless, bring Brooke to counseling and does, in fact, tell Flowers that she has questioned the child about being abused.

For this reason it is not unreasonable to believe that Audrey has an interest in helping her daughter to thrive and to ameliorate her acting out behaviors. In addition, and more importantly, Audrey has diligently brought Brooke to therapy sessions and has committed to her own personal therapy. That Audrey has an interest in maintaining her relationship with Brooke appears unquestionable to Flowers.

Flowers is also motivated by the fact that Brooke's welfare depends, in large part, on her being in a trustworthy therapeutic relationship. Flowers wonders whether telling Audrey about Brooke's allegations could possibly be construed by the child as a breach of trust. Since Brooke has been sexually abused by her adult cousin, a beloved family member, she already has had her trust betrayed. If she suspects that Audrey has any clue about the abuse and does not act to protect her, this may well compound her feelings of betrayal and disempowerment. Flowers has to tread very carefully so as not to further such feelings and to avoid jeopardizing the trusting and empowering therapeutic bond that she has successfully forged with Brooke.

As she diligently tries to avoid further disempowering Brooke, Flowers also remains cognizant of her status as a minor child and understands that she must honor her commitment to be candid, respectful, and empowering with Brooke. Will informing Brooke's mother create a situation where one client is disempowered at the expense of empowering another?

As a benevolent therapist, Flowers strives to empower all her clients as much as possible. She is justifiably concerned that Audrey may feel disempowered if she is not informed of the impending report beforehand. Although Audrey has been informed that she will not be privy to everything that transpires in the sessions, she is told that she will be broadly informed of her child's progress and if her child is in danger. As a candid therapist, Flowers may owe it to Brooke's mother to give her advanced warning about an impending report to protective services. Audrey appears to trust Flowers with her daughter's well-being, and Flowers does not want to violate that trust. Since Audrey might feel disempowered by not being forewarned, and might develop resentful feelings toward Flowers, Flowers faces a dilemma. Loyalty to her clients is a serious concern, and she is in the position of ostensibly appearing to be disloyal to Audrey.

Further, the decision to not notify Audrey beforehand may not only appear to be disloyal, but, on another practical level, it may result in Audrey terminating therapy with Flowers even if Brooke's allegations come back founded. This could result in all parties being left without viable counseling services and feeling betrayed on some level. Accordingly, Flowers weighs all the foreseeable outcomes of her decision and decides to inform Audrey of her intent to report Brooke's allegations prior to actually making the report.

This chapter has illustrated how a therapist's personal interests such as the keeping of one's job can be pitted against protecting the welfare and dignity of the client. In the case of Flowers, the therapist exercised courage in remaining loyal to her client notwithstanding personal risk. In this case, the conflict of interest between her clients' welfare and dignity and Flower's interest in keeping her job arose as a natural consequence of Flowers exercising due diligence in doing her job. In some cases, however, conflicts of interest may arise in the context of pursuing problematic dual or multiple role relationships that place an undue strain on the therapist's loyalty to her client, or at least create the appearance of such a conflict. For example, a therapist might take on, as a client, someone with whom he has a business relationship. The next chapter explores such problematic dual or multiple role relationships.

Questions for Review and Reflection

1. Who perpetrates most child sexual abuse? Why might this make reporting the abuse more complicated?

2. When children actually disclose sexual abuse, what is the usual nature of their disclosures?

3. Flowers courageously puts her job on the line by refusing to follow her agency's newly adopted rule of terminating clients for missing sessions. Could she potentially have jeopardized the welfare of her other clients by risking being dismissed from her job? Explain.

4. Flowers's courage eventually results in her being allowed to keep Audrey and Brooke as clients, but does not change the overall future direction of the agency in considering exceptions to its new policy. Does Flowers have an ethical obligation to address this as well?

5. Flowers is intent to provide equitable counseling services for Brooke and Audrey. What types of future roadblocks might her agency create for her with their new policy? Are there any other viable ethical routes that Flowers can take besides directly challenging the policy?

6. Although Brooke is a 7-year-old child, Flowers includes her in the informed consent process. Explain the significance of this. What therapist virtue(s) does this illustrate?

7. Discuss the agency's rule to terminate clients who miss three consecutive sessions regardless of reasons. Could such a policy ever be considered virtuous?

8. What do you consider to be therapists' ethical obligations in challenging an agency's rules and practices they deem to be antithetical to a client's interests?

9. Does Flowers have an ethical obligation to inform Audrey about Brooke's allegations and to forewarn her that she is going to report them? Could Flowers be ethically justified in not forewarning Audrey?

10. Discuss Flowers's loyalty both in the context of informing Audrey before reporting Brooke's allegations as well as keeping her word not to terminate her clients even though she risked losing her job.

11. Two fellow therapists told Flowers that she was violating agency policy and that although some people might be hurt by these rules, in the long run, these rules would be helpful. From the perspective of an ethically virtuous therapist, can this perspective be defended? Discuss this in detail.

Cases for Analysis

Using the concepts discussed in this chapter, discuss and reflect on virtuous practice in the following cases.

1. Ceci is a 30-year-old woman who has shared with her therapist, Dr. Stanton, that she was molested by her child psychologist, Dr. Little, when she was 9 years old. Dr. Little, unbeknownst to Ceci, is Stanton's best friend. How should Stanton ethically proceed? What are his ethical and legal responsibilities?

2. Brandon is a 70-year-old widowed male. He recently informed his therapist, Dr. Melton, that he had sexually molested his two children when they were young. He had threatened them with retaliation if they ever came forth, and neither of them ever disclosed. Brandon told Melton that he regretted what he did, but that he does not want to be punished. How should Melton ethically proceed? Explain.

3. Henry, age 15, has been in therapy with Hayley Helmsworth for 6 months because of a suspension from school due to truancy. Henry has repeatedly told Helmsworth that he hates his parents and can't wait until he turns 18 so he can live on his own. He has not alleged any type of abuse but has stated that his parents are overly strict and unfriendly to him. Henry's parents have been recently asking Helmsworth how their son is progressing in treatment. Helmsworth is unsure how to handle the situation and fears violating Henry's confidentiality if he informs his parents of Henry's feelings. How can this therapist ethically proceed with this case?

References

American Counseling Association. (2014). *ACA code of ethics.* Alexandria, VA: Author. Retrieved from counseling.org/resources/aca-code-of-ethics.pdf

Kelley, S. J. (1986). Learned helplessness in the sexually abused child. *Comprehensive Child and Adolescent Nursing, 9*(3), 193–207.

London, K., Bruck, M., Ceci, S. J., & Shuman, D. W. (2005). Disclosure of child sexual abuse: What does the research tell us about the ways that children tell? *Psychology, Public Policy, and Law, 11*(1), 194–226.

Miller, K. L., Dove, M. K., & Miller, S. M. (2007, October). *A counselor's guide to child sexual abuse: Prevention, reporting and treatment strategies.* Paper based on a program presented at the Association for Counselor Education and Supervision Conference, Columbus, OH.

Polowy, C. I., & Felton, E. (2014). *Working with children: The many layers of consent to treatment.* Sacramento, CA: National Association of Social Workers, California News. Retrieved from http://naswcanews.org/working-with-children-the-many-layers-of-consent-to-treat/

RAINN. (n.d.). *Children and teens statistics.* Washington, DC: Author. Retrieved from https://www.rainn.org/statistics/children-and-teens

Sinanan, A. N. (2015). Trauma and treatment of child sexual abuse. *Journal of Trauma and Treatment, S4,* 24. Retrieved from https://www.omicsgroup.org/journals/trauma-and-treatment-of-child-sexual-abuse-2167-1222-S4-024.pdf

PART V

COUNSELING ACROSS MULTIPLE ROLES AND CULTURES

9

BEING LOYAL AND FAIR TO CLIENTS

Case Study: Sex With a Former Client

Client loyalty requires maintaining independence of judgment (Cohen & Cohen, 1999). This means that therapists practice mindful of personal interests or aversions that prevent them from being objective in the provision of therapy, and, therefore, do not take on professional roles when their

> personal, scientific, professional, legal, financial or other interests or relationships could reasonably be expected to (1) impair their objectivity, competence or effectiveness in performing their functions as psychologists or (2) expose the person or organization with whom the professional relationship exists to harm or exploitation. (American Psychological Association [APA], 2016, 3.06)

Fairness, as equitable distribution of counseling services, sets important limits on what a therapist can ethically do for one client at the expense of another. For example, therapists who become personally involved with particular clients not only lose independence of judgment by allowing their personal interests to cloud their professional judgment, but they also fall short of being fair, by virtue of their unjustified, differential treatment of their clients, especially those clients with whom they become personally involved.

In some cases, a therapist's personal aversion to a certain client population may make it prohibitive to work with such clients. For example, some therapists may find it difficult to exercise objectivity in working with clients with pedophilia. In other cases, the therapist may have a visceral dislike for an individual client. As human beings, therapists are not immune from having such personal emotional responses. Here, the greatest danger lies not in having the aversion, but instead in the refusal to acknowledge it and take appropriate action to refer the client to a therapist who can be objective in the provision of counseling services.

CONFLICTS OF INTEREST

Independence of judgment can be compromised when a therapist has a *conflict of interest*. Such conflicts exist when therapists have one or more interests that place a strain on their ability to remain objective in the provision of competent counseling services (Davis, 1982). For example, a therapist may have a conflict of interest if the therapist's interest in continuing to receive payment from the client (say due to financial difficulties) inclines the therapist to keep the client in therapy longer than necessary.

Conflicts of interest can be actual or apparent. A therapist has an *apparent* conflict of interest when the client perceives the therapist to have a conflict of interest even if she actually does not. For example, an agnostic therapist who is counseling a religious client may not have any personal problem counseling a believer; however, the client may perceive the therapist to have such a problem. In this case, the appearance of a conflict can be just as problematic, in the provision of effective counseling services, than that of an actual conflict of interest, and, as such, may be just cause for referring the client to another therapist who does not have a real or apparent conflict of interest related to counseling the client.

Dual or Multiple Role Relationships

Conflicts of interest, real or apparent, often arise in the context of *dual or multiple role relationships* (APA, 2016, 3.05.a; National Association of Social Workers [NASW], 2017, 1.06). A dual role relationship exists when a therapist has *exactly one additional relationship*, such as a business or social relationship, with a client or someone closely associated with the client; for example, when a therapist becomes a friend of a current or former client, or of the client's close friend or partner. A multiple role relationship exists when a therapist has *one or more additional relationships* with a client or someone closely associated with the client; for example, when a therapist is a business associate of the client's close friend and a fellow parishioner of the client.

Multiple or dual role relationships may occur *simultaneously* or *consecutively* (NASW, 2017, 1.06[c]). The former type of relationship exists when two or more roles are assumed or ongoing at the same time. For example, such a relationship exists when the instructor of a student is also simultaneously the student's therapist, or when a therapist is having a sexual relationship with a current client. In contrast, consecutive multiple or dual role relationships exist when the roles occur consecutively, that is, one after the other. Such a relationship would exist if an instructor who also counsels takes on a former student as a client. A therapist who begins a sexual relationship after the therapy has terminated would also assume a consecutive dual role relationship.

As emphasized in this book, constructive client change can occur within the therapeutic relationship only if clients can trust their therapists. While healthy therapist-client relationships empower clients to make their own decisions, they are, by their nature, *fiduciary* relationships, that is, ones founded on trust (Bayles, 1989). As discussed in Chapter 2, the trust-based character of the relationship provides the climate under which client empowerment thrives. As an essential part of this fiduciary climate, clients must trust their therapists to apply, with undivided devotion, their professional expertise (knowledge and skills) to facilitate constructive client change rather than to advance personal self-interest through client manipulation and deception. Consequently, any dual or multiple role relationship (simultaneous or consecutive) involving even the appearance of conflict of interest can potentially undermine this sacred bond of trust. As such, therapists should avoid such relationships inasmuch as there is risk of exploitation or harm to clients or former clients (Kitchener, 1988; NASW, 2017, 1.06[c]).

Dual role relationships are also problematic to the extent that role expectations conflict or compete (Kitchener, 1988). For example, business associates expect that transactions be mutually beneficial wherein clients expect their therapists to act in ways that promote clients' welfare, not their own. Similarly, friends are mutually self-interested; and students expect their teachers to be objective in assigning grades, whereas clients expect their therapists to be concerned about their emotional welfare. So the expectations in a teacher-student relationship or that of friends diverge greatly from that of a therapist-client relationship. In general, "the greater the incompatibility of expectations is, the greater the role strain for the individual in the role" (Kitchener, 1988, p. 218).

Dual or Multiple Role Relationships in Rural Communities

Some dual or multiple role relationships may not easily be avoided, however. For example, in rural areas where there is only one psychologist serving the community at large, there is strong probability that the psychologist may assume multiple dual role relationships with others in the community. Thus, the psychologist may buy his groceries from the owner of the town market who happens to attend the same church as the psychologist. In such a case, it may not be feasible, in a practical sense, to avoid such multiple role relationships when the grocer is also the psychologist's client. Where such conditions arise, the therapist should mitigate factors that may potentially contribute to client harm. This would include avoiding overlap of interaction as much as possible (e.g., not going to a social function if it could be avoided) and making a concerted effort on the part of both the client and the therapist to keep the expectations of each role separate (e.g., not expecting a client teacher to give one's child special treatment). Accordingly, it is important that the therapist discuss with the client such relationship boundaries at the inception of therapy as part of the informed consent agreement and reinforce this understanding throughout the counseling process (Burgard, 2013).

Nonelective Dual or Multiple Role Relationships

Dual or multiple role relationships may also be *nonelective*; that is, therapists may not intentionally choose to take them on. Instead, the additional relationships may arise as a result of the unforeseen actions of others or by unanticipated changes in circumstances. For example, a therapist who teaches may have a client sign up for one of his classes, thereby placing the therapist in the precarious situation of counseling a current student. Or a therapist whose child attends elementary school might be counseling a client who ends up being the therapist's child's teacher. Or a therapist might counsel a client whose child ends up becoming best friends with the therapist's child. While, in such nonelective cases, it may not have been the therapists' wish to end up in such relationships, the therapists ordinarily still have the power to terminate the therapy (except for unusual cases such as judge-ordered counseling) and refer the client to a therapist who does not have any known conflicts of interest. Further, the therapist can also take precautions against ending up in such relationships. For example, the therapist who has reason to believe that a prospective client may be poised to take one of his classes can choose not to accept this individual as her client, or she can inform the prospective client in advance that it is not her policy to counsel students. Indeed, where there are conditions ripe for such potential conflicts of interest, therapists can act proactively by including a disclaimer (e.g., not counseling students, or not counseling clients with close familial connections to the therapist) as part of the client's informed consent.

Sexual Relationships

Among the most harmful relationships are ones involving sex with current or former clients. Clearly, the role expectations of a sex partner seeking sexual gratification are incompatible with that of a therapist, and the potential for loss of objectivity or independence of judgment is therefore extremely high. Yet, notwithstanding that such relationships are avoidable (unlike some arising as a result of living and practicing in a small rural community, for instance), the most frequent professional liability allegations made against counselors involve inappropriate sexual relationships with their clients or the partners or family members of their clients (CNA & HPSA, 2014). The following case illustrates the serious danger of conflicts of interest, competing or incompatible expectations, loss of independence of judgment, client manipulation, and harm generated by a therapist's succumbing to sexual attraction.

A CASE OF SEXUAL ATTRACTION TO A CLIENT

> George Langston, LCSW, in the state of Florida, was seeing Antonio Carlson for depression. Antonio's partner, Karl, had passed away 2 years prior from metastatic liver cancer. Previously, a well-regarded fashion designer, Antonio had refused to move on with his life. Living a solitary lifestyle, he was unwilling to return to the work for which he once harbored strong passion. Nor was he willing to date or engage in other social activities. Most of his "friends," who were more interested in his celebrity and wealth than in him personally, had since abandoned him. His younger sister, Gina, was the only one with whom Antonio kept in contact, and it was she who convinced him to seek counseling with George Langston, a close friend of Gina.
>
> After about 2 months of therapy, Antonio began to open up to Langston about pervasive personal issues in his life: his struggle with being gay in a homophobic world, being rejected by his parents, intimate details of his relationship with Karl, and how Karl had inspired him to pursue his dream of becoming a fashion designer. Antonio talked about how the two would meet each day for lunch at an outdoor café called the Gemini, where he said he made contact with his muse.
>
> As Antonio began to speak freely, Langston resonated with Antonio's life story, which reawakened his own unresolved painful feelings: his parent's refusal to accept that he was gay, his personal struggle with coming out, and his recent breakup with a man whom he deeply loved. This similar history and set of feelings formed a deepening emotional bond between the two, which eventually turned into reciprocal sexual attraction. Here there was ongoing transference and

counter-transference, but Langston still believed that there was remarkable progress and remained convinced that he could continue to facilitate constructive client change through the counseling relationship.

However, Antonio began to express his love for Langston and a renewed desire to return to work. Rebuffed by Langston, who cautioned Antonio about the importance of keeping their relationship professional, Antonio became enraged, and in the midst of a session, left Langston's office in tears. Fearful that Antonio might do something foolish, he contacted him. Antonio offered to see Langston over lunch and suggested meeting at the Gemini. Unable to convince Antonio to schedule an appointment at the office, Langston reluctantly agreed to meet at the Gemini, and the two dined.

It was evident to Langston that he could no longer counsel Antonio and offered to be friends. Antonio said that he wanted more from the relationship than friendship, and Antonio left the café abruptly leaving Langston sitting alone. Two days later Langston called Antonio; the two agreed to discontinue the counseling relationship, and they began a sexual relationship.

The romantic relationship appeared to be going well. Antonio returned to work, Langston moved in with him, lunched regularly at the Gemini, and Antonio claimed to have, once again, found his muse. However, the depression began to return as the relationship became increasingly contentious. In a particularly heated argument, Langston told Antonio that he "needed to stop feeling sorry for himself because he was gay." Langston collected his belongings, moved out, and the two parted. Six months later, Langston listened to the evening news, which announced that the famous fashion designer had taken his life.

Shaken by the news, Langston referred his clients to another therapist who agreed to take them on and closed his practice. However, after 2 months of quietly grieving the loss of his former client and partner, Langston returned to his practice, this time vowing never again to counsel single, attractive gay men.

SEXUAL RELATIONS WITH CURRENT CLIENTS

The case of Antonio is edifying with respect to the risks and dangers of entering into sexual relationships with clients. In fact, all states legally proscribe sexual relationships with *current* clients based on the palpable fact that clients, by virtue of their vulnerability, are subject to exploitation by therapists (Morgan, 2013). And all codes of ethics governing psychotherapy back up this proscription. For example, according to the ACA Code (2014, A.5.a), "[s]exual and/or romantic counselor–client interactions or relationships with current clients, their romantic partners, or their family members are prohibited." The American Psychological Association (2016) states succinctly, "Psychologists do not engage in sexual intimacies with current therapy clients/patients" (10.05). And the National Association of Social Workers makes plain that there are no exceptions, even with the claimed "consent" of the client. "Social workers should under no circumstances engage in sexual activities or sexual contact with current clients, whether such contact is consensual or forced" (NASW, 2017, 1.09[a]).

SEXUAL RELATIONS WITH FORMER CLIENTS

This proscription, with qualification, also legally applies to sexual relations with *former* clients. For example, according to Florida statute, "Any psychotherapist who commits sexual misconduct with a client, or former client when the professional relationship was terminated primarily for the purpose of engaging in sexual contact, commits a felony of the third degree . . ." (FS 491.0112[1]); where "sexual conduct" means "the oral, anal, or vaginal penetration of another by, or contact with, the sexual organ of another or the anal or vaginal penetration of another by any object" (FS 491.0112[4][c]). Accordingly, as a Florida mental health practitioner, George Langston is potentially guilty of sexual misconduct, a third degree felony, when he terminates therapy with his client Antonio for purposes of beginning a sexual relationship with him. Further, the legal case may be complicated by the fact that Antonio subsequently commits suicide. Arguably, if a causal connection can be proved to exist between the commission of the felony of sexual misconduct and the subsequent client suicide, it may meet the standards set by Florida statute for third degree murder (FS 782.04[4]). In fact, there is evidence to suggest a possible connection. According to one study of 958 individuals who had engaged in sexual relations with a therapist, 14% attempted suicide and 1% succeeded in committing suicide (Pope & Vetter, 2001).

Further, according to the Florida Administrative Code (64B4-10.003), for purposes of determining whether sexual misconduct has been committed, the therapist-client relationship is "deemed to continue for a minimum of 2 years after termination of psychotherapy or the date of the last professional contact with the client." However, the code adds, "the psychotherapist shall not engage in or request sexual contact with a former client at any time if engaging with that client would be exploitative, abusive or detrimental to that client's welfare." This means that waiting a minimum of 2 years after termination of the therapist-client relationship to have a sexual relationship with the client may not be sufficient to avoid a charge of sexual misconduct. What is also requisite is that such a relationship cannot be shown to be harmful to the client. However, according to the aforementioned study, most of the harms due to sexual intimacy (80% for females, 86% for males), including hospitalization, suicide, and attempted suicide, occurred in cases in which the sexual relationship began *after* termination of the therapist-client relationship (Pope & Vetter, 2001). In our opinion, this evidence militates against establishing a sexual relationship with clients even after waiting a set amount of time.

According to the ACA Code of Ethics (2014, A.5.c), a sexual relationship with former clients or their romantic partners or family members is prohibited for a period of 5 years after the last professional contact. Further, the therapist must document in writing whether the sexual relationship would in any way be exploitive or harmful to the former client. However, the therapist is arguably not a credible witness regarding whether the relationship would be exploitative or potentially harmful to the client inasmuch as he may have an actual or apparent conflict of interest. Hence, a therapist contemplating a sexual relationship with a former client, even after 5 years, may be justly advised to seek consultation from an impartial colleague about whether the relationship would, indeed, be in any way exploitative or harmful to the former client.

The APA is less stringent than the ACA regarding the length of time a therapist must wait in order to have sexual intimacy with a former client. According to the APA (2016,

10.08), "Psychologists do not engage in sexual intimacies with former clients/patients for at least two years after cessation or termination of therapy." Further, after the 2-year period, the therapist does not engage in a sexual relationship with the client "except in the most unusual circumstances." Again, the practitioner must demonstrate that there has not been exploitation.

However, the APA provides criteria for determining whether the therapist has exploited the client by beginning a sexual relationship. They include: (a) the amount of time transpiring since termination of therapy; (b) the "nature, duration, and intensity" of therapy; (c) the circumstances under which therapy was terminated; (d) the "personal history" and (e) "current mental status" of the client; (f) the probability of "adverse impact" on the client; and (g) any statements the therapist may have made prior to termination about the possibility of beginning a sexual relationship after termination (APA, 2016, 10.08). While the aforementioned criteria appear to provide constructive standards for determining sexual misconduct (e.g., pursuant to Florida statute), the reliance on the therapist, who may be conflicted, to document that these standards have been safely satisfied is problematic, in our opinion. Requiring that the therapist seek consultation with a qualified therapist who can confirm or disconfirm the satisfaction of these standards would offer a more objective determination. Quite clearly, Langston is not prepared to make such an objective determination given his own unfinished business and seeming inability to transcend his countertransference. Inasmuch as the risks of serious consequences arising from sex with former clients are substantial, including attempted suicide and commission of suicide, a virtuous practitioner would avoid a sexual relation with a former client in the first place and, in the very least, would not venture to make such an awesome decision without a competent ethics consult.

The case of George Langston also illustrates the firm basis in both law and ethics for a strong proscription against establishing sexual relationships with former clients. As human beings, therapists are not immune from having strong emotions in their personal relationships, which may be irrational or misdirected. Given the very clear incompatibility of expectations in the role of therapist and that in sexual relationships, it is not remarkable that a therapist who engages in a sexual relationship with a former client might confuse the two to the detriment of the former client and sex partner. In Langston's case, he admonishes Antonio to "stop feeling sorry for himself because he was gay." Here, Langston uses a deeply painful and personal fact disclosed in confidence by a client to his therapist to castigate Antonio for not meeting up to his expectations in their personal relationship. Such a confusion of role relationships is not only a potential problem of having sexual relationships with former clients, but it also is a predictable one, given the imperfect nature of humans. Indeed, it is expecting too much to require therapists never to say or do what they ought not, or to keep their composure without exception, even in the most emotionally and behaviorally challenging occasions of an intimate relationship. This is simply expecting too much; and this underscores the profound importance of not mixing close personal relationships (including but not limited to sexual intimacy) with a therapist-client relationship.

Further, the Langston case demonstrates the magnitude of discriminatory and unfair treatment of clients that can arise in the context of sexual involvement with them. Langston not only fails to help Antonio, but also his personal relationship with him deprives him of the competent therapy he so sorely needs. Thus, there is an inherent inequity arising out of having forged a personal relationship with Antonio. On the one hand, Langston's other clients, with whom he maintains independence of judgment, receive competent counseling services. On the other hand, Antonio, whom he finds to be sexually attractive, receives inferior counseling services, and, in the end, no professional help whatsoever. This treatment is not only damaging to Antonio's best interest (in the end, it cost him his life), but it also is grotesquely unfair.

SEXUAL ATTRACTION TO CLIENTS

But it is not the sexual attraction per se that creates the problem. As human beings, it is not unexpected that a therapist will occasionally be sexually attracted to certain clients. In itself, sexual attraction need not present a problem so long as the attraction does not impair the therapist's ability to maintain independence of judgment (Cohen & Cohen, 1999). However, this is not the case with George Langston. Unfortunately, his own unfinished business (including parental rejection, his struggle with living authentically as a gay person, and his recent breakup) provides the occasion for countertransference and loss of independence of judgment. Realizing that this is the case is sufficient for referring the client rather than continuing to work with him. Here, the therapist harbors a rationalization that because there has been "remarkable progress" he could continue, under the present circumstances, to facilitate further constructive client change by preserving the counseling relationship. No doubt, it is difficult for Langston to make an appropriate referral. Indeed, he is personally invested; however, the personal investment is what blurs his objectivity. The essential boundary between helping his client overcome his depression and helping himself work through his own psychological problems is breached; thus, there is client manipulation rather than client respect. The client becomes a mere means to promote the therapist's own perceived self-interest rather than an end in itself. Therefore, the sacred trust by which the client trusts the therapist to act to promote his welfare rather than his own self-interest is breached.

In the aftermath of Antonio's suicide, Langston decides not to counsel single, attractive gay men. Clearly, a gay man does not present with a tag that says "I'm gay," and Langston would not necessarily surmise that a prospective client is, indeed, gay. Nor would it be appropriate to ask a client if he is gay before accepting him as a client. The problem here underscores the more general problem with attempting to deal with unfinished business by avoiding working it through. Langston is correct that he ought not counsel clients with whom he has a problem that would impair his professional judgment; however, the issue may also be whether he is capable of counseling *any* clients if he cannot work through his issues. For example, Langston's issue includes having been rejected by his parents. However, heterosexuals can also be rejected by their parents. Parental rejection is a *human* issue wherefore the potential for countertransference may still be present across the gamut of client populations. Unfortunately, Langston does not himself seek appropriate counseling, even after the tragic consequences of not having worked through his issues. However, therapists who practice within the boundaries of competence are aware of, and monitor their physical, mental, or emotional problems. They seek assistance when such problems impair their professional judgment, *and*, when necessary, they suspend, terminate, or appropriately limit their practices until such problems have been adequately addressed (American Counseling Association [ACA], 2014, C.2.g).

Therapists who confront such potential conflicts appropriately take an inventory of the relevant welfare and interests that are at stake. As discussed in Chapter 3, this can be done by taking account of the stakeholders involved and the welfare and interests that are at stake. Table 9.1 provides an illustration.

Clearly, a careful, objective articulation of the relevant welfare and interests at stake, as presented in Table 9.1, points to the need to refer the client to another therapist who can competently counsel him. Acting on the sexual interests shared by both stakeholders fueled by transference and countertransference would have been seen as destructive of both party's welfare and legitimate interests. Langston has a legitimate interest in providing competent counseling services, and his welfare lies in working through his problems through appropriate channels—by seeking professional help. Continuing to counsel Antonio accomplishes neither. Instead, it has the potential to adversely affect Antonio's welfare—his ability to work through his depression and avoid the injury suffered by the termination of much needed therapy. In this light, the best interest of the client is served by terminating the counseling relationship and making an appropriate referral. The option of terminating only to embark on a sexual relationship would have been seen as unequivocally wrong from not only a client-oriented perspective but also from a self-interested and social perspective. From a self-interested perspective, Langston risks criminal charges of sexual misconduct. From a social perspective, he risks contributing to a negative stereotype of therapists as willing to "jump into bed" with their clients. As a mental health professional, Langston owes his profession more than this.

TABLE 9.1 ■ Stakeholder/Welfare/Interests

Stakeholder	Welfare (Positive/Negative)	Interests
Antonio	• Working through his depression • Not being harmed by therapy	• Sexual attraction to Langston and starting an affair with him (due to transference) • Being served by a competent therapist • Having a therapist who does not manipulate or deceive him
Langston	• Working through his own problems by seeking professional help • Not being charged with a felony for sexual misconduct	• Providing competent counseling services • Sexual attraction to Antonio (due to countertransference) • Not contributing to a negative image of the counseling profession

Further, Langston has a responsibility to Antonio to inform him of his personal issues when it becomes evident to him that his professional judgment has been impaired by them. Because there may be potential for a client to blame himself for the discontinuation of therapy, Langston needs to be candid with his client. "I have emotional problems dealing with my own personal issues related to my life experiences as a gay man, and I am having a difficult time keeping my personal life separate from the problems you are confronting. When such conflicts arise, it is my professional responsibility to refer you to another therapist." Here, Langston would have made sufficient disclosure so that Antonio would not be misled by his decision to terminate counseling. Unfortunately, Langston chooses to mislead Antonio by presenting the façade that he is acting consistently to promote the welfare and legitimate interests of his client in having a competent therapist who would not manipulate or deceive him.

ONLINE RELATIONSHIPS

The case of Langston would not have been substantially different if the counseling relationship was a distance one via the Internet. Cyber relationships can involve sexually stimulating chat sessions and conversation and/or cybersex, such as capturing mutual masturbation through a web camera (Smith, 2011). Online sexual relationships with current or former clients have similar proscriptions as do in-person sexual relationships (ACA, 2014, A.5.c). This is because they raise similar emotional issues of attachment and discordant role expectations as do in-person sexual relationships, including jealousy and betrayal (Smith, 2011).

Social Media Relationships

Social media such as Facebook, Twitter, and Pinterest have also created the occasion for the sharing of personal facts about oneself. While privacy used to be a highly prized value, it has become increasingly less so in cyberspace. One can now "friend" hundreds and thousands of people whom one does not know in person and share with the connected universe very personal facts about oneself. Therapists who get involved with posting to social media need to keep in mind that they may be setting the stage for confusing professional relationships with personal ones. In therapy, personal disclosure is appropriately restricted to information that is relevant to the client's situation. There is, therefore, opportunity to control the extent to which personal information is disclosed. However, social media websites typically permit members of their online communities to post very personal facts about themselves—from provocative photos to anecdotes about sexual encounters to intimate details about their likes and dislikes. Such information, therefore, exceeds the modest limits of disclosure in the professional context. Inasmuch as the Internet is a public facility and these posts may be publicly accessible, therapists who post to such websites raise the potential for blurring the lines between personal and professional relationships.

As discussed, apparent conflicts of interests can be just as problematic as actual ones, which means that a therapist who shares intimate personal information online may still feel comfortable with counseling another individual who may have had access to this information. However, the client may not feel comfortable with it or it may have repercussions on the therapist-client relationship. For example, a client who learns about her therapist's sexual desires from the Internet or sees the therapist in a sexually provocative pose online may come to think of the therapist as having sexual interests in them or otherwise entertain ideas about the therapist's sexuality that impede therapeutic progress. There is, therefore, abundant need for constraint by therapists in posting things to the Internet. Inasmuch as it is safe to suppose that what gets posted to the Internet stands a strong chance of remaining in some form online, the need for exercise of discretion cannot be overstated.

Therapists should not establish "personal virtual relationships" with their current clients (ACA, 2014, A.5.e), for example, friend them on Facebook; nor should they accept requests from them on professional social media networks such as LinkedIn. Again, such virtual interactions raise the risks of blurring the lines between personal and professional roles. Because LinkedIn or other collegial websites create occasion for establishing professional relationships, which have a different set of expectations than those of the therapist-client relationship (e.g., the exchanging of professional services and employment opportunities), therapists who do not keep such lines separate risk finding themselves in the crosshairs of potentially problematic dual role relationships such as bartering for fees (American Psychological Association, 2016, 6.05) or entering into business or employer-employee relationships with current clients (Cohen & Cohen, 1999).

Conversely, therapists should avoid accepting as clients individuals with whom they already have personal virtual relationships. For example, a therapist should avoid accepting a personal Facebook friend as a client. Again, even if the therapist can maintain independence of judgment, the client may not be so inclined, and the appearance to the client that the therapist has a conflict may be just as damaging as a real conflict.

Therapists should also avoid entering into personal virtual relationships with former clients to the extent that such relationships portend harm to the clients (ACA, 2014, A.5.e). As in nonvirtual (in-person) relationships, embarking on such a consecutive dual role relationship can provide the occasion for blurring of lines between personal and professional relationships because the expectations of each relationship may conflict. Thus, the client may continue to view the therapist as one with whom he can share confidential information to help him confront his behavioral or emotional problems; whereas the therapist may now be seeing the client as an online friend and, thus, no longer a professional charge. In our opinion, because the risks are significant for such role confusions, possible misuse of confidential client information in the context of the personal virtual relationship, and the appearance if not the reality of conflicts of interest, we would caution against entering into such relationships as a general policy.

The American Counseling Association enjoins that therapists who wish to maintain both a professional and personal social media presence should keep separate their personal and professional websites and profiles (2014, H.6.a). However, this may not be sufficient to address the problem of confusing the therapist-client relationship with personal virtual relationships. Therapists may not exercise caution regarding what they post to their personal websites, with whom they share what they post, and how restricted they make access to the personal information on their personal websites. For example, the public option on Facebook permits anyone, even those who do not have a Facebook account, to view one's information while the friends setting permits only friends to see one's personal information (Facebook, n.d.). However, restricting information, as by using the friends setting, still requires meticulous care as to whom one accepts as friends. So keeping personal virtual relationships separate from professional ones is not cut and dried. Of course, having only a professional presence on social media may be the best option for keeping one's personal information separate from one's professional profile.

Respect for clients' self-determination also requires that therapists respect the boundaries of client's privacy regarding their online identities. This means that therapists should avoid initiating social media contacts with clients such as attempting to friend a client. It further requires that therapists do not attempt to view clients' personal online information without their prior consent (ACA, 2014, H.6.c).

BARTERING FOR FEES

Bartering, that is, exchanging counseling services for goods or services provided by the client, can be potentially problematic because there is potential for confusion of expectations and the perception of conflicts of interest. A client expects her therapist to give undivided attention to her welfare and interests, while there is also potential for the bartering arrangement to create the perception of divided loyalties. For example, the client may believe that the therapist is dissatisfied with the quality of services she has rendered and that this will, in turn, affect the quality of the therapist's counseling services. Further, therapists who truly are dissatisfied with the goods or services provided by the client may encounter an actual conflict of interest. For example, suppose the client is providing lawn services in exchange for counseling; however, the client is not trimming bushes adequately or leaving trimmings on the property instead of hauling them off according to their agreement. Under such a situation, the therapist may be hard put to express dissatisfaction with the client's lawn services without alienating him or otherwise introducing a potentially damaging element into the therapist-client relationship.

On the other hand, according to Zur (2016), bartering can have positive therapeutic benefits, such as helping a poor client overcome low self-esteem and shame by proving to the therapist that she has talents and/or resources that can be beneficial. Further, it is already a norm for some cultures such as Hispanic, Native American, and some agricultural communities (Zur, 2016). However, being a norm does not necessarily mean that it does not create the potential for harm. Nor is it necessarily the case that a client who gains a sense of self-worth through the provision of goods or services is necessarily making therapeutic progress; for the sense of self-worth attained is a conditional one based on such abilities or resources rather than one of unconditional self-acceptance (Ellis, 2001).

Nevertheless, in poor communities where money is a scarce resource, but talents, skills, and tradable assets are plentiful, bartering for fees may be an accessible option for receipt of needed counseling services. According to the ACA (2014, A.10.e), in such cases, therapists should enter into a bartering arrangement only if the client requests it, the arrangement has not resulted in client exploitation or harm, and it is an accepted practice in the given community. Further, therapists should discuss with the client potential problems that can arise when distinct roles having competing expectations are combined and document the arrangement in a clearly articulated, written contract.

PRO BONO COUNSELING SERVICES

While therapists are not reasonably expected to work entirely without compensation, a possible alternative to bartering for fees in certain cases is the provision of *pro bono* counseling services to a percentage of indigent individuals who are in serious need of therapy. Such services are provided free of charge. Indeed, a fair-minded therapist welcomes the opportunity to help clients who are in serious need of therapy who would otherwise not receive it. For, it is not the amount of money clients have that determines whether or not they are worthy of receiving therapy; it is their psychological need for such services. The fair therapist understands this, and is willing to sacrifice some measure of monetary gain for promotion of client best interest.

Codes of ethics in the mental health professions have also recognized the value of providing pro bono counseling services. For example, in its Introduction, the ACA Code of Ethics states, "[C]ounselors are encouraged to contribute to society by devoting a portion of their professional activities for little or no financial return (pro bono publico)." In explicating its core aspirational principles or values, the NASW's Code of Ethics (2017) similarly states, "Social workers are encouraged to volunteer some portion of their professional skills with no expectation of significant financial return (pro bono service)." However, these codes provide no explicit guidelines on how to fulfill such virtuous aspirations. For example, what sort of work might qualify? How many hours of pro bono services would be appropriate?

In contrast, there are professional standards that have been set elsewhere. For example, the legal profession recognizes a professional responsibility to render 50 hours of pro bono legal services each year. According to Rule 6.1 of the American Bar Association's Model Rules of Professional Conduct (2016),

> [e]very lawyer has a professional responsibility to provide legal services to those unable to pay. A lawyer should aspire to render at least (50) hours of pro bono publico legal services per year.

Using 50 hours as a benchmark, therapists might similarly strive to advance the service goal encouraged by codes of ethics such as the ACA and NASW codes.

Programs such as the Pro Bono Counseling Project (2016), established in 1991 to provide pro bono counseling services to Maryland residents in need, can serve as a model for focusing attention on underserved populations. For instance, it has special programs for:

- Caring for the Caregivers
- Parenting Alone: Building Healthy Families
- Private Counseling for Public Service
- The Jean Steirn Cancer Program
- Transition & Depression: Elderly & Underserved
- Victims of Violence

Therapists can contact organizations (e.g., hospitals, nursing homes, assisted living facilities, prisons, Veterans Affairs, and other federal or state agencies) that serve underserved, indigent populations who would otherwise not receive needed therapy. Here, the standard for determining whether pro bono counseling services are warranted is the seriousness of the need. Thus, an individual who is having a crisis coping with an end-of-life decision may need pro bono counseling more immediately than an individual who is temporarily unemployed but not in crisis mode.

SLIDING SCALES

Fair practitioners are also prepared to provide a sliding scale of fees commensurate with the client's ability to pay (Cohen & Cohen, 1999). The ACA Code of Ethics (2014, A.10.C) provides that, when legally permitted, counselors adjust their fees to accommodate client's ability to pay. Similarly, according to the NASW's Code of Ethics (2017, 1.13[a]), in setting fees, "consideration should be given to clients' ability to pay." Here, we are referring to clients who do not have mental health insurance. Clients who have mental health insurance would still need to pay for deductibles unless the health care company was willing to waive the fee (Chamberlin, 2009).

There has, however, been controversy in the past about the fairness of sliding scales. For example, in 2008, the ACA Chief Professional Officer stated,

> Nothing in the ACA Code of Ethics prohibits the use of a sliding fee scale. However, the ACA Ethics Committee recommends against using a sliding scale. Why? Because it is discriminatory. A sliding fee scale charges people with larger incomes more for the exact same service that is being provided to clients with lesser incomes. (Walsh & Dasenbrook, 2008)

We submit that this argument engenders a confusion between equity and equality. While a wealthier individual may pay more for the same service under a sliding scale arrangement, this inequality is not necessarily an iniquity. As discussed in Chapter 2, the Justice Standard enjoins that *relevantly* like cases be treated alike and relevantly unlike cases be treated differently (Feinberg, 1973). For the purpose of the provision of counseling services, the standard of relevance is the need for counseling, not the amount of money one has. The fact that two clients with different financial means may be treated differently does not, therefore, necessarily make the disparate treatment unjust unless one of the two is being deprived of needed services or is receiving inferior services. To the contrary, it is unjust to provide competent counseling services to one individual but not to another because the former has more money than the latter. If relying on a sliding scale in distributing mental health care is "discriminatory," it is not *unfairly* discriminatory. It is unfairly discriminatory to allow the wealthy to receive competent (mental or physical) health care services while allowing those with less money but equal need to go without such services. Again, need, not money, is the ethically relevant criterion for doling out health care. While fair-minded therapists cannot eliminate the systemic iniquity that currently pervades our health care system, they can contribute to a more equitable system by providing a sliding scale commensurate with clients' ability to pay.

RECEIVING GIFTS FROM CLIENTS

Not uncommonly, therapists are also the recipients of gifts from clients. Unlike bartering, which always involves reciprocal arrangements discussed and agreed on in advance, therapists may not anticipate or agree in advance to accept a gift from a client. The client's motivation for offering the gift may be to express gratitude or respect, and it may be motivated by custom or ritual according to the client's culture (Corey, Corey, & Callanan, 2011; Zur, 2015). As such, therapists should consider the cultural context in which the gift is offered (ACA, 2014, A.10.f). Ordinarily, accepting small gifts having symbolic import whose monetary value is low, such as candy, flowers, or fruit, would be acceptable; whereas accepting gifts that have relatively high monetary values, for example, a television set, airline tickets, or a computer, would be unacceptable. As in bartering for services, accepting valuable gifts runs significant risk of generating competing expectations that can strain independence of judgment of both client and therapist. For example, a client may expect his therapist to give him priority over other clients; or he may worry that the therapist may not like the gift enough. Conversely, the therapist may have an uncomfortable feeling that she "owes" the client a debt of gratitude, or that the client has such expectations (Cohen & Cohen, 1999).

The timing of gift giving can also be significant (Zur, 2015). For example, after termination of therapy, receiving a small symbolic gift is more likely to be innocuous than if the gift is given in the midst of a client's working through her issues. In the latter case, the gift itself may take on additional meanings related to the client's issues. For example, a client who is working through a self-destructive demand for approval may be seeking the therapist's approval in providing a gift, even if it is an inexpensive one, such as a homemade cake.

Thus, in deciding whether or not to accept a gift from a client, a therapist should consider such facts as the gift's cultural significance, its monetary value, the motivation for offering it, and the timing of the offer. Empathetic, morally sensitive therapists understand that rejecting the client's gift can chill the therapist-client relationship. However, if the therapist determines that it would be inappropriate to accept the client's gift, the therapist should discuss with the client her reasons for not accepting the gift. As in the case of multiple or dual relationships where there is significant potential for loss of independence of judgment, actual or apparent conflicts of interest, or conflicting expectations, the virtuous therapist acts mindful of the client's best interest in maintaining the therapist-client trust.

As discussed in this chapter, the cultural background of clients can be an important factor in deciding how to treat gift giving or other dual or multiple role relationships that may place a strain on the therapist's independence of judgment or lend an appearance of such. The next chapter, accordingly, examines more closely the need to demonstrate respect for the cultures of diverse client populations (multiculturalism) in the counseling relationship. More specifically, it examines the importance of multicultural training for beginning therapists in the context of the supervisory relationship.

Questions for Review and Reflection

1. What does it mean to maintain independence of judgment, and why is it important in counseling?

2. What does it mean to have a conflict of interest? What is the difference between an actual and an apparent conflict of interest? Does the fact that the latter conflict of interest is only apparent mean that it cannot be problematic? Explain.

3. What is a dual role relationship? What is a multiple role relationship? Provide an example of each that is not provided in this chapter. Does either of these relationships involve a conflict of interest, real or apparent? Is either of these relationships problematic? Explain.

4. What factors can make a dual or multiple role relationship problematic?

5. How might a counseling relationship in a rural community lead to potentially problematic dual or multiple role relationships? What can be done to avoid or reduce the possibility of such problems?

6. What is a nonelective dual or multiple role relationship and how can they be problematic? Provide at least two examples. What can be done to avoid or reduce the possibility of such problematic relationships?

7. In the case of George Langston, Antonio's sister, Gina, is a close friend of Langston. Is such a dual role relationship potentially problematic? Explain.

8. What type of dual role relationship discussed in this chapter is encumbered by an exceptionally high number of liability claims filed against counselors? Why are such relationships so problematic?

9. What do state laws and codes of ethics unequivocally have to say about sex with current clients? What does the American Counseling Association (ACA) Code of Ethics state about sex with former clients? What does the American Psychological Association (APA) Code state?

10. What standards does the APA provide for determining whether sex with a former client is exploitative? List them.

11. In your estimation, does a therapist have at least an appearance of conflict of interest in attempting to document the acceptability of entering into a sexual relationship with a former client? If not, explain. If so, what might a therapist in such a situation do to avoid the appearance of conflict with respect to documenting the decision?

12. In the case of George Langston, in your estimation, does Langston commit sexual misconduct pursuant to Florida state statute? Explain.

13. Is there any empirical evidence that sex with former clients can be harmful?

14. After Langston begins a personal relationship with Antonio, at one juncture he states, "Stop feeling sorry for yourself because you are gay." What problem does this illustrate about establishing personal relationships with former clients?

15. In what way or ways is Langston's personal involvement with Antonio unfair or unjust?

16. Is sexual attraction to a client in itself a sufficient reason to refer a client? Is sexual attraction in the case of George Langston problematic? Explain.

17. What role does Langston's countertransference play in the problematic nature of his dual role relationship with his client?

18. In the aftermath of Antonio's suicide, Langston decides not to counsel single, attractive gay men. Is this a satisfactory way of dealing with his issues? Explain.

19. What is the advantage of doing a stakeholder analysis such as the one provided in Table 9.1? If Langston had, contrary to fact, prepared such an analysis, what ethical decision would it have supported? Why? In answering this question, consider the primary client responsibilities as well as the other-regarding and self-regarding responsibilities discussed in Chapter 3.

20. Does Langston have a responsibility to Antonio to inform him of his personal issues when it becomes evident to him that his professional judgment has been impaired by them? Explain.

21. Can online sexual relationships with clients be as problematic as physical ones? Explain.

22. What potential problems are raised when counselors post very personal facts about themselves or photos of themselves (not necessarily restricted to sexually provocative ones) on the Internet? How should therapists address such potential problems?

23. Is it acceptable for therapists to establish virtual friendships with current clients? What about former clients? Explain.

24. Is it acceptable for therapists to accept as clients individuals with whom they have had virtual friendships? Explain.

25. What does the ACA maintain about having both a personal as well as professional presence on the Internet? Is the ACA's response adequate? Explain.

26. Is it okay for therapists to view clients' personal online information or to friend their clients? Explain.

27. Is bartering for fees ever acceptable? Are there any potential risks in such arrangements? Can they have any positive value? Explain. What does the ACA say about bartering for fees?

28. Do therapists have a professional responsibility to provide pro bono counseling services, that is, services rendered without remuneration to poor clients? If not, why not? If so, in what ways might a therapist discharge such a responsibility?

29. Is it fair for therapists to provide sliding scale fees to their clients based on their ability to pay for counseling services? Why or why not? What did the ACA Ethics Committee in 2008 claim about such fee arrangements? Was its argument for its position a convincing one? Explain.

30. Is it ever ethically acceptable to accept a gift from a client? If not, why not? If so, what factors should be considered in deciding whether or not to accept the gift? Provide examples of gift giving to illustrate your response.

Cases for Analysis

1. Alberta Seabrook is a licensed mental health counselor who has a large teenage clientele. One of her clients, Bettina, age 15, was referred to counseling as part of a misdemeanor diversion program because she is caught shoplifting. Seabrook is developing a good rapport with her client, and Bettina is beginning to make progress toward her goals in therapy. Yesterday, Seabrook heard her own daughter's phone ring and looked at the screen. The missed caller's name was displayed and it read "Bettina." Alberta stood still in shock. "How many teenage *Bettinas* could there be in our town?" she asked herself. Alberta now wants to question her daughter about her new friend, but doesn't want to disclose that she has a client with the same name. Furthermore, Seabrook is alarmed that her daughter may be friends with a girl who shoplifts and Seabrook does not want her daughter to associate with Bettina. All this is further complicated by the fact that if Seabrook's daughter is, indeed, friends with Seabrook's client, then a nonelective dual role relationship will be in place. What should Seabrook do? What are her ethical responsibilities? To whom does Seabrook have primary responsibility, her client or her daughter? Should Seabrook mention to her daughter or her client that she knows that her daughter has a new friend named Bettina. Could this question, if asked of Seabrook's daughter, violate client confidentiality in any way?

2. Diana Duncan is a clinical psychologist who is a professor in a private college. She also maintains a small private practice. Duncan is careful not to take as clients anyone who is presently a student at the college or who plans to attend her college. At the very beginning of the fall semester this academic year, a student in one of Duncan's classes waits after class to speak to her. "Hi, Dr. Duncan. My name is Dennis Burgess. I'm so glad to finally meet you. You were my wife's therapist. She's Isla Burgess. She still talks about you, and it's been a year already since she finished therapy."

Duncan is very surprised by this disclosure and tells Dennis that she is glad to meet him, but that she has concerns about having him as a student in light of his relationship with a former client of hers. She suggests that he register for another section of the same class with another instructor. Dennis states that his wife is fully aware that he is enrolled in Duncan's class and she is okay with it. He maintains that he wants to remain in Duncan's class. Duncan remembers that Dennis's wife had worked on issues relating to verbal abuse and is concerned because the class that he is now enrolled in covers that topic. She wonders whether Dennis might bring up topics in class that have relevance to his own marital situation. What do you think Duncan should do in this situation? Does she have a legal or ethical right to acknowledge that Isla, Dennis's wife, was, in fact, her client? Does Duncan have an ethical right or responsibility to contact Dennis's wife? Who are the stakeholders in this situation? What are some of the possible dangers of this dual role relationship?

3. Simeon Lemon is a 28-year-old male who is receiving counseling from Irene Waters, a licensed mental health intern. Waters is 26 years old. Both Lemon and Waters are single. One Friday night, the two happen to be at the same local club and Lemon strikes up a conversation with Waters. Waters is at first hesitant to socialize with Lemon and tells him that their socializing is unprofessional. Later that night, after both consume several drinks, Lemon

asks her to dance and she consents. At his next session the following week, Lemon tells Waters that he "really likes her" and is discontinuing his therapy with her so that the two can date. Waters explains that she should not have danced with Lemon and must refer him to another therapist because of the nature of what happened on Friday night. Lemon states that he will not see another therapist and will report Waters to her supervisor if she refuses to date him. Waters fears that her conduct will lead to professional censure and that she will not be able to become licensed. What should she do at this point? What are her ethical or legal responsibilities at this juncture? What might be the possible role of Waters' clinical supervisor? How would a virtuous therapist proceed?

References

American Bar Association, Center for Professional Responsibility. (2016). *Model rules of professional conduct*. Chicago, IL: Author. Retrieved from https://www.americanbar.org/groups/professional_responsibility/publications/model_rules_of_professional_conduct/model_rules_of_professional_conduct_table_of_contents.html

American Counseling Association. (2014). *ACA code of ethics*. Alexandria, VA: Author.

American Psychological Association. (2016). *Ethical principles of psychologists and code of conduct*. Washington, DC: Author. Retrieved from http://www.apa.org/ethics/code/?item=11#805

Bayles, M. D. (1989). *Professional ethics* (2nd ed.). Belmont, CA: Wadsworth.

Burgard, E. L. (2013). Ethical concerns about dual relationships in small and rural communities: A review. *Journal of European Psychology Students, 4*, 69–77.

Chamberlin, J. (2009). How to offer a financial break: Six ways psychologists can help patients who can no longer afford therapy. *Monitor on Psychology, 40*(1). Washington, DC: American Psychological Association. Retrieved from http://www.apa.org/monitor/2009/01/fees.aspx

CNA & HPSA. (2014). Understanding counselor liability risk. Retrieved from http://www.hpso.com/Documents/pdfs/CNA_CLS_COUNS_022814p_CF_PROD_ASIZE_online_SEC.pdf

Cohen, E. D., & Cohen, G. S. (1999). *The virtuous therapist: Ethical practice of counseling and psychotherapy*. Belmont, CA: Wadsworth.

Corey, G., Corey, M., & Callanan, P. (2011). *Issues and ethics in the helping professions*. Belmont, CA: Brooks/Cole.

Davis, M. (1982). Conflict of interest. *Business and Professional Ethics Journal, 1*(4), 17–27.

Ellis, A. (2001). *Feeling better, getting better, staying better: Profound self-help therapy for your emotions*. Atascadero, CA: Impact.

Facebook. (n.d.). Privacy facts. [Facebook Privacy Basics]. Retrieved from https://www.facebook.com/about/basics/manage-your-privacy/posts#1

Feinberg, J. (1973). *Social philosophy*. Englewood Cliffs, NJ: Prentice-Hall.

Kitchener, K. S. (1988). Dual role relationships: What makes them so problematic? *Journal of Counseling & Development*, *67*(4), 217–221.

Morgan, S. (2013). *Criminalization of psychotherapist sexual misconduct*. Washington, DC: National Association of Social Workers. Retrieved from http://c.ymcdn.com/sites/www.naswca.org/resource/resmgr/imported/7_13_legal_issue.pdf

National Association of Social Workers. (2017). *Code of ethics of the National Association of Social Workers*. Retrieved from https://www.socialworkers.org/About/Ethics/Code-of-Ethics/Code-of-Ethics-English.aspx

Pope, K. S., & Vetter, V. A. (2001). Prior therapist-patient sexual involvement among patients seen by psychologists. *Psychotherapy*, *28*(3), 429–438. Retrieved from https://www.kspope.com/sexiss/sex2.php

Pro Bono Counseling Project. (2016). About us. Baltimore, MD: Author. Retrieved from http://probonocounseling.org/about_us

Smith, B. L. (2011). Are internet affairs different? *Monitor on Psychology*, *42*(3). Washington, DC: American Psychological Association. Retrieved from http://www.apa.org/monitor/2011/03/internet.aspx

Walsh, R. J., & Dasenbrook, N. C. (2008). The complications of sliding scale fees. *Counseling Today*. Alexandria, VA: American Counseling Association. Retrieved from https://ct.counseling.org/2008/04/private-practice-in-counseling-the-complications-of-sliding-fee-scales/

Zur, O. (2015). *Gifts in psychotherapy & counseling: Ethics, cultural and standard of care considerations*. Sebastopol, CA: Zur Institute. Retrieved from http://www.zurinstitute.com/giftsintherapy.html#cultural

Zur, O. (2016). *Bartering in psychotherapy & counseling: Complexities, case studies and guidelines*. Sebastopol, CA: Zur Institute. Retrieved from http://www.zurinstitute.com/bartertherapy.html

10

BEING RESPECTFUL ACROSS DIVERSE CULTURES

Case Study: Supervising a Supervisee Doing Cross-Cultural Counseling

According to the American Counseling Association (ACA) Code of Ethics (2014, Preamble), a core value of the counseling profession is that of "honoring diversity and embracing a multicultural approach in support of the worth, dignity, potential, and uniqueness of people within their social and cultural contexts." Indeed, such a multicultural perspective, or "multiculturalism," is prescribed by the standards of Client Autonomy and Welfare and goes to the heart of what it means to treat a client with respect.

As guardians of professional core values, counselor educators and supervisors "actively infuse multicultural/diversity competency in their training and supervision practices" to promote awareness, knowledge, and skills in the competencies of multicultural practice" (ACA, 2014, F.11.c). This chapter focuses on the role of supervisors in "actively infusing" such competencies in their supervisees. It begins with a case of a Muslim client who is being counseled by a therapist in training who comes from a different cultural orientation than his client.

A CASE OF CROSS-CULTURAL COUNSELING

> A member of the Hazara, a Persian-speaking Shia ethnic group, Abdul Mohammed came from Afghanistan to Brooklyn, NY, in 1995, when he was a young man, to escape religious persecution by the Taliban. A medical lab technician, he and his wife, Maya, both college graduates, had two children, Ahmad and Adela. While Abdul and his wife were not unaccustomed to religious discrimination in the early days of settling in the city, the intensity and frequency of this discrimination increased to frequent bouts with hate speech and mistreatment, especially after the World Trade Center was bombed in 2001. Since the Mohammeds' neighborhood

had a large community of Muslims, most of this discrimination occurred when the family ventured outside the confines of this area of Brooklyn.

One year ago, Abdul's son, Ahmad, an infantryman in the U.S. army, was killed in Iraq when he attempted to save the life of another U.S. soldier. After Ahmad's death, overcome with grief, Abdul took leave from his job at a Brooklyn lab where he had worked for over 15 years. Still unable to cope with the loss of his son, Maya urged Abdul to seek counseling. Although he was very skeptical about the possibility that counseling could ever help him, Abdul reluctantly agreed to try counseling. Maya then scheduled an appointment at Safe Harbor Counseling Center in a nearby locality of Brooklyn, which arranged for her husband to see Maxwell Stuart, a counselor intern working toward his master's degree in mental health counseling at a New York state university and eventual state licensure as a mental health counselor. A politically conservative Baptist, residing in a section of Brooklyn that was predominately Christian, Maxwell was under the supervision of Art Berman, PhD, LMHC, an Orthodox Jew.

On the first session, Mohammed sat stoically, listening attentively, nodding occasionally, and avoiding eye contact with Maxwell, all of which Maxwell took to be signs of resistance and/or low self-esteem. It was not until the third session when Mohammed began to make some personal disclosures:

"I always believed that New York City was basically a tolerant city," said Abdul, "but I am now starting to feel unsafe when I leave the neighborhood. I am starting to feel like a prisoner."

"So you are having some anxiety about leaving your home?" queried Maxwell.

"Not my home. I go to the market in the neighborhood."

"This is interesting. During 9/11 I bet you can recall how New Yorkers all banded together to help each another. I don't think any of the first responders were asking whether someone trapped in a building was a Muslim, Christian, or Jew when they risked their lives to save them."

"I am aware of that. They were very courageous."

"People are often afraid of what they don't know. You wear a turban. This is your custom and your right to dress as you please."

"I am aware of that. My son gave his life for our freedom."

"Tell me about that."

"He was an American soldier on his second tour in Iraq. He attempted to save another American soldier and was killed by friendly fire. He received the Purple Heart."

"You must be very proud."

"I am. And I now question whether it was worth it in the end. My only son died defending this country, and there is still so much hatred in the hearts of so many. Even the American president!"

"What do you mean?"

"The president wishes to ban Muslims from entering the country. This could have been me."

"I think he just wants to protect the nation."

"He once said he wanted a total ban on Muslims entering the country. That could have been my son, too, who paid the ultimate price for freedom. And now the president wants to ban my brothers and sisters, and their children, from coming here."

> "It sounds like you are feeling very upset because you think your son died in vain."
>
> "Yes. That is correct."
>
> "But your son was an American hero. You should be proud."
>
> "I am, sir."

THE ROLE OF THE SUPERVISOR

According to the ACA Code of Ethics (2014), a primary obligation of a counseling supervisor is to "monitor client welfare and supervisee performance and professional development" (F.1.a). As such, the role of Art Berman, in the given multicultural context, includes monitoring his supervisee's handling of the multicultural issues that might affect the quality of his counseling services. Indeed, counselor competence includes knowledge of the diverse cultures across which the supervisee counsels.

In fact, the choice of modality being used, even the client's diagnosis (ACA, 2014, E.5.b), may be profoundly influenced by such knowledge. In Abdul's case, consideration needs to be given to the fact that the client comes from Afghanistan where men are discouraged from expressing emotion. This fact can explain Abdul's perceived "stoic" affect (Mehraby, 2002). This knowledge can also help determine what modality would be most effective for this particular client. For example, a modality such as Gestalt therapy, which is highly emotional, would probably be a less suitable choice than cognitive-behavior therapy (CBT), which requires less emotional expression (Gladding, 1996).

Further, knowledge of Afghan etiquette and social customs can help explain Abdul's averted eye contact, inasmuch as it is considered best in this culture to only occasionally look someone in the eyes (Commisceo Global, n.d.). Hence, Maxwell's hypothesis that Abdul is resistant and/or has low self-esteem is hastily constructed without due knowledge or consideration of the facts about Abdul's ethnic background.

Supervisory competence in overseeing the supervisee's performance and professional development must therefore include multicultural understanding. Otherwise the supervisor is incapable of monitoring client welfare, especially in cases where the supervisee and the client come from disparate cultural backgrounds and key nuances and distinctions affecting counseling performance may not be evident to the supervisee.

The Concept of Culture

It is arguable that the client's cultural background is always a key factor in the provision of competent supervisory and counseling services (Diller, 2004, p. 17). Here, the concept of *culture* means "a lens through which life is perceived" as distinguished by differences in "language, values, personality and family patterns, worldview, sense of time and space, and rules of interaction," which "generates a phenomenologically different experience of reality" (Diller, 2004, p. 4). On this definition, different cultures can be distinguished not just according to demographic factors such as race, nationality, and religion, but also according to sexual orientation and age. For example, insofar as teenagers, as distinct from older persons, share common practices, language, music, interests, and rules of interaction through which they perceive the world, we can speak of a teenage or "youth" culture. The same can be said of "gay or LGBT culture" (Owens, 2016).

The Supervisor's Critique

A therapist who is culturally sensitive would therefore have the capacity to enter the phenomenological world of the client and perceive the world through his cultural perspective. Clearly, this requires understanding the client's cultural background, including the challenges that it may have presented in the client's life. In the case of Abdul Mohammed, this includes a history of oppression, discrimination, and iniquity related to authentically living according to his values, religious beliefs, practices, worldview, rules of interaction, and other aspects of his culture. It requires knowing that not all Muslims are the same in their beliefs and practices and that there can be oppression of subgroups of Muslims by other Muslims (Hopfe & Woodward, 2009). In Abdul's case, he is a member of the Hazara group, a Shi'ite minority group among the worldwide community of Muslims with a history of oppression by Sunni Muslims (Esposito, 2011).

Promoting development of such cultural sensitivity in the supervisee is an important part of the role of the supervisor. As such, in the present case, as a culturally competent supervisor himself, Dr. Berman would recommend that Maxwell research the customs, worldviews, religious beliefs, practices, and history of the Hazara people and their relationships to other Muslim groups. This can help Maxwell improve his capacity to enter the subjective world of his client; reflect back, more insightfully what he is experiencing; gain his trust; and, consequently, help him address his issues.

Second, Maxwell, who perceives the world through the lens of Christianity and (presumably) political conservatism, must learn to bracket his own religious and political biases. Post 9/11 New York may, from his perspective, appear to be tolerant, but this is not necessarily how another experiences it. For example, Maxwell may not have lived through seeing his house of worship defiled with hateful epithets, being mocked, or called vile names by individuals who do not even know him. Still, he can imagine how he might feel if these things were to happen to him or his loved ones. Indeed, while there is cultural diversity, on a human level, one can appreciate how such degrading and demeaning attacks on one's personhood can promote a jaundiced reality perspective. Add to this the loss of one's beloved child, who died defending the right to live freely; yet at the same time, feeling like a prisoner, being fearful to venture outside the confines of one's neighborhood enclave. Then add to this a government administration that appears (from the client's perspective) to be insensitive to the suffering and persecution of his people, and we can better sense the profound sadness that Abdul has experienced. In this endeavor, there is no room for judging whether the client's politics is right, or wrong, or whether it agrees or disagrees with one's own. To the contrary, the goal is to resonate with the client's phenomenological world, grasping it on a deep emotional level enlightened by knowledge of the client's plight. Such resonance is an essential aspect of what it means to respect one's client. In Maxwell's case, there is considerable need for improvement.

BARRIERS TO RESONATING WITH THE CLIENT'S PHENOMENOLOGICAL WORLD

Stereotypes

As a virtuous supervisor, Dr. Berman would himself need to transcend the popular stereotypes that breed disrespect for the humanity of others. A stereotype is a form of oversimplified thinking that categorizes reality, particularly human beings, into overly broad categories through the use of universal (and quasi-universal) quantifiers such as "all," "no," and "most" (Cohen, 2017). For example, the stereotype, "all Muslims are terrorists (or terrorist supporters)," is behind much of the discrimination that Muslim Americans experience in the United States, especially since the 9/11 attacks (Brooklier, 2015). Sadly, the person who stereotypes perceives the other through such a rigid conceptual framework and therefore does not see the other as an individual. In this way, stereotypes can dehumanize the other and, as a result, permit the stereotype holder to treat the other in dehumanizing or degrading ways without taking responsibility for it (Bandura, Underwood, & Fromson, 1975). After all, if a Muslim is subhuman, an animal, a murderer, a terrorist, or other form of lowly creature, then it is okay to treat this individual as such, and therefore no need to blame oneself for any transgression. Indeed, the stereotype can conceal the transgression behind a veil of self-righteousness.

In fact, no one is immune to stereotyping. The term *stereotype*, itself, was first introduced into the literature by media scholar Walter Lippmann (1946) in his influential book, *Public Opinion*. In this profoundly astute work, Lippmann argued that stereotyping is the human being's way of dealing with the complex and often risky nature of reality. Stereotypes are, by their nature, prejudgments and provide a premade solution to handling a litany of diverse phenomena. Thus, if all people can be divided into a relatively small number of categories, then processing relationships with them is manageable. Solutions to interpersonal problems and relationships can thereby be "stamped out" mechanically like using a printing plate or so-called stereotype to mechanically create multiple high-speed copies of printed matter (Lippmann, 1946).

As a virtuous supervisor, Dr. Berman would be aware of this human propensity to stereotype and would be sensitive to identifying his own particular stereotypes and those of whom he trains. Clearly, Maxwell stereotypes New Yorkers when he takes all New Yorkers to be tolerant and not prone to prejudgment. As a result, he is blinded to the manner in which stereotypes of Muslims since 9/11 have negatively impacted the manner in which Muslim Americans have been treated. Dr. Berman should therefore instruct Maxwell about the human propensity to stereotype and to be self-aware of this tendency.

Mind-Sets

Stereotypes also tend to be held as mind-sets. A mind-set is a frame of mind that is resistant to evidence to the contrary. Believing that "all Muslims are terrorists" is held as a mind-set when any evidence offered against it is summarily dismissed. For example, pointing out that a particular individual whom the stereotype holder knows not to be a terrorist may prompt the response, "Oh but he's an exception." As such, a supervisor needs to be aware of this tendency to dismiss evidence in helping a supervisee address their stereotypes. Otherwise, the stereotype may continue to play in the background of the provision of counseling services to the detriment of client welfare.

Instruction in the avoidance of stereotypes should also include the manner in which they tend to be sustained by their holders. Typically, the stereotype arises through socialization. For example, children are taught to distrust black people, to expect Jewish people to haggle about prices, or to expect gay men to be flamboyant and effeminate (Cohen, 2009). Unfortunately, the mass media (television shows, movies, etc.) tend to reinforce such stereotypes. Further, a confirmation bias is used to sustain the stereotype. "If what we are looking at corresponds successfully with what we anticipated, the stereotype is reinforced for the future . . ." (Lippmann, 1946, p. 74). For example, when a terrorist attack occurs and the terrorist is a Muslim, it is used to support and to continue to hold the stereotype that all Muslims are terrorists; or when a gay man acts flamboyantly, the instance is again used to support and continue to hold the stereotype; while, as mindsets, instances of individuals that do not fit the stereotype in question are summarily dismissed, ignored, or played down. Virtuous supervisors and therapists are adeptly aware of the flawed logic of stereotyping and work diligently to expose this flawed logic in supervisees and to avoid its commission in the provision of counseling services. This is especially the case when supervisees are engaging in cross-cultural counseling, as in the case of Maxwell; but, since stereotypes are endemic to humankind, such keen awareness, diligence, and reflective practice in overcoming stereotypes should be at the forefront in the rendering of all supervision, educational, and counseling services (ACA, 2014, F.11.c; C.2.a).

CLIENT INFORMED CONSENT IN THE SUPERVISORY CONTEXT

Treating clients with respect in the supervisory context unequivocally requires receiving informed consent from the client about the nature of the supervision. Thus, in addition to the other information regularly provided (see Chapter 6), Maxwell would need to disclose that he is a counselor intern, that he is being supervised by another counselor, and that he will be discussing their sessions with his supervisor (ACA, 2014, E.1.b; F.1.c).

Further, the quality of the supervisory critique clearly depends on the ability of the supervisor to gain adequate knowledge of how the supervisee is conducting himself in sessions. This knowledge can be gleaned from discussions with the supervisee who provides first person accounts of what has transpired in the sessions. Another approach is to audio and visually record the sessions so that the supervisor can review them with the supervisee. Both approaches have both positive and negative aspects. On the one hand, discussing rather than recording the sessions can be less intimidating for at least some clients who may feel uncomfortable about their private lives being recorded. On the other hand, the supervisor may miss important problems in the conduct of the session that he would have otherwise found had he had an opportunity to view a recording of the session (Haggerty & Hilsonroth, 2011). The positive and negative aspects of recording the session are the converse: possibly more intimidating but more informative. Because recording the counseling sessions of supervisees in supervised training tends to be more informative, it is widely accepted (Baltrinic, O'Hara, & Jencius, 2016). However, because it has potential to violate the confidentiality of the client (e.g., if the recordings are shared with unauthorized third parties), it is important for the client to receive explicit information about how the recordings will be used, who will have access to them, and how they will be treated after termination of therapy (Ford, 2006, p. 46). Such informed consent must be given prior to recording any sessions (ACA, 2014, B.6.c.), and it is preferable if given in writing to clearly establish that legal permission was provided for the recording.

As such, Maxwell would need to explain to Abdul the rationale for recording the sessions, namely that it is a more effective way for the supervisee to learn, that the recording would be shared only with his supervisor, and that it would be destroyed when the counseling relationship ends. In the event that Abdul is uncomfortable with the recording of his sessions, then he should not insist on it. Here, as elsewhere, Client Welfare comes first. Indeed, the client is already reluctant to disclose his personal life history to a person he does not know. In the present case, this may have much to do with the client's cultural perspective inasmuch as Afghan men tend not to bare their souls to others, especially to those whom they do not know (Mehraby, 2002).

THE SUPERVISORY RELATIONSHIP

According to the ACA Code of Ethics (2014, F.2.b), supervisors must also be aware of and address multiculturalism and diversity as it relates to the supervisory relationship. In the present case, Art Berman is an Orthodox Jew, Maxwell Stuart, a Baptist. Indeed, while Maxwell, as a New Yorker, may have known other Jewish people, this need not prevent him from harboring prejudice toward Jewish people. For example, when among other Baptists, he might partake in popular stereotypes about Jewish people, for example, making anti-Semitic jokes. As Gordon W. Allport (1985) astutely surmised, this is still a form of prejudice, albeit a covert one. Conversely, as an Orthodox Jew, Berman might harbor his own subtle prejudices against Baptists.

Further, stereotypes can drive problematic misperceptions about the prejudices of others. For example, it is popularly assumed that if one is Jewish then one hates Muslims, and conversely. However, despite the hostility between these groups in the Middle East, relying on a mind-set driven stereotype rather than assessing people on their own merit can lead to false and self-defeating conclusions. Thus, Maxwell might assume that Dr. Berman must hate his Muslim client because Berman is a Jew; and this assumption could lead Maxwell to question the credibility of Berman's assessment of his performance. It is therefore important that supervisors candidly discuss with their supervisees the potential for respective stereotypes and prejudices to adversely affect the supervisory relationship, the supervisee's learning experience, and the quality of counseling the client receives.

As in the case of the therapist-client relationship, the supervisory relationship requires that both parties maintain independence of judgment. If the supervisor is unable to objectively evaluate the performance of the supervisee, or the supervisee is unable to work cooperatively with the supervisor, due to personal bias, irreconcilable differences, or other conflicts, then the supervisor should provide appropriate referral to other potential supervisors (ACA, 2014, F.4.d). For example, if Dr. Berman is unable to competently assess Maxwell's performance, due to his inherent biases toward Maxwell or his client, then he should terminate the relationship. In such a case, Berman would need to resolve his issues before assuming the supervisory role.

Similarly, as gatekeepers of the profession, supervisors have a responsibility to insure that supervisees are competent to enter the profession. Thus, if supervisees are "unable to demonstrate that they can provide competent professional services to a range of diverse clients," then their supervisors recommend dismissal from the training program or help supervisees to obtain remedial assistance. In such cases the supervisors also seek consultation and document their decisions (ACA, 2014, F.6.b; F.6.c). For example, in the end, if Maxwell were uncomfortable with counseling anyone who did not share his Christian values, then he would either be referred for assistance and/or dismissed from the counseling program in question. Indeed, as a state licensed mental health counselor (in contrast to an unlicensed, pastoral counselor working for a Christian church), Maxwell would be expected to counsel a culturally diverse client population. As such, it would be unjust to turn away clients in need of mental health services based on their ethnicity or religion.

Supervisors do not counsel their supervisees, however (ACA, 2014, F.6.c). Thus, if Maxwell needs counseling to overcome personal problems he has in relating to non-Christian clients, then Dr. Berman would need to refer him to another competent therapist for such assistance. This is because counseling a supervisee can lead to a problematic dual role relationship (see Chapter 9). Thus, Dr. Berman's role as Maxwell's supervisor was to assess Maxwell's competence to advance his future clients' welfare and dignity and to adhere to professional values and ethical standards (ACA, 2014, F.6.c). On the other hand, Berman's role as Maxwell's therapist would be to promote *Maxwell's* welfare and dignity. Inasmuch as these distinct roles can create inconsistent expectations for both supervisor (therapist) and supervisee (client), it would therefore be unacceptable to mix them (Kitchener, 1988). Similar considerations apply to mixing the supervisory relationship with personal or sexual relationships (ACA, 2014, F.3.a; F.3.b; F.3.d).

Supervisee Informed Consent

Supervisors also respect the rational self-determination of their supervisees by providing them with the opportunity to give their informed consent to the supervisory relationship (ACA, 2014, F.4.a). Inasmuch as the supervisee has the option of choosing to work with different supervisors, they are entitled to give their informed consent to the relationship before undertaking it. In fact, some state statutes (Counselor-License, n.d.; Washington Administration Code [WAC] 246-810-025, 2017) and codes of professional ethics, such as the American Mental Health Counseling Association Code of Ethics (AMHCA, 2015, III), require the informed consent agreement to be in writing. To forestall any misunderstandings between supervisor and supervisee such agreements should be in writing (Baily, 2005).

The following set of topics provides a comprehensive list of topics that should be included in the supervisory informed consent contract (AMHCA, 2015, III; Leddick, 1994; Syracuse University, 1999; WAC 246-810-025; Zur, 2015):

- Information about the supervisor, including business address, telephone number, list of degrees, licenses and credentials and/or certifications, areas of competence, training in supervision, and supervisory experience
- Supervisor's theoretical orientation(s)
- Types of activities in supervision (e.g., role play, reviewing recordings, homework assignments, journaling)
- Time and place where supervision will be conducted
- Supervision model or approach (e.g., development, integrated, or orientation-specific models)
- Goals of supervision

- Expectations of both parties
- Evaluation procedures
- Limits and scope of supervisee confidentiality
- Procedures for emergencies and supervisor absence
- Frequency of supervision
- How the supervisory agreement is to be used
- How and where records are to be kept and protected
- Procedures and conditions of supervisee endorsement for certification, licensure, or employment
- The limits of the supervisory relationship (e.g., policies concerning conflicts of interest, dual role relationships, supervisees needing counseling)
- Financial arrangements

The provision of such information at the inception of the supervisory relationship permits the supervisee to have a clear understanding of what to expect in the relationship. For example, if Dr. Berman lists CBT as his orientation, and later recommends that Maxwell use CBT with his client, this would not come as a surprise. While supervisees should be flexible about use of modalities appropriate for a diverse client population, it is still possible that the theoretical orientation of a particular supervisor may not provide a good fit for a particular supervisee. Knowing this information in advance before agreeing to the arrangement can therefore be helpful to the supervisee in making an informed decision about whether to work with the supervisor in question.

According to the Association for Counselor Education and Supervision (1990), the supervisor and supervisee should cooperate to develop goals of supervision that are realistic, measurable, and attainable within the particular supervisory context. Such goals should include cultural competence and the other core areas of counselor competence such as relationship building and professionalism, as well as traditional supervision goals such as counseling performance and cognitive skills, diagnosis, treatment planning, and self-awareness. Such goals should be framed in a manner that "directly benefit the therapeutic alliance between the supervisee and client and the effectiveness of services provided" (Association for Counselor Education and Supervision, 1990, 2). Thus, in the context of the present case, Dr. Berman would set as a core goal, among others, the development of cultural awareness consistent with the promotion of client welfare and dignity.

ONLINE SUPERVISION

In the present case, the supervisory relationship between Dr. Berman and Maxwell is conducted face-to-face in an office located at a specific physical address. In this case, the two can see each other, sense the presence of the other, notice the expressions on the other's face, and the posture of each other's body in response to verbal cues. This is the traditional forum for conducting supervision of therapists in training. However, supervision is also increasingly being conducted online where the supervisor and supervisee are located in different geographic locations and are communicating across distances through the use of communications technologies. According to the ACA (2014), when using such technologies in supervision, supervisors are competent in their use. Further, they act diligently in protecting the confidentiality of all information transmitted through such technologies (2014, F.2.c). The next chapter examines the challenges raised in protecting confidential, online information against unauthorized access. The subsequent and final chapter examines the challenges involved in providing competent online counseling services.

Questions for Review and Reflection

1. What does *multiculturalism* mean in the context of counseling?
2. How does multiculturalism support Client Autonomy?
3. What does the term *culture* mean as used in this chapter?
4. What does it mean to be "culturally sensitive"? Why is such sensitivity toward clients important for demonstrating respect for clients? Why is it important for demonstrating Compassionate Caring?
5. Is Maxwell culturally sensitive to Abdul? Provide examples to support your response.
6. Does Maxwell's own cultural and political perspectives affect his ability to counsel Abdul? Explain.
7. What roles does a supervisor serve according to the American Counseling Association? How does multicultural knowledge figure in competently fulfilling such roles? What implications does this have for Berman's responsibilities in supervising Maxwell?
8. Why is multicultural knowledge necessary in providing competent supervisory services?
9. What is a stereotype?
10. What is the confirmation bias and how does it tend to support one's stereotypes?
11. Is anyone truly immune from stereotyping? Explain.
12. What is a mind-set?
13. How can stereotypes and mind-sets impair the provision of competent supervisory services as well as counseling services? How might have Maxwell's and Berman's respective, possible stereotypes of each other adversely affected the supervisory relationship?
14. What, if any, action should a supervisor take if he is unable to objectively evaluate the performance of his supervisee, or if the supervisee is unable to work cooperatively with the supervisor?
15. What should a supervisor do if she concludes that her supervisee is unable to provide competent counseling services to a range of diverse client populations?
16. Is it acceptable for a supervisor to counsel his supervisee? Why or why not?
17. Should the supervisory informed consent agreement be in writing or is a

verbal agreement sufficient? Explain.

18. What items should be included in the supervisory informed consent agreement?

19. According to the Association for Counselor Education and Supervision, what sort of goals should be included in the supervisory agreement?

20. In conducting supervision online, what expectations does the American Counseling Association explicitly include in its Code of Ethics?

Cases for Analysis

Using concepts discussed in this chapter, discuss and reflect on virtuous practice in the following scenarios.

1. Martina Silva completed her master's degree in mental health counseling and sought to become a registered mental health intern. She had been searching for a suitable supervisor and was recently referred to Dr. Barbara Beckworth, a mental health counselor with 15 years' experience. Silva and Beckworth decide to work together and to use Beckwith's office space. The use of this office space is a plus for Silva as is the location of Beckworth's office because it is close to Silva's children's school, and she has to pick them up 2 days per week. Although Silva is bilingual in English and Spanish, Beckworth only speaks English. Over time, about two thirds of Silva's clients express a preference to have their sessions conducted in Spanish (their first language), although most of them speak English as well. Beckworth is becoming increasingly frustrated because she is unable to understand what transpires in the recordings of Silva's sessions and needs Silva to translate for her. Beckworth believes that this is not responsible supervision and has requested that Silva only conduct sessions in English. Discuss the following: What elements of the supervisor-supervisee relationship should be discussed prior to a supervisor agreement being formalized? What are the therapeutic, ethical, and professional implications of Beckworth's requests? What are Silva's ethical and professional responsibilities to her clients? How would you proceed with the situation if you were Silva or Beckworth?

2. Ellie Greer, a mental health counselor intern, is being supervised by Sabrina Martinelli in a private secular counseling agency. Recently, the question of religious affiliation came up during the lunch hour as all the agency therapists were together. Martinelli mentioned that she is agnostic and has not attended church in 10 years. Greer stated that she was a devout evangelical Christian and that she no longer wanted Martinelli to supervise her because she could no longer respect her. Greer requested that the clinical director appoint another supervisor for her or she was going to quit the agency. Discuss the possible implications that Greer's aversion to working with others who do not share her religious view might have on her clients. What are the ethical implications of her position? What are the responsibilities of the clinical director in handling this situation? How should the director proceed?

3. Simone Abrams is a social work intern whose supervisor is Dr. Denny Clemson. Abrams, an observant Jew, does not see clients after 3:00 PM on Friday in preparation for observance

of the Sabbath, which begins at sunset. Recently, several clients with atypical diagnoses have expressed a strong preference for appointments on Friday evenings, and Clemson believes that the experience of working with these clients would be beneficial for Abrams. He strongly suggests that she modify her schedule for several months to accommodate the clients. Abrams becomes very upset and irate at Clemson's suggestion and accuses him of violation of the social work code of ethics and accuses him of religious discrimination. Discuss the ethical implications of Clemson's request. How could this situation have been handled differently?

References

Allport, G. W. (1985). *The nature of prejudice*. Reading, MA: Addison-Wesley.

American Counseling Association. (2014). *ACA code of ethics*. Alexandria, VA: Author.

American Mental Health Counseling Association. (2015). *AMHCA Code of Ethics*. Alexandria, VA: American Mental Health Counseling Association. Retrieved from http://connections.amhca.org/HigherLogic/System/DownloadDocumentFile.ashx?DocumentFileKey=d4e10fcb-2f3c-c701-aa1d-5d0f53b8bc14

Association for Counselor Education and Supervision. (1990). *Standards for counseling supervisors*. Alexandria, VA: American Counseling Association. Retrieved from https://www.acesonline.net/sites/default/files/aces_stds_for_counseling_supervisors_jcdv69n1-1.pdf

Baily, D. S. (2005). Get it in writing. *GradPsych Magazine*. American Psychological Association. Retrieved at http://www.apa.org/gradpsych/2005/11/writing.aspx

Baltrinic, E. R., O'Hara, C., & Jencius, M. (2016). Technology-assisted supervision and cultural competencies. In T. Rousmaniere & E. Renfro-Michel (Eds.), *Using technology to enhance clinical supervision* (pp. 47–66). Alexandria, VA: American Counseling Association. Retrieved from https://www.counseling.org/resources/library/ERIC%20Digests/94-08.pdf

Bandura, A., Underwood, B., & Fromson, M. E. (1975). Disinhibition of aggression through diffusion of responsibility and dehumanization of victims. *Journal of Research in Personality*, 9(4), 253–269.

Brooklier, N. (2015, December). Islamophobia: The stereotyping and prejudice towards Muslims since 9/11. *Law and Justice in Real Time*. Pullman: Washington State University. Retrieved from https://hub.wsu.edu/law-justice-realtime/2015/12/17/islamophobia-the-stereotyping-and-prejudice-towards-muslims-since-911/

Cohen, E. D. (2009). *Critical thinking unleashed*. Lanham MD: Rowman & Littlefield.

Cohen, E. D. (2017). *Logic-based therapy and everyday emotions*. Lanham, MD: Rowman & Littlefield.

Commisceo Global. (n.d.). Afghanistan guide to language, culture, customs and etiquette. Retrieved from http://www.commisceo-global.com/country-guides/afghanistan-guide

Counselor-License. (n.d.). Counselor licensing requirements by state. Counselor-License: A State by State Counselor Guide. Retrieved from http://www.counselor-license.com/resources/state-counselor-license.html#context/api/listings/prefilter

Diller, J. V. (2004). *Cultural diversity: A primer for the human services*. Belmont, CA: Brooks/Cole.

Esposito, J. L. (2011). *Islam: The straight path*. New York, NY: Oxford University Press.

Ford, G. G. (2006). *Ethical reasoning for mental health professionals*. Thousand Oaks, CA: Sage.

Gladding, S. T. (1996). *Counseling: A comprehensive profession* (3rd ed.). Englewood Cliffs, NJ: Prentice-Hall.

Haggerty, G., & Hilsonroth, M. J. (2011). The use of video in psychotherapy supervision. *British Journal of Psychotherapy*, *27*(2), 193–210. Retrieved from http://onlinelibrary.wiley.com/doi/10.1111/j.1752-0118.2011.01232.x/abstract

Hopfe, L. M., & Woodward, M. R. (2009). *Religions of the world*. New York, NY: Vango Books.

Kitchener, K. S. (1988). Dual role relationships: What makes them so problematic? *Journal of Counseling & Development*, *67*(4), 217–221.

Leddick, G. R. (1994, April). Models of clinical supervision. *Eric Digest*. Retrieved from https://www.ericdigests.org/1995-1/models.htm

Lippmann, W. (1946). *Public opinion*. New York, NY: Macmillan.

Mehraby, N. (2002, May). Counseling Afghanistan torture and trauma survivors. *Psychotherapy in Australia*, *8*(3). Retrieved from http://www.startts.org.au/media/Research-Doc-Counselling-Afghan-Survivors-of-TT.pdf

Owens, J. (2016, June). Beyond sex: What is gay? *Huff Post*. Retrieved from http://www.huffingtonpost.com/james-owens/beyond-sex-what-is-gay_b_6951926.html

Syracuse University. (1999). Ethical issues in clinical supervision. School of Education. Retrieved from http://soe.syr.edu/academic/counseling_and_human_services/modules/Common_Ethical_Issues/ethical_issues_in_clinical_supervision.aspx

Zur, O. (2015). *Professional organizations' codes of ethics on supervision in psychotherapy and counseling*. Sebastopol, CA: Zur Institute. Retrieved from http://www.zurinstitute.com/ethics_of_supervision.html

PART VI

COUNSELING IN CYBERSPACE

11

BEING DILIGENT IN THE DIGITAL AGE

Case Study: A Case of Record Hacking

The changing technological terrain has ushered in a host of problems related to the maintaining and transmission of clients' deepest secrets as contained in their counseling records. This chapter looks at how to be a diligent practitioner amid the complex challenges posed by counseling in a digital age. It does so through the lenses of a case study involving the mass hacking of client records stored on an online network.

Indeed, given the risks to client privacy posed by maintaining client records in a digital environment, there may be some traditionalists inclined to confine client records to paper copies. A less extreme view may be to keep client records on local media unconnected to the Internet. Unfortunately, both of these approaches have their own special challenges. For example, the traditionalist is likely to encounter problems submitting client information to be processed for third party payment. Likewise, the unconnected therapist is likely to find it impractical not to transmit any client information over the Internet or to successfully communicate with clients who are, in fact, connected. Ironically, as demonstrated in this chapter, all these approaches, one way or another, depend on a key element that is now, as it has been in the past, largely responsible for breaches in security: this is *human* responsibility. Further, there is something else on which the traditionalist, the unconnected, and the connected alike can agree. This is the profound importance of maintaining client records in a manner that fulfills its vital purpose, while competently (albeit humanly) protecting client privacy. So why, in the first place, is the keeping of client records so important?

THE PRIMARY PURPOSE OF COUNSELING RECORDS

The American Counseling Association (ACA) succinctly sums it up: "Counselors create, safeguard, and maintain documentation necessary for rendering professional services"

(2014, A.1.B). Such records are necessary for documenting and monitoring treatment plans, implementing courses of treatment, and tracking client progress (American Psychological Association [APA], 2007, Intro to Guidelines). They are important resources for keeping the therapist's memory fresh between sessions and in providing continuity when a client changes therapists. Such documentation can also provide legal protection for a therapist in case of legal challenges, and accurate counseling records are generally required for third party reimbursement for services rendered (APA, 2007, Intro to Guidelines). However, the virtuous practitioner perceives the latter values as secondary. Indeed, for such a practitioner, the client's best interest is paramount, and diligently maintaining records is a highly effective means of promoting constructive client change.

WHAT COUNSELING RECORDS INCLUDE

Counseling records may include prescribed medications and monitoring, treatment plan, counseling session histories (dates, times, etc. of services), modalities used, test results, diagnoses, current client status, symptoms, and prognosis. However, they may also include "psychotherapy notes," which, as discussed in Chapter 5, are notes in any medium documenting and/or analyzing what has transpired in counseling sessions. Such notes may include therapist's tentative hypotheses explaining information gleaned from such sessions. These notes are to be kept separate from other counseling records and, in contrast to other counseling records, may be legally withheld from a client who has requested copies of her counseling records (Health Insurance Portability and Accountability Act [HIPAA], 2013, Subpart E, 164.524). This is not to confuse the legal requirement to turn over counseling records when court ordered. If a therapist is unsuccessful in her motion to protect client records that have been subpoenaed (see Chapter 6), a judge may find a therapist in contempt of court for refusing to comply with the order. In this regard, for purposes of complying with a court order, in the absence of any reasons to the contrary, it is reasonable to assume that psychotherapy notes, together with e-mail messages, text messages, and other client documents related to the provision of counseling services, which may be stored on separate media in diverse locations, are still parts of the client's records (Zur, 2016).

Electronic Client Records

Clearly, use of digital technologies can make the storage and transfer of client information more convenient. However, this convenience has come with a price. In times past, the main concern with storage and retrieval of clients' private information was whether the office file cabinet and facility was secure and kept under lock and key. Today, however, there are also a plethora of issues surrounding the use of computers to store records, especially when these computers are connected to the Internet. As examined in what follows, comprehensive HIPAA (Health Insurance Portability and Accountability Act) security regulations have been created to address a number of such concerns. These include requirements for transfer, removal, disposal, reuse of, and access to electronic storage means.

In this context, diligence in the handling of client counseling records has taken on new meanings. Starting with the case of computer records that are saved on a vulnerable computer that gets hacked, this chapter addresses these emerging issues and their implications for the protection of client privacy.

THE HACKING OF A VULNERABLE NETWORK

> Jackson Pierce is a mental health counselor who works in a large behavioral and mental health facility called Fair Lands, which serves thousands of clients in a suburb of the New York metropolitan area. Jackson went to work on Monday morning only to find that a staff meeting had been called for a breach in security. Over 4,000 records had been stolen including mental health test results and entire records of therapy sessions including ones from sex offenders and sexual abuse victims. The records contained names, birth dates, social security numbers, addresses, phone numbers, employers, race, family histories, and psychiatric and medical histories, among other highly personal information. Even worse, the criminal who identified himself as "Boris" had put the information up for sale on the "dark web," which, given its highly encrypted and guarded nature, makes tracing extremely difficult. Worse, Boris's last post was to announce that the records had been sold for $50,000.
>
> However, the plot thickened. At the meeting, Jackson was reprimanded in front of his colleagues by a very irate executive director who informed him that the hackers had penetrated the system through Jackson's computer by cracking his password.
>
> "But I regularly change my password," Jackson defensively responded.
>
> "Apparently your password was not very difficult to crack!" scowled the Director.
>
> Jackson left the meeting despondent and guilt-ridden. What he failed to mention was that his password was "FairLands#1."

As the Fair Lands case demonstrates, a computer system is as strong as its weakest link. Often, it is the human element that is such a link. This means that therapists who work in organizations that utilize online systems to store confidential client records have a responsibility to each other, as well as to their clients, to steadfastly protect their systems from unauthorized breaches. In Jackson's case, the failure was in having entered a password that was easy to crack through the use of abundantly available software. Such password cracking software can be downloaded from the Internet and is often available as freeware ("10 most popular password cracking tools," 2017).

THE HIPAA SECURITY RULE

Unfortunately, the Fair Lands case represents an increasing number of instances in which health care records, including mental health records, have been hacked (DataBreaches.net, 2017). Responsive to this burgeoning challenge, the "Security Standards for the Protection of Electronic Protected Health Information" contained in Subpart C of HIPAA has provided a substantial set of standards that regulate the protection of electronic health care records. HIPAA has also been strengthened with the passage of the Health Information Technology for Economic and Clinical Health (HITECH)

Act, passed by Congress in 2009. Among other things, HITECH expands enforcement of HIPAA, allows for breach notification of clients (when at least 500 client records are breached), requires that clients have access to their records in electronic form, and requires business associates of counseling organizations to comply with the HIPAA Security Rule (Department of Health and Human Services, 2013).

According to Subpart C, 164.308 ("Administrative safeguards") of HIPAA, facilities that store and transmit electronic health care information ("covered entities") or companies that assist health care organizations in these activities ("business associates") must establish policies and procedures "to prevent, detect, contain, and correct security violations." This includes conducting accurate and thorough risk assessments or analyses of "potential risks and vulnerabilities to the confidentiality, integrity, and availability of electronic health information"; and to implement measures to reduce these risks and vulnerabilities to the extent reasonably possible.

According to the HIPAA Security Standards (2013), covered entities or their business associates are tasked with establishing policies and procedures to

1. Create, change, and safeguard passwords
2. Implement a mechanism to encrypt electronic protected health information whenever deemed appropriate
3. Determine which employees should have access to electronic health care records, to permit only those with access to have it, and to prevent those without it from gaining access
4. Create and maintain retrievable, exact, backup copies of all electronic protected health information
5. Guard against, detect, and report malicious software
6. Implement security awareness and training programs for all employees
7. Implement physical safeguards for all workstations that access electronic protected health information, to restrict access to authorized users
8. Address the final disposition of electronic protected health information and/or the hardware or electronic media on which it is stored
9. Provide periodic security updates
10. Monitor information system activities through regular inspection of system activity records such as audit logs, access reports, and security incident tracking reports
11. Terminate access when the employment or work relationship ends
12. Monitor log-in attempts and report discrepancies
13. Identify, respond to, and document suspected or known security incidents, and address their harmful effects
14. Respond to emergencies such as fire, vandalism, system failure, or natural disaster that damages protected health care information systems

15. Limit physical access to electronic information systems and the facility or facilities in which they are housed, while ensuring authorized access

16. Automatically terminate an electronic session after a predetermined time of inactivity

17. Record and examine activity in the information system using appropriate hardware and software

18. Protect electronic protected health information from improper alteration or destruction

The above standards represent some, among other standards, that are federally mandated by HIPAA. With regard to password security, in Jackson's case, either Fair Lands lacked a sufficient company policy about how to "create, change and safeguard passwords" pursuant to HIPAA, or Jackson simply did not comply with it. Indeed, a reasonable interpretation of what it means to "safeguard" passwords would include more than simply physically protecting them (Center for Financial Industry Information Systems, 2009, 017.1). The strength of the password itself is an inherent factor in securing the password against unauthorized access to it. A strong password would include 12 to 14 characters, special symbols, varied capitalization, no dictionary words, combination of dictionary words, or variations of dictionary words ("d0g" instead of "dog"). There are also mnemonic devices for creating a memorable password that meets these stringent criteria (Hoffman, 2015). For example, one could simply remember the sentence, "How to make 22 million five hundred dollars legally in America" and use the first letters and numbers to generate "Htm22000500$liA" as your password. Unfortunately, with the rise of cybercrime, even strong passwords, not to mention easy to guess ones, along with a user name, are becoming increasingly less secure against hackers. Consequently, so-called "two-factor authentication" has been proposed for the protection of clients' mental health records (Lustgarden, 2016). This system provides an additional layer of protection in safeguarding passwords. For example, use of numerical access codes that are randomly generated and text-messaged to the authorized individual's cell phone provides a mechanism that is increasingly being used by organizations handling confidential information. Because the code is only used once, it tends to be more secure than a personal identification number. A physical token such as a key or card or biometric data such as retina or fingerprint scan could also uniquely authenticate a user (Elliott, 2017).

Encryption provides a further measure for safeguarding electronic client information (American Counseling Association [ACA], 2014, H.5; APA, 2007, 6). According to HIPAA (2013, Subpart C, 164.302), "[e]ncryption means the use of an algorithmic process to transform data into a form in which there is a low probability of assigning meaning without use of a confidential process or key." Pursuant to the HIPAA Security Standards (2013; Item 2 above), therapists, or their business associates, who store and/or transmit client information online need to provide for encrypting of this information, both in storing as well as transmitting it. As discussed in Chapter 12, while offering some protection (including a mechanism for encryption), free e-mail and videoconferencing services, such as those of Gmail and Skype, are still not HIPAA compliant.

However, encryption of e-mail messages and attachments containing protected health care information does not address the problem of protecting such information when stored on a computer network, flash drive, or in the cloud. While strong authentication procedures as well as firewalls provide important components of a system of protection, the files themselves can also be encrypted for added protection. Clearly, this was a major problem in the Fair Lands case. If the client files that were stored on the facility's network were encrypted, then even if Boris was able to get past authentication, he would have also needed to figure out how to decrypt the files to read them. This underscores the importance of having a strong encryption mechanism in place to prevent unauthorized access to online client records, even if the authentication mechanism is breached.

The HIPAA Security Standards (2013, Subpart C, 164.308) also enjoin that covered entities "[i]mplement a mechanism to encrypt and decrypt electronic protected health information." A decryption mechanism is an algorithmic key that converts the encrypted information back to a readable form. Encryption programs can link the key to a user generated password, which can, in turn, be used to decrypt an encrypted file. Here, a major challenge to cryptography is how to safely store the decryption key or password. Clearly, it would be self-defeating to store the key, or a password that generates the key, alongside the very information it decrypts. Instead, the password or key should be stored offline, and, pursuant to the HIPAA Security Standards (2013; see Item 3 above), made accessible only to those who are authorized to access the client information. Here, again, the weakest link in the system may be an employee who fails to keep the password, or the key, safe. Human beings forget or lose passwords, too, not infrequently, which requires a secure mechanism for resetting passwords ("Forgot password cheat sheet," 2017).

Diligence in the digital age clearly involves a defensive posture with diverse tentacles. Cyberattacks such as "brute force" attacks aim at cracking password codes thereby gaining unauthorized entry. Malware and viruses can infect and destroy client files. Hence there is need for implementing a consistent policy providing for backup copies of all electronic client records pursuant to HIPAA Security Standards (2013; Item 4 above), maintaining up-to-date virus and malware protection (Item 5 above), and having strong authentication and encryption policies in operation. Such policies and procedures are not optional; they are legally as well as ethically sanctioned.

Pursuant to the HIPAA Security Standards (2013), training and awareness of the aforementioned security risks are essential for all employees having access to client records (Item 6 above). Security awareness applies offline as well as online. Keeping passwords accessible where unauthorized individuals can find them is proscribed by the HIPAA regulation to safeguard passwords. According to HIPAA Security Standards (Subpart C, 164.304), "[c]onfidentiality means the property that data or information is not made available or disclosed to unauthorized persons or processes." Wherein, "[d]isclosure means the release, transfer, provision of access to, or divulging in any manner of information outside the entity holding the information" (Subpart A, 160.103). As such, any therapist or member of the office staff who exposes, *even unintentionally*, client records to unauthorized individuals, including other clients, has disclosed such records to such individuals in breach of confidentiality and is, therefore, in violation of HIPAA Security Standards. For example, an office staff member who has a client's records displayed on a computer monitor where other clients can see them is violating federal law. Accordingly, security awareness and training needs to stress the practical import of respecting client confidentiality in avoiding making client records accessible to, or otherwise divulging client records to, unauthorized persons or other unauthorized entities.

Pursuant to HIPAA Standards (2013; see Item 7 above), physical safeguards for all workstations need to be implemented that restrict access to electronic protected health information to authorized users. For example, placing privacy filters on all workstation monitor screens, blocking side views, can help prevent unauthorized individuals from seeing protected client information displayed on monitor screens. However, physical privacy safeguards are as useful as the individuals utilizing them and cannot substitute for keen security awareness among therapists and their office staff.

MAINTAINING AND DESTROYING RECORDS

Guideline 7 of the APA Record Keeping Guidelines (APA, 2007) states that

> [i]n the absence of a superseding requirement, psychologists may consider retaining full records until 7 years after the last date of service delivery for adults or until 3 years after a minor reaches the age of majority, whichever is later. In some circumstances, the psychologist may wish to keep records for a longer period, weighing the risks associated with obsolete or outdated information, or privacy loss, versus the potential benefits associated with preserving the records.

State statutes can vary on how long they must be kept. The Florida Administrative Code (64B4-9.001) requires that counseling records be maintained for 7 years after the date of the last contact with the client or user. Virginia law requires that client records of adults be maintained for a minimum of 5 years from the date of termination of the counseling relations. However, counseling records of a minor child must be maintained for a minimum of 5 years after the child attains the age of majority (18), or 10 years following termination, whichever comes later (Virginia Board of Counseling, 2016). So, in the case of a child whose counseling terminated at age 5, the child's records would need to be kept for 18 years. Because state statutes supersede HIPAA regulations when the former are stricter, a therapist needs to check state statutes in deciding how long to maintain them.

The longer records are maintained, the greater the probability that privacy can be breached. This may especially be true when the records are stored on outdated technologies. Accordingly, diligent therapists are sensitive to the need to update technologies protecting these records; they keep track of the number of years the records have been maintained and appropriately provide for the final disposition of client records and/or the hardware or electronic media on which they are stored, pursuant to HIPAA Security Standards (2013, see Item 8 above).

Files stored in the cloud are especially problematic since copies of deleted files may still exist somewhere on the cloud server (Sheldon, 2014). Cloud services are especially reticent to permanently delete files because there is potential liability in losing customer files. This has inclined such services to err on the side of keeping data around rather than destroying it. As a result the destruction of client files that have been saved in cyberspace may not always be straightforward. This realm of uncertainty adds a further wrinkle to the prospect of keeping client information completely safe.

Smaller organizations or individual providers may choose to store some or all of their client records on "air-gapped" computers. These are computers that are neither directly nor indirectly (via other computers) connected to the Internet. Since these computers are offline, the logic is that they are less vulnerable to being hacked. However, information stored on computers that are not connected to the Internet still counts as electronic protected health information and is subject to the provisions of the HIPAA Security Standards (2013, Subpart A, 160.103). Such electronic information must therefore be protected from unauthorized access, password protected, encrypted, and placed in a secure physical location. USB ports are an area of particular vulnerability with respect to air gapped computers, whereby unauthorized individuals with physical access to the computer can insert a flash drive into its USB to access and steal client information, and/or infect the computer with a virus. USB ports on such computers should therefore be locked by password protecting them (Wallen, 2017).

Some therapists also use laptops, tablets, smart phones, or other mobile devices to store and/or send client information. Inasmuch as these devices are connected to the Internet, they are not only subject to all the risks of other online computers, but they also encompass additional risks. Because they are smaller and mobile, they may also be more easily lost or stolen. For example, a tablet might be accidentally left behind in a car while the car is being repaired, thereby subjecting the records to unauthorized access. Accordingly, such devices need to be password protected, data encrypted, and great care taken not to place them outside arm's length. When these devices are not being used, they can be locked away in a secure filing cabinet to prevent unauthorized access.

The legal, ethical, and technological challenges of protecting client records in a digital age are not the only challenges raised by mental health practice in a digital age. Not only are clients' records stored in networks connected to the Internet, or in the cloud, but counseling sessions themselves are increasingly being conducted online. In the next chapter, the ethical, legal, and technological challenges of online counseling are examined.

Questions for Review and Reflection

1. What are the primary purposes for keeping client counseling records? What are the secondary purposes?

2. What items are included in counseling records?

3. What are "psychotherapy notes"? Are they part of the other counseling records? If a therapist is court ordered to turn over counseling records, should this be understood to include psychotherapy notes as well as e-mail, text messages, and other forms of notations?

4. Would you agree that when the security of client records is breached, it is usually the result of the failure of technology to keep the records safe? What does the Fair Lands

case suggest about the weakest link in the protection of client records?

5. What is HITECH, and what are some of its provisions?

6. What do the Security Standards of the Health Information Portability and Accountability Act (HIPAA) require regarding the use of passwords to protect electronic health information? In the Fair Lands case, is Jackson in compliance? What measures could he have taken to better protect his electronic files?

7. What is encryption, and how, in general, does it work? What does HIPAA require about encryption of electronic health care information? Was Jackson in compliance with HIPAA? Explain.

8. What is decryption? What does HIPAA say about it? What security risk is raised by decryption, and how should it be addressed?

9. Why does HIPAA require that backup copies of all electronic health records be maintained? In other words, what sort of threats to cyber security does the maintenance of backup copies protect against? Where should the backup copies themselves be stored? Explain.

10. In the chapter it is stated, "Security awareness applies offline as well as online." What are at least two major offline safeguards that therapists as well as their office staff need to be aware of?

11. For how long does the American Psychological Association recommend that counseling records be maintained in the case of adults and in the case of minors? Have state laws necessarily followed the same guidelines? Explain.

12. How often should the technology on which client records is stored be updated?

13. What potential problem is there for disposal of client records stored in the cloud?

14. What is an "air-gapped" computer? What is the main virtue of storing client records on such computers? What is a major vulnerability of such computer storage, and how can it be addressed?

15. What are some of the additional risks encountered by storing client data on mobile devices and tablets? What safety measures should be implemented to protect against these risks or vulnerabilities?

Cases for Analysis

1. Cyril Bennett is a mental health counselor in an increasingly growing private practice. He has decided to hire part-time office help and places an online ad for this. Several candidates respond, and Cyril interviews three of them, ultimately hiring Deidre Sherring, a former office clerk for a local insurance agency. Cyril reasons that since Deidre has worked with confidential information in her previous job, she will appropriately protect client information and perform diligently in this position as well. He instructs her to "be careful" with protecting client information and immediately puts her to work. On her third day on the job, a client states that she does not remember her health insurance policy number but can access it online. Deidre subsequently allows the client to

use the office computer for this purpose. What, if any risks is Deidre taking regarding the security of Cyril's records? How is Cyril failing to take due diligence with the protection of his client records and information? What would you do if a client approached you with a similar request as was posed to Deidre?

2. Dr. Amelia Armstrong is a psychologist working for a medium size mental health agency. As part of ongoing efforts to protect the privacy of client records, Armstrong is required to change her password every 30 days. Since Armstrong also has a private practice and has to regularly change her password in that capacity as well, she often gets confused about her passwords and gets shut out of the systems. This causes her frustration and loss of work time. Armstrong decides to keep track of her changing passwords by storing them on a "Notes" application on her cell phone. One morning, Armstrong forgets her phone in the agency restroom, and it is retrieved by a custodian. Since Armstrong's phone screen lock is set on the longest time limit, 5 minutes, she does not know if the custodian saw her stored passwords. What should Armstrong do? Does she have a responsibility to inform her supervisors and coworkers of a potential Internet breach?

3. Clarence Upton worked as a mental health counselor at Healthy Life Counseling for 5 years before resigning. Because he had been a model employee, Rina Morales, his supervisor allows him access to agency and client records for 2 weeks after his employment ends to "tie up loose ends with clients." During this time, Morales discovers that Upton is copying some protected information from agency files and using it to recruit clients for his new private practice. Discuss the legal and ethical dimensions of Morales's decision to allow Upton access to files. What should Morales do now? Is what Upton did considered to be an ethical breach even though he was a recent employee, and are his actions illegal, unethical, or both?

References

American Counseling Association. (2014). *ACA code of ethics*. Alexandria, VA: Author.

American Psychological Association. (2007). *Record keeping guidelines*. Washington, DC: Author. Retrieved from http://www.apa.org/practice/guidelines/record-keeping.aspx

Center for Financial Industry Information Systems. (2009). *FISC security guidelines on computer systems for banking and related financial institutions* (7th ed.). Tokyo: Author. Retrieved from https://www.unifiedcompliance.com/products/search-controls/control/514/

DataBreaches.net. (2017). Highly confidential psychotherapy records from Maine center listed on the dark web. Author. Retrieved from www.databreaches.net/highly-confidential-psychotherapy-records-from-maine-center-listed-on-the-dark-web

Department of Health and Human Services. (2013). Modifications to the HIPAA privacy, security, enforcement, and breach notification rules under the health information technology for economic and clinical health act and the genetic information nondiscrimination act; other modifications to the HIPAA rules; final rule. *Federal Register, 78*(17). Retrieved from https://www.gpo.gov/fdsys/pkg/FR-2013-01-25/pdf/2013-01073.pdf

Elliott, M. (2017, March). *Two-factor authentication: How and why to use it.* San Francisco, CA: C/Net. Retrieved from https://www.cnet.com/how-to/how-and-why-to-use-two-factor-authentication/

Forgot password cheat sheet. (2017). Bel Air, MD: OWASP. Retrieved from https://www.owasp.org/index.php/Forgot_Password_Cheat_Sheet

The Health Insurance Portability and Accountability Act (HIPAA). Administrative Simplification. 45 CFR Parts 160, 162, and 164. (2013). Retrieved from https://www.hhs.gov/sites/default/files/ocr/privacy/hipaa/administrative/combined/hipaa-simplification-201303.pdf

Hoffman, C. (2015, May). How to create a strong password (and remember it). *How-to Geek.* Retrieved from https://www.howtogeek.com/195430/how-to-create-a-strong-password-and-remember-it/

Lustgarden, S. D. (2016). New threats to client privacy. *Monitor on Psychology, 47*(1). Washington, DC: American Psychological Association. Retrieved from http://www.apa.org/monitor/2016/01/ce-corner.aspx

Sheldon, R. (2014, September). *Deleting files in the cloud.* Cambridge, UK: Redgate Hub. Retrieved from https://www.red-gate.com/simple-talk/cloud/cloud-data/deleting-files-in-the-cloud/

10 most popular password cracking tools. (2017). Elmwood Park, IL: InfoSec Institute. Retrieved from http://resources.infosecinstitute.com/10-popular-password-cracking-tools/#gref

Virginia Board of Counseling. (2016). Ethical & legal resources: Licensing board regulations. *The Center for Ethical Practice.* Retrieved from http://www.centerforethicalpractice.org/ethical-legal-resources/virginia-legal-information/licensing-board-regulations/

Wallen, J. (2017, January). 6 ways to secure air-gapped computers from data breaches. *TechRepublic.* Retrieved from http://www.techrepublic.com/article/6-ways-to-secure-air-gapped-computers-from-data-breaches/

Zur, O. (2016). *Subpoenas and how to handle them: Guidelines for psychotherapists and counselors.* Sebastopol, CA: Zur Institute. Retrieved from http://www.zurinstitute.com/subpoena.html#responding

12

PROVIDING COMPETENT ONLINE COUNSELING SERVICES

Case Study: A Suicidal Client

There is presently a dearth of mental health practitioners available relative to the need. Online therapy increases the availability of therapists substantially. Clients whose work schedules preclude them from scheduling face-to-face appointments with local counselors, who are homebound, or who otherwise would not have access to therapy now have an online option. In rural areas, clients may know the therapist and encounter multiple role relationships. For example, the client may be the therapist's neighbor, children's teacher, pharmacist, or fellow parishioner. There may be very few, if any, therapists living in the area, making lengthy trips to the closest metropolis the only other viable option. Clients who perceive therapy as stigmatizing might be more inclined to seek online therapy than face-to-face therapy.

Still, it would be ethically irresponsible for a therapist who undertakes online counseling to proceed without due understanding and consideration of the unique character of online counseling. Beginning with the case of JC, an online, at-risk client, this chapter highlights some of the major ethical considerations that therapists need to take into account in undertaking online counseling.

A CASE OF A SUICIDAL, ONLINE CLIENT

> JC is a 48-year-old single, heterosexual male inventory clerk who lives alone. A resident of Austin, Texas, he has sought online counseling from Gene Stanton, a licensed mental health counselor residing in Los Angeles and holding licenses in New York and California. Counseling sessions were scheduled on a weekly basis through video conferencing calls via Skype. Because there is a 2-hour time

difference and JC works until 5:00PM Central Time, Gene did not meet with JC until 6:00PM, which was 4:00PM in California. JC's presenting problem was an inability to forge lasting personal relationships. He was married once before for 6 months, after which his wife filed for divorce. It has been 6 years since the divorce, and JC maintains that he has been unable to date anyone else for more than a couple of times. "No one ever likes me. At first they seem to be interested but then they refuse to go out with me. I know I will never find anyone." After 4 weeks of counseling, JC began to express suicidal ideation. "There is nothing to live for. No one will even care if I die. I have a dead-end job and a dead-end life. I can't go on any more like this." When Gene asked JC if he is thinking of hurting himself, JC paused a moment and then said,

"Yes. I don't want to live anymore."

"Do you have a plan to kill yourself?" asked Gene.

JC pauses again. "I have some sleeping pills. It would be better that way," said JC.

JC's situation is one that would be challenging for any therapist if the therapist and client were sitting across from each other in the same physical space. However, because the client is sitting in a room in Austin, and the therapist in another room in LA, the dynamics of the situation are significantly changed. The therapist presents to the client as an image on a screen that can be "turned off" with the click of a mouse, not a warm body sharing common physical space. The therapist cannot lean forward, touch the client gently on the hand, and reassure him. His gestures, forward lean, facial expressions, and other care-oriented body language are blunted through their virtual transmission. The therapist cannot delay the client's departure from his office because the client is already home, sitting there, probably with the potentially lethal medication at his disposal. It is evening in Austin but still afternoon in LA. Referral to another, local therapist cannot wait until tomorrow. The client can go to his medicine cabinet, reach for the pills, take them, get into bed, shut off the night light, and "go to sleep." As a skilled therapist, Gene can attempt to negotiate a waiting period with JC; but he cannot spontaneously reach into his desk drawer, produce a no-suicide contract, and present a real-time copy to JC to sign. True, one can be downloaded from the cloud, or e-mailed to JC, but that requires extra steps, which can take more time, whereas spontaneity is crucial.

Emergency Planning

If Gene approached online counseling with due regard for the possibility of such a crisis occurring, he would have an emergency plan in place. For one, he would know the physical address of the client, not just his e-mail address. He would have at his immediate disposal the Austin Police Department phone number. Gene would also have handy JR's phone numbers, both his home as well as his cell phone. He would further have a contact number for JR's closest relative or friend. Such information can best be assembled in one place on a form that can be accessed immediately. So should Gene contact the Austin police?

Assessing Suicide

The client has expressed a desire to kill himself. He indicates a plan. He has the means to carry out his plan. He has low self-esteem, feelings of hopelessness, and relationship problems as well as career issues. These are salient indicators that the client may attempt to commit suicide (American Counseling Association, 2011). Still, Gene does not know the client well. Indeed, he has never (literally) met him. His history may not include prior suicide attempts, and he may not have been thinking about killing himself very long. Perhaps he is especially distraught at the moment. It may also be harder to read the client's body language and generally more challenging to assess suicidal tendencies in online clients. Clearly, based on the presenting facts (the client's response to questions about harming himself and his admitting to having a plan), Gene has reasonable belief that JC may attempt suicide. But is this a legally sufficient basis to breach confidentiality?

STATE LAW AND ETHICAL RESPONSIBILITY

The case of JR involves counseling across state lines. JR is in Texas, and Gene is in California. So which law should Gene obey; that of Texas, California, or both? In fact, the laws of these two states say different things, which are not entirely consistent. Texas does not recognize a duty of a mental health practitioner to disclose confidential client information to an endangered third party to protect this individual from harm. Instead, it *permits* a mental health practitioner to disclose the information only to police or other medical personnel if there is an *imminent and probable* threat of physical harm by the patient to the patient or others. However, pursuant to the California Supreme Court ruling in *Tarasoff*, as discussed in Chapter 5, California recognizes a duty to protect (including by disclosing the threat directly to the endangered third party), if there is a *reasonable* assessment of harm. Adding to the problem is that, whereas California provides immunity against legal liability in the case of disclosure, disclosure in Texas carries legal risk, including criminal liability (National Conference of State Legislatures, 2015). As such, pursuant to California law, Gene would be on firm ground in seeing himself as having a legal duty to disclose to the authorities whatever information necessary to protect JC from harming himself, inasmuch as he has reasonable belief that his client presents a danger to himself. However, pursuant to Texas law, Gene has no such duty. In fact, Gene would be in violation of Texas law if he contacted a close friend or neighbor of JC, without JC's consent, to come to JC's house to dissuade him from harming himself. And, unless Gene could show that JC posed a probability of imminent harm to himself, there could even be a legal basis for holding him civilly and/or criminally liable for disclosing to the police.

According to the Texas State Board of Examiners of Psychologists, *Guidelines for the Practice of Telepsychology* (1999),

> an individual who is physically located in another state shall be considered to be practicing psychology in Texas and, therefore, subject to the Act, if a recipient of psychological services provided by the individual is physically located in the state of Texas.

So, legally, it would appear that Gene is subject to the laws of Texas. But does Gene even know what these laws say?

According to one study, 74% of therapists who provided counseling across state lines were mistaken or uncertain about the laws governing the states across which they practiced (Barnett & Kolmes, 2016). Accordingly, therapists who practice across state lines are admonished to check the laws of other states before they counsel online clients who reside in those states. As a rule of thumb, it is also safe to assume that the therapist will be legally liable for violations of such state laws.

Further, with the exception of limited guest licenses to practice in a state for a brief time (e.g., 30 days per year), all, or almost all, states require that mental health practitioners who practice across state lines possess a valid state license in the state in which the client resides. This would mean that Gene would also need to be validly licensed in Texas; however, he is licensed to practice only in California and New York. As such, a therapist who takes on clients who reside across state lines, and who reside in states in which the therapist is not licensed, is likely to be in violation of those states' licensing laws and, therefore, subject to the punitive measures (fines and/or imprisonment) attached to such violations (Barnett & Kolmes, 2016).

Some states have also adopted laws specific to distance therapy that address issues such as informed consent, confidentiality of information, and competence to practice in the provision of distance mental health services (Epstein Becker Green, 2016). For example, in addition to requiring that specific types of pertinent information be included as a condition of informed consent (see this chapter under informed consent), Delaware requires psychologists to conduct a risk-benefit analysis to see whether the client can benefit from telepsychology and whether the client has sufficient knowledge and skills in the use of the communication technology to be used (Delaware Administrative Code, 2014, 18.6.1).

In contrast, in Texas, there are presently no additional legal requirements identified for psychologists and other mental health providers who are providing distance therapy. And, in California, with the exception of requiring documentation of clients' informed (verbal) consent to distance therapy, there are presently no additional legal requirement identified for mental health practitioners who provide distance therapy (Epstein Becker Green, 2016). However, it is important to emphasize that all other state laws governing face-to-face therapy apply.

As such, therapists who practice across state lines may be subject to the laws governing *both* face-to-face and distance therapy, in the states wherein they reside, *as well as* the states wherein their clients reside. Inasmuch as these laws may conflict, the therapist may sometimes need to exercise moral discretion. This is the challenge that confronts Gene. He can do his best to work with his client without disclosing to the authorities, which would be consistent with Texas law. However, if he concludes, pursuant to California law, that he has a duty to protect his client from self-harm, then he may choose to risk legal sanctions pursuant to Texas law. Here, it may present less legal risk, pursuant to Texas law, to avoid disclosure to the Austin police to prevent a possible suicide attempt by JR. But in simply assuming less legal risk, Gene would place his personal welfare above that of his client. Instead, the virtuous therapist would follow his moral lights. Thus, Gene may seek to treat his client as an autonomous person as much as possible, by informing JC of his intention to notify the Austin police; and if, consequently, the client is willing to sign a non-suicide agreement, Gene could agree to hold off on notifying them. Otherwise, he might proceed to contact the police, disclosing only information that is essential to protecting the client from self-harm. (For example, the fact that the client is having relationship problems would not be appropriate to disclose.) The possibility that, in making appropriate disclosure, the therapist might be taking legal risks pursuant to Texas law would then be insufficiently weighty to override the perceived duty to disclose. Here, questions about "probability" and "imminent harm" would need to be interpreted after the fact, in a legal context. However, Gene's reasonable assessment of the possibility of client self-harm (relative to his less than ideal viewpoint as JC's online therapist) coupled with his respect for JC's autonomy and confidentiality as much as reasonably possible, would provide a strong moral defense. While having a strong moral basis for one's decision does not necessarily mean that one will prevail legally, it can, indeed, strengthen one's case.

INTERSTATE AGREEMENTS

One approach to addressing some of the legal challenges of mental health practice across state lines via communication technology is through the establishment of mutual agreements between states. One such agreement is "Psypact," a new initiative of the Association of State and Provincial Psychology Boards (ASPPB), which seeks to standardize licensure requirements between member states by setting up "E-Passport Certificates" for telepsychology (The Association of State and Provincial Psychology Boards [ASPPB], n.d.). For example, a psychologist who is eligible must hold a valid state license in a member state and a doctoral degree in psychology from a regionally accredited university ("ASPPB Mobility program e.passport overview," n.d.). According to the Council of State Governments (n.d.),

> the Interstate compacts are powerful, durable, flexible tools to promote and ensure cooperation among the states, while avoiding federal intervention and preemption of state powers. Compacts offer the following benefits: They settle interstate disputes. They provide state-developed solutions to complex public policy problems, unlike federally imposed mandates. They respond to national priorities in consultation or in partnership with the federal government. They retain state sovereignty in matters traditionally reserved for the states. They create economies of scale to reduce administrative costs. In other words, the interstate compact is a constitutionally authorized means of implementing and protecting federalism and the states' role in the federal system.

While it remains to be seen how such an agreement will settle jurisdictional matters arising between member states such as that described in the case of Gene and JC, there is clear need for a systematic approach to the provision of mental health services across state lines that protects the integrity of the relationship between the therapist and client, while alleviating the strain of jurisdictional conflict and ambiguity.

THREE POSSIBLE MODELS FOR RESOLVING INSTATE CONFLICT AND AMBIGUITY

One possible way in which jurisdictional boundary conflict and ambiguity can be settled among compact member states would be for the law of the state to apply that offers the strongest legal protection of clients. For example, according to this approach, in the case of Gene and JC, Texas law would supersede California law because the former provides the strongest protection of client confidentiality. This approach is sometimes used when state and federal law conflict. For example, the Health Insurance Portability and Accountability Act (HIPAA) provides that, in matters of protecting personal health information, when state requirements conflict with the federal legislation, the latter supersedes the former unless the former offers stronger privacy protection. However, by concentrating exclusively on client privacy (namely protection of client confidentiality), this model does not consider the welfare of third parties or that of clients whose lives may be endangered. More generally, while laws in one state may provide stronger legal protection than another state in one respect (such as with respect to therapist-client confidentiality), they may provide less legal protection in another respect (such as less protection against client or third party harm). As such, attempting to settle jurisdictional conflicts and ambiguity according to the state law that provides the greatest legal protection for clients can itself lead to further ambiguity and conflict.

A second model would be to apply the law of the state in which the therapist resides and is licensed. This model has the advantage of applying law that is most familiar to therapists, thereby making it likely that therapists will know and efficiently follow this law. However, these laws may fail to work efficiently with the agencies of the state in which the client resides. For example, reporting laws governing reporting abuse and neglect of minors in the state in which the client resides may be significantly different than that of the state in which the therapist resides. More specifically, they may differ in "how abuse and neglect are defined, the threshold to be followed for making reports, in which jurisdiction the report should be filed, the age of majority in that state, and more" (Barnett & Kolmes, 2016). As such, state agencies tasked with investigating reports may find the nature of these reports to be vastly at odds with their own knowledge and understanding and manner of proceeding. For example, the age of the child may fall outside case workers' understanding of reportable actions; or the nature of the act itself may fall outside case workers' understanding of what constitutes abuse or neglect. As such, attempting to make the laws of a different state work efficiently in another state with substantially different laws and agency processes for implementing them would create considerable confusion and loss of efficiency.

A third model would be for the laws governing the state in which the client resides to apply exclusively. For example, on this model, Texas law would supersede California law in the case of Gene and JC. Indeed, there is precedent for this approach. For example, in criminal law, jurisdictional issues are settled according to the state in which the alleged crime is committed, not the state in which the accused resides if from a different state. In like manner, according to the third model, any alleged malfeasance committed by a therapist against a client would be settled pursuant to the laws of the state in which the injury was said to occur. As such, these are the laws with which the therapist would be required to comply. Unlike the second model, this model offers a process consistent with the laws and practices governing the state in which the client resides. Of course, on this model, therapists who practice across state lines would need to know the laws of the states across which they practice. This is a reasonable expectation of therapists who practice distance therapy across state lines inasmuch as it has the potential to most efficiently promote the welfare of both clients and endangered third parties pursuant to the laws of the state (or states) in which such parties reside. Therefore, ethically, as well as legally, possessing such multistate knowledge should be a minimum expectation of competent distance practitioners, whether or not they practice under the umbrella of a pact designed to regulate distance therapy across state lines. However, this third model still does not eliminate the potential strain of interstate legal conflict and may even intensify it. As in the case of Gene and JC, a therapist who resides and primarily practices in a state such as California may feel uncomfortable about disclosing potential client or third party harm when the endangered party resides in a state such as Texas. For one, there is greater legal risk of disclosing confidential information pursuant to Texas law than pursuant to California law. Moreover, the California therapist may feel duty-bound to disclose pursuant to his own state law. Such tensions are inevitable regardless of what interstate model is embraced. As such, virtuous practice across state lines requires the exercise of moral discretion (and courage) in balancing prevention of client or third party harm with respect for client autonomy.

INFORMED CONSENT IN DISTANCE COUNSELING

In Chapter 6, the provisions of informed consent were considered when counseling clients face-to-face. These provisions also apply in the case of distance counseling. However, due to the unique challenges of distance counseling arising from the use of technology to speak and interact with clients who are distant, there is a further set of related information that should, ethically, be provided to the distant client. In fact, in some states, the provision of this additional information is legally required.

For example, in Delaware psychologists are required to include the following information in obtaining the informed consent of clients prior to providing telepsychology (Delaware Administrative Code, 2014, 18.6.8):

- The limitations and innovative nature of using distance technology in the provision of psychological services;

- Potential risks to confidentiality of information due to the use of distance technology;

- Potential risks of sudden and unpredictable disruption of telepsychology services and how an alternative means of re-establishing electronic or other connection will be used under such circumstances;

- When and how the licensee will respond to routine electronic messages;

- Under what circumstances the licensee and service recipient will use alternative means of communications under emergency circumstances;

- Who else may have access to communications between the client and the licensee;

- Specific methods for ensuring that a client's electronic communications are directed only to the licensee or supervisee; and

- How the licensee stores electronic communications exchanged with the client.

The American Psychological Association (APA) has proposed a similar set of information in its ethical "Guideline" on informed consent in distance counseling (2013, Guideline 3). The American Counseling Association (ACA) has done the same in its Code of Ethics (2014, H2.a). The above set of guidelines encapsulates information that a reasonable client would want to know when embarking on distance counseling.

Inasmuch as the use of communication technology carries its own limitations and risks, clients should be apprised of such limitations and risks. Thus, as discussed in this chapter, counseling from a distance is limited by the extent to which communications technology can provide a medium through which to acquire sufficient information for making sound clinical judgments. Clients should be apprised of such limitation such as the increased challenge of keying in to client body language, gestures, and intonation. Indeed, some technologies such as e-mail and text messaging are especially limited in these respects and, in our opinion, fall below the minimum standard of acceptability for conducting distance counseling. While these may be used to set up a meeting or to cancel one, they are themselves unsuitable for purposes of conducting actual counseling sessions.

Reasonable clients would also want to be apprised of the risks accompanying distance counseling such as the potential for confidential information to be acquired by unauthorized third parties (e.g., hackers, third party advertiser, and others who seek the private information of others for personal gain). Clients therefore need to be apprised that there are inherent risks in communicating using information technologies and, therefore, that there can be no guarantee that such information will be secure. On the other hand, the therapist should apprise the client of what precautions she is taking to protect the privacy of the client. For example, "[c]ounselors use current encryption standards within their websites and/or technology-based communications that meet applicable legal requirements" (ACA, 2014, H.2.d). Such legal standards include the use of HIPAA compliant video and e-mail services. Because therapists are subject to HIPAA regulations, it is not lawful for a therapist to practice online unless the technology she uses is compatible with HIPAA regulations. This includes compliance with current encryption standards, but there are further requirements. Pursuant to HIPAA, therapists must also document that they are taking adequate precautions to guard against any unauthorized acquisitions of the protected information being transferred across distances. Ordinarily, this can be accomplished when the therapist contracts with a HIPAA compliant "business associate" to provide a secure means of transmitting the electronic protected health information on the therapist's behalf. Pursuant to HIPAA regulations, such service providers must have the facility to monitor who is receiving the protected health care information, thereby keeping an audit trail, and to notify the therapist of any security breaches. The therapist must, accordingly, receive a contract or other written documentation from the service provider assuring the therapist that it is providing such services, as required by HIPAA (1996, §164.308[b][1]). Because free video conferencing services such as Skype do not offer such business associate contracts, therapists who use them in the provision of distance counseling assume greater legal risk. Ethically, in risking breaching clients' confidentiality to save money, a therapist such as Gene who uses a free version of Skype violates the Client Best Interest standard. Further, inasmuch as this amounts to treating clients as mere means to advancing therapists' self-interest, such action also violates the ethical standard of Client Autonomy. As such, from both ethical and legal perspectives, therapists are advised to seek out a service provider that is fully HIPAA compliant, that is, offers all the protections required by HIPAA, and provides written documentation of the same. In turn, therapists should inform their clients that they have taken such necessary measures to protect their confidentiality but that, notwithstanding, this does not guarantee that there will not be any confidentiality breaches.

Therapists should also inform clients about the risks of sending personal information via e-mail. Like video conferencing services, e-mail services may not be HIPAA compliant. Thus, while free e-mail services such as Google's Gmail offers some safeguards, only its paid version, included in its so-called G Suite, can be considered to satisfy HIPAA security requirements. This service has ways to safeguard against messages and attachments containing confidential information being shared with unintended recipients (Google, 2017). However, *clients'* e-mail services are not usually HIPAA compliant. For example, when a client sends an e-mail message from some free e-mail accounts, it is scanned by the service for purposes of collecting advertising information. This means that the confidentiality of the information has already been breached. Therapists need to inform clients of this vulnerability so that they are aware that they may be violating their own security by sending and opening e-mail messages using an unsecure e-mail service (Dear, 2017). So informed clients may choose to install a software program that allows them to view and send encrypted e-mail messages (Strom, 2015).

While not currently in abundant use in mental health practice, physicians are increasingly beginning to use patient portals, which permit patients to view their health care information in a relatively secure environment. Some of these services also allow patients to send and receive messages to and from their health care providers (Clarke, 2015). Inasmuch as mental health providers deal with exceptionally personal and private information, such information portals may hold promise for helping protect confidential client information in the provision of distance mental health therapy. Indeed, as information portal technologies expand, such an option may also be possible for conducting audio visual exchanges within such secure infrastructures, thereby further increasing client privacy protection.

Therapists should also discuss with clients, as part of informed consent, the safeguards that will be implemented to assure that information exchanges are sent to the appropriate recipient. Thus, the therapist should be clear about the specific address to which personal information may be sent. For example, a therapist may have several e-mail addresses, some of which are not private; the same may be true of the client.

Further, therapists should discuss with clients alternative means of communication in case there is an interruption in services. For example, consider what might have happened if the connection between JR and Gene's communication lines were severed at the moment when JR expressed a desire to take his own life and there was not a mutually agreed on avenue for resuming the communication. For example, given interruption in services, the two might have agreed that Gene would call JR's cell phone. Thus, while not ideal, such a measure could still offer a failsafe measure in such an emergency situation.

Finally, therapists should inform the client about the precautions they are taking in storing information that is electronically sent and received. Accordingly, they assure clients that policies and procedures are in place to control access to client information that is being stored in information systems. This includes encryption of the stored information, robust passwords, and safe hardware and/or software (APA, 2013, Guideline 5).

PRACTICING RESPONSIBLY IN CYBERSPACE

While cyberspace presents a new and promising frontier for the delivery of counseling services, it also raises serious ethical challenges for distance practitioners. As the case of Gene and JR underscores, such practitioners must approach this new frontier mindful of these challenges, which include: the unique and limited character of cyberspace as a medium for conducting therapy; the importance of having emergency plans in place to deal with possible crises, such as client threats to harm themselves or others; the potential for legal conflicts, ambiguity, and insufficient legal knowledge in practicing across state lines; and the enhanced character of informed consent. Practitioners who are not prepared to meet these and related challenges appropriately limit their practice to physical space. Those who find daunting the legal challenges of practicing across state lines may appropriately choose to limit their cyber practices within the boundaries of their home states. In any event, virtuous therapists who choose to extend their practices to cyberspace practice with integrity and due regard for Client Welfare and Autonomy.

Questions for Review and Reflection

1. What are some benefits of online counseling? What are some drawbacks?

2. Can time differentials in online counseling across states or nations present a potential problem? Explain.

3. Should online counselors have an emergency plan in place? If not, why not? If so, what things should be included in it?

4. Are there any potential problems in attempting online assessment of a client's dangerousness to self or others? Explain.

5. What legal questions might be raised in conducting online counseling across state lines?

6. With what laws should a therapist, who does counseling across state lines, be familiar? Do most therapists who do such counseling possess this knowledge?

7. What state laws appear to apply in the case of Gene? Does Gene possess the appropriate license to practice under the laws in question?

8. In Gene's situation, what legal conflict does Gene have? If you were in Gene's situation, how would you approach the situation?

9. What is "Psypact," and what issues is it intended to address? What benefits does such an arrangement have? What potential challenges might it face? In your estimation, would such an arrangement resolve all the legal challenges Gene confronts in counseling JR?

10. Describe briefly the three models presented in this chapter for resolving interstate conflict and ambiguity. Which of these models would you recommend? Why would this model be preferable to the other two? Is this model

capable of eliminating the need for the therapist to exercise moral discretion? Explain.

11. In obtaining informed consent of online clients, what information, over and above the information ordinarily contained in face-to-face consent, should be included?

12. What HIPAA security requirements are there in conducting online counseling? Based on what you know about Gene's online practice, is Gene in compliance with all these requirements? Why or why not?

13. What should therapists tell their online clients as part of their informed consent about the e-mail services they may be using to communicate with their therapists?

14. What are patient portals and how might they be potentially useful in the online counseling environment?

15. With what you now know about distance counseling across state lines, would you be willing to engage in such a practice? Explain.

Cases for Analysis

Using concepts discussed in this chapter, discuss and reflect on virtuous practice in the following scenarios.

1. Dr. Emmett Jones, a psychologist, has been treating some of his clients using telepsychology. Recently, he began working with Bob Rinehart, a 35-year-old, single male who states that he resides with his widowed mother, 300 miles away from Jones, in another state. Bob's stated presenting problem is his dependent relationship with his mother, whom he describes as a "controlling bitch." Into the third month of counseling, based on a compilation of things that Bob has said and done, Jones begins to suspect that Bob does not have a living mother. Concerned, he conducts an online background search on both Bob and his mother and discovers that she had passed away 5 years ago. What would you do if you were Dr. Jones? What are the ethical and legal issues and problems that he may have to navigate?

2. Jerri Michaels, a newly licensed mental health counselor, has decided to add telephone counseling to the services she provides to clients. One of her clients, Karen Kittle, a 50-year-old female who is wrestling with issues of emotional and physical isolation, has a very low voice, and Michaels has difficulty hearing her accurately even after turning up the volume on her phone. Michaels has tried to diplomatically ask her client to speak more loudly, to no avail. Frustrated, Michaels decides to put Karen's calls on speaker, increasing the volume to its maximum capacity. Michaels reasons that although Karen's voice can now be heard in Michaels's reception area, the chances of clients hearing the conversation are minuscule because she is usually finished with Karen's session before clients physically arrive for appointments. For this reason, Michaels decides that she does not have to inform Karen that her voice is on speaker. To do so, she believes would be intimidating and counter therapeutic. Discuss Michaels's decision to not inform Karen that the speaker volume is on while she talks. What are the justifications for this, if any? What are the ethical and legal ramifications of this behavior? Discuss also the suitability of using telephone counseling for the types of issues with which Karen is presenting.

3. Kirwin Kelsey, a licensed clinical social worker, has been using his Yahoo e-mail account to remind his clients of their upcoming appointments. It is a free e-mail server, and Kelsey believes that using it, in this capacity, is ethical and legal because details of sessions are not included. Last week, Kelsey received notification that his server had been hacked by a foreign government. He quickly changed his password but did not notify his clients of the intrusion. Kelsey wonders if it's necessary to switch to a more secure but costly network in the future. Does Kelsey have an ethical or legal obligation to notify his clients of the breach? Was he justified in using the unsecured network in the first place?

References

American Counseling Association. (2011). *Suicide assessment*. Alexandria, VA: Author. Retrieved from https://www.counseling.org/docs/trauma-disaster/fact-sheet-6---suicide-assessment.pdf?sfvrsn=2

American Counseling Association. (2014). *ACA code of ethics*. Alexandria, VA: Author.

American Psychological Association. (2013). *Guidelines for the practice of telepsychology*. Washington, DC: Author. Retrieved from http://www.apa.org/practice/guidelines/telepsychology.aspx

ASPPB Mobility program e.passport overview. (n.d.). Retrieved from https://c.ymcdn.com/sites/asppb.site-ym.com/resource/resmgr/PSYPACT_Docs/E.Passport_Overview_2015.pdf

The Association of State and Provincial Psychology Boards. (n.d.). Psypact. Retrieved from https://asppb.site-ym.com/mpage/micrositehp

Barnett, J. E., & Kolmes, K. (2016, May). Avoiding a disconnect with telemental health. *Monitor of Psychology*, *47*(5). Washington, DC: American Psychological Association. Retrieved from http://www.apa.org/monitor/2016/05/ce-corner.aspx

Clarke, C. (2015). Patient portals secure PHI better than email. *Security Metrics*. Retrieved from http://blog.securitymetrics.com/2015/06/patient-portal-security.html

Council of State Governments. (n.d.). What is an Interstate Compact? *National Center for Interstate Compacts*. Retrieved from http://www.csg.org/knowledgecenter/docs/ncic/FactSheet.pdf

Dear, B. (2017). Therapy client emails can get you in trouble with health privacy. *Couch Therapy Simple*. Retrieved from https://simple.icouch.me/blog/therapy-client-emails-can-get-you-in-trouble-with-health-privacy

Delaware Administrative Code. (2014). Title 24, Regulated Professions and Occupations. Retrieved from http://regulations.delaware.gov/AdminCode/title24/3500.shtml

Epstein Becker Green. (2016). *50-State Legal Survey of Telemental Health*. Retrieved from http://psychology.ohio.gov/Portals/0/MISC%20PDFs/EPSTEIN-BECKER-GREEN-50-STATE-TELEMENTAL-HEALTH-SURVEY.pdf

Google. (2017). HIPAA Compliance with G Suite, G Suite HIPAA Implementation Guide. Retrieved from https://static.googleusercontent.com/media/gsuite.google.com/en//terms/2015/1/hipaa_implementation_guide.pdf

The Health Insurance Portability and Accountability Act. (HIPAA). Administrative Simplification. 45 CFR Parts 160, 162, and 164. Retrieved from https://www.hhs.gov/sites/default/files/ocr/privacy/hipaa/administrative/combined/hipaa-simplification-201303.pdf

National Conference of State Legislatures. (2015). *Mental health professional's duty to warn*. Washington, DC: Authors. Retrieved from www.ncsl.org/research/health/mental-health-professionals-duty-to-warn.aspx

Strom, D. (2015, July). Review: Best tools for email encryption. *Networkworld*. Retrieved from http://www.networkworld.com/article/2948183/security/best-tools-for-email-encryption.html

Texas State Board of Examiners of Psychologists. (1999). Guidelines for the practice of telepsychology. Retrieved from https://www.tsbep.texas.gov/files/forms/Guidelines%20for%20the%20Practice%20of%20Telepsychology.pdf

PART VII
DEFINING LIMITS OF CONFIDENTIALITY

13

BEING BENEVOLENT

Case Study: A Terminally Ill Client Contemplating Suicide

In the previous chapter, a case was examined in which a client had expressed an *irrational* desire to kill himself. In such a case, the virtuous therapist acts with due care for the welfare of his client and, pursuant to applicable state law, may even be required to breach confidentiality to prevent the client from killing himself. But what happens when a client has an arguably *rational* desire to die? What if the client is already dying of a debilitating and irremediable disease and will soon be rendered totally (or almost totally) incapacitated by the disease? According to the ACA Code of Ethics (American Counseling Association [ACA], 2014, B.2.b),

> [c]ounselors who provide services to terminally ill individuals who are considering hastening their own deaths have the option to maintain confidentiality, depending on applicable laws and the specific circumstances of the situation and after seeking consultation or supervision from appropriate professional and legal parties.

Indeed, the conventional wisdom of mental health practice has been to treat all suicidal clients as needing an intervention to prevent the suicide. However, there is presently a growing trend in the United States in medicine and law toward recognition of a right to die. For example, in several states including California, Montana, Oregon, and Washington there are statutes that make physician-assisted suicide a legal option. In tandem with this trend in medical law and ethics, there has been a belief among an increasing number of mental health practitioners that not all clients who have a desire to die are irrational and in need of an intervention aimed exclusively at preventing them from acting on their desire (Rogers, Gueulette, Abbey-Hines, Carney, & Werth, 2001; Werth, 1996). Beginning with a case of a terminally ill client who is considering hastening his death, this chapter develops ethical guidelines for counseling clients in such difficult circumstances within the constraints of applicable law.

A TERMINALLY ILL CLIENT CONTEMPLATING SUICIDE

Consider the case of Roger Titus, a 55-year-old retired professor of literature who had ALS (Lou Gehrig's Disease).

> For the past month, Roger had been seeing New York state licensed mental health counselor John Bartleby about how to cope with the inevitability of his imminent death. While he was still ambulatory using a motorized wheelchair, he was quadriplegic. Other previously intact abilities, especially his ability to speak, were degenerating rapidly.
>
> "Hello Roger," said John, as he pulled up a chair next to him.
>
> "I decided. I'm doing it before out of hands," said Roger as he strained to get all his words out.
>
> "You're going to end your life?"
>
> "Yes, I decided."
>
> "You ruled out hospice care? You can die in your own home."
>
> "No control. No dignified death. Totally helpless!" said Roger, defensively, as he gasped for air.
>
> "What do you think about discussing this with Emily [Roger's wife]?"
>
> "I considered . . . but decided no. She wouldn't let go."
>
> In their last meeting, the two also explored so-called "methods of deliverance," that is, ways to successfully end one's life, and the risks and dangers of unsuccessfully attempting suicide. Undeterred, Roger had managed to obtain a lethal dosage of the barbiturate, Nembutal, which he ordered from Mexico over the Internet. Now, notwithstanding the risks of consuming a drug obtained online, Roger was determined to end his life with this drug.
>
> John paused to think about what he should do in a case like this. He had received no specific training pertaining to working with end-of-life decisions such as this; and in the past, when a client expressed a desire to kill himself and had a plan, he had intervened to prevent it. Moreover, John was aware that in the state of New York, where he practiced, he had a duty to report in cases where a client poses an imminent and serious danger to himself. But, in the present case, John was torn between what was usual, customary, and legal and what he thought was morally right. In the end, John did not attempt to stop Roger from going forward with hastening his own death.
>
> Roger looked John in the eyes. "Thank you," he said.
>
> The two locked eyes and deeply engaged for a brief moment. This was the last time John was to see Roger, who ended his life later that evening.

THE CONVENTIONAL MORAL VIEW OF SUICIDE

Many people, especially those schooled in the Judeo Christian traditions, believe that suicide is never morally defensible, even if it is to end a tortured existence such as that experienced by Roger. For example, according to the National Conference of Catholic

Bishops, "life is the most basic gift of a loving God—a gift over which we have stewardship but not absolute dominion" ("Euthanasia and assisted dying," 2009).

The rejection of suicide has also been arrived at through the use of the medieval ethical principle known as the Principle of Double Effect. First introduced by the Roman Catholic Saint, Thomas Aquinas, according to this principle, an act that has two effects, one good and the other bad, is morally justified if and only if: (1) the act itself is morally good or at least not morally bad, (2) the agent does not intend or aim at the bad effect but merely tolerates it, (3) the agent does not use the bad effect as a means to bring about the good effect, and (4) the good effect is sufficiently good to compensate for allowing the bad effect (McIntyre, 2014). According to this principle, suicide cannot ever be morally justified even if it aims at a good effect such as the alleviation of pain and suffering. This is because, arguably, the act of killing oneself is itself a morally bad act. Moreover, the agent does not merely tolerate the bad effect (the death of oneself), but intends the bad effect and also uses it as a means to bring about the good effect—the alleviation of pain and suffering (Battin, 1995).

Another classical attempt to prove that suicide is immoral is provided by philosopher Immanuel Kant. According to Kant, suicide is morally wrong because it is motivated by self-love, which is supposed to improve life, not destroy it. As such, the act of committing suicide engenders a contradiction because in attempting suicide one tries to improve one's life by destroying it. According to Kant, this inherent contradictory nature of suicide shows that it is immoral. Moreover, according to Kant, to kill oneself to relieve one's pain or suffering is to treat oneself as a "mere means," that is, as an object manipulated rather than as a center of intrinsic worth and dignity. Such degradation of humanity, says Kant, is immoral (1964, pp. 95–96).

However, the above classical perspectives on the morality of suicide have tended to treat all suicides the same, despite the fact that the circumstances may be significantly different. For example, in the previous chapter, a case of a suicidal client was considered in which the client contemplates suicide because he is depressed about not having found a suitable life partner or job. In this case, the client has irrational ideation, for example, that "there is nothing to live for." In such a case, the client can still acquire new interests, eventually meet somebody compatible with him, or find a new job. He can go back to school for training in a new field; he can learn new social skills; he can overcome his depression through therapy; so the inference from his current situation to the conclusion that there is nothing to live for is not rational. In the present case, Roger is suffering from a terminal illness and may also be suffering from clinical depression. Insofar as this is the case, Roger is also a proper subject of a therapeutic intervention; however, insofar as he is not experiencing any similar kinds of irrational ideation, his desire to end his life may well be rational.

RATIONAL SUICIDE

As a number of mental health organizations, including the American Counseling Association (ACA, 2014), The National Association of Social Workers (NASW, 2017), and the American Psychological Association (APA, 2000), have maintained, some suicides in response to serious physical illnesses can be rational (The APA Working Group on Assisted Suicide and End-of-Life Decisions, 2000; Werth & Gordon, 2002). Whether or not they are rational can be determined by applying specific standards of rational suicide (Cohen, 2001).

Clearly, a therapist who is considering whether a client's decision to end his own life is rational needs to consider whether this decision is based on *sound reasoning*. As a minimal condition, the client needs to have the capacity to make rational decisions, which includes orientation to time, place, personal identity, and other basic aspects of reality. The therapist may administer a mental status examination such as the Mini-Mental State Examination (Upton, 2013; see also Mini-Mental State Examination [MMSE], n.d.) to determine decision-making capacity. Second, the client must not be suffering from a diagnostic mental disorder that impairs the ability to think or reason such as Major Depressive Disorder. Third, the client's reasoning that supports his decision to end his life cannot contain any false factual statements such as medical claims that lack evidentiary support ("I will lose control of my bowels" or "There are no palliative measures that will relieve my pain"). Fourth, the inferences from empirically verifiable factual claims need themselves to be valid or reliable. For example, it would be irrational to deduce that "the only way to end my suffering is suicide" from the fact that "suicide will end my suffering." As such, John cannot conclude that Roger's decision to end his life is rational because he has a terminal illness. It also matters what inferences Roger draws about this illness and whether he has an accurate understanding of his illness.

Further, decisions to commit suicide may be based on worldviews such as religious ones. Since religious beliefs rely largely on faith, they cannot ordinarily be confirmed empirically in the same way as medical or other factual claims. Nevertheless, suicides can be assessed as rational or irrational *in relation* to the client's worldview depending on whether or not it is shared by other members of his culture. According to Battin (1995) "in order that a suicide count as rational, it is only necessary that it be based on a world view that is consonant with the surrounding culture" (p. 136). For example, if Roger comes from a culture according to which killing himself before he becomes completely debilitated would preserve some measure of self-determination in the hereafter, then this would be a rational worldview for him to embrace. On the other hand, if he comes from a Judeo Christian culture but still believes that he will suffer in the hereafter unless he kills himself, then his worldview would not be a rational one for him because it is inconsistent with his surrounding (Judeo Christian) culture. As such, the rationality of a client's worldview must be assessed relative to his surrounding culture and not according to some absolute standard.

Also, a rational suicide decision must seek to avoid *irremediable pain and suffering*. That is, the client seeks to avoid pain and suffering that cannot otherwise be avoided (Battin, 1995). Here, the concept of *pain* refers to unpleasant physical sensations while *suffering* refers to existential distress (Cohen, 2001). For example, for Roger, the indignity of losing total control of his life may rationally count as suffering to be avoided through the act of suicide, even if the distress in question did not include physical pain.

Further, a rational suicide decision must be consistent with the client's "basic interests" or values (Battin, 1995, p. 146). For example, if Roger has a strong religious conviction about the unconditional sanctity of life, then, absent some reasonable explanation for the disparity, the decision to end his life would not be rational. Similarly, if Roger had a goal of completing a novel he had dedicated much of his life to writing, and he now chooses to end his life rather than complete the novel, then his suicide would be irrational save for some reasonable explanation, for example, that he lacks the physical stamina to complete the project.

Since suicide decisions that are inconsistent with basic values, or that do not truly reflect the client's own interests, can be the result of prescribed medications, as well as substance abuse, the therapist needs to check for the presence of such factors in determining the rationality of a suicide decision (Cohen, 1986). For example, Roger's judgment, as well as his emotional and behavioral responses, may be impaired by an anti-anxiety medication he is taking ("Anti-anxiety drug side effects," n.d.).

Suicide decisions can also be the result of external social or economic pressures, perceived or actual. For example, Roger's judgment may be the result of his perception of what others want and not what he himself truly wants. Accordingly, in determining the rationality of a suicide decision, the therapist needs to explore with the client his perception of others (such as friends and family) regarding his ending his life. In some cases, a client may harbor guilt about being a burden on significant others and falsely believe that they want him to end his life. The client may also harbor shame and perceive suicide as a means of self-punishment. For example, clients who are dying of HIV may believe that they are getting what they deserve (The APA Working Group on Assisted Suicide and End-of-Life Decisions, 2000).

Table 13.1 summarizes the standards of rational suicide decisions discussed in this chapter. Because suicide is final, and there is no opportunity to rectify a mistake in

TABLE 13.1 ■ Standards of Rational Suicide Decisions

Standard
1. The decision is based on sound reasoning. • The client has capacity to make rational decisions. • The client does not have a cognition-impairing mental disorder such as Major Depressive Disorder. • The client's decision does not rely on any false claims or misperceptions. • The client is not making any irrational inferences.
2. If the client is relying on a nonempirical worldview such as a religious perspective, it is consistent with the client's surrounding culture.
3. The client seeks to avoid physical pain or existential suffering through the commission of suicide. • The pain or suffering is irremediable, that is, cannot otherwise be avoided.
4. The suicide decision is consistent with the client's basic interests, goals, and values.
5. The client is not taking or addicted to any medication or drug that appears to be adversely affecting the client's cognition, emotions, or behavior.
6. The client's decision is not being influenced by any external social or economic pressures. • The client is not being influenced by guilt, such as that of being a burden to others. • The client is not being influenced by shame related to the client's illness or disease. • The client does not view suicide as a means of self-punishment.

judgment, therapists should exercise due care when determining if the decision in question is rational. Rationality (as well as irrationality) can admit degrees, and some decisions can be more (or less) rational than others, say when more (or less) standards are met. For example, a decision of a client who lacks decision capacity due to a psychosis may be less rational than that of a client who feels guilty about being a burden on his family. It would also seem that, when one standard is not satisfied, others will probably also not be satisfied. For example, if a client is clinically depressed, then there is likely to be faulty thinking in his belief system ("No one cares about me anyway").

Whether or not a standard is met can itself be subject to interpretation. Even clinical diagnoses such as Major Depressive Disorder may be assessed differently by different clinicians.

> Bias in the mental competence evaluation may result, because those who support assisted suicide as an option may be more willing to find a dying person's judgment to be unimpaired while opponents indicate that even if they found the person's judgment to be unimpaired, they would attempt to prevent the person from receiving assisted suicide. (The APA Working Group on Assisted Suicide and End-of-Life Decisions, 2000, p. 45)

This is one reason why it is important that therapists who are counseling seriously ill clients who are considering ending their lives seek consultation with other qualified therapists. In cases where, even after consultation, there is still a question about the rationality of a client's suicide decision, we submit that it is better to err on the side of caution since the client's life hangs in the balance.

Mental health professionals also "need to assess their own personal and professional beliefs about the dying process and different end-of-life decisions and consult with others regarding the degree to which their attitudes, values, and beliefs could affect or bias the review process" (The APA Working Group on Assisted Suicide and End-of-Life Decisions, 2000, p. 80). Indeed, in applying the standards of rational suicide decisions, all therapists, especially those who may have personal reservations about the morality of suicide, should take due care not to confuse their personal values with cognitive dysfunction, faulty thinking, or false premises (Appelbaum & Gutheil, 1991). On the other hand, an inconsistency, or other logical mistake in the client's belief system, might appropriately be challenged by the therapist in determining the rationality of the suicide decision (Cohen, 2001).

LEGAL CONCERNS

Inasmuch as therapists weigh client welfare and self-determination against their own personal welfare, therapists need also to consider the lawfulness of permitting clients to end their lives, even when the decision appears to be quite rational. First, it is important to emphasize here that *assisting* suicide is distinct from *permitting* suicide (Cohen, 2001). The former implies that the therapist takes an active measure that contributes causally to the client's death, such as providing a lethal dose of medication or other means of ending life.

Presently, in most states, assisted suicide is still unlawful. Further, even where it is lawful, the practice is carefully regulated by the state. For example, according to the Oregon Death with Dignity Act (2015), for a patient to qualify to receive medication to end his or her life,

> a consulting physician shall examine the patient and his or her relevant medical records and confirm, in writing, the attending physician's diagnosis that the patient is suffering from a terminal disease, and verify that the patient is capable, is acting voluntarily and has made an informed decision. (127.820 s.3.02)

In fact, unless the medication is prescribed by the attending physician in consultation with another physician pursuant to the said Act, the individual dispensing the medication may be guilty of a criminal offense. According to Oregon state law (ORS 163.193, 2015),

> [a] person commits the crime of assisting another person to commit suicide if the person knowingly sells, or otherwise transfers for consideration, any substance or object, that is capable of causing death, to another person for the purpose of assisting the other person to commit suicide.

Further, according to the Oregon Death with Dignity Act (2015), mental health professionals currently serve only a confirmatory role in the qualification process. The Oregon statute declares,

> If in the opinion of the attending physician or the consulting physician a patient may be suffering from a psychiatric or psychological disorder or depression causing impaired judgment, either physician shall refer the patient for counseling. No medication to end a patient's life in a humane and dignified manner shall be prescribed until the person performing the counseling determines that the patient is not suffering from a psychiatric or psychological disorder or depression causing impaired judgment. (127.825 s.3.03)

In contrast, permitting suicide does not involve the prescribing of lethal medication or otherwise providing the client with the means of obtaining such medication. Instead, in the case of permitting a client's suicide, the mental health provider does not intervene to prevent the suicide, such as by involuntarily detaining the client for observation in an inpatient facility, or by setting up a family vigil to monitor the client. According to Cohen (2001),

> [a] mental health provider (P) *permitted* a client (C) to commit suicide when, (1) C successfully attempted suicide; (2) P reasonably anticipated that C would attempt suicide; (3) P was aware of at least one accessible intervention which could have thwarted C's anticipated suicide attempt; (4) P intentionally elected *not* to employ any such intervention; and (5) the proximate cause of C's death was C's lethal act. (emphasis added)

It is remarkable that the omission in question is *intentional*, that is, the mental health practitioner intentionally deciding not to intervene. Accordingly, a permitted suicide must be distinguished from cases in which the therapist simply misjudges or disregards (e.g., due to negligence) the client's likelihood of committing suicide. Roger's suicide can be accurately characterized as a permitted suicide according to Conditions 1 through 5 given above inasmuch as John quite clearly anticipated with high probability that Roger would take the barbiturate he had obtained for the purpose of ending his life, and he clearly chose not to intervene to prevent this foreseen lethal act. John was also (presumably) aware of interventions that might have successfully prevented Roger from killing himself, such as informing his wife of his plan or contacting the authorities to involuntarily detain him for evaluation. Finally, the proximate (legal) cause of Roger's death was, apparently, the ingestion of the lethal medication, a determination that would need to be confirmed by the medical examiner. So, while John has not *assisted* Roger in committing suicide by providing him with the means of ending his life, has he still done something unlawful by virtue of his intentional omission?

The lawfulness of such an omission depends on the state in which John practices. As discussed in Chapter 4, whether or not disclosure of confidential information to prevent harm to self or other depends on whether the state in which the therapist practices requires or permits disclosures. In states such as California, Colorado, Delaware, Idaho, Illinois, Indiana, Iowa, Kentucky, Louisiana, Maryland, Massachusetts, Michigan, New York, New Jersey, Pennsylvania, Vermont, Virginia, and Washington, among others, where there is a mandatory reporting requirement, therapists do not have the discretion afforded them legally to decide not to disclose information necessary to prevent the intended suicide. On the other hand, in states such as Alaska, Arkansas, the District of Columbia, Connecticut, Florida, Kansas, Maine, Mississippi, Nevada, North Carolina, North Dakota, Oregon, South Dakota, Texas, West Virginia, and Wyoming, among others, where there are no mandatory reporting laws, therapists may have such discretion legally afforded them (National Conference of State Legislatures, 2015). However, even in the latter states, therapists should not assume the legality of exercising such discretion without first checking case law and statutes for other laws that might bear on its legal status. For example, according to Connecticut statute (952.53a-56), "a person is guilty of manslaughter in the second degree when . . . he intentionally causes or aids another person, other than by force, duress or deception, to commit suicide." According to New York state statute (PEN 120.30), "[a] person is guilty of promoting a suicide attempt when he intentionally causes or aids another person to attempt suicide," where "[p]romoting a suicide attempt is a class E felony," which can carry up to 4 years in prison. So does exploring end-of-life issues with a terminally ill, potentially suicidal client, and intentionally not intervening should the client rationally decide to end his life, qualify as "promoting a suicide" or "aiding another person, other than by force, duress, or deception"?

While it may be arguable that such an application of the statute would not be consonant with its original intent, the court is still out on such matters. In the meantime, professional associations such as the ACA have supported the option of assisting terminally ill clients in exploring their end-of-life issues without a duty to disclose the client's autonomous decision to end her own life. According to Vilia Tarvydas and Christine Moll, who were members of the 2005 ACA Ethical Code Revision Task Force, "counselors cannot be brought up on charges to the ACA Ethics Committee of doing harm by helping a terminally ill client explore end-of-life decisions" (Kaplan, 2008). While state laws do not necessarily conform to professional standards and codes of ethics, they can be decisive in determining the outcome of legal decisions. For example, according to the majority opinion in *Tarasoff*,

> once a therapist does in fact determine, or under *applicable professional standards* reasonably should have determined, that a patient poses a serious danger of violence to others, he bears a duty to exercise reasonable care to protect the foreseeable victim of that danger. (emphasis added)

Similarly, professional negligence in civil suits is always established by showing that the defendant failed to act in a manner that exhibits "a level of professionalism and standards commonly held by those in the profession" ("Professional negligence facts," n.d.). Inasmuch as the code of ethics of the counseling profession establishes such standards for counselors, practicing within the scope of the code provides a basis for avoiding professional malpractice (CNA & HPSA, 2014). Accordingly, standards such as ACA B.2.b. (2014), "Confidentiality Regarding End-of-Life Decisions," which affords therapists who counsel "terminally ill individuals who are considering hastening their own deaths" the "option to maintain confidentiality," may well play a decisive role in foreseeable legal cases involving therapists who permit the suicide of such clients.

Still, as has been emphasized in this book, codes of ethics are often ambiguous, subject to interpretation, and have latitude for the exercise of discretion. Thus, while ACA rule B.2.b (2014) provides an option to maintain the confidentiality of clients who are considering hastening their deaths, it also qualifies this option with the proviso, "depending on applicable laws and the specific circumstances of the situation and after seeking consultation or supervision from appropriate professional and legal parties." So what are these "specific circumstances of the situation" to which the code refers, and who are the "appropriate professional and legal parties" with whom to consult? Answers to such questions, among others, require the exercise of discretion that can only be guided by broader ethical standards such as those developed and applied in this text. As such, mindful of the legal risks and ethical ambiguity of current codes of ethics, therapists who counsel clients who entertain ending their own lives should be guided by pertinent ethical standards. These standards include Client Nonmaleficence, Client Welfare, Client Autonomy, and Compassionate Caring.

APPLYING THE ETHICAL STANDARDS

In permitting Roger's suicide, did John violate the standard of Client Nonmaleficence? In other words, did John intentionally stand by and let Roger harm himself? After all, he could have intervened to prolong his life but failed to do so. Here it depends on whether all human life is taken to be a positive value in itself, no matter how bad off one might be. This is what Immanuel Kant (1964) believed when he claimed that one cannot improve life by destroying it. On this view, since all life has positive value, the destruction of a life always destroys this positive value, leaving the individual worse off ("harmed"). To illustrate the point in mathematical terms, if the value of a person's life is +10 (just by virtue of being alive), then death only subtracts this positive value leaving the value at 0 (nonexistence). However, there are some who would disagree with Kant. For example, Richard Brandt (1986) has argued that some people's lives have negative value due to the irremediable pain and suffering they experience. Therefore, in killing themselves these individuals are not truly harmed because they have ended their pain and suffering. In mathematical terms, 0 (nonexistence) is better than -10 (a life of pain and suffering). Inasmuch as both these views about the value of life are coherent and rational, it is not the therapist's place to impose either one of them on the client. Thus, the latter approach can provide a rational basis for a client's ending his own life. So, even if the therapist believes that all human life has positive value, this is not a satisfactory reason to intervene to prevent the client from hastening his death. As long as it is rational, it is the client's value judgment, not that of the therapist, that takes precedence. Otherwise, the therapist imposes her own values on the client, which is not her prerogative.

So when John allowed Roger to commit suicide, did he violate the standard of Nonmaleficence? *From Roger's value perspective*, the answer is no; and it is the client's (rational) value perspective that counts in such cases, not the therapist's or anyone else's.

Did John also act beneficently toward Roger? The standard of Client Welfare tells therapists to maximize the client's net positive welfare, which means to choose the option that produces the greatest balance of positive welfare over negative welfare for the client than any available alternative option. For Roger, remaining alive would produce a greater balance of *negative* welfare (pain or suffering) over positive welfare (pleasure or happiness) than ending his life. However, hospice care was also a possibility. Palliative sedation was another option, which involves rendering a patient unconscious, especially in cases of intractable, physical pain (Lo, 2013). However, in Roger's case, the suffering was largely existential or emotional in nature. For Roger, being rendered unconscious would not have respected his dignity as an autonomous agent since it would have been tantamount to having relinquished complete and total control. As such, from Roger's viewpoint, concern for his own welfare together with respect for his own dignity or autonomy provided a rational justification for choosing to hasten his own death. Of course, since Roger ended his own life, Roger, not John, removed his own pain or suffering and respected his own dignity. Nevertheless, insofar as these two standards of client care—Client Welfare and Autonomy—constitute the primary responsibilities of therapists, John arguably best honored these responsibilities by not intervening to forcibly prevent Roger from ending his life. Insofar as John afforded Roger the opportunity to freely explore his end-of-life options and to come to a rational, autonomous conclusion of his own, John served Roger's (rational) interest in resolving his end-of-life crisis, consistent with Roger's own values.

QUALIFICATIONS FOR CONDUCTING END-OF-LIFE COUNSELING

John's service in facilitating rational resolution of Roger's end-of-life crisis also required *competence* in conducting end-of-life counseling with seriously, irremediably ill clients like Roger. Such competence assumes understanding of the unique issues and challenges raised in working with this population. At this juncture, this knowledge and insight is not ordinarily acquired through conventional degree programs in mental health (The APA Working Group on Assisted Suicide and End-of-Life Decisions, 2000, p. 22). As such, therapists who wish to work in this area should obtain further training. There is presently a growing body of knowledge in the interdisciplinary area of thanatology (the study of death, dying, and bereavement) as well as certification programs in the field such as that offered by the Association of Death Education and Counseling (2017). Subject matter includes cultural, socialization, and gender issues related to death and dying; different death systems and views on death; demographics of aging; religious and spiritual issues; the process of dying; loss, grief, and mourning; assessment and intervention; traumatic death; family dynamics; professional issues on dying; end-of-life decision making; quality of care issues; and the effects and/or incidences of end-of-life depression, dementia, and delirium (The APA Working Group on Assisted Suicide and End-of-Life Decisions, 2000, p. 22; Association for Death Education and Counseling, 2017).

Such multidisciplinary knowledge can be useful in acquainting therapists working in the field with the diverse perspectives and attitudes toward death and dying that can influence terminally ill clients' end-of-life decisions. This knowledge can, in turn, help promote compassionate caring by enabling therapists to see where their clients are coming from and, thus, to empathize with what they are going through. Such deep empathetic understanding was evident in the case of Roger when, at the end of the last session, the two locked eyes and Roger thanked his therapist. Here there was nonjudgmental, authentic relating, not intimidation or condemnation.

In this context of authentic, nonjudgmental relating, and compassionate caring and understanding, Roger was afforded an opportunity to reach his decision *autonomously* without subtle (or not so subtle) influence or manipulation by his therapist. "Do you think Emily would be *seriously traumatized* if you didn't tell her about your plan to kill yourself?" would have been manipulative and alienating. It would have attempted to instill guilt as a means of influencing Roger's decision. In contrast, John asked, "What do you think about discussing this with Emily?" This was open-ended, avoided the use of emotively charged language ("seriously traumatized"), and encouraged the client to think for himself.

Clearly, such deep caring and nonjudgmental engagement with a terminally ill client who is considering hastening the end of his life is not something that can be expected of all therapists. A therapist who feels strongly about the moral impropriety of suicide may be incapable of forging such a relationship. In this case, such a therapist should refer the client to a therapist who is competent to work with the client. It is not acceptable to retain the client and attempt to dissuade the client. This is a violation of the standard of Autonomy, and it is not consonant with helping the client reach a decision with which she is comfortable. Therapists are free to have conscientious objections to counseling such clients, but they are not free to coerce, manipulate, deceive, force, or otherwise impose their own value perspectives on them. As professionals trained in diagnosis, they can identify mental illnesses such as depressive or anxiety disorders that may be affecting the client's rational judgment. But this training does not qualify the therapist to determine that a terminally ill client must be mentally ill simply because the client is entertaining committing suicide.

PERMITTED SUICIDE WITH IRREMEDIABLY ILL PATIENTS WHO ARE NOT TERMINALLY ILL

Can a client who is *not* terminally ill be a proper candidate for permitted suicide? For example, can a client who is quadriplegic qualify?

There is evidence to suggest that moderate to high levels of anxiety and depression exist in patients who have quadriplegia, which also appears to vary with age (Kumar &

Raghav, 2012). There is also evidence to suggest that up to 50% of persons with spinal cord injuries (which include persons with quadriplegia) have cognitive impairments including deficits in memory, decision making, concentration, and abstract reasoning (Dezarnaulds & Ilchef, 2014, p. 5). Still, the possibility of clients in this population who have decision-making capacity cannot be ruled out *a priori*. Further, because such individuals may not be terminally ill, given a life expectancy of 6 months or less (Oregon Death with Dignity Act, 2015, ORS, 127.800 1.01[12]), existential suffering in this group may be sustained over a longer period of time. This suggests that such clients may have a stronger claim to permitted suicide than clients who are terminally ill, and will therefore die sooner, in any event. A parallel point has been expressed in *Quill v. Vacco* (1996), in which a New York statute that criminalized physician assisted suicide was found to be in violation of the Equal Protection Clause of the Fourteenth Amendment because it allowed terminally ill patients on life support to end their lives by having the equipment removed, but left terminally ill patients *not* on life support to suffer longer by foreclosing help in ending their lives. Here, the morally significant fact is not the contingent one of whether or not the patient is being mechanically sustained, but rather patients' desire to be relieved of their pain. Analogously, whether or not a client is terminally ill may be less morally significant than a rational client's desire not to prolong her irremediable suffering.

There is also legal precedent for recognizing the right to die of physically debilitated patients who are *not* terminally ill. For example, in *McKay v. Bergstedt* (1990), the Nevada Supreme Court found in favor of a 31-year-old quadriplegic, Kenneth Bergstedt, who sought to have a ventilator removed that had kept him alive for 23 years. Bergstedt had limited ambulation but could read, watch television, and orally operate a computer (Cohen, 2001). Clearly, the *Bergstedt* case can be distinguished from permitted suicide of a non–terminally ill client because it involved the removal of life support. However, the case established that *non–terminally ill* patients can have a legal right to end their suffering. Further, it also set a precedent for the right of such clients to end their existential suffering, not just physical pain. The court stated,

> It appeared that Kenneth's suffering resulted more from his fear of the unknown than any source of physical pain. After more than two decades of life as a quadriplegic under the loving care of parents, Kenneth understandably feared for the quality of his life after the death of his father, who was his only surviving parent. . . . His quadriplegia left him not only ventilator-dependent, but entirely reliant on others for his bodily functions and needs. (II.1)

Quadriplegic clients who seek suicide in an effort to avoid the indignity of being helplessly dependent on others resemble Bergstedt in morally significant respects. Such clients are entirely or almost entirely dependent on others to feed, clothe, clean, and assist them in the bathroom. Their range of activities is circumscribed by the availability of computers, electronic sensors, power wheelchairs, and other technologies to which they may or may not have access. The fact that Bergstedt was sustained by a respirator, but such other individuals breathe without such equipment, may be beside the point. Depriving the latter group the right to end their lives without being stopped by their therapists, while allowing physicians to help patients like Bergstedt die, seems unfair, discriminatory, arbitrary, and perhaps also an abridgment of their constitutional right to equal protection. Nevertheless, the ACA, APA, NASW, and other mental health practitioners associations do not presently recognize the option of permitting non–terminally ill, physically disabled clients to hasten their lives. Accordingly, therapists who permit the suicides of such clients do not have professional standards to support their cases should they confront legal challenges.

STANDARDS FOR PERMITTING SUICIDE IN MENTAL HEALTH PRACTICE

Currently, professional standards addressing permitted suicide in mental health practice are very broad and in need of greater specificity. Cohen (2001) has provided a more articulate set of standards or "model rules" to guide the decisions of mental health practitioners who have terminally ill or profoundly disabled clients who are considering ending their lives. The model rules presented in Table 13.2 have been adapted from the proposed standards.

TABLE 13.2 ■ Model Rules for Permitting Suicide

1. The therapist has obtained the medical records (pursuant to a signed, written release) from a qualified physician, and from a second, qualified, independent consulting physician, documenting that the client is terminally ill (likely to die within 6 months), or has an incurable, irreversible, and profoundly disabling disease.

2. The therapist determines that the client's decision is rational (see Table 13.1) and obtains confirmation from at least one independent, qualified mental health practitioner.

3. The therapist's determination of the rationality—or irrationality—of the client's decision is not based on or influenced by the therapist's own personal moral outlook on suicide.

4. The therapist facilitates the client's autonomous, informed exploration of hastening or ending the client's life and does not coach, deceive, trick, intimidate, coerce, frighten, coax, or otherwise manipulate the client's decision.

5. The therapist is certified or otherwise sufficiently trained in the area of death, dying, and bereavement (thanatology) or seeks supervision from such a qualified therapist.

6. The therapist neither provides the client with the means to end the client's life, nor advises or counsels the client on where or how to obtain such means.

7. The therapist who has a conscientious objection to permitting clients to end or hasten their lives, or who is otherwise incapable of competently working with such end-of-life issues, assesses the client's likelihood of committing suicide and, mindful of the client's safety, refers the client to a therapist who does not have a similar objection.

8. The therapist considers applicable state as well as federal laws before proceeding to permit a client's suicide.

Applying the Model Rules

Inasmuch as John did not consult with a qualified colleague on whether Roger's decision was rational, he was not in compliance with Rule 2. The latter rule requires consultation with at least one qualified mental health practitioner. Here, "qualified" may include mental health practitioners who have been trained and practice in the area of end-of-life decisions. For example, according to the American Psychological Association, "there is a significant number of psychologists who have attained stature as authorities" in thanatology and who "may be in a position to serve as teachers and mentors" (The APA Working Group on Assisted Suicide and End-of-Life Decisions, 2000, p. 24). As the role of mental health practitioners in end-of-life care and decisions becomes more mainstream, we can expect the number of trained professionals in the field to expand. *In addition* to consultation with at least one trained mental health practitioner, other professionals who specialize in end-of-life care or decisions, or who are able to provide further insight into the issues confronted by clients considering ending their lives, might be consulted. For example, Cohen (2000) has argued that philosophical counselors, who hold a master's or doctorate degree in philosophy and who are certified to help their clients address problems of living, including moral problems, could provide some useful insight. For instance, such practitioners are trained in logic and critical thinking and may assist the therapist in determining whether a client's reasoning is sound. They may also be able to help therapists disambiguate their own personal biases in the assessment of clients' thinking.

Indeed, end-of-life decisions go beyond the ability to diagnose mental illness such as clinical depression and anxiety disorders and require the exercise of prudence or practical reasoning. Thus, John appropriately challenged Roger to consider the risks of ingesting an unregulated medication obtained over the Internet, in compliance with Rule 4. Similarly, the exercise of prudence would require that John adequately document Roger's disease, in compliance with Rule 1. Further, prudence would also demand that therapists avoid practicing in an area in which they are not trained especially without adequate supervision. In the present case, John was not trained to work with clients confronting end-of-life decisions and apparently failed to seek out supervision from a trained colleague in compliance with Rule 5.

Because John practiced in New York, which recognizes a duty to report when a client poses a serious and imminent threat to himself, he also confronted a significant legal challenge. Appropriately, John considered the potential legal consequences in compliance with Rule 8, but chose to do what he thought was morally right notwithstanding the significant legal risk. For example, he did not disclose to Roger's wife her husband's plan to kill himself, which may have left him open to a civil suit. To the extent that John failed to comply with all provisions of the rules set forth in Table 13.2, the persuasiveness of his moral position would arguably have been lessened. As suggested earlier in this chapter, in such instances the chances of prevailing legally can depend on the strength of one's moral argument. Indeed, it is through morally responsible action that laws failing to square with respect for client welfare and autonomy can be challenged and improved.

Presently, laws (case law as well as statutes) and professional standards (codes of ethics and guidelines) addressing permitting suicide of clients with seriously debilitating or terminal illnesses are ambiguous, vague, absent, or (arguably) unjust. In this legal climate of uncertainty and inadequacy, professional standards such as those provided in Table 13.2 may be useful to therapists who counsel clients in confronting their end-of-life issues.

This chapter has explored the limits of confidentiality regarding a client who has a rational desire to end his own life due to irremediable pain and suffers from a physical disease. In the next and final chapter the limits of confidentiality are again tested by the case of a client who is HIV positive and having sexual intercourse with an unsuspecting sex partner.

Questions for Review and Reflection

1. What does the ACA Code of Ethics say about counseling terminally ill clients who are considering hastening their own deaths? How does this compare to the traditional stance on counseling clients who are considering killing themselves?

2. Would the National Conference of Catholic Bishops agree with the ACA's position? Why or why not?

3. What is the Principle of Double Effect? Can this principle be used to justify terminally ill clients hastening their own deaths? Why or why not?

4. Would the philosopher Immanuel Kant approve of terminally ill clients hastening their own deaths? Explain. Do you agree with Kant? Why or why not?

5. In your judgment, are there any morally significant differences between the case of Roger and that of JC in Chapter 12? Explain.

6. What are the six standards proposed in this chapter for assessing whether a suicide is rational? Give an example of each where the standard would not appear to be satisfied.

7. Is rationality an all or nothing concept, or are there degrees of rationality? Explain and provide an example.

8. Is the determination of whether the standards themselves are satisfied itself subject to interpretation? Explain.

9. Should a therapist seek consultation from another therapist regarding the rationality of a client's suicide decision even if the therapist feels confident that the decision is rational? Why or why not?

10. What if the client correctly believes that her continued existence is a burden to loved ones, for example, a financial drain on family resources or an emotional burden? In your judgment, is a client being irrational if she decides to end her life primarily because she feels guilty about being such a burden and does not want to continue to be such? Explain.

11. Is John providing Roger with assisted suicide or permitted suicide? What is the difference?

12. What is the role of mental health professionals according to the Oregon Death with Dignity Act? In your estimation, should assisted suicide (or "death with dignity") be provided only if the patient is first evaluated by a mental health professional? Explain.

13. In what state does John practice? Is there any reason to think that he may have violated New York state law in permitting Roger to take his own life? Explain.

14. In your opinion, would John's role in counseling Roger about his end-of-life decision qualify as the crime of "promoting a suicide"? Why or why not?

15. How would the American Counseling Association's Ethics Committee view John's case based on prior ACA history?

16. According to this chapter, some members of the 2005 ACA Ethical Code Revision Task Force stated that "counselors cannot be brought up on charges to the ACA Ethics Committee of doing harm by helping a terminally ill client explore end-of-life decisions." What role might such professional standing serve in defending against a charge of criminally "aiding" or "promoting" suicide in a case such as John's?

17. Is ACA rule B.2.b itself subject to interpretation? Explain.

18. If you were John, would you have taken the legal risk of not breaching confidentiality? Why or why not?

19. In permitting Roger to take his own life, does John transgress the Standard of Client Nonmaleficence? What is Kant's position? What is Richard Brandt's position? What is your position? Explain.

20. In permitting Roger to take his own life, does John respect the Standard of Client Welfare? What about Client Autonomy? Explain.

21. What qualifications are requisite to counseling clients such as Roger in end-of-life decisions? Does John possess the requisite training? If so, what is his training that so qualifies him? If not, should John have agreed to counsel Roger? Explain.

22. Are there any *ethical* arguments for broadening permitted suicide in mental health counseling to include irremediably ill clients who are not terminally ill such as clients who are quadriplegic? Are there any legal cases that may support the option of permitted suicide for such non–terminally ill clients? Does the ACA *Code of Ethics* currently support this broader justification of permitted suicide?

23. Briefly describe the standards introduced in this chapter for guiding therapists in conducting end-of-life counseling? Does John satisfy all these standards? Explain.

Cases for Analysis

1. Ava is a 45-year-old divorced mother of an adult daughter and was diagnosed with fibromyalgia by her family physician 2 years ago. She has been in counseling with Freida Fallon, LMHC, since shortly after her diagnosis. Ava suffers from extreme fatigue, muscle aches, difficulty in concentration, and sleep disturbances. Her physician has prescribed antidepressants to help to ease her symptoms, but Ava reports to Fallon that her life is a "living hell" and she wants to die. She indicates to Fallon that she intends to overdose on her antidepressants and that she has already prepared her last will and testament. Fallon, a devout Catholic, is concerned that allowing Ava to commit suicide would be a sin, so she alerts Ava's 25-year-old daughter to her mother's plan. Discuss the following: How could the medical and mental health treatment of Ava have been better coordinated? Specifically, discuss the role of antidepressants prescribed by Ava's family physician. Examine whether Fallon has any responsibility to recommend that Ava

consult another physician for a second opinion regarding her diagnosis of fibromyalgia (e.g., a rheumatologist). Discuss whether Fallon acted beneficently in warning Ava's daughter about Ava's plan to commit suicide.

2. Terry Bigelow, an 80-year-old widow and former nurse, is in relatively good health physically, but is disillusioned about the quality of her existence. Terry has been in therapy with Cameron Keaton for the last 3 months. Terry does not have any children, and both her siblings have died in the past 5 years. All her friends have either died or are in nursing homes, and Terry expresses loneliness and lack of purpose. Keaton diagnoses her with persistent depressive disorder. A few days ago, during session, she expressed the desire to end her life. "I was a nurse, and I know the way to carry this out," she relates to Keaton. When Keaton attempts to get Terry to brainstorm about possible life changes that she might make to lessen the feelings of estrangement and lack of purpose, she becomes angry and leaves the session. "And don't try to stop me!" she yells as she exits his office. Does Terry's potential suicide qualify as a rational one using the above discussed criteria? Why or why not? How would you proceed if you were Keaton?

3. Milagro Smith, age 72, is a former librarian who has been diagnosed with moderate Alzheimer's disease. He is often lucid and able to engage in lively discussions, only to later become confused and disoriented. Smith's doctor has prescribed medication to slow down the progression of the disease, but Smith states that he is experiencing uncomfortable side effects from the drug. With the medication, Smith's physician estimates that he may have several years of moderate functioning before he goes into more serious cognitive decline. Smith has been in therapy with Silvy Newton, a clinical psychologist. Lately, Smith has been speaking in sessions about committing suicide. He relates, however, that if he does kill himself, his daughter will not be able to collect on his life insurance policy because it has an exclusion for this. Smith suggests to Newton that he has found out how to make his suicide look like a natural death and that, sometime soon, he will end his life. Does Newton have an ethical responsibility to warn Smith's daughter of his plan? What are her responsibilities to Smith? What are her responsibilities to the life insurance company? How can she avoid imposing her own values on her client in this case?

References

American Counseling Association. (2014). *ACA code of ethics.* Alexandria, VA: Author. Retrieved from counseling.org/resources/aca-code-of-ethics.pdf

American Psychological Association. (2000). Report from the APA working group on assisted suicide and end-of-life decisions: Formation of the APA working group on assisted suicide and end-of-life decisions. Washington, DC: Author. Retrieved from http://www.apa.org/pubs/info/reports/aseol.aspx

Anti-anxiety drug side effects. (n.d.). CCHR International. The Mental Health Watchdog. Psychiatryic Drugs. Retrieved from https://

www.cchrint.org/psychiatric-drugs/antianxietysideeffects/

The APA Working Group on Assisted Suicide and End-of-Life Decisions. (2000, May). *Report to the board of directors of the American Psychological Association (APA)*. Retrieved from http://www.apa.org/pubs/info/reports/aseol-full.pdf

Appelbaum, P., & Gutheil, T. (1991). *Clinical handbook of psychiatry and the law*. Philadelphia, PA: Williams & Wilkens.

Association for Death Education and Counseling. (2017). Certification in thanatology. Retrieved from http://www.adec.org/adec/Main/Earn-Certification/ADEC_Main/Earn-Certification/Certification_Home.aspx?hkey=605cb70f-dd67-4dd3-82c5-297b8881532f

Battin, M. P. (1995). *Ethical issues in suicide*. Englewood Cliffs, NJ: Prentice-Hall.

Brandt, R. B. (1986). The morality and rationality of suicide. In T. A., Mappes & J. S. Zembaty (Eds.), *Biomedical Ethics* (2nd ed., pp. 337–343). New York, NY: McGraw-Hill.

CNA & HPSA. (2014). Understanding counselor liability risk. Retrieved from http://www.hpso.com/Documents/pdfs/CNA_CLS_COUNS_022814p_CF_PROD_ASIZE_online_SEC.pdf

Cohen, E. D. (1986). Paternalism that does not restrict individuality: Criteria and applications. *Social Theory and Practice*, *12*(3), 309–335.

Cohen, E. D. (2000, Summer). Permitting suicide in philosophical counseling. *International Journal of Philosophical Practice*, *1*(1). Retrieved from http://npcassoc.org/docs/ijpp/cohen.pdf

Cohen, E. D. (2001). Permitted suicide: Model rules for mental health counseling. *Journal of Mental Health Counseling*, *23*(4), 279–294.

Dezarnaulds, A., & Ilchef, R. R. (2014). *Psychological adjustment after spinal cord injury. Useful strategies for health professionals*. Sidney, AU: Agency for Clinical Innovation. Retrieved from http://docplayer.net/8818264-Psychological-adjustment-after-spinal-cord-injury-useful-strategies-for-health-professionals.html

Euthanasia and assisted dying: General Christian view. (2009). BBC. Retrieved from http://www.bbc.co.uk/religion/religions/christianity/christianethics/euthanasia_1.shtml

Kant, I. (1964). *Groundwork of the metaphysics of morals* (H. J. Paton, trans.). New York, NY: Harper & Row.

Kaplan, D. (2008, June). End-of-life care for terminally ill clients. *Counseling Today*. Alexandria VA: American Counseling Association. Retrieved from https://ct.counseling.org/2008/06/ct-online-ethics-update-3/

Kumar, A., & Raghav, D. (2012). Anxiety & depression among the spinal cord injury patients. *International Journal of Pharmacy, Biology and Medical Sciences*, *1*(1), 1–4. Retrieved from http://www.academia.edu/14709093/Anxiety_and_Depression_among_the_Spinal_Cord_Injury_Patients

Lo, B. (2013). *Resolving ethical dilemmas*. Philadelphia, PA: Lippincott Williams & Wilkens.

McIntyre, A. (2014, Winter). Doctrine of double effect. In E. N. Zalta (Ed.), *The Stanford Encyclopedia of Philosophy*. Retrieved from https://plato.stanford.edu/archives/win2014/entries/double-effect/

McKay v. Bergstedt, 801 P.2d 617 (1990). Retrieved from http://law.justia.com/cases/nevada/supreme-court/1990/21207-1.html

Mini-Mental State Examination (MMSE). (n.d.). Retrieved from https://www.uml.edu/docs/Mini%20Mental%20State%20Exam_tcm18-169319.pdf

National Association of Social Workers. (2017). *Code of ethics of the National Association of Social Workers.* Retrieved from https://www.socialworkers.org/About/Ethics/Code-of-Ethics/Code-of-Ethics-English.aspx

National Conference of State Legislatures. (2015). *Mental health professional's duty to warn.* Washington, DC: Authors. Retrieved from http://www.ncsl.org/research/health/mental-health-professionals-duty-to-warn.aspx

The Oregon Death with Dignity Act. Revised Statutes ORS 127.800-127.897 (2015). Retrieved from http://www.oregon.gov/oha/ph/ProviderPartnerResources/EvaluationResearch/DeathwithDignityAct/Pages/ors.aspx

Professional negligence facts. (n.d.). Negligence Laws. Retrieved from http://negligence.laws.com/professional-negligence

Quill v. Vacco, 80 F.3d 716 (2d Cir. 1996). Retrieved from https://supreme.justia.com/cases/federal/us/521/793/case.html

Rogers, J. R., Gueulette, C. M., Abbey-Hines, J., Carney, J. V., & Werth, J. L. (2001). Rational suicide: An empirical investigation of counselor attitudes. *Journal of Counseling & Development, 79*(3), 365–372.

Upton, J. (2013). Mini-mental state examination. In M. D. Gellman & J. R. Turner (Eds.), *Encyclopedia of Behavioral Medicine* (pp. 1248–1249). New York, NY: Springer.

Werth, J. L., Jr. (1996). *Rational suicide.* Washington, DC: Taylor & Francis.

Werth, J. L., Jr., & Gordon, J. R. (2002). Amicus curiae brief for the United States Supreme Court on mental health issues associated with "physician-assisted suicide." *Journal of Counseling & Development, 80*(2), 160–172.

14

BEING NONMALEVOLENT

Case Study: A Sexually Active Client With HIV

The previous chapter considered whether the general confidentiality requirement applies to disclosures of rational, terminally ill clients who are considering hastening the end of their lives; and guidelines were proposed for therapists who counsel such end-of-life issues. This chapter explores another challenge to the general confidentiality requirement: Under what conditions, if ever, should a therapist disclose confidential client information about the client's HIV status, against the client's wishes, for purposes of protecting the client's sex partner(s) from the potential harm posed by the disease? In addressing this question, a case study is presented of an HIV positive client who is sexually active in a monogamist relationship. As in the previous chapter, ethical guidelines are proposed within the context of applicable state and federal law. Given the present HIV pandemic, it is highly probable that, over time, therapists will confront such cases in their practices, especially therapists who work with populations of clients who are IV drug users (Centers for Disease Control, 2016b). The chapter begins with pertinent facts about HIV.

HIV AND AIDS

HIV is the virus that causes Acquired Immunodeficiency Disease Syndrome (AIDS). It attacks immune cells in the human immune system known as CD4 T cells, reproduces itself in these cells, and destroys them. At a certain point in the destruction process, the individual's immune system becomes unable to fight off opportunistic infections such as Kaposi's Sarcoma, Tuberculosis, and Pneumocystis Carinii Pneumonia. At this progressed stage in the disease, the individual is said to have AIDS ("Opportunistic infections," 2017). Today, there are drugs that can slow the progression of the disease, but these do not cure it, unfortunately.

The virus is carried in bodily fluids, especially blood, semen, and vaginal secretions. Saliva has very low counts of virus load and is generally not capable of causing infection. The primary means of spreading the disease are sex and the sharing of infected hypodermic needles, where there is contact of a permeable membrane with the infected bodily fluid. Intercourse using protection such as a condom is generally not high risk for contracting the virus ("Good counselling vital for clients with STDs," n.d.). A single episode of intercourse carries a risk of .5% for female to male transmission and 1% for male to female transmission. Anal sex per sex act is much riskier, 13 times higher for the nonpositive receptive partner, according to the Center for Disease Control (CDC, 2016a). As discussed later, these risks increase with each additional sexual episode.

Tests for the virus generally test for the antibodies to the virus. While there are also rapid tests available, the gold standard consists of two positive enzyme immunoassay (EIA) tests, which can detect antibodies between 2 to 12 weeks after becoming infected; and one positive Western Blot test to confirm the diagnosis.

DISCRIMINATION AGAINST PERSONS WITH HIV

Presently, HIV is prevalent in pandemic proportions in heterosexual as well as homosexual populations. In the mid to late 1970s, when the disease became prevalent, its cause was unknown, hence creating widespread panic leading to persons with HIV being discriminated against in housing, employment, health care, education, and other social spheres of human interaction. The fear of even having casual contact with a person with HIV created an atmosphere of ostracism and severe discriminatory practices against persons with the disease. Professional codes of ethics as well as legal standards provided little or no guidance for professionals such as physicians, nurses, dentists, mental health practitioners, attorneys, and early childhood educators in confronting the ethical and legal challenges raised by working with HIV positive individuals (Cohen & Davis, 1994).

In 1998, in *Bragdon v. Abbott* (1998), the Supreme Court ruled that persons with HIV are protected under the Americans with Disabilities Act (ADA). This case involved an HIV positive woman who filed suit against a dentist for refusing to treat her in his office. "From the moment of infection and throughout every stage of the disease," the court declared, "HIV infection satisfies the statutory and regulatory definition of a 'physical impairment'" (§ 625[b]). Not only did the court point to inability to perform economic and public tasks, as defining the sphere of protected disabilities, but it also pointed to the inability of someone to reproduce sexually as an impairment of a "major life activity" as understood by the ADA. "[A]n HIV-infected woman's ability to reproduce is substantially limited in two independent ways" (§ 625[c]), the court explained. If she tries to conceive a child, (1) she imposes on her male partner a statistically significant risk of becoming infected, and (2) she risks infecting her child during gestation and childbirth (i.e., perinatal transmission).

Clearly, *Bragdon v. Abbott* made substantial strides in clarifying the private as well as public challenges faced by persons with HIV and helped build legal protections against social discrimination against this ever increasing population. Unfortunately, the social stigma attached to having this disease has not lost its original taint, and persons with HIV are commonly negatively stereotyped and thought condemnable for their moral turpitude (Barnhart, 2014). It is such discriminatory attitudes that still prevail, notwithstanding laws aimed at quelling their outward manifestations.

At the same time, state laws have also emerged that criminalize sexual activities of HIV positive persons with unaware sex partners. Presently, there are 33 states that have HIV specific criminal laws. Some of these laws make it a felony for HIV positive persons to have sex with other persons without first disclosing their HIV status to the person (Lehman et al., 2014). As such, federal regulations such as the ADA militate against discrimination against persons with HIV, while state criminal laws aim at protecting others from contracting the disease from those already infected.

Some professional associations have also addressed the challenge of counseling sexually active clients who have HIV. In 1995, the American Counseling Association (ACA) added a "Fatal and Contagious Diseases" rule to its Code of Ethics as an exception to confidentiality (Section B.1). This rule, modeled after the rule proposed earlier by Elliot D. Cohen (1990), has provided general conditions under which it would be permissible for a counselor to notify the unsuspecting sex partners of HIV positive clients that they are at risk of contracting the disease. In addition, as discussed below, states have also added a further layer of laws that regulate mental health practice with respect to this client population. It is in this context of negative stereotypes, federal antidiscrimination legislation, criminal laws, codes of ethics, and state professional regulations that the ethical challenges confronted by mental health practitioners regarding HIV positive clients who are sexually active with unaware sex partners arise.

THE CASE OF AN HIV POSITIVE CLIENT AND HIS UNSUSPECTING FIANCÉE

Consider, for instance, the case of Ralston Infield, who is a 37-year-old male in therapy with Barrett Wilson, PhD, a licensed clinical psychologist practicing in Maryland.

> Employed as a manager at a technology firm, Ralston was married for 3 years, divorced, and now engaged to a local high school English teacher, Bonnie Collins, whom he has been seeing for about 1 year. Coming from a strict Roman Catholic background, he had entertained the possibility of becoming a priest but decided against it because he did not think he was "worthy of such a high calling." Nevertheless, he became an ordained minister and practiced as a pastoral counselor for a while.
> "I felt like such a fraud," he said. "I just couldn't keep up the façade."
> "So you stopped practicing?"
> "Yes."
> "It sounds like you had some strong feelings that led you to this decision."
> "I did."
> "You said you couldn't keep up the façade. Tell me about that."
> "It isn't my faith. I never stopped believing. It is how I think others would judge me if they found out who I really am."

"What do you mean by 'who you really are'?"

"It's not that I don't have sexual feelings for women."

"So it's about your sexuality?"

"When my first wife found out, she divorced me. I thought I could live a straight life, but I had an affair with a guy and she found out. I really loved her, and I ended the affair, but she wouldn't have anything to do with me after that. It's not that I didn't have sexual feelings for her. It's not like that at all."

"So you're bisexual?"

[pause]

"Yes, you could say that."

"It sounds like you're facing some challenges?"

"Yes, Bonnie doesn't know, and I struggle with this, but there is something much worse."

"Tell me about it."

"There's an X-rated bookstore not far from where I live. I stopped going, but I was meeting some men there. It was just sex, but I think that's where I got it."

"Got it?"

"HIV. I tested positive! What am I going to do?"

"Are you receiving treatment?"

"Yes, I'm seeing a doc regularly."

"That's good. Have you told Bonnie that you are HIV positive?"

"No, I haven't."

"Are you having sex with her?"

"Yes, we have great sex."

"Tell me about that."

"We both have great timing, like we're meant for each other. The orgasm is incredible. And she says the same thing!"

"So you're having intercourse?"

"Yes, we also have oral sex."

"How often do you sleep with your fiancée?"

"Once a week, on Saturday night."

"Do you use protection?"

"She's on the pill."

"Do you intend to tell her about your HIV status?"

"I tried telling her, but just couldn't get the words out. She was being so affectionate, and I was about to destroy everything with just three words: 'I have HIV.'"

"What about using a condom?"

"Well suddenly I start wanting to use a condom!? She'll get suspicious and leave me just like my ex did. I don't know what I'd do if that happened."

"Tell me about that."

"When my wife left me, I became very depressed. I attempted suicide. Took a bunch of sleeping pills. When I got out of the hospital, I lived with my parents for a while. That was the worst part of my life. I'm just getting back on my feet. I can't go through this again. I love her so much. I don't want to lose her. Are you going to tell her what I told you? This is all still confidential, right!?"

"We talked about a couple of exceptions to confidentiality."

"Yeah, right, but I thought that was if someone's going to kill himself or someone else. It's not like that! I love her. I just don't want to lose her. I couldn't go on without her!"

THE ETHICAL CHALLENGE

The ethical question of what a therapist in Wilson's shoes should do is complex and not easily reduced to the logic of the *Tarasoff* case, which says, "the protective privilege ends where the public peril begins" (see Chapter 5). Clearly, Ralston's interpretation of the limits of confidentiality cuts to the heart of an ongoing debate within the legal community. HIV is a life-threatening disease, but is breaching the confidentiality of the HIV positive client the most efficacious way to prevent its spread when the client, stigmatized by this disease, lives in fear of being rejected by his beloved as well as others? Is this a matter best dealt with in treatment, and what should be done if the client still refuses to disclose? Will such disclosure, if legally required, alienate and keep those with the virus from seeking therapy in the first place?

STATE PROFESSIONAL REGULATIONS

Pursuant to Maryland Statute (MS 18-337, 2005), a health care provider, whose practice may include "diagnosing, healing, treating, preventing . . . any mental, or emotional ailment or supposed ailment of an individual" (MS14-101, 2005) may disclose to the client's sex partner and/or to the health department "the individual's identity" and "the circumstances giving rise to the notification." In "acting in good faith," the health care provider would be immune from civil and criminal liability, whether or not he makes the disclosure ("HIV/AIDS reporting and partner notification," 2011). Accordingly, the ethical decision of whether or not to disclose the identity and circumstances of notification to the client's sex partner is not settled by Maryland law. Instead, this law leaves the moral decision squarely in the hands of the health care provider. Nor is this situation unique to Maryland. For example, Florida (FS 456.061, 2016) provides a similar permissive legal framework for disclosure. However, in contrast to Florida, Maryland does recognize a therapist's *duty* to protect in cases where clients inform their therapists of "the patient's intention to inflict imminent physical injury on a specified victim or group of victims" (General Assembly of Maryland [GAM], 2017, 5-609). As such, it cannot be assumed that the logic that drives a state's duty to protect in cases of threatened physical injury also automatically applies to cases concerning notification of the sex partners of HIV positive clients.

This does not mean there are no legal constraints on a therapist in states like Maryland and Florida with permissive laws. For instance, according to Maryland law (GAM 5.609, 2017), a therapist has a duty to "take action" in cases where the client poses a threat of violent behavior toward another. This duty may be

> discharged if the mental health care provider or administrator makes reasonable and timely efforts to . . . formulate a diagnostic impression and establish and

undertake a documented treatment plan calculated to eliminate the possibility that the patient will carry out the threat.

As applied to the case of a client who is sexually active with an unwitting sex partner, this would imply at least a duty to act discharged by working diligently to help the client resolve the mental issues preventing him from disclosing his HIV status to his partner in the first place. As such, Wilson would arguably have a duty to treat if he did not take action to disclose. This assumes that, in Maryland, the harm posed by an HIV positive client may appropriately be addressed in a similar manner as the harm posed by a violent client. As discussed below, some states distinguish between these two kinds of potential harms. However, in the case of an HIV positive client who is sexually active with an identifiable partner, diligent treatment in lieu of disclosure would appear to be a reasonable interpretation of "acting in good faith."

In New York, physicians and others who order tests for or diagnose HIV (such as nurse practitioners, physician assistants, medical examiners, pathologists, and coroners), or their agents, are required to report the names and addresses of all known HIV contacts to the health department, which in turn, notifies the subject's sexual and/or needle-sharing contacts, giving priority to more recent contacts (New York Laws and Regulations, Title 10, Chapter II, Subchapter G, Part 63.8, 2017). In addition to reporting these contacts to the health department, physicians in New York may also notify them on their own pursuant to New York Public Health Law on "Confidentiality and Disclosure" (§ 2782[5]). On the other hand, psychologists, social workers, and other mental health providers are not permitted to disclose the HIV status to the client's sex partner(s) (New York State Department of Health, 2013).

This is consonant with Massachusetts, insofar as it also *prohibits* disclosure by mental health practitioners (Burke, 2015). The Massachusetts law (Part I, Title XVI, Ch. 111, § 70F) enjoins that

> a health care provider [including psychologist or social worker] shall not... disclose the results of [a test for the HIV antibody or antigen] to any person other than the subject of the test without first obtaining the subject's written informed consent; or... identify the subject of such tests to any person without first obtaining the subject's written informed consent.

However, the Massachusetts law (Ch. 123, § 36 B) also prescribes a "duty to warn patient's potential victims" in certain cases where the patient poses "an explicit threat to kill or inflict serious bodily injury upon a reasonably identified victim or victims and the patient has the apparent intent and ability to carry out the threat." So while Massachusetts prescribes a duty to warn potential victims of those who make explicit threats to kill or seriously harm them, it also *prohibits* warning the sexual or needle-sharing contacts of HIV positive subjects.

Apparently, in the latter class of cases, Massachusetts does not consider the potential harm sufficient to justify breaching confidentiality. For example, Ralston does not make an "explicit threat to kill or inflict serious bodily injury" upon an identifiable victim; nor does he have the intent to do such harm. True, Ralston can and should be able to foresee the likelihood of infecting his fiancée over time, but this is a consequence of having a sexual relationship with her, not his explicit intention in carrying out a threat. Further, as discussed in more detail later, the question of whether there is an imminent probability of serious harm is complicated by a number of biological and situational factors (e.g., whether there are bleeding disorders) that determine probability of transmission. In any event, in Massachusetts as well as New York, Dr. Wilson would have been barred from breaching confidentiality to warn Ralston's fiancée. On the other hand, as a Maryland therapist, he has the option of disclosing or not disclosing. So which approach makes the most sense?

There are clearly alternative perspectives about which reasonable persons can agree to disagree. Apparently, according to New York law, the harm in question is imminent, probable, and serious enough to justify disclosure by physicians (and other medical clinicians) to the endangered sexual or needle-sharing partner, regardless of whether there was an explicit threat that was made to the client's partner and regardless of what the client's intention was. Yet mental health practitioners are prohibited from making such disclosure. This apparent discrepancy may be explainable due to medical clinicians' roles in testing and/or diagnosing the disease and, therefore, their knowledge and competence to determine that the patient in question has, indeed, tested positive for HIV antigens or antibodies. In contrast, a mental health professional typically learns about the client's HIV positive diagnosis indirectly, from the client's confidential disclosure, which may not be complete or accurate.

Pursuant to Section 8 of the Ryan White Care Act of 1996 (last amended in 2009), states that receive federal funds under Part B of Title XXVI of the Public Health Service Act must show that they are making a "good-faith effort . . . to notify a spouse of an HIV-infected patient that such spouse may have been exposed to the human immunodeficiency virus and should seek testing." While this Act refers specifically to "spouses," most states have implemented more inclusive programs applying to all sex and needle-sharing partners. For example, Florida Statute 455.216 (1991) referred exclusively to the notification of the patient's spouse, but subsequently was revised to include any sex or needle-sharing partner (FS 456.061, 2016). Nevertheless, the impact of the Act has been to encourage changes in existing law promoting disclosure. This includes freedom from legal liability in making disclosure, offering counseling to the partners of HIV-positive clients or patients, and permitting or requiring physicians and/or counselors to participate in contact identification and notification (Office of Inspector General, Department of Health and Human Services, 1999, Appendix C).

RESPECT FOR CLIENT SELF-DETERMINATION

While the virtuous therapist has an interest in complying with such state laws that encourage disclosure to unwitting partners of HIV positive clients, also weighing heavily in the ethical decision is respect for the client's self-determination and welfare, which can be undermined through disclosure. Still, within legal boundaries, there is considerable room for balancing these competing values.

Ralston has confronted Wilson about the limits of confidentiality in his case. Unfortunately, his view of exceptions to confidentiality did not include having HIV and sleeping with his fiancée; nor did Wilson clarify such potential grounds for breach of confidentiality. Consequently, there is the real danger that the client could lose trust in his therapist and stop confiding in him. This would portend lost opportunity to help the client work through his issue.

So should Wilson have been more thorough in the provision of informed consent? Indeed, had he explored possible case scenarios in which disclosure of confidential information would be permissible, including one involving partner notification, Ralston would not have had a cogent reason to feel betrayed in the event of such disclosure. Of course, there is the possibility that the client would then have been more reticent to be forthright with the therapist about his HIV status in the first place. However, deception as a mode of encouraging a client to disclose is a self-defeating approach because it forecloses a trusting relationship, which destroys the prospect for successful therapy in the long run. Accordingly, for therapists practicing in states permitting or requiring partner notification in such cases, we recommend including an example of such a scenario as part of the client's informed consent.

FACILITATING CLIENT SELF-DISCLOSURE

Respect for client self-determination is therefore paramount in such cases. Here, the goal is not to use disclosing the client's HIV positive status as a threat or device of manipulation. To the contrary, it is to help the client work through his issue and make disclosure on his own. This holds true regardless of whether partner notification is permitted, required, or forbidden in the state in which the therapist practices. In disclosing himself because he believes it is the right course of action, the client acts autonomously and is not manipulated.

As a facilitator of self-disclosure, the virtuous therapist demonstrates compassionate caring for the client. Thus, as a virtuous practitioner, Wilson would be there for his client, resonating with his plight: the struggle with fear of abandonment, the loneliness of confronting this formidable and socially stigmatizing disease on his own, the gnawing guilt of not having disclosed his HIV status to a beloved, conflicting sexual desires, and the confusion over his true sexual identity. As such a compassionate caring therapist, Wilson would listen empathetically to his client's story, asking open-ended questions ("So how do you feel about not disclosing this information to Bonnie?"), thus encouraging Ralston to key into his own emotions and reflecting back the anguish he is communicating in a manner that brings his conflict into focus ("It sounds like you are feeling afraid to tell her and guilty about not telling her"). Here, there is opportunity for building the client's trust, and a virtuous therapist would do his utmost not to lose this trust. Indeed, Ralston has confided in Wilson in the first place only because he trusted him, and it is important that the therapist not sabotage this trust.

Ralston's ongoing trust of his therapist is clearly on the line. "Are you going to tell her what I told you? This is all still confidential, right!?" he asked. In this delicate situation, ethically, Wilson must avoid lying to or misleading his client about the confidential nature of his disclosure. The fact that Maryland law does not require that the therapist disclose this information needs, therefore, to be disclosed in response to Ralston's question. At the same time, the therapist walks a narrow tight rope in avoiding alienating his client. Thus, he might say, "While Maryland law allows me to disclose this information to your fiancée, this is really your responsibility, and it would be far better for you both if you told her." Then, assuring his client that he will be there to support him, Wilson might add, "I am here for you, Ralston, to help you work this through."

Then, Wilson's challenge would be to help Ralston appreciate, both cognitively and emotionally, that informing his fiancée about his HIV status would be far better than not informing her. This could be accomplished by asking questions to help the client carefully explore the implications of withholding the information:

- "What would happen if you kept this information from Bonnie while continuing to have sexual intercourse with her?"
- "What if she got HIV from you and didn't get the medication that you yourself are now on?"
- "Would it be better for her to get the medicine sooner rather than later?"
- "Would she eventually find out anyway, especially if she contracted HIV from you?"
- "How would she feel if she found out that you knew you were HIV positive but continued to sleep with her without telling her?"
- "How would you feel if she got HIV from you?"
- "How would you feel if you were her?"

In challenging his client to think through the answers to these questions, the therapist avoids the implication that his client is a bad person. "What kind of person would sleep with someone when he knows he has HIV" is the language of intimidation and disempowerment. To the contrary, the point is to empower the client to disclose on his own. In globally condemning his client, a therapist would imply that the client is incapable of moral conduct, for how could a totally worthless person do anything worthwhile!

Still, such questions would not address the painful emotions the client is experiencing; for, all the while, there is need to move between the affective and cognitive dimensions of the client's predicament. "It sounds like you think telling Bonnie is the right thing to do but it's still really hard for you to bring yourself to do it." Here, through such reflection, Wilson demonstrates unconditional positive regard for Ralston and resonates with his client's subjective world. Connecting emotionally, this strengthens the bond of therapist-client trust, which increases the probability the client will work through his issues and disclose.

"I tried telling her, but just couldn't get the words out. She was being so affectionate, and I was about to destroy everything with just three words, 'I have HIV.'" Here, the therapist can offer the client assistance. "Would you feel more comfortable if you came with Bonnie to a session and you told her then? That way, I would be there to support you both." Offering the client such assistance, while not insisting on it, can further fortify the message that the therapist is there for the client.

But what if the client is still unwilling to disclose on his own? What if, no matter how much support and encouragement Ralston receives, he is still reticent to disclose?

THERAPIST DISCLOSURE

In states in which disclosure is not permitted, such as Massachusetts, the virtuous therapist weighs the personal legal risks of disclosure against the welfare and interests of the client and at-risk sex partner and acts accordingly. In states in which disclosure is required or permitted, the therapist also acts mindful of the welfare and interests of the client and at-risk sex partner. As a Maryland practitioner, Wilson can avoid legal liability, whether or not he notifies Bonnie about her risk of contracting HIV, insofar as he acts in "good faith." As a virtuous therapist, Wilson's first priority is to facilitate Ralston's self-disclosure, since this seeks both to promote Ralston's autonomy and avoid harm to Bonnie. Pursuant to Maryland law, Wilson would presumably act in good faith by virtue of working toward Ralston's self-disclosure through provision of competent treatment. But where it becomes evident that timely self-disclosure is not likely to occur, Wilson can no longer act in good faith by failing to notify Bonnie. In such a case, he neither helps his client nor his client's fiancée by not taking further action. In Maryland, as mentioned earlier, a therapist has the option to disclose "the individual's identity" and "the circumstances giving rise to the notification" to the client directly or with the assistance of the health department ("HIV/AIDS reporting and partner notification," 2011).

When to Disclose

Cohen (2003) has provided a set of six conditions of disclosure that are necessary for disclosure, either by the therapist or through the health department. These conditions are provided in Table 14.1.

The importance of the evidentiary requirement, as provided in Condition 1, cannot be overstated. Inasmuch as clients can draw hasty conclusions on their own, without

TABLE 14.1 ■ Conditions of Justified Disclosure

1. The practitioner must be aware of *conclusive* medical evidence indicating that the client is HIV positive, such as two EIA tests and a confirmatory Western Blot.

2. The client's sex partner must be engaging in a relationship with the client that, according to current medical standards, places the third party at high risk of contracting HIV from the client such as ongoing, unprotected sexual intercourse.

3. In addition to the client, there must be no one else who has or is likely to disclose to the client's sex partner in the near future.

4. Prior to making disclosure, the practitioner candidly informs the client of his or her intention to notify the client's sex partner, or the health department, and gives the client a reasonable opportunity to make self-disclosure.

5. It must be possible for the client's sex partner(s) to be identified and contacted without intervention of law enforcement.

6. The client's sex partner is not negligently engaging in high-risk sexual activity for which he or she can reasonably be expected to foresee or comprehend the high risk of HIV infection.

sufficient medical information, it is the therapist's responsibility to have reasonable belief that such evidence exists prior to deciding to disclose. For example, the client may have used an at-home, do-it-yourself saliva test, which is less accurate than laboratory blood tests and, therefore, always requires follow-up with a medical center (Schattner, 2012). A client may not have had a confirmatory Western Blot test, or the client may be assuming that he has HIV because he has engaged in high-risk sex. In such situations, the therapist should encourage the client to follow up with conclusive testing before deciding to disclose the client's HIV status to his sex partner. Arguably, without such conclusive evidence that the client, in fact, has HIV, the presumption of respecting client confidentiality is overriding. This appears to be a rationale for permitting only medical practitioners who order tests for or diagnosis HIV to disclose (either directly or through the health department) the patient's HIV positive status to the patient's sex partner. Whereas medical practitioners have the knowledge and competence to determine conclusively whether the patient has HIV, mental health practitioners do not generally possess the same knowledge and competence by virtue of their training in mental health.

In Ralston's case, he has confided to Wilson that he is being treated for HIV by a medical doctor. While this assumes that the client does, in fact, have the disease, the virtuous practitioner would still query his client about the medical tests performed and document this information in the client's record. Further, in our opinion, it is not being too cautious for the therapist to ask the client to provide a copy of, or to release, the lab results to the therapist. If the client is uncooperative, then the therapist exercises prudence in concluding that there is such conclusive evidence.

The therapist also should not act precipitously in concluding that the client's sex partner is in danger of contracting HIV from the client, unless she has reasonable belief that the client is engaging in risky sex. As discussed earlier in this chapter, such sexual activities involve a high probability of a bodily fluid carrying the virus contacting a permeable membrane. So while the use of condoms (both male and female types) for vaginal intercourse do not provide certainty that the virus will not be transmitted (accidents can happen, and condoms can sometimes break), the disease is rarely spread when condoms are used properly (CDC, 2016c). Shallow kissing is also not a high-risk sexual activity. Nor is deep mouth kissing high risk unless the HIV positive individual has an oral disease in which the mouth is prone to bleed. Oral sex is not, in itself, high risk unless the HIV positive individual has vaginal bleeding (including menstrual bleeding and fissures) or oral bleeding. In the latter cases, oral sex can be considered high risk (CDC, 2016d). In Ralston's case, he is having unprotected vaginal intercourse, which places his sexual activity in the high-risk category, thus satisfying Condition 2 in Table 14.1.

Condition 3 in Table 14.1 also appears to be satisfied in Ralston's case inasmuch as there does not appear to be anyone else but the client likely to disclose his HIV status to Bonnie in the near future. This assumption would need to be confirmed before Wilson would be justified in disclosing. Clearly, when someone else (a friend or a relative, for example) is already likely to make timely disclosure, it would be self-defeating for Wilson to unnecessarily risk losing his client's trust by also disclosing.

Inasmuch as trust is paramount to a successful therapeutic relationship, sacrificing that trust through disclosing "behind the client's back" would be self-defeating and unethical. The virtuous therapist respects the client as a self-determining person and does not treat him as a mere object manipulated. Respect for client autonomy therefore requires that the therapist disclose his intention to contact the client's sex partner about the client's positive HIV status (Condition 4, Table 14.1). As discussed earlier, here the emphasis should be on the client's responsibility to disclose and the therapist's willingness to be there for them both. Still, there is an honest reckoning with the client that, regrettably, the therapist is prepared to disclose if the client continues to refuse.

In our opinion, the therapist's notifying the client's sex partner rather than involving the health department for this purpose tends to be preferable. For one, assigning the task to the health department sends the message, intended or not, that the therapist does not care enough about the client's significant other to notify her himself. Second, in placing the onus on the health department, the therapist relinquishes the opportunity to offer the client's partner an opportunity to receive support from the therapist, who, due to his relationship with the client, may be in a better situation to offer such support. So because Wilson is Ralston's therapist, he is not simply a health department caseworker assigned to the case. His status is a special one due to his knowledge of the couple's relationship and his history of support. Of course, there can be exceptions. For example, in some cases, the sex partner may have a history of domestic abuse or violence, and it may be less risky for one's client to have assistance from the health department in notifying the client's sex partner. The therapist should therefore act accordingly. In Ralston's case, insofar as there is no likelihood of domestic violence, or other exceptional circumstance for which the assistance of the health department is indicated, Wilson acts appropriately in notifying Bonnie on his own.

It is remarkable that all legal and professional standards of disclosure restrict disclosure to *identifiable* third parties (e.g., American Counseling Association [ACA], B.2.c, 2014; FS 456.061, 2016). As such, these rules would not apply if the client were routinely having one night stands with sex partners, the names and contact information of whom were not known, even by the client. Thus, in such cases, the therapist is not permitted to contact law enforcement to catch the client having unlawful, infectious sexual encounters with unwitting sex partners. Setting up such sting operations would be manipulative and deceptive; it would destroy therapist-client trust and create a public image of mental health practitioners as police informants, which would discourage sexually active, HIV positive clients from seeking therapy in the first place. Far from helping protect their sex partners from contracting the disease, such a policy would chill off the opportunity to provide the therapy needed to help these clients give up their dangerous sexual activities (Cohen, 1990).

Further, individuals who have unprotected intercourse with sex partners, whom they do not know, take unreasonable health risks, for which they bear some responsibility. In contrast, those who have faithful monogamist sexual relationships with sex partners who fail to disclose their HIV positive status are more vulnerable, and arguably less responsible, because they lack the foreknowledge to avoid the danger. It therefore stands to reason that the latter group merits protection more than the former group, insofar as one's responsibility to protect others increases with their degree of vulnerability (Cohen, 1990). This does not mean that those who take unreasonable health risks deserve to get sick. Nevertheless, in situations where protecting such individuals, who already have reason to avoid their dangerous behavior, requires breaching the therapist-client trust, the weight of the latter trust would be overriding. On the other hand, where the third party is vulnerable and there is no one else but the therapist who could protect this individual from contracting a life threatening disease, the therapist may be justified in notifying the third party about the danger. As discussed earlier, in states such as Massachusetts, which do not permit therapists' disclosure of the client's HIV status, the therapist would need to act mindful of the legal risks.

How to Disclose

Table 14.1 states *when* disclosure is justified; but of equal ethical importance is *how* one makes disclosures. Accordingly, Table 14.2 identifies general guidelines for how to proceed in making disclosure to the endangered third party (Cohen, 1990, 2003; Cohen & Cohen, 1999).

Timeliness of Disclosure

The risk of HIV infection can be increased by a number of different risk factors. In addition to the type of sex (e.g., vaginal, anal, or oral) as well as whether the inserting partner is HIV positive or negative, and whether protection is used, these factors include

> the presence of sexually transmitted infections (STIs), a high viral load, a man being uncircumcised, a woman menstruating, other bleeding and activities that can cause tearing and inflammation, such as rough sex, longer sex, douching, enemas before anal sex, and tooth brushing, flossing or dental work before oral sex. (Wilton, 2012)

Such factors can increase the risk beyond average risks. For example, the risk of transmission from an HIV positive female to an HIV negative male in a single episode of vaginal sex may be significantly more than .5% if the HIV woman is menstruating. It also matters how many sexual episodes occur. The greater the number of sexual episodes the higher the probability of transmitting the disease. For example, the average risk (not allowing for additional risk factors) of an HIV positive male transmitting the disease to an HIV negative female through 100 episodes of (insertive) vaginal sex is approximately 10% (Wilton, 2012). Thus, the timeliness of the disclosure is a function of the number

TABLE 14.2 ■ Procedures of Disclosure

Ethical Guideline

- Disclosure is *timely* in light of risk factors.
- The therapist notifies the client's sex partner (or legal guardian of the client's sex partner) *directly*.
- The therapist *limits disclosure* to general information sufficient to inform the third party of the imminent danger.
- The therapist offers *therapy assistance or an appropriate referral* to the at-risk sex partner.
- The therapist takes reasonable measures to *safeguard the client* from physical harm such as self-inflicted harm or domestic violence occasioned by disclosure.

of sexual episodes over the period of time during which the endangered sex partner is not informed, in light of additional risk factors such as those listed above. For example, if Ralston also has a sexually transmitted disease, has lengthy sexual episodes, or has rough sex, then Wilson's waiting additional time (say an additional week) would be more significant than if such factors were absent. In fact, the CDC (n.d.) has provided an HIV risk calculating tool on its website that takes into account certain additional risk factors in helping make such determinations. However, even if the third party has already contracted the disease, notifying her sooner rather than later can still make a difference, because starting treatment sooner can affect the HIV positive patient's prognosis, including her longevity ("Considerations before starting HIV treatment," 2016).

Directly Notifying the Client's Sex Partner(s)

As discussed previously, while contact notification through the health department is sometimes a legal option, it may not be the best therapeutic option. Assigning messengers such as a secretary or assistant would be inappropriate because there is an inherent therapeutic element to conveying such disturbing information, and those not trained as therapists are therefore not qualified for this assignment. Electronic communications such as text messaging or e-mail are also inappropriate because such means are inappropriate for conveying such highly emotional information in an empathetic manner. Moreover, such technology does not provide the individual with any immediate support. Leaving one's contact information for the client's sex partner can be appropriate as long as it is presented discreetly and confidential information is not included in the message. Informing the client's sex partner about the problem by leaving a message on voicemail or on an answering machine is indiscreet and self-defeating from a therapeutic perspective. While setting up a face-to-face meeting tends to be preferable therapeutically, the sex partner may be unwilling to cooperate. Under such circumstances, a therapist may convey the information via a phone conversation.

Limiting Information

The primary goal of notifying the client's sex partner is to help prevent continued exposure to HIV and to allow the person to be tested for the disease as soon as possible. As provided by the ACA Code of Ethics (2014, B.2.e), "[w]hen circumstances require the disclosure of confidential information, only essential information is revealed." In the present case, conveyance of "essential information" would be that required to enable the person to avoid continued exposure. Such information would typically require the therapist to provide the client's identity and HIV positive status, general information about the potential for the disease to be transmitted sexually, and a brief explanation about why it is urgent to be tested for the disease such as the potential benefits of being treated sooner rather than later if the test turns out to be positive. While recommending that the individual see a physician to be tested is a reasonable recommendation, some people may prefer to purchase a rapid test purchased over the counter because of privacy concerns. In such a case, the therapist should inform the client that further testing may be necessary if this test comes back positive. As such, any further details the client may have disclosed in the course of therapy are nonessential and would violate the client's trust if disclosed. For example, Wilson would not disclose to Bonnie that her fiancée has been sexually active with other men and that is how he thinks he acquired HIV.

Offering Therapy Assistance or Referral

Understandably, the client's sex partner may experience shock, incredulity, anger, denial, and a wide range of other reactions, including the potential for violence (Disclosure and HIV, 2016). The client may therefore benefit from an opportunity to receive therapy to work through such feelings. In cases in which the individual declines the offer of therapy, the therapist should offer to provide a referral (Cohen, 1990). In any event, the therapist should exercise compassionate caring and strive to be with the individual in this time of crisis.

Safeguarding the Client From Harm

Violence against women with HIV perpetrated by their sexual partners is an increasing, worldwide problem (World Health Organization [WHO], 2006). In one U.S. study of HIV positive women, 12% of HIV positive women reported fear of violence as a barrier to disclosing their HIV status to their sex partners (WHO, 2003). The problem is even more intense in other nations. For example, in one Kenyan study, nearly one third of the respondents experienced emotional abuse or violence by their partners (Colombini, James, Ndwiga, & Mayhew, 2016). As discussed earlier, where there is already a history of emotional abuse or physical violence, it is reasonable to involve the health department in making disclosure. In cases in which a potentially violent reaction of the partner was unexpected based on prior history, the therapist should take appropriate steps to protect the client from the potential violence. This includes providing information about resources and options such as contact information for accessible domestic violence shelters or safe houses. The therapist must therefore exercise discretion in determining if there is a credible threat of violence and act accordingly. Similarly, the client may be disposed to harm herself after the disclosure occurs. In such cases, the therapist assesses the risk prior to disclosure and takes appropriate measures to protect the client from self-harm. When the therapist-client relationship is based on trust, the inherent risk is lower because the client may be willing to continue treatment. On the other hand, if the therapist does not already have the trust of the client and then discloses, the client is likely to feel betrayed, and the opportunity is likely lost for continuing therapy. Unfortunately, in some cases where the client is rejected by the sex partner after being notified, involuntarily detaining the client for psychiatric evaluation may be the only means available to protect the client. However, this intervention diminishes client autonomy and can dissuade the client from seeking therapy in the future (Sederer, 2013). As such, the importance of maintaining client trust and being there and for the client in such a time of distress is paramount.

BUILDING TRUST AND PREVENTING HARM

Building trust is, therefore, the best way to avoid harm to clients and their sex partners. When the HIV positive client trusts her therapist, the probability of promoting self-disclosure is greatest. Indeed, these clients will be more likely to stay in therapy, speak candidly to their therapists, and, consequently, work through the personal issues (low self-esteem, fear of rejection, depressions, and anger, for example) that sustain their self-defeating, potentially harmful sexual conduct.

Legal regulations, which prescribe the conditions under which therapist disclosure is permitted, required, or forbidden, provide a failsafe when client self-disclosure is not a reasonable option. However, when therapists do their job well, when their HIV positive clients can confide in them without feeling degraded, manipulated, or deceived, then the need for therapist disclosure is eliminated, or substantially reduced. In this manner, therapists act as facilitators of such constructive change and to reduce client suffering and the chances of transmitting the disease to others.

In the event that the therapist is unable to facilitate such constructive client change, and disclosure is a legal option, virtuous therapists make disclosure mindful of the welfare and interests of both their clients and their clients' sex partners. Here, as always, there is respect for client self-determination in the process of notifying sex partners. The client is informed about the decision to disclose, offered a final opportunity to disclose, and only essential information is conveyed, thereby avoiding unnecessary breaches of client confidentiality. Regard for at-risk third parties follows suit. The therapist offers her professional assistance but does not insist on it, acts in a timely way to inform the sex partner, and does so directly, without violating individual privacy or otherwise precipitating unnecessary pain or suffering.

Questions for Review and Reflection

1. What is the difference between HIV and AIDS? In what bodily fluids is the virus most prevalent? What are the primary means of spreading the disease?

2. What are the risks of male to female transmission of the disease in a single episode of vaginal intercourse? What about female to male transmission in a single episode of vaginal intercourse? What about in anal sex?

3. What is/are the most reliable test(s) for detecting the disease?

4. What did the Supreme Court rule in *Bragdon v. Abbott*, and what is the significance of this decision for persons with HIV?

5. What is the present legal status of having sexual intercourse without first informing one's sex partner of one's HIV positive status?

6. Consider the case of Ralston. What similarities does this case bear to the landmark *Tarasoff* case discussed in Chapter 5? What dissimilarities does it have? In your judgment, does the conclusion reached in *Tarasoff* apply to cases such as Ralston's? Explain.

7. In the state in which Ralston's therapist, Winston, practices (Maryland), what does the law provide regarding notification of sex partners of HIV positive clients? How does this compare to Maryland's law concerning the threatening of imminent physical harm? Why do you think Maryland treats these two types of cases differently?

8. What does New York state law governing physicians say about notification of the sex partners of HIV positive patients? How does this compare to New York's law governing mental health practitioners? Why do you

think New York treats physicians and mental health practitioners differently?

9. What rationale might justify Massachusetts in *prohibiting* notification of sex partners of HIV positive patients of the patients' HIV positive status, yet recognizing a duty to warn potential victims when a patient threatens to do serious bodily harm to them?

10. What is the Ryan White Care Act of 1996, and what impact has it had on partner notification activities?

11. Did Winston provide Ralston with adequate informed consent about exceptions to confidentiality? Explain. What possible impact could Winston's manner of addressing such exceptions have had on the therapist-client relationship?

12. Is it best that Winston notify Ralston's fiancée, Bonnie, of Ralston's HIV positive status, or is this better left to Ralston? Explain.

13. What approach might Winston take in encouraging Ralston's self-disclosure to Bonnie? Is it okay for Winston to threaten to tell Bonnie if Ralston refuses? Explain.

14. What should Winston do if Ralston refuses to inform Bonnie of his HIV status? Are there conditions under which it would be appropriate for Winston to make the disclosure to Bonnie?

15. In your judgment, would it be better for the health department or for Winston to notify Bonnie of Ralston's HIV status?

16. What if Ralston agrees to use a condom going forward? Does that make disclosure of Ralston's HIV positive status to Bonnie unnecessary? Explain.

17. What if Ralston is routinely having oral sex rather than intercourse with Bonnie? Does that make disclosure of Ralston's HIV positive status unnecessary?

18. In the event Winston decides to disclose to Bonnie, what guidelines recommended in this chapter should he follow in determining *how* to disclose?

Cases for Analysis

1. Matilda is a 30-year-old, married female who resides in New York with her husband, Ignatz. She has a history of intravenous drug use. After 5 years of unsuccessful treatment, she has finally been clean for 14 months. Upon arriving at work one morning, she discovers a "pink slip" on her desk. She has been fired because her company is downsizing. Matilda soon finds out, however, that two other coworkers, who were on-the-job for far less time, are not terminated. Feeling distraught and embarrassed, Matilda leaves the building without even retrieving her personal belongings and travels to one of the "shooting galleries" that she had previously frequented. She remains there using IV drugs, prostituting herself for 3 days, and eventually overdosing and requiring hospitalization. Matilda subsequently admits herself to an in-patient substance abuse treatment program. Upon successful completion of the program, she returns home to Ignatz. As part of her recommended medical follow-up, Matilda is receiving follow-up tests for STIs

3 months following her relapse. Her 3-month testing confirms that she is HIV positive. Matilda is in out-patient aftercare at the facility where she just completed treatment and immediately schedules an emergency session with her counselor, Monroe Jackson. She discloses her HIV status to Jackson and states that Ignatz has become both physically and emotionally abusive since her relapse, often striking her and calling her a whore. She tells Jackson that she feels guilty and wants to inform Ignatz about her health status but is terrified to tell him because of the domestic abuse. Matilda discloses that the two have regular unprotected vaginal sex because Ignatz wants her to conceive. What are Jackson's ethical responsibilities to Matilda, Ignatz, and a possible unborn child? How does the alleged domestic abuse complicate Jackson's decision? How does New York law affect what Jackson should do?

2. Harry is a single heterosexual male client, age 40, who lives in Florida. He has been in therapy for 1 year for generalized anxiety disorder with Dr. Lynn Yang, a clinical psychologist. Harry describes himself as a "swinging" bachelor and has multiple, ever changing sex partners, often engaging in threesomes with women. He uses no protection because he considers his behaviors to be low risk. He estimates that he has had intercourse with about 300 women. Recently, Harry has been chronically ill and has had a series of tests, including those for HIV. The results reveal that he is not only HIV positive, but also has full-blown AIDS. Harry is becoming increasingly depressed and speaks of trying to find out who infected him. He asks Yang if he should try to contact all his partners to see if he can detect the source of his infection. Yang is concerned about Harry's preoccupation with finding out the source of his illness and is also wondering if she has ethical responsibilities to notify any of Harry's partners, if they are identifiable. What are Yang's ethical and legal responsibilities to Harry and his partners? Discuss how Florida law might affect the way she proceeds.

3. Lisa and Mitch Sylvester, both age 35, have been in couples counseling for 3 months with Lydia Roma, a licensed mental health counselor in Maryland. At the start of therapy, Roma asks that the two agree that nothing said to her in any individual sessions be withheld from each other. The couple's treatment consent form clearly articulates this provision. Recently, Mitch has disclosed to Roma that he found out during routine testing that he is HIV positive. He emphasizes that he never cheated on Lisa and likely contracted the virus during his youth when he experimented with IV drugs. Mitch maintains that there is "no way" that Lisa can contract the disease from him because he always wears a condom. He explains that the two do not want to have children, so he will be using protection for the "next 25 years until Lisa goes into menopause." Mitch implores Roma to not disclose his status to Lisa because she will "be emotionally destroyed." What do you think Roma should do? What are her responsibilities under Maryland law? How much weight should the consent agreement have in guiding Roma's course of action? Would withholding such information from Lisa constitute a violation of the therapist-client trust? What are her ethical responsibilities to both Lisa and Mitch?

References

American Counseling Association. (1995). *Code of ethics*. Alexandria, VA: Author. Retrieved from https://www.counseling.org/Resources/Library/ACA%20Archive/Code%20of%20Ethics%201995.pdf

American Counseling Association. (2014). *ACA code of ethics*. Alexandria, VA: Author.

Barnhart, G. (2014, December). The stigma of HIV/AIDS: HIV/AIDS-related stigma exerts a direct negative impact on the health of those who have HIV. In the Public Interest. Washington, DC: American Psychological Association. Retrieved from http://www.apa.org/pi/about/newsletter/2014/12/hiv-aids.aspx

Bragdon v. Abbott, 524 U.S. 624 (1998). Retrieved from https://www.hivlawandpolicy.org/sites/www.hivlawandpolicy.org/files/Bragdon%20majority—Kennedy.pdf

Burke, J. (2015). Discretion to warn: Balancing privacy rights with the need to warn unaware partners of likely HIV/AIDS exposure. *Boston College Journal of Law and Social Justice, 35*(1), 89–116. Retrieved from http://lawdigitalcommons.bc.edu/cgi/viewcontent.cgi?article=1077&context=jlsj

Centers for Disease Control. (2016a). *Anal sex and HIV risk*. Atlanta, GA: Author. Retrieved from https://www.cdc.gov/hiv/risk/analsex.html

Centers for Disease Control. (2016b). *HIV and injection drug use*. Atlanta, GA: Author. Retrieved from https://www.cdc.gov/hiv/pdf/risk/cdc-hiv-idu-fact-sheet.pdf

Centers for Disease Control. (2016c). *HIV risk and prevention: Condoms*. Atlanta, GA: Author. Retrieved from https://www.cdc.gov/hiv/risk/condoms.html

Centers for Disease Control. (2016d). *HIV risk and prevention: Oral sex and HIV risk*. Atlanta, GA: Author. Retrieved from https://www.cdc.gov/hiv/risk/oralsex.html

Centers for Disease Control. (n.d.). *HIV Risk reduction tool: Beta version*. Atlanta, GA: Author. Retrieved from https://wwwn.cdc.gov/hivrisk/estimator.html#

Cohen, E. D. (1990). Confidentiality, counseling, and clients who have AIDS: Ethical foundations of a model rule. *Journal of Counseling & Development, 68*(3), 282–286.

Cohen, E. D. (2003). Lethal sex: Conditions of disclosure in counseling sexually active clients with HIV. *International Journal of Applied Philosophy, 17*(2), 253–265.

Cohen, E. D., & Cohen, G. S. (1999). *The virtuous therapist: Ethical practice of counseling and psychotherapy*. Belmont, CA: Wadsworth.

Cohen, E. D., & Davis, M. (1994). *AIDS: Crisis in professional ethics*. Philadelphia, PA: Temple University Press.

Colombini, M., James, C., Ndwiga, C., & Mayhew, S. H. (2016). The risks of partner violence following HIV status disclosure, and health service responses: narratives of women attending reproductive health services in Kenya. *Journal of the International AIDS Society*,

19(1), 20766. Retrieved from https://www.ncbi.nlm.nih.gov/pmc/articles/PMC4819069/

Considerations before starting HIV treatment. (2016). *The Well Project.* Retrieved from http://www.thewellproject.org/hiv-information/considerations-starting-hiv-treatment#Starting%20Sooner%20Rather%20than%20Later

Disclosure and HIV. (2016). *The Well Project.* Retrieved from http://www.thewellproject.org/hiv-information/disclosure-and-hiv

Good counselling vital for clients with STDs. (n.d.). *General Health Topics.* Retrieved from http://generalhealthtopics.com/good-counselling-vital-clients-stds-232.html

HIV/AIDS reporting and partner notification. (2011). *Center for a Healthy Maryland.* Retrieved from http://healthymaryland.org/wp-content/uploads/2011/05/10-Reporting-and-Notifying-Partners.pdf

Lehman, S., Carr, M. H., Nichol, A. J., Ruisanchez, A., Knight, D. W., Langford, A. E., Gray, S. C., & Mermin, J. H. (2014). Prevalence and public health implications of state laws that criminalize potential HIV exposure in the United States. *AIDS and Behavior*, *18*(6), 997–1006. Retrieved from https://link.springer.com/content/pdf/10.1007%2Fs10461-014-0724-0.pdf

New York State Department of Health. (2013). HIV reporting and partner notification questions and answers. Retrieved from https://www.health.ny.gov/diseases/aids/providers/regulations/reporting_and_notification/question_answer.htm

Office of Inspector General, Department of Health and Human Services. (1999). *The Ryan White Care Act Implementation of the Spousal Notification Requirement.* Washington, DC: Author. Retrieved from https://oig.hhs.gov/oei/reports/oei-05-98-00391.pdf

Opportunistic infections. (2017). HIV.gov. Retrieved from https://www.hiv.gov/hiv-basics/staying-in-hiv-care/other-related-health-issues/opportunistic-infections

Ryan White Care Act of 1996. Pub. L. 104-146, 110 Stat. 1346, codified as amended at 42 U.S. Code 300ff-27a. Retrieved at https://www.law.cornell.edu/uscode/text/42/300ff-27a

Schattner, E. (2012). This at-home HIV test looks simple, but is it accurate? *The Atlantic.* Retrieved from https://www.theatlantic.com/health/archive/2012/07/this-at-home-hiv-test-looks-simple-but-is-it-accurate/259558/

Sederer, L. I. (2013, October). Involuntary psychiatric hospitalization. *Psychology Today.* Retrieved from https://www.psychologytoday.com/blog/therapy-it-s-more-just-talk/201310/involuntary-psychiatric-hospitalization

Wilton, J. (2012, Summer). Putting a number on it: The risk from an exposure to HIV. Canadian AIDS Treatment Information Exchange. Retrieved from http://www.thebodypro.com/content/68672/putting-a-number-on-it-the-risk-from-an-exposure-t.html

World Health Organization. (2003). *Gender dimensions of HIV status disclosure to sexual partners: Rates barriers and outcomes.* Geneva, Switzerland: Author. Retrieved from http://apps.who.int/iris/bitstream/10665/42717/1/9241590734.pdf

World Health Organization. (2006). *Addressing violence against women in HIV testing and counselling: A meeting report.* Geneva, Switzerland: Author. Retrieved from fhttp://www.who.int/gender/documents/VCT_addressing_violence.pdf

INDEX

AAMFT. *See* American Association of Marriage and Family Therapists
Abuse victims
   adults, 115–123
   advocacy for, 125–133
   case studies, 115–123
   emotional abuse, 119–123
   empowerment, 115, 117–123, 131
   with HIV, 235
   physical abuse, 115–119
   safety, 118–119
   See also Child abuse; Sexual abuse
ACA. *See* American Counseling Association
ADA. *See* Americans with Disabilities Act
AIDS, 221
   See also HIV
Air gapped computers, 180
Allport, Gordon W., 163
American Association of Marriage and Family Therapists (AAMFT) Code of Ethics, 109
American Bar Association Model Rules of Professional Conduct, 149
American Counseling Association (ACA) Code of Ethics
   counseling records, 173–174
   couples and family therapy, 108
   disclosure of confidential information, 82–83, 234
   disclosure of disease status, xvi, 223
   diversity and multiculturalism, 157, 163
   end-of-life counseling, 208, 209
   ethics consultations, 72
   online counseling, 192
   online supervision, 166
   Preamble, 40, 57, 157
   pro bono services, 149
   rational suicide, 203
   responsibilities of counselors, 50
   sexual relations with clients, xviii, 141, 142
   sliding scale fees, 150
   supervisor roles, 159, 163, 166
   terminally ill clients, 201
   virtual relationships, 147
American Mental Health Counseling Association (AMHCA) Code of Ethics, 164
American Psychological Association (APA)
   Ethical Principles of Psychologists and Code of Conduct, 68, 137, 141, 142–143
   Record Keeping Guidelines, 179
   telepsychology guidelines, 192
   Working Group on Assisted Suicide and End-of-Life Decisions, 203, 206, 214
Americans with Disabilities Act (ADA), 222, 223
AMHCA. *See* American Mental Health Counseling Association
APA. *See* American Psychological Association
Aristotelian mean, 4, 7, 9, 16, 74, 86
Aristotle, 3, 4, 8, 39, 53, 70
ASPPB. *See* Association of State and Provincial Psychology Boards
Association for Counselor Education and Supervision, 165
Association of Death Education and Counseling, 211
Association of State and Provincial Psychology Boards (ASPPB), 189
Authenticity, xv–xvi, 7–8
Autonomy
   Client Autonomy standard, 41, 45–46, 50, 66, 91, 210, 211
   of clients, 91–92, 97, 107, 227–228
   confidentiality and, 91–92, 227–228
   of counselors, 41, 46, 51
   individual, 11, 45–47
   standards, 41, 45–47
   of third parties, 46–47, 52
   See also Empowerment

Basic client responsibilities, 50–52, 51 (diagram)
Battin, M. P., 204
Beneficence
   Client Welfare standard, 41, 43, 50, 66, 210
   standard, 40, 41, 42–44

Benevolence, 5–6, 41, 42–43
Bergstedt, Kenneth, 212
Beyer, Karen, 90
Bok, Sissela, 70–71, 72, 73
Bragdon v. Abbott, 222
Brandt, Richard B., 209–210
Brown v. Board of Education of Topeka, 48

California state laws
   on client capacity, 105–106
   on online counseling, 188
   on suicidal clients, 187, 188
Candor
   case study, 97–99, 100, 104, 109
   informed consent and, 10–11, 99, 100–104
   as virtue, 10–11
   See also Honesty
Canterbury v. Spence, 10, 11, 100, 103
Case studies
   abuse victims, 115–123
   applying ethical standards, 40, 52–53
   child abuse, 97–99, 104, 109, 126–133
   confidentiality, 82, 84–89
   counseling records, 175, 177
   cross-cultural counseling, 157–161, 162–164
   dangerous client, 82, 84–89
   empowerment, 117–123
   end-of-life counseling, 202, 208, 209–210, 211, 214
   ethical decision-making, 58–59, 60–65, 66–74
   fundamentalist Christian family, 40, 52–53
   hacking of electronic records, 175, 177
   hateful client, 58–59, 60–65, 66–74
   HIV positive client, 223–225, 226–230, 231
   informed consent, 97–99, 100, 104, 109
   Muslim client, 157–161, 162–164
   online counseling, 185–187, 188–189, 193
   sexual abuse, 126–133
   sexual relations with client, 140–141, 142, 143–146
   suicidal client, 185–187, 188–189, 193
   supervision, 159–161, 162–164
   terminally ill client, 202, 208, 209–210, 211, 214
   trustworthiness, 25–33
CBT. *See* Cognitive behavioral therapy
Centers for Disease Control (CDC), 222, 234
Child abuse
   case studies, 97–99, 104, 109, 126–133
   family therapy and, 108
   mandatory reporting, 15, 91, 97–99, 126–127, 131, 190

   sexual abuse, 125–133
   victims, 125
   See also Abuse victims; Sexual abuse
Children
   counseling records, 179
   custody decisions, xix–xx
   informed consent by, 106, 107, 126, 131
Circumstantial information, informed consent and, 104–105
Client Autonomy standard, 41, 45–46, 50, 66, 91, 210, 211
Client Nonmaleficence standard, 44, 50–51, 209–210
Clients. *See* Counseling records; Counseling relationship
Client Welfare standard, 41, 43, 50, 66, 210
   See also Beneficence
Clinton, William Jefferson, 10
Codes of ethics. *See* American Counseling Association; Ethics codes
Cognitive behavioral therapy (CBT), 13, 42, 102
Cohen, E. D., 57, 207, 213, 214, 223, 230
Cohen, G. S., 57
Compassionate Caring standard, 41, 49–50, 61, 66, 211
Competence
   assessment by supervisors, 163–164, 165
   in end-of-life counseling, 210–211
   multicultural knowledge, 159–160
   as virtue, 17–18, 43
Computer records. *See* Electronic client records
Confidentiality
   autonomy and, 91–92, 227–228
   case study, 82, 84–89
   in couples and family therapy, 108–109
   discretion, 14–15
   duty to protect and, 83–84, 187, 225
   in end-of-life counseling, 208, 209
   ethical limits, 82–83
   exceptions, 14–15, 99, 104, 223, 225–232
   laws protecting, 89–91, 190
   legal limits, 15, 83–84, 86, 89, 90, 208
   in online counseling, 192–193
   of online information, 104–105, 166, 173, 192–193
   privileged communication, 89–92
   as virtue, 81
   See also Counseling records; Disclosure of information
Conflicts of interest
   actual or apparent, 138, 147
   bartering for fees, 147, 148
   dual or multiple role relationships, 15, 138–140, 146–148

identifying, 69–70
loyalty and, 15–16
self-regarding, 69–70
in supervision, 164
virtual relationships, 146–148
See also Sexual relations
Congruence, 7, 122
Connecticut state law, 208
Council of State Governments, 189
Counseling ethics
consultations, 17–18, 72, 143
definition, xv
dilemmas, xvi–xvii, xix–xx
personal ethics and, xv–xvi
See also Standards of ethical practice; Virtuous practice
Counseling records
case study, 175, 177
contents, 174
electronic storage or transmission, 104–105, 173, 174–180, 192–194
legal requirements for access, 99–100, 103, 174
maintaining and destroying, 179–180
patient portals, 193
psychotherapy notes, 91, 174
purpose, 173–174
See also Informed consent
Counseling relationship
authenticity in, xv–xvi, 7
in couples and family therapy, 108–109
fiduciary, 19, 138–139
gifts from clients, 151
intrinsic regard for clients, 5, 12
multiple roles, 104, 138–140, 146–148
privileged communication, 90–92
responsibilities, 50–52, 51 (diagram)
sexual relations with clients, xvii–xviii, 44, 140–146
treatment length, 102
trust in, xv–xvi, 7, 19–20, 25–33, 81, 109, 138–139
See also Informed consent; Virtuous practice
Counselor Autonomy standard, 41, 46, 51
Counselor Nonmaleficence standard, 44–45
Counselor virtues. *See* Virtues
Couples therapy, 108–109
Courage, 8–9
Cross-cultural counseling
case study, 157–161, 162–164
challenges, 160–162
supervisor roles, 157, 159–164, 165
See also Cultural differences

Cultural differences
attitudes on bartering, 148
effects on counseling, 159
gift giving, 151
knowledge of, 18, 159–160
respect for, 157
stereotypes, 160–162
See also Cross-cultural counseling
Culture, meaning, 159
Cybersex, 146
Cyberspace. *See* Electronic client records; Online counseling; Social media

Death, right to die, 201, 212–213
See also Suicide; Terminally ill clients
Deception, 9–10, 47
Decision-making, ethical
acting on decision, 74
applying standards, 39
case study, 58–59, 60–65, 66–74
challenges, 57
compromises, 73
ethical analysis, 65–73
models, 57–58
morally relevant information, 64 (table), 64–65
overriding conditions, 70–72, 71 (table)
steps, 58, 61–74
Delaware state laws, informed consent, 191
Digital records. *See* Electronic client records
Diligence, 16–17, 173
Disclosure of information
limited to essential information, 92, 188, 234
mandatory reporting of child abuse, 15, 91, 97–99, 126–127, 131, 190
preventing harm, 81, 82–89, 91, 92, 186–187, 188–189, 208, 225–226
to third party payers, 102
See also Confidentiality; HIV status disclosure
Discretion, 14–15
See also Confidentiality
Distance therapy. *See* Online counseling
Diversity. *See* Cultural differences
Division of Corrections v. Neakok, 69
Documentation. *See* Counseling records
Domestic abuse. *See* Abuse victims; Child abuse; Sexual abuse
Dual or multiple role relationships, 15, 138–140, 146–148, 164
See also Sexual relations
Dudley, D. R., 118

Duties
  morality of, xvii
  prima facie, 41–42
  to protect, 83–84, 187, 225
  See also Responsibilities

Electronic client records, 104–105, 173, 174–180, 192–194
  See also Counseling records
E-mail, 192, 193
  See also Online counseling
Emotional abuse. *See* Abuse victims
Empathy
  compassionate caring, 41, 49–50, 61, 66, 211
  in end-of-life counseling, 211
  as virtue, 6–7, 41, 61, 117–118
Empowerment
  of abuse victims, 115, 117–123, 131
  case studies, 117–123
  as virtue, 13–14
  See also Autonomy
Encryption, 177–178, 180, 192, 193
End-of-life counseling
  case study, 202, 208, 209–210, 211, 214
  confidentiality, 208, 209
  ethical standards and, 209–210, 211
  irremediably ill clients, 211–213
  model rules, 213 (table), 213–214
  qualifications, 210–211, 214
  terminally ill clients, 201, 202, 208, 209–210, 211, 214
  See also Suicide
Equity. *See* Fairness
Ethical analysis, 65–73, 66 (table), 71 (table)
Ethics
  meanings, xv
  personal, xv–xvi
  professional, xv
  virtue, 3–5
  See also Counseling ethics; Standards of ethical practice
Ethics codes
  American Association of Marriage and Family Therapists, 109
  American Mental Health Counseling Association, 164
  American Psychological Association, 68, 137, 141, 142–143
  conflicts with laws, xviii–xx
  inconsistencies, xvii–xviii
  National Association of Social Workers, xvii–xviii, 83, 141, 149, 150, 203
  professional, xv

standards and, 65
  See also American Counseling Association
Ethics consultations, 17–18, 72, 143
Euthanasia. *See* Physician assisted suicide
Existential therapy, 7–8

Facebook, 147–148
  See also Social media
Fairness
  of sliding scale fees, 150–151
  as virtue, 18–19, 41, 47, 137
Family therapy, 108–109
Faulty thinking, 72 (table), 72–73
Fees
  affordability, 48–49
  bartering, 147, 148
  disclosure of, 102
  sliding scales, 19, 150–151
Felton, E., 126
Florida state laws
  disclosure of HIV status, xvi–xvii, 225, 227
  disclosure of information, 84
  patient records, 99, 179
  Patient's Bill of Rights, 107
  privileged communication, 90
  sexual relations with clients, xviii, 142
  therapist responsibilities, 122
Fourteenth Amendment, 107, 212
Fredericks v. Jonsson, 69–70
Fundamentalist Christian family case study, 40, 52–53

Gifts from clients, 151
Golden Rule, 71
Google, 193

Hacking of electronic records case study, 175, 177
Hammonds v. Aetna Casualty and Surety Company, 89
Harm. *See* Abuse victims; Disclosure of information; Interests; Violence
Health departments, HIV status disclosure by, 225, 226, 230, 231, 232, 235
Health Information Technology for Economic and Clinical Health (HITECH) Act, 175–176
Health Insurance Portability and Accountability Act of 1996 (HIPAA)
  client access to records, 103
  confidentiality of patient information, 91, 174, 190
  disclosure to third party payers, 102
  Security Standards, 175–177, 178–179, 180, 192, 193

HITECH Act. *See* Health Information Technology for Economic and Clinical Health Act
HIV
  discrimination based on status, 222–223
  shame associated with, 205
  tests, 222, 231, 234
  transmission, 222, 227, 231, 233–234
HIV status disclosure
  case study, 223–225, 226–230, 231
  by client, 228–229, 230, 235–236
  conditions justifying, 230 (table), 230–233
  by health departments, 225, 226, 230, 231, 232, 235
  laws on, xvi–xvii, 223, 225–227, 230, 232, 235–236
  by medical professionals, 225, 231
  preventing harm to client, 235
  procedures, 233 (table), 233–235
  by therapist, 221, 225–228, 230–233, 234–236
  timeliness, 233–234
Homeless population, 48
Honesty, 7, 9–10
  See also Candor; Truthfulness
Human services delivery system
  ethical standards and, 43–44
  injustice in, 48

Immigrants. *See* Cross-cultural counseling; Cultural differences
Incompetent clients, 106–107
Information technology. *See* Electronic client records; Online counseling
Informed consent
  candor and, 10–11, 99, 100–104
  case study, 97–99, 100, 104, 109
  circumstantial information and, 104–105
  client capacity and, 105–107
  in couples and family therapy, 108–109
  disclosure of information and, 11, 102, 227–228
  exceptions, 99–100
  legal guidelines, 99–101, 105–107
  online counseling, 104, 188, 191–194
  as process, 99, 104, 109
  for recording sessions, 103, 162–163
  risks of potential treatments, 11, 100–101
  scope, 46
  for supervision, 162–163, 164–165
  termination of therapy and, 107–108
  trust and, 109
Insurance companies, 10, 43–44, 47, 48, 102
  See also Third party payers
Interests, 60, 62–64, 63 (table)
  See also Conflicts of interest; Stakeholders

Internet. *See* Electronic client records; Online counseling; Patient portals; Social media
Irremediable illnesses, 209–210, 211–213
  See also End-of-life counseling
Islam. *See* Cultural differences; Muslim client case study

Jaffee v. Redmond, 90–91
Justice standard, 41, 47–49, 150

Kant, Immanuel, 11, 12, 45, 46, 203, 209
Kustron, D. A., 118

Laws
  age of consent to treatment, 126
  anti-discrimination, 222
  assisted suicide, 201, 206–207
  client capacity, 105–107
  confidentiality, 83–84, 86, 89–91, 190
  conflicts with ethics, xviii–xx
  disclosure of HIV status, xvi–xvii, 223, 225–227, 230, 232, 235–236
  disclosure of information, 84, 86, 102, 187, 208, 225–227
  electronic record security, 175–177, 178
  in ethical analysis, 65
  informed consent, 11, 99–101, 105–107
  interstate agreements, 189–191
  licensing, 188, 189
  mandatory reporting of child abuse, 15, 91, 97–99, 126–127, 131, 190
  online counseling and, 187–191
  patient records, 99–100, 103, 174, 179
  privileged communication, 90–91
  sexual relations with clients, xviii, 142
  state jurisdictions, 187–191
  suicide prevention, 187, 188–189, 208, 214
Legal responsibility
  distinction from moral responsibility, xx
  liability, xx, 69–70, 187–188, 209
Lies, 9–10, 47
LinkedIn. *See* Social media
Lippmann, Walter, 161
Loyalty, 15–16, 137

Malpractice, 11, 44, 209
Married couples. *See* Abuse victims; Couples therapy; HIV status disclosure
Maryland state laws, disclosure of information, 225–226, 228–229, 230
Massachusetts state laws, HIV status disclosure, 226
McCloskey, K., 118

McKay v. Bergstedt, 212
Medical professionals
   HIV status disclosure, 225, 231
   physician-assisted suicide, 201, 206–207, 212
Mind-sets, 161–162, 163
Minors. *See* Children
Mobile technology, 180
Moll, Christine, 208
Moore, Lawrence, 83
Morality
   conventional view of suicide, 202–203, 209
   of duty vs. aspiration, xvii
   professional ethics and, xv
   See also Ethics; Virtues
Moral problems, 59–64
   See also Decision-making, ethical
Moral responsibility, xx
Moral sensitivity, 61, 62
Multicultural perspective. *See* Cross-cultural counseling; Cultural differences
Multiple role relationships, 15, 104, 138–140
   See also Sexual relations
Muslim client case study, 157–161, 162–164

National Association of Social Workers (NASW), Code of Ethics, xvii–xviii, 83, 141, 149, 150, 203
National Conference of Catholic Bishops, 202–203
New York state laws
   disclosure of information, 84
   HIV status disclosure, 226, 227
   Mental Hygiene Law, 84, 99
   physician assisted suicide, 212
   promoting suicide, 208, 214
Nietzsche, Friedrich, 13
Nonelective dual or multiple role relationships, 139–140
Nonmaleficence standards, 41, 44–45, 209–210
Nonmalevolence, 5–6, 41, 42–43

Objectivity, 6, 70, 137
Online counseling
   advantages, 185
   case study, 185–187, 188–189, 193
   challenges, 194
   informed consent, 104, 188, 191–194
   limitations, 192
   security issues, 192–194
   state laws, 187–191
   suicidal clients, 185–187, 188–189, 193

Online records. *See* Electronic client records
Online supervision, 165–166
Oregon Death with Dignity Act, 207

Passwords, 177, 178
Patient portals, 193
   See also Electronic client records
Personal ethics, xv–xvi
   See also Morality; Virtues
Philosophical counselors, 214
Physical abuse. *See* Abuse victims; Sexual abuse; Violence
Physician-assisted suicide, 201, 206–207, 212
Plessy v. Ferguson, 48
Poddar, Prosenjit, 83
Polowy, C. I., 126
Powelson, Harvey, 83
Pretermination therapy, 108
Principle of Double Effect, 203
Privacy, 91–92
   See also Confidentiality; Discretion
Privileged communication, 89–92
   See also Confidentiality
Problem solving. *See* Decision-making, ethical; Moral problems
Pro Bono Counseling Project, 149
Pro bono counseling services, 149–150
Professional ethics, xv
Psychotherapy notes, 91, 174
   See also Counseling records
Psypact, 189

Quadriplegia, 211–212
Quill v. Vacco, 212

Racial segregation, 47–48
Rational suicide, 201, 203–206, 205 (table), 209–210, 212–213
Records. *See* Counseling records
Redmond, Mary Lu, 90
Religious differences
   case study, 157–161, 162–164
   stereotypes and prejudice, 163
   See also Cross-cultural counseling
Respect
   for cultural differences, 157
   self-, 12–13
Respectfulness, 11–13, 41
Responsibilities, xx, 50–52, 51 (diagram)
   See also Duties

Right to die, 201, 212–213
  See also Suicide
Risks
  HIV transmission, 231, 232, 233–234
  informed consent and, 11, 100–101
  online security, 177–180, 192–193
  reasonable judgments, 86
Rogers, Carl, 6, 7, 12, 118
Ross, W. D., 41–42
Rural communities
  dual or multiple role relationships, 139
  online therapy, 185
Ryan White Care Act of 1996, 227

Sartre, Jean-Paul, 7–8, 73
Self-determination. *See* Autonomy
Sexual abuse
  case study, 126–133
  of children, 125–133
  couples and family therapy and, 108
  See also Abuse victims
Sexual relations
  attraction to clients, 144–146
  case study, 140–141, 142, 143–146
  with clients, 44, 140–141, 143–146
  with former clients, xvii–xviii, 142–144
  online, 146
  state laws on, xviii, 142
  See also HIV
Social media, 146–148
Social Welfare standard, 41, 43–44, 52
Social workers. *See* National Association of Social Workers
Stakeholders, 61, 62–64, 63 (table), 84
  See also Interests
Standards of ethical practice
  applying, 39, 41–42
  autonomy, 41, 45–47
  balancing conflicts, 41, 50, 52
  beneficence, 40, 41, 42–44, 210
  case study, 40, 52–53
  compassionate caring, 41, 49–50, 61, 66, 211
  decision-making and, 65
  in end-of-life counseling, 209–210, 211
  in ethical analysis, 65–67
  ethics codes and, 65
  justice, 41, 47–49, 150
  nonmaleficence, 41, 44–45, 209–210
  overview, 40–42
  responsibilities, 50–52, 51 (diagram)
  virtues and, 41

State laws. *See* Laws; *and individual states*
Stereotypes, 160–162, 163, 223
Substance abuse, 88
  See also HIV
Suicidal clients
  assessing, 186–187
  case study, 185–187, 188–189, 193
  emergency planning, 186
  end-of-life counseling case study, 202, 208, 209–210, 211, 214
  online counseling, 185–187, 188–189, 193
  sexual misconduct of therapist and, 142
Suicide
  conventional moral view of, 202–203, 209
  legal issues, 201, 206–209, 214
  permitting, 207–209, 211–214, 213 (table)
  physician-assisted, 201, 206–207, 212
  rational, 201, 203–206, 205 (table), 209–210, 212–213
Supervisors
  case study, 159–161, 162–164
  informed consent of client and, 162–163
  informed consent of supervisees, 164–165
  online supervision, 165–166
  recording sessions for, 162–163
  relationships with supervisees, 163–165
  roles in cross-cultural counseling, 157, 159–164, 165

Tarasoff, Tatiana, 83
Tarasoff v. the Regents of the University of California, 83–84, 86, 187, 209, 225
Tarvyda, Vilia, 208
Technology. *See* Electronic client records; Online counseling; Social media
Terminally ill clients
  case study, 202, 208, 209–210, 211, 214
  right to die, 201
  See also End-of-life counseling
Termination of therapy
  gift giving, 151
  informed consent, 107–108
Texas State Board of Examiners of Psychologists, 187
Texas state laws
  online counseling, 188
  suicidal clients, 187, 188–189
Thanatology, 210
Therapists, autonomy of, 41, 46, 51
  See also Counseling relationship; Supervisors; Virtues
Third Party Autonomy standard, 46–47, 52
Third party payers, 10, 91, 102, 173, 174
  See also Insurance companies

Thomas Aquinas, Saint, 203
Transference, 46, 140–141, 145
Treatments
   cognitive behavioral therapy, 13, 42, 102
   lengths, 102
   potential risks, 11, 100–101
Trust
   in counseling relationship, xv–xvi, 7, 19–20, 25–33, 81, 109, 138–139
   informed consent and, 109
Trustworthiness
   case studies, 25–33
   as virtue, 19–20
   See also Confidentiality
Truthfulness, 3–4, 9
   See also Honesty

Video conferencing. See Online counseling
Violence
   dangerous client case study, 82, 84–89
   disclosure of information, 82–84, 92, 225–226
   HIV status and, 235
   predicting, 86–89, 87 (table)
   preventing, 89
   See also Abuse victims
Virtue ethics, 3–5
Virtues
   authenticity, 7–8
   benevolence/nonmalevolence, 5–6, 41, 42–43
   candor, 10–11
   competence, 17–18, 43
   confidentiality, 81
   courage, 8–9
   developing, 3–5
   diligence, 16–17, 173
   discretion, 14–15
   empathy, 6–7, 41, 61, 117–118
   empowerment, 13–14
   fairness, 18–19, 41, 47, 137
   honesty, 9–10
   ideals, xix–xx
   loyalty, 15–16, 137
   moderation and, 4
   respectfulness, 11–13, 41
   standards of ethical practice and, 41
   trustworthiness, 19–20
   truthfulness, 3–4, 9
Virtuous practice
   applying standards, 39
   ideals, xv, xvii
   moral responsibility, xx

Websites. See Patient portals
Welfare
   Client Welfare standard, 41, 43, 50, 66, 210
   positive or negative, 60, 63 (table), 63–64
   social, 41, 43–44, 52
Women, with HIV, 235

Zur, O., 148

ABOUT THE AUTHORS

Elliot D. Cohen, PhD, Brown University, is professor and chair of the Department of Humanities at Indian River State College, and adjunct professor of Clinical Ethics at Florida State University College of Medicine. He is also executive director of the National Philosophical Counseling Association (NPCA), president of the Institute of Critical Thinking Center for Logic-Based Therapy (LBT), and editor-in-chief of the International Journal of Applied Philosophy. Author of 23 published books and numerous articles in diverse areas of applied and professional ethics and philosophical counseling, Dr. Cohen has developed and proposed model rules for professional codes of ethics, including the American Counseling Association (ACA). He also writes a popular blog for *Psychology Today* called "What Would Aristotle Do?"

Gale Spieler Cohen, EdD, LMHC, NCC, is professor and chair of the Human Services Department at Indian River State College. She is a licensed mental health counselor in Florida and a National Certified Counselor with clinical experience in a wide array of areas, including child sexual abuse and domestic abuse and intimate partner violence. She holds a doctorate in Child, Youth, and Human Services with a specialization in Family Systems and Services from Nova Southeastern University.